SENSELESS SECRETS

★★★★★

SENSELESS SECRETS

The Failures of U.S. Military Intelligence from the Revolution to Afghanistan

★★★★★

Lt. Col. (Ret.) Michael Lee Lanning

STACKPOLE
BOOKS
Essex, Connecticut
Blue Ridge Summit, Pennsylvania

STACKPOLE BOOKS

An imprint of Globe Pequot, the trade division of
The Rowman & Littlefield Publishing Group, Inc.
4501 Forbes Blvd., Ste. 200
Lanham, MD 20706
www.rowman.com

Distributed by NATIONAL BOOK NETWORK

British Library Cataloguing in Publication Information available

Library of Congress Cataloging-in-Publication Data

Names: Lanning, Michael Lee, author.
Title: Senseless secrets : the failures of U.S. military intelligence from the
    Revolution to Afghanistan / Lt. Col. (Ret.) Michael Lee Lanning.
Description: 2022 edition. | Essex, Connecticut : Stackpole Books, 2022. |
    Includes bibliographical references and index.
Identifiers: LCCN 2022014890 (print) | LCCN 2022014891 (ebook) | ISBN
    9780811771931 (cloth) | ISBN 9780811772105 (ebook)
Subjects: LCSH: Military intelligence—United States—History.
Classification: LCC UB251.U5 L36 2022 (print) | LCC UB251.U5 (ebook) |
    DDC 355.3/4320973—dc23/eng/20220405
LC record available at https://lccn.loc.gov/2022014890
LC ebook record available at https://lccn.loc.gov/2022014891

♾™ The paper used in this publication meets the minimum requirements of
American National Standard for Information Sciences—Permanence of Paper
for Printed Library Materials, ANSI/NISO Z39.48-1992.

To Thomas R. Hargrove,
who was taken hostage by Columbian guerillas on
September 23, 1994,
and finally freed on August 22, 1995

and

Susan Sheldon Hargrove,
who vigilantly worked for his release

★★★★★

Contents

Acknowledgments   viii
Author to Reader   ix
Introduction to the 2022 Edition   xv

1. Desert Storm and Somalia   3
2. Beginnings: The American Revolutionary War   22
3. The Second War for Independence: The War of 1812   47
4. Expansionism: The Mexican War   60
5. Brother Against Brother: The Civil War   75
6. Combat on the Plains: The Indian Wars   100
7. Remembering the *Maine*: The Spanish-American War   118
8. Over There: The First World War   138
9. World War II: The Pacific Theater   162
10. World War II: The European Theater   196
11. The Unknown War: Korea   221
12. The Only War We Had: Vietnam   243
13. Weekend Wars: Grenada, Panama, and More   269
14. Today and Tomorrow: Can Failures Become Successes?   290

Source Notes   307
Index   317

★★★★★
Acknowledgments

Research for this book was assisted by the staff of the National Archives and Records Administration in Washington, D.C.; the Director of Public Affairs, Central Intelligence Agency; Office of Public Affairs, Department of Defense; Office of Public Affairs, U.S. Army; Office of Information, U.S. Navy; Air Intelligence Agency, U.S. Air Force; and the Public Affairs Office, U.S. Marine Corps.

Library resources were provided by the U.S. Army Intelligence Center and School (USAICS), Fort Huachuca, Arizona; the Arizona State University Library, Tempe, Arizona; and the public libraries of Phoenix, Scottsdale, and Tempe, Arizona.

Acquisition of valuable reports was expedited by the offices of Representative Norman Sisisky (D-Va.), chairman of the House of Representatives Committee on Armed Services Subcommittee on Oversight and Investigations; and Representative Gary A. Condit (D-Calif.), chairman of the House of Representatives Subcommittee on Information, Justice, Transportation, and Agriculture of the Committee on Government Operations.

Research assistance, advice, and encouragement were provided by my good friend Dan Cragg of Springfield, Virginia.

As with all my books, my best editor and critic remains my wife, Linda.

Author to Reader

Intelligence, simply defined, is information about an adversary. This information falls into political, economic, technical, and military categories, with the lines of demarcation among them vague, depending on the situation. Military intelligence further separates into two categories. Strategic intelligence is information required for the formation of policy and military plans at national and international levels. Tactical intelligence is information required for the planning and conduct of military operations. Again, the distinction between the two is often difficult to determine. The purpose of military intelligence is to provide knowledge about the capabilities, intentions, and vulnerabilities of the enemy as well as facts about the terrain and climate of the proposed area of operations. This book focuses on those instances in American history where intelligence, particularly tactical intelligence, has failed to accomplish these objectives.

"Military intelligence," used throughout this text for the reader's ease of understanding, is a term of recent origin. George Washington wrote about the necessity of procuring good "intelligence," but after the American Revolution the more frequently used term was "information." During the Civil War, commanders on both sides spoke of "military information." The U.S. Navy favored "intelligence" when it established the Office of Naval Intelligence in 1882, but the U.S. Army in 1885 named its newly formed intelligence organization the Military Information Division. The first recorded use of the term "intelligence information" appeared with publication of the memoirs of General Philip Sheridan in 1888. It was not until World War I that "intelligence" became the standard term for military information and for the organizations that deal in the subject.

From 1968 to 1988, I served as an infantry and public affairs officer in the U.S. Army. This book in part was inspired by the failures of military intelligence I observed during my twenty-year career. As much as I was fulfilled by my time in the service of my country, I was constantly troubled, and often angered, by the inept performance of our intelligence organizations and the arrogance of the officers who led them. As a combat commander I was trained to report as much information as possible, yet little processed intelligence of benefit to us was ever returned.

My first unit assignment was with the famed 82d Airborne Division at Fort Bragg, North Carolina. As a second lieutenant, my intelligence requirements were, of course, limited. Yet I did make some observations. The battalion S-2 (intelligence officer) was "the ghost," for he was seldom seen and rarely spoke. Although we were frequently on alert for hot spots around the globe, no intelligence data was ever made available to us, the infantrymen who needed it most.

Surely, I thought, this will change when I arrive in a real combat zone. Unfortunately, Vietnam only reinforced my opinion about the U.S. intelligence community. During my tour as a platoon leader, reconnaissance platoon leader, and rifle company commander with the 199th Light Infantry Brigade, I did not receive a single bit of accurate, useful intelligence. Often we were ordered, on the basis of intelligence, into specific areas where we encountered enemy booby traps that maimed our soldiers rather than the predicted enemy.

As a platoon leader, I had the mission to find and destroy the enemy. On one occasion, we were told by intelligence that the Viet Cong were operating in our area in groups no larger than three to five. I consequently led six men deep into the jungle as the point element of a company sweep and encountered an elaborate base camp of more than 100 well-armed North Vietnamese regulars. One hundred instead of five is an intelligence failure that even an inexperienced lieutenant can understand.

Later in my tour, I led an infantry company of 120 men into remote jungle areas where intelligence said we would find the enemy in great numbers. After days of hacking through thick, leech-infested vegetation and finding no hint of recent enemy activity, I was told by the brigade intelligence officer that surely we were wrong and his information was correct. This was the same intelligence section that sent us to follow up aerial sensor information that yielded a band of monkeys rather than the Viet Cong.

On my return from Vietnam, I served on the staff of the Florida Phase of the Infantry School's Ranger Department. Undoubtedly the most difficult training school in the U.S. armed forces, Ranger School produces the military's strongest leaders and most outstanding intelligence-gathering and -exploitation personnel. Unfortunately, many of these superior soldiers have been killed because of intelligence failures at such locations as Desert One in Iran, Grenada, Panama, the Persian Gulf, and Somalia.

By 1974, I was a captain and back in command with a company of the 3rd Mechanized Infantry Division in Schweinfurt, Germany, less than an hour from the East German border. We trained on the exact ground we would defend if the Soviet army crossed the border. Although we were told that the Soviet and East German order-of-battle experts were so efficient that they maintained biographical sketches of U.S. commanders down to captain level, we received no specific information on the enemy. All we were told was to expect artillery, tanks, and armored personnel carriers to outnumber us ten to one. We were not even provided the unit designations of the enemy in our sector; our intelligence officers said we had no "need to know."

In the late 1970s, I joined the battle-tested 1st Cavalry Division at Fort Hood, Texas, where, as a major, I was the executive officer of a mechanized infantry battalion and later a tank battalion. I quickly discovered that field-grade officers received no better intelligence than captains and lieutenants did. At the time, the mission of the 1st Cav was "to fight anywhere, anytime, and win." Simple enough, yet never was a single piece of intelligence provided at the battalion level to ensure the "and win" part. We were aware of our role as reinforcements to Europe, as well as other world-crisis areas, but our requests for specific intelligence met with the now-familiar response that we had no "need to know."

By the time I arrived in the war plans section of the G-3 operations division of I Corps at Fort Lewis, Washington, in 1982, I was becoming suspicious that no "need to know" was a euphemism for "we have no idea." As the war planner for the corps mission to reinforce the defense of Korea, I asked our intelligence section for information to assist in the planning process. I was told to read after-action reports and other documents from the Korean War in the early 1950s. Current information remained inaccessible behind the triple-locked vaults of the intelligence offices.

At Fort Lewis, I later joined the Corps Command Group as the secretary of the general staff and had access to every piece of paper in the headquarters. With a top secret clearance, I reviewed and prioritized the message traffic to the commanding general and sat in on classified planning and training exercise briefings. I also had access to the "Black Book," a classified weekly intelligence update for the commanding general. In two years of reading this three-inch-thick record of information, I did not in a single instance see a shred of information not available in the daily newspapers or the weekly news magazines. Accompanying the corps commander and chief of staff in 1983, I sat in on a private briefing by the commander of the Fort Lewis–based ranger battalion that had returned only hours earlier from Grenada. The ranger battalion commander's briefing centered on two aspects of the mission—the bravery of his men and the inadequacies of the intelligence that he had been provided.

In my final tour of duty I served as a public affairs officer with the Department of Defense staff. For the first time, I worked daily with officers from the other services. I found the airmen, sailors, and marines to have the same dedication and spirit as their soldier counterparts. One thing we all shared was a lack of confidence in our intelligence system.

While on active duty, I based my opinions about military intelligence on personal experiences. I zipped up body bags, and I evacuated soldiers with lifetime disabilities because of actions that I directly attributed to failures of intelligence. Since retiring, I have spent six years studying military history and writing seven books on the subject. I have visited many battlefields so that I could better understand the fighting that took place and comprehend the impact of military intelligence failures. (Additional information on these visits appears in the Source Notes section at the end of this book.)

From these experiences, studies, and visits I have learned that an inept intelligence community that does not properly serve combat forces is nothing new; it is as old as the United States itself.

The inability to provide accurate, timely intelligence about the size, capabilities, and intentions of the enemy to frontline ground, air, and sea forces has been a constant shortcoming of the U.S. military intelligence community throughout history. Time and time again, the U.S. armed forces have snatched victory from the jaws of defeat, not because of good—or even adequate—intelligence but rather despite continual intelligence failures.

In fact, the greatest "success" of the extremely expensive American military intelligence community has been in maintaining secrecy about its actions and mistakes. Military and government vaults are crammed with shelf after shelf of classified documents, some dating back as far as World War II. Few significant intelligence documents for actions during the past twenty-five years have as yet been declassified. By classifying literally billions of documents as pertinent to national security, intelligence personnel prevent access to information, not so much by potential enemies but rather by the American press and public.

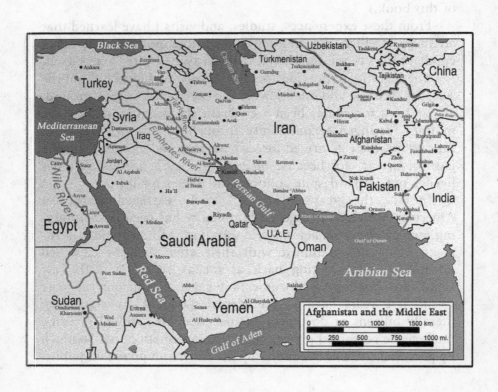

Afghanistan and the Middle East

★★★★★

Introduction to the 2022 Edition

The military-intelligence-academia-corporate complex has become an all-but-ungovernable—and certainly unaccountable—conglomerate of power-hungry, ambitious, and predatory actors. The first two entities—the military and the intelligence—are inextricably linked in that, at their core, they both serve to protect the United States. Without the military, the intelligence gathering is aimless; without intelligence, the military is blind. Hence, the term *military intelligence* is actually redundant when both function properly. The country is safe and sovereign. However, when either, or both, misstep, the other—and the country—suffers.

And suffer it did when Americans lost much of their confidence in their military forces following the turbulent Vietnam War of the 1960s and 1970s. Operation Desert Storm in 1991 appeared to restore that confidence. The Stars and Stripes once again proudly flew throughout the country in a united effort to put the negative aftermath of the 1960s decidedly in the past. From a polling low of 23 percent of Americans having "a great deal" of confidence in the military in 1977, the confidence ranking in armed forces rose to 52 percent after the liberation of Kuwait in 1991. The American people trusted that the success of the "shock and awe" operation would end U.S. intelligence failures.

Such was not the case then, nor is it now. Intelligence failures over the past three decades continue to be the norm, endangering the safety of American citizens and sacrificing blood and treasure—from the 1998 surprise nuclear weapons test firing in India to the unexpected bombing of the U.S.S. *Cole* in 2000; from the shocking 9/11 attacks on the World Trade Center and the Pentagon that killed more than 3,000 Americans to the 2003 invasion of Iraq in pursuit of verified-yet-nonexistent weapons of mass destruction; from the 2012 murder and mutilation of the U.S. ambassador in

Libya to the 2013 release of thousands of classified documents by NSA analyst Edward Snowden; and finally, from the 2021 surrender and humiliating retreat from Afghanistan to the realities of the southern border invasion from Mexico.

All the while, the United States has had—and continues to have—the most sophisticated intelligence gathering systems in the world, operated by countless dedicated and efficient analysts. Yet the intelligence system continues to fail, either because the territorial analysts are unable—or unwilling—to convert vast amounts of data into actionable information for decision-makers at the highest levels or because the intelligence community (IC) has correctly synthesized material, only to have ranking officers blatantly ignore or incompetently deny the evidence. Information, no matter how accurate, is useless if it is not shared and believed.

Most recently, the proliferation of cable television twenty-four-hour news cycles and the massive expansion of internet news sites, blogs, and reports expose intelligence fiascos and present them to the public. Intelligence catastrophes no longer lurk behind claims of classified labels and the veil of "need to know"—or, at least, not for long.

Compounding incompetence within the intelligence community and misdirection of information outside the system has been the politicization of the intelligence brands, including the National Security Agency (NSA), the Central Intelligence Agency (CIA), and the Federal Bureau of Investigation (FBI). The politically appointed cabinet members heading these organizations have lied under oath to Congress on national television, and they have overtly interfered with elections, eroding even more of American citizens' confidence in the government and the military. Not only has this partisan bias corrupted their fellow countrymen's belief in the alphabet bureaucracies but it has also resulted in a lack of trust from our allies and fear from our enemies.

The last twenty years of intelligence failures have been illuminated by spectacular imagery. On one side of the haunting score of years is September 11, when news videos exploded with images of people throwing themselves from the burning World Trade Center in New York City before the Twin Towers collapsed upon themselves. At the opposite end of the timespan is the recent incredulous sight of Afghans falling from the wheel wells of evacuation planes flying from Kabul in their attempt to escape the Taliban. Intelligence analysts anticipated neither disaster.

One glaring reason for the unending debacles is that succeeding administrations have avoided addressing the fact that the intelligence community is, in fact, not a community at all. That reality is the singular most salient issue of all. The enemy may change, the size and shape of the opposition may shift, and the goals of the warriors may differ. Yet the American intelligence system remains fractured—and deliberately so. Each initialism prefers to operate independently, refusing to share information or coordinate with any other except on the most superficial level. Whether driven by jealousy or petty power plays—or more nefarious plots—this strategy serves only to portray all intelligence agencies as inefficient—and ultimately unintelligent.

This ruptured intelligence system is the very structure upon which Americans depend for their national security. The outcomes have been inevitable and dire. For one thing, there were ample warnings of attacks against Americans following Operation Desert Storm; they went unheeded. The sand had barely shifted back into place from the war before a group led by Pakistani terrorist Ramzi Yousef attempted to bring down the World Trade Center in New York for the first time with a truck bomb on February 26, 1993. Although unsuccessful in its desired scale, the attack did kill six and wound hundreds. Yousef's stated objectives, similar to those of other Muslim terrorists, included ending American military, economic, and political aid to Israel and forcing the withdrawal of the United States from the internal affairs of all Middle East countries.

Following on the heels of the "Blind Sheik" Yousef's bomb came the Iranian-supported terrorist attack on the Khobar Towers apartment complex in Dhahran, Saudi Arabia, which housed American servicemen. Nineteen of them were killed and many more wounded. U.S. intel folks did not foresee that either.

By 1997, Osama bin Laden, the son of a billionaire Saudi Arabian construction magnate, had become the primary non-state Muslim leader in the fight against the United States. In addition to his hatred of Westerners, bin Laden harbored ambitions to control the entire Middle East region, dominating all the opposing Muslim sects. So blatant was bin Laden's positioning of himself at the forefront of a movement to eradicate the West that, for once, the intel analysts identified him as a person to watch. Ultimately though, they dismissed him as strictly a financier of terrorism rather than an actual operator or leader. As usual, they were wrong. It was not until bin Laden publicly declared that every Muslim should fight against the "occupation" of Islam's holy places by killing American military personnel and civilians anywhere in the world that the intelligence community recognized him as a threat. In an interview with CNN's Peter Arnett in March of 1997, bin Ladin made it clear that he and his al-Qaeda followers had declared jihad on the United States. Arnett asked, "What are your future plans?" Bin Laden responded, "You'll see them and hear about them in the media, God willing."

Despite being aware of bin Ladin's announcement and his activities, the intelligence community failed to prevent the all but simultaneous truck bombings at the U.S. embassies in Nairobi, Kenya, and Dar es Salaam, Tanzania, on August 7, 1998. The attacks killed 224, including twelve Americans, and wounded hundreds more.

The intelligence failures continued, in large part because intelligence analysts were slow to recognize that bin Ladin and his followers had declared war against the West. On October 12, 2000, the U.S.S. *Cole*, a guided missile destroyer, sailed into Yemen's Aden harbor to refuel. In the routine undertaking, the ship was unescorted and unprotected. No one challenged a small fiberglass boat with two passengers that sailed calmly up to the side of the larger vessel. It was not until the suicide bombers aboard unleashed C-4 explosives that blew a forty-by-sixty-foot hole in the port side that anyone sensed danger. The blast killed seventeen sailors and injured thirty-seven more. Evidence revealed that al-Qaeda was responsible.

According to the National Commission on Terrorist Attacks Upon the United States report completed in August 2004, "By September 2001, the executive branch of the U.S. government, the Congress, the news media, and the American public had received clear warning that Islamist terrorists meant to kill Americans in high numbers." The commission report continued, "During the spring and summer of 2001, U.S. intelligence agencies received a stream of warnings that al-Qaeda planned, as one report put it, 'something very, very, very big.' Director of Central Intelligence George Tenet told us, 'The system was blinking red.'"

Other intelligence agents spotted several men suspected of terrorism in Southeast Asia, but this finding served to convince analysts that the threats extended only to targets overseas and not at home. In the late summer of 2001, U.S. officials arrested Zacarias Moussaoui after he aroused suspicions when he sought training in flying large jet airliners. Despite clear warnings that al-Qaeda was preparing for a major attack against Americans, the intelligence community continued to dismiss the idea of direct attacks in the United States. According to the commission report, "These cases did not prompt urgent action. No one working on these late leads in the summer of 2001 connected them to the high level of threat reporting. In the words of one official, no analytic work foresaw the lightning that could connect the thundercloud to the ground."

Even as late as the early days of September 2001, no information about any attacks directly on U.S. soil alerted analysts about al-Qaeda activities. When asked on September 4 about the coordination between intelligence agencies, Richard Clark, the White House staffer responsible for counterterrorism policy, replied that the government had not yet determined how to answer the question, "Is al-Qaeda a big deal?"

Clark's answer arrived a week later when two commercial jetliners struck the Twin Towers of New York's World Trade Center and another crashed into the Pentagon in Washington, D.C. Still another plane went down in southern Pennsylvania as passengers fought with their hijackers. Its target was likely the White House or the Capitol.

In fewer than two hours, more than 3,000 Americans—more than the number who died in the Japanese attack against Pearl Harbor in 1941—lay dead in the rubble of the World Trade Center, the Pentagon, and in a Pennsylvania field.

The successful al-Qaeda attacks once again revealed the ineptness of the intelligence community. Despite an annual budget of more than $30 billion (an amount that would increase to over $84 billion by 2021), the intelligence community had failed to provide any warning of the aerial attacks. In response, rather than providing actionable intel, the intelligence agencies made excuses. No senior official, or junior one for that matter, was fired or relieved of his or her duties for failure to anticipate and detect the attack of 9/11. Instead, they quipped about hindsight being 20/20 and hid behind their favorite question: "How could anybody have known?" They ignored the fact that their specific job is to have known.

In its general findings, the 9/11 commission concluded, "Since the plotters were flexible and resourceful, we cannot know whether any single step or series of steps would have defeated them. What we can say with confidence is that none of the measures adopted by the U.S. government from 1998 to 2001 disturbed or even delayed the progress of the al-Qaeda plot. Across the government, there were failures of imagination, policy, capabilities, and management."

The findings continued, "The intelligence community struggled throughout the 1990s and up to 9/11 to collect intelligence on and analyze the phenomenon of transnational terrorism. The combination of an overwhelming number of priorities, flat budgets, an outmoded structure, and bureaucratic rivalries resulted in an insufficient response to this new challenge."

While acknowledging that "many dedicated officers worked day and night for years to piece together the growing body of evidence" about terrorist threats, the report concluded that "there was no comprehensive review of what the intelligence community knew and what it did not know, and what that meant. There was no National Intelligence Estimate on terrorism between 1995 and 9/11."

In its recommendations, the commission report stated, "The U.S. government has access to a vast amount of information. But it has a weak system for processing and using what it has. The system of 'need to know' should be replaced by a system of 'need to share.'"

To accomplish these goals, the commission recommended combining intelligence-gathering agencies into a single organization headed by the director of national intelligence (DNI). Congress passed a law to this effect in 2004. However, as quickly became obvious, the final approved legislation lacked adequate powers for the DNI to manage, lead, or improve the overall intelligence community. The law also left the NSA, the National Reconnaissance Office (NRO), and the National Geospatial-Intelligence Agency (NGIA) under the control of the Department of Defense (DOD).

The 9/11 commission report thoroughly details the methods and procedures used by the terrorists in the 9/11 aerial attack as well as the intelligence failures that led to the attackers' success. Few Americans read the extensive report. What Americans remember about that day is the images of two planes flying intentionally into the Twin Towers, the fires from the Pentagon where a third plane struck, and the black hole in the Pennsylvania field into which the fourth hijacked plane disappeared. Each of those images represents a bit of data or a fragment of suspicion ignored, misunderstood, or discounted by intelligence specialists.

In the aftermath of 9/11, the United States was the most united it had been in recent history in its desire to secure itself from terrorism and to seek vengeance against bin Laden and al-Qaeda. The commission report summed up these objectives, concluding, "We call on the American people to remember how we all felt on 9/11, to remember not only the unspeakable horror but how we came together as a nation—one nation. Unity of purpose and unity of effort are the way we will defeat the enemy and make America safer for our children and grandchildren."

Before the completion of the commission investigation, President George W. Bush took more immediate measures to bolster U.S. security in the weeks following 9/11 by forming the Office of Homeland Security (DHS). The official announcement of its formation stated, "The mission of the Office will be to develop and coordinate the implication of a comprehensive national strategy to secure the United States from terrorist threats or attacks. The Office will coordinate the executive branch's efforts to detect, prepare for, prevent, protect against, respond to, and recover from terrorist attacks within the United States." Included in the DHS are various agencies responsible for border security, immigration, customs, and anti-terrorism.

President Bush also took action to punish bin Laden and his followers. On October 7, 2001, he launched Operation Enduring Freedom to force the Taliban, which controlled Afghanistan, to turn over the terrorist leader. When they refused, the United States and its allies took military action, bombing al-Qaeda and the Taliban and forcing them out of most of the country and into the remote mountainous caves of Tora Bora in eastern Afghanistan. However, despite all their "lessons learned" analysis, the intelligence agencies once again managed to bungle the results when they failed to anticipate that bin Laden, most of al-Qaeda, and the Taliban would easily escape into neighboring Pakistan.

A report to the U.S. Senate Foreign Relations Committee, chaired by Senator John Kerry, on November 30, 2009, detailed the significance in the failure to find bin Laden. It stated, "When we went to war less than a month after the attacks of September 11, the objective was to destroy al-Qaeda and kill or capture its leader, Osama bin Laden, and other senior figures in the terrorist group and the Taliban, which had hosted them. Today, more than eight years later, we find ourselves fighting an increasingly lethal insurgency in Afghanistan and neighboring Pakistan that is led by many of those same extremists. Our inability to finish the job in late 2001 has contributed to a conflict today that endangers not just our troops and those of our allies, but the stability of a volatile and vital region."

It took nearly a decade for the intelligence community to finally determine that bin Laden was possibly hiding in a compound near Abbottabad, Pakistan. Even then, they hedged their bets by employing the usual intelligence analysis tactic of stating that the information had a 50-50 chance of accuracy. This way, the agencies would be correct regardless of the outcome. On May 1, 2011, President Barack Obama, acting against the recommendation of Vice President Joe Biden, ordered an attack by U.S. special operations troops that resulted in the death of bin Laden. The intelligence community proudly claimed a success—validating their 50-50 analysis.

The death of bin Laden helped heal a part of the lingering tears and tribulations of 9/11. It did not, however, end U.S. involvement in Afghanistan. Instead of going home and declaring victory, the United States, acting on diplomatic and military intelligence, decided to remain in the country in its nation-building efforts to bring democracy, diversity, women's rights, and other "Western" ideas to Afghanistan—a country dominated for 1,400 years by Islam and divided by dozens of tribal and ethnic groups, characterized by a history of defeating the powerful armies of Great Britain and the Soviet Union. What resulted was the longest war in American history that, after two decades, finally concluded with yet another inglorious intelligence disaster.

★ ★ ★

While the intelligence community took a decade to find "the most wanted man in the world," it also continued to fail in other areas. After U.S. and coalition forces expelled Saddam Hussein's army from Kuwait in 1991 in what became known as the Gulf War, the intelligence community continued to focus on the possibility of Iraq developing weapons of mass destruction—chemical, biological, or radioactive weapons capable of causing widespread death and carnage.

On December 21, 2002, the director of the CIA briefed the president, the vice president, and the national security advisor on the possibilities of Iraq having weapons of mass destruction and missiles to deliver them. President George W. Bush was not convinced by the evidence and asked CIA director George Tenet, "Is this the best we've got?" Tenet assured him the weapons existed, declaring, "Don't worry; it's a slam dunk case!"

Critics of the intelligence, including former United Nations inspectors, declared that Hussein had eliminated his nuclear and chemical weapons programs after the Gulf War. Investigations proved the intelligence reports of Iraq purchasing uranium for nuclear weapons from Africa were false. The intelligence community stood firm, however, and convinced President Bush and his cabinet that the weapons did, in fact, exist and were a threat to American troops and their allies.

On February 5, 2003, U.S. Secretary of State Colin Powell presented President Bush's overall rationale for the invasion of Iraq to the United Nations. Armed with intelligence reports, satellite images, and audio tapes of intercepted telephone conversations, Powell liberally interspersed his briefing with reassurance, such as "we know" and "we know from intelligence." He confirmed his statements to the U.N. delegates, saying, "These are not assertions. They are facts, collaborated by many sources."

Powell emphasized his points, noting, "We know that Saddam Hussein is determined to keep his weapons of mass destruction; he's determined to make more. Given Saddam Hussein's history of aggression, given what we know of his grandiose plans, given what we know of his terrorist associations, and given his determination to exact revenge on those who oppose him, should we take the risk that he will not someday use these weapons at a time and a place and in the manner of his choosing—at a time when the world is in a much weaker position to respond? The United States will not and cannot run that risk to the American people. Leaving Saddam Hussein in possession of weapons of mass destruction for a few more months or years is not an option, not in a post-September 11th world."

Canada, France, Germany, and other longtime allies opposed military action against Iraq, asserting that, regardless of the claims by Powell and U.S. intelligence, there was not ample evidence to go to war. President Bush ignored their concerns and opened his invasion of Iraq with an airstrike on Hussein's presidential palace in Bagdad on March 20, 2003. American troops then rapidly swept across the country. Major combat concluded on April 30 and the occupation began.

On May 1, President Bush made his "mission accomplished" speech aboard the flight deck of the aircraft carrier U.S.S. *Abraham Lincoln*. He said, "In the battle of Iraq, the United States and our allies have prevailed." The president was far from accurate in his assumption—but then, that was inevitable because he was relying upon and at the mercy of his own intelligence departments.

Although American forces and coalition had performed well and easily defeated the Iraqi army, the overall mission was a complete failure. Despite an enormous number of searches by countless units from multiple countries, no weapons of mass destruction were discovered. Likewise, no proof of the development of chemical, biological, or nuclear weapons turned up. The most notable finds were Hussein's multiple luxurious palaces he had built across the country.

In 2003, the *Commission on the Intelligence Capabilities of the United States Regarding Weapons of Mass Destruction:*

Report to the President declared the Iraqi invasion as "one of the most public—the most damaging—intelligence failures in recent American history."

Not only had the intelligence community been woefully incorrect about weapons of mass destruction, but the agencies had also failed to locate Hussein himself. It was not until December 13, 2003, that American infantrymen found Hussein hiding in a hole on a farm near Tikrit. On June 30, 2004, the Americans turned Hussein over to the interim Iraqi government, which tried their former leader for crimes against humanity. The court found him guilty on November 5, and executed him by hanging on December 30, 2006.

U.S. troops remained in Iraq to fight pockets of resistance until December 2011. It was not until 2020 that the United States finally withdrew from the country. American blood and treasure had been shed for nearly two decades in Iraq because of an intelligence failure. Powell, who admitted his U.N. speech was a "blot" on his career, said, "Our failure was that our intelligence community thought [Saddam Hussein] had stockpiled weapons of mass destruction. That was a mistake."

While the conflict raged in Iraq, other intelligence failures continued around the world. With no advance warning, or at least with none that American leaders accepted as valid, the Islamic terrorist group Ansar al-Sharia attacked two U.S. facilities in Benghazi, Libya, during the night of September 11–12, 2012. The terrorists burned and looted the U.S. diplomatic compound, killing the American ambassador to Libya, J. Christopher Stevens, and U.S. Foreign Information Management Officer Sean Smith. They then attacked an annex a mile away manned by CIA contractors, where they killed two and wounded ten more.

Intelligence failures plagued operation both during and after the assault. Conflicting intelligence about the attackers and the ongoing battles resulted in no reinforcements being sent to Benghazi, even though communications were maintained and the fight lasted more than thirteen hours. Confusion and failure only grew when the attack ended. President Barack Obama, Secretary of State Hillary Clinton, and U.S. Ambassador to the United Nations Susan Rice all claimed the assault was a spontaneous attack by Libyans protesting an anti-Islam video. Later investigations revealed that the administration made the claims based on incorrect intelligence reports.

The Investigative Report on the Terrorist Attacks on U.S. Facilities in Benghazi, Libya by the U.S. House of Representatives Permanent Select Committee on Intelligence stated, "The Committee concludes that after the attacks, the early intelligence assessments and the Administration's initial public narrative on the causes and motivations for the attacks were not fully accurate. There was a stream of contradictory and conflicting intelligence that came in after the attacks. The Committee found intelligence to support the CIA's initial assessment that the attacks had evolved out of a protest in Benghazi; but it also found contrary intelligence, which ultimately proved to be correct intelligence. There was no protest. The CIA changed its initial assessment about a protest on September 24, 2012, when closed caption television footage became available on September 18, 2012, and after the FBI began publishing its interview with U.S. officials on September 22, 2012."

Other than the many false claims attributing the Benghazi attacks to a reaction to an obscure video, the most memorable words about the incident came from Secretary of State Clinton. In her testimony to the Senate Foreign Relations Committee on January 23, 2013, Clinton, frustrated and angry about questioning concerning the video and claims of protests, responded, "With all due respect, the fact is we had four dead Americans. Was it because of a protest or was it because of guys out for a walk one night who decided that they'd go kill some Americans? What difference at this point does it make?" Although she continued to press the need "to figure out what happened" and to prevent it from occurring again, she offered no suggestions on preventing future intelligence failures.

★ ★ ★

The intelligence community has continued to accumulate even more fiascoes. One contributing factor to its long and lackluster history may well be the selection and vetting of its personnel. One noteworthy example is Edward J. Snowden, born in North

Carolina on June 21, 1983, who dropped out of high school before attempting to become a member of the U.S. Special Forces in May 2004. The army discharged him after only four months, before he completed his training.

Snowden worked as a security guard at the University of Maryland before he applied his computer skills to secure a position in the CIA in 2006—despite his lack of formal education and failure to complete his army training. With a top secret clearance, the CIA posted Snowden to Geneva, Switzerland, with diplomatic cover as a network security technician. Snowden later claimed, "I was trained as a spy in sort of the traditional sense of the word—in that I lived and worked undercover, overseas, pretending to work in a job that I'm not—and even being assigned a name that was not mine." U.S. intelligence officials deny that Snowden was ever a "spy."

In 2009, Snowden left the CIA for a position as a private contractor with the firm Booz Allen Hamilton in Hawaii, where he worked for the NSA. He soon became disgruntled and concerned with the NSA's secret mass surveillance programs, including those surveilling the American public. In May 2013, he flew to Hong Kong, where he began releasing information and conducting interviews with U.S. and world media outlets. He revealed that the NSA was monitoring the telecommunications of Verizon customers and that the agency, in concert with the FBI and British intelligence organizations, was data mining information, including audio and video chats, photographs, emails, and other materials from internet companies such as Microsoft, Facebook, and Google.

The scope of Snowden's disclosures remains unknown. Estimates range from several hundred thousand documents to more than 1.7 million. While the revelation that the NSA was illegally monitoring the activities of U.S. citizens was an embarrassment to the intelligence community, Snowden did not expose any greatly useful secrets to the United States' enemies. However, to prove that the documents about surveillance were true, Snowden had to include sensitive, detailed blueprints on the NSA's procedures and how it carried them out.

The general consensus by U.S. officials is that Snowden's actions did "grave damage" to the intelligence community. Army

Gen. Martin Dempsey, chairman of the Joint Chiefs of Staff, told the House Armed Services Committee in March 2014, "The vast majority of the documents that Snowden . . . exfiltrated from our highest levels of security . . . had nothing to do with exposing government oversight of domestic activities. The vast majority of those were related to our military capabilities, operations, tactics, techniques and procedures." On February 23, 2015, NSA director Adm. Michael Rogers admitted that the leaks had had a "material impact" on the agency's ability to detect and prevent terror plots.

To some Americans, Snowden became a hero whistleblower for exposing the intrusion into the privacy of private citizens, while others called him a traitor. On June 14, 2013, the U.S. Justice Department charged Snowden with espionage and filed extraction procedures. Snowden flew to Moscow where he sought and received asylum.

In addition to direct intelligence failures and poor vetting of employees, several directors have shown their lack of integrity and honesty by directly lying to committees of the U.S. Congress about the performance of their agencies. In the past, directors misdirected and dodged questions without regard for which party was in the White House. Failures were nonpartisan. However, more recent intelligence appointees have become much more political, even to the point of attempting to undermine the power of a president they oppose.

James R. Clapper, Jr., as an air force lieutenant general, became the director of the Defense Intelligence Agency in 1992. After his retirement from active duty in 1995, he served in several other important intelligence positions before President Barack Obama appointed him director of national intelligence in 2010. In a hearing of the Senate's Select Committee on Intelligence on March 12, 2013, Senator Ron Wyden asked Clapper, "Does the NSA collect any type of data at all on millions, or hundreds of millions, of Americans?"

Clapper responded, "No, sir."

Wyden continued, "It does not?"

Clapper continued, "Not wittingly. There are cases where they could inadvertently, perhaps, collect, but not wittingly."

Two months after Clapper's testimony, Edward Snowden fled the United States and released hundreds of thousands of classified documents to the media. The archives clearly revealed that the NSA was spying on U.S. citizens on a vast scale. In a Moscow television interview on January 26, 2014, Snowden was asked when he decided to release the classified documents. He replied, "Sort of the breaking point was seeing the Director of National Intelligence, James Clapper, directly lie under oath to Congress. . . . Seeing that really meant for me there was no going back."

Clapper attempted to justify his perjury by claiming the surveillance was "inadvertent." He justified his lying to Congress using the old fallback intelligence standard: the "need to know." Ultimately, Clapper apologized to the Senate Intelligence Committee, stating, "My response was clearly erroneous—for which I apologize." Several members of Congress called for Clapper's resignation. He ignored the demand, remaining in his position until the end of President Obama's term the following January.

In an interview on CNN on December 19, 2013, Senator Rand Paul explained the impact of the falsehood, saying, "Clapper lying to Congress is probably more injurious to our intelligence capabilities than anything Snowden did. Clapper has damaged the credibility of the entire intelligence apparatus and I'm not sure what to believe anymore when they come to Congress."

Paul continued by calling upon Clapper to resign, saying, "I don't know how you can have someone in charge over intelligence who has known to lie in a public forum to Congress, to lie without repercussions. If the intelligence community says we're not spying on Americans and they are, and then they say we're not collecting any data, it's hard to have confidence in them."

Another intelligence community leader also lied to Congress. John Brennan should never have been cleared to join the CIA, much less to become the director of the agency. In 2016, Brennan stated that in 1976, during a polygraph test as part of the vetting process for admission into the CIA, he had admitted to voting for Gus Hall, the Communist Party presidential candidate that year. He explained, "I said I was neither Democratic or Republican, but it was my way, as I was going to college, of signaling my unhappiness with the system, and the need for change." He continued, "I said I'm not a member of the Communist Party, so the polygrapher looked at me and said, 'OK,' and when I was finished with the polygraph and I left and said, 'Well, I'm screwed.'"

Despite the admission, the agency accepted Brennan, and he moved up the ranks to become the CIA's daily intelligence briefer to President Bill Clinton and the White House in 1994. He left the CIA in 2005 and became the intelligence advisor to Barack Obama in the 2008 presidential campaign. In 2013, President Obama nominated him to become the director of the CIA. The nomination was not popular either outside or within the agency. Brennan's history was well known, and he was often referred to as "Comrade Brennan."

Brennan's falsehoods to Congress began even before he became the CIA director. In 2011, in his capacity as the assistant to President Obama for homeland security and counterterrorism, he claimed that drone strikes abroad had not killed a single noncombatant. At the time he—and most of the intelligence community—were well aware of multiple civilian collateral deaths.

After becoming the CIA director, Brennan continued his deceitful practices. In March 2014, Brennan replied to a question by NBC News's Andrea Mitchell about the CIA spying on the offices of U.S. senators by hacking into their computers. He emphatically replied, "As far as the allegations of CIA hacking into Senate computers, nothing could be further from the truth. I mean, we wouldn't do that. I mean, that's—that's just beyond the scope of reason in terms of what we would do."

When evidence was revealed that the CIA was, in fact, looking into the computers of U.S. senators, Brennan, on July 31, apologized to the Senate Intelligence Committee but claimed there was no malicious intent in the actions. Senator Ron Wyden, a member of the committee, said, "The CIA Inspector General has confirmed what senators have been saying all along: The CIA conducted an unauthorized search of Senate files and attempted to have Senate staff prosecuted for doing their jobs. Director Brennan's claims to the contrary were simply not true."

The American Civil Liberties Union was also dissatisfied with Brennan's response. A spokesman said, "An apology is not enough—the Justice Department must refer the CIA inspector general's report to a federal prosecutor for a full investigation into any crimes by CIA personnel or contractors. It is hard to imagine a greater threat to the Constitution's system of checks and balances than having the CIA spy on the computers used by the very Senate staff carrying out the Senate's constitutional duty of oversight over the executive branch. It was made worse by CIA Director John Brennan's misleading the American people in denying any wrongdoing."

Brennan continued to be untruthful after leaving the CIA. He also revealed how politics had become a part of his directorship. In May 2017, Brennan testified before a congressional committee about a report written in late 2016, compiled as "opposition research" by Republican presidential candidate Donald Trump's opponents and known as the Steele Dossier, which contained unsubstantiated allegations of conspiracy and collusion between Trump's campaign and the Russian government. Brennan claimed that he did not know who commissioned the document nor had the CIA had taken any actions based on its contents. In 2019, Department of Justice Inspector General Michael Horowitz released a report that showed Brennen was incorrect in both statements.

On July 24, 2018, Charles S. Faddis, a thirty-year veteran of the CIA who before retirement was head of the agency's Weapons of Mass Destruction Department, wrote a letter to Brennan detailing his opinion and that of many others. He stated, "Everything that has transpired in your professional career since [being the CIA's White House briefing officer] has been based on your personal relationship with the former president, his wife Hillary, and their key associates. Your connection to President Obama was, in fact, based on you having established yourself by the time he came to office as a reliable, highly political Democratic Party functionary."

Faddis concluded, "Meanwhile, Senator Rand Paul's assessment of you stands: 'John Brennan started out his adulthood by voting for the Communist Party presidential candidate. He's now ending his career by showing himself to be the most biased, bigoted, over-the-top, hyperbolic sort of unhinged director of the CIA we've ever had.'"

After leaving the CIA, Brennan continued to show his political bias by joining James Clapper as an "intelligence analyst" on MSNBC. There, he continued his criticism of Trump and his administration.

The Horowitz IG Report also revealed that FBI director James Comey was a member of the senior intelligence triumvirate who had no scruples about lying to Congress and the American public. According to the report, Comey lied when he said that the FBI did not investigate the Trump campaign. The report also noted that Comey fostered an environment within the FBI where subordinates exchanged text messages that "clearly showed a biased state of mind" that was "antithetical to the core values of the FBI." With biases such as these, it is no wonder that the public has no confidence in the leaders of our primary intelligence-gathering agencies. The fact that officials were never punished for lying under oath is stunning.

Former-agent Faddis, author of *Beyond Repair: The Decline and Fall of the CIA*, best summarized the problems at the highest levels of the intelligence community in an interview on Steve Bannon's *War Room* on November 13, 2021. He said, "Our intelligence apparatus is broken. You don't any longer have operators running ops and recruiting spies. We've gone through this phase where we have replaced them with bureaucrats. And now we have replaced them with ideologues who are focused on what's going on inside the capital city of our country."

Faddis also offered guidance on fixing the problems, saying, "At the senior levels you need to get a big broom and clean the place out."

★ ★ ★

"Chaotic." "Debacle." "Pandemonium." "Bedlam." "Embarrassment." "Profound Intelligence Failure." These are but a few of the headlines describing the U.S. evacuation from Afghanistan. Congressman Ami Bera, whose district contains one of the largest Afghan populations in the United States, said in an interview to *The Hill*, "How did we get Afghanistan so wrong after 20 years and hundreds of billions of dollars in investment. Clearly mistakes were made for the analysis of how stable the Afghan government was. How stable the Afghan security forces were when we pulled out was clearly misassessed. Certainly in briefings we received, the worst-case scenario was six months post August; obviously we saw complete collapse in a week."

Images of the first Afghans falling to earth after attempting to hold on to the landing gear and wings of evacuation aircraft had barely begun to fill television screens before finger-pointing began. There was plenty of blame go around.

On August 15, Michael Rubin, the resident scholar at the American Enterprise Institute, wrote in an op-ed, "The Taliban's rapid conquest of Afghanistan following President Joe Biden's order to withdraw US forces is a strategic disaster and, no matter how hard Biden seeks to cast blame elsewhere, will shape his legacy.

"For the United States, however, it represents not only a military failure but also an intelligence one. Not only did the Central Intelligence Agency and other US intelligence agencies wildly underestimate the speed of the Taliban advance, but they also appear to have been blind to the extent of political dealings the Taliban had made as the withdrawal loomed and the military prepositioning the Taliban achieved to begin a near-simultaneous assault on provincial capitals. They appear to have missed the fact that Taliban shadow governors were already in place, alongside their staff, to take over provincial functions.

"The question of what went wrong with US intelligence is not simply Monday morning quarterbacking. Both the Trump administration and then Biden's team prefaced America's withdrawal on the notion that US intelligence capabilities would enable the United States to maintain an over-the-horizon strike capability against both insurgents and terrorists. The CIA's failure, however, shows that as US forces withdrew, they were essentially blind and that the White House built America's post-withdrawal strategy on a rotten foundation."

American presidents had been looking to withdraw from Afghanistan ever since finding and killing Osama bin Laden a decade earlier. On February 29, 2020, President Trump agreed to a planned withdrawal of U.S. troops from Afghanistan by May 1, 2021. When Biden became president, he concurred with the withdrawal but apparently adopted no plans for its execution. On April 14, he announced, "Time to end the forever war." The withdrawal would begin on May 1; it would not be completed until September 11.

In a speech, Biden explained that he "inherited a diplomatic agreement" between the United States and the Taliban, saying, "It is perhaps not what I would have negotiated myself, but it was an agreement made by the United States government, and that means something. We will not conduct a hasty rush to the exit, we'll do it responsibly, deliberately, and safely." He concluded that Americans had "trained and equipped a standing force of over 300,000 Afghan personnel" who will "continue to fight valiantly, on behalf of the Afghans, at great cost."

The next day, the Taliban released a statement concerning failure by the United States to complete the withdrawal by May 1, saying it "opens the way for [the Taliban] to take every necessary countermeasure, hence the American side will be held responsible for all future consequences."

Over the following months, intelligence agencies noted increased attacks on Afghan government forces and Taliban and al-Qaeda preparations for "large scale offensives." On June 8, a Taliban spokesman stated that their goal was to create an Islamic government after the departure of the United States and its allies. He said, "We will be compelled to continue our war to achieve our goal."

Despite these warnings, neither President Biden nor the intelligence community anticipated the possible outcome of the withdrawal. On July 6, the U.S. military abandoned Bagram Airfield, the most secure area from which to manage a withdrawal. Two days later, President Biden, citing "speed is safety" as the reason, announced he had moved the date of the complete withdrawal to August 31.

He added that the takeover by the Taliban of Afghanistan "is not inevitable." When asked if he saw any parallels between the withdrawal from Afghanistan with that of the departure from Vietnam in 1975, he replied, "None whatsoever. Zero. . . . The Taliban is not the south—the North Vietnamese army. They're not—they're not remotely comparable in terms of capability. There's going to be no circumstance where you see people being lifted off the roof of an embassy in the—of the United States from Afghanistan. It is not at all comparable."

On August 6, the Taliban took control of its first province. As late as August 10, the U.S. intelligence community continued to claim that it would take the Taliban at least ninety days to take Kabul. Five days later, on August 15, Taliban forces entered the city and surrounded its airport. The Afghan president fled the country. Helicopters evacuated diplomats from the U.S. embassy. Former Afghan officials and those who had worked for the United States stormed the Kabul airport seeking escape from Taliban vengeance. Most were turned back by the Taliban cordon.

In a speech on August 16, President Biden said he did not regret his decision to end America's warfighting in Afghanistan. Rather than accepting the fiasco as a leadership or intelligence failure, he placed the blame on the Afghan government's hasty collapse. He said, "The truth is: This did unfold more quickly than we had anticipated. So what's happened? Afghanistan political leaders gave up and fled the country. The Afghan military collapsed, sometimes without trying to fight."

These excuses that "this did unfold quicker than anticipated" and the unexpected rapid collapse of the Afghan military were repeated by both military and civilian officials over the next weeks and months. They often added, "No one could have known." Few admitted that with the billions of dollars spent on multiple intelligence agencies, someone should have known.

Intelligence failures continued during the final days of the withdrawal. On August 26, a suicide bomber killed thirteen American service members and 169 Afghan civilians at the Kabul airport. Three days later, a U.S. drone attack destroyed an automobile that officials claimed posed an "imminent threat" on the evacuation airfield. When asked about the attack, General Mark Milley, chairman of the Joint Chiefs of Staff, declared to reporters that it was a "righteous" strike and that at least one of the vehicle's occupants was a "facilitator" for the August 26 suicide bombing. Within hours, the world learned that the drone attack had erroneously killed a longtime employee of an American humanitarian organization along with two other innocent adults and seven children.

The last evacuation aircraft lifted off from the Kabul airport on August 31, leaving behind hundreds of American citizens and thousands of former Afghan employees to face the revenge-seeking Taliban. An Associated Press story on November 30, 2021, reported, "Taliban fighters have summarily killed or forcefully 'disappeared' more than 100 former police and intelligence officers since taking power in Afghanistan, Human Rights Watch said in a report Tuesday. The group pointed to continuing retaliation against the armed forces of the ousted government despite an announced amnesty. Taliban forces have hunted down former officers using government employment records . . . local Taliban commanders have drawn up lists of people to be targeted, saying they committed 'unforgivable' acts."

Also abandoned to the Taliban were more than 75,000 vehicles, 200 aircraft, 600,000 weapons, U.S. military identification printing equipment, and 162,000 pieces of encrypted military communications gear.

Along with the billions of dollars of equipment and weapons left to the Taliban, the United States lost the confidence and support of many of its allies. David Lidington, chair of the Royal United Services Institute and former deputy prime minister of the United Kingdom, said, "What made support from the West so attractive to countries around the world was the underpinned commitment to helping countries build liberal, open democracies and a society grounded in the rule of law. One of the consequences of the defeat in Afghanistan is the lack of confidence in the West, which can only be a good thing for China and Russia who can offer their support with zero regard for rule of law or human rights."

Finally, left on the tarmac of the Kabul airport were the last vestiges of any belief by the U.S. public that its intelligence community could properly perform its duties in keeping the United States and Americans safe. Kabul was another entry in the long line of intelligence failures that has cost the United States the blood of its defenders and the treasures of its people.

Sources for 2022 Introduction

The intelligence failures over the past two decades are found in the headlines of daily newspapers and internet sites. A simple internet search for "intelligence failures in Afghanistan" yields more than 17 million results. Of particular help was the 9/11 commission report, the report of the National Commission on Terrorist Attacks Upon the United States, and the Senate Committee on Foreign Relations's *Tora Bora Revisited: How We Failed to Get Bin Laden and Why It Matters Today* and the *Final Report of the Select Committee on the Events Surrounding the 2012 Terrorist Attack in Benghazi.*

SENSELESS SECRETS

★ 1 ★

Desert Storm and Somalia

Early in 1991, after forty-three days of war in the air and 100 hours of fighting on the ground, coalition forces led by the United States routed Saddam Hussein's Iraqi army from Kuwait in a decidedly one-sided battle. The first major conflict of the post–Cold War era clearly showed that the United States had assumed the position of the single remaining world power.

However, while the war appears to have been a turning point in U.S. history—and perhaps in modern warfare, with its use of highly sophisticated technology—the conflict suffered under an age-old stigma: the failure of U.S. military intelligence. In a tradition dating back more than two centuries, starting with the Revolutionary War, the actions of brave soldiers, sailors, airmen, and marines were thwarted by the repeated failures of military intelligence.

The specific intelligence blunders of Operation Desert Storm will likely be hidden under Top Secret covers for years to come. The general intelligence failures, however, have been detailed in the writings and interviews of participants and by the U.S. House of Representatives Committee on Armed Services Subcommittee on Oversight and Investigations. In an August 1993 report, the subcommittee stated that collection of tactical intelligence during Desert Storm was often substantial but the information did not reach the fighting units that needed it. The report also said that damage by air and ground forces to Iraqi military equipment and manpower was greatly overestimated and that some of the intelligence assets of the U.S. Army, Air Force, Navy, and Marine Corps had no means of compatible communications. Still another portion of the report noted that existing intelligence about the battle area prior to hostilities was almost nonexistent and the little that was available was mostly incorrect.

Operation Desert Storm benefited from the lesson learned by the American military in Korea and Vietnam and already applied in Panama and Grenada: There is no such thing as limited war if victory is the objective. Military planners of the 1990s did not have to contend with limitations on combat units and firepower. Unlike Vietnam, where Washington hampered military leaders in their decision-making processes, Desert Storm was a mission directed by a president who did not interfere with the uniformed services while they accomplished their objectives. Failures of military intelligence, however, continued.

Intelligence failures in the war with Iraq actually predated the invasion of Kuwait by Saddam Hussein's forces. The United States ignored the Iraqi record of human rights violations and supported Iraq's long war with Iran, sharing intelligence with the Iraqis and training their intelligence personnel. Although Iraq had the fourth largest land army in the world after its war with Iran ended, the United States failed to recognize that Saddam's forces could be a threat.

The United States was not alone in supporting Iraq in its war with Iran. Because the Arab world considered Saddam a hero for fighting their ancient Persian enemies, Kuwait and Saudi Arabia had provided more than $120 billion in financial aid to Iraq. Neither the United States nor its allies seemed to recognize that large, successful armies headed by tyrannical kings or dictators rarely remain at peace.

By the summer of 1990, Iraq and Kuwait were at odds about Kuwait's increase in oil production and the resulting lower crude oil prices. Saddam initially asked only for a share of the oil revenue from fields in Kuwait jointly claimed by Iraq in a long-standing dispute. Kuwait refused. Saddam was now left with the option of backing down and reducing his recently gained position as a leader of the Arab world or taking military action. Saddam

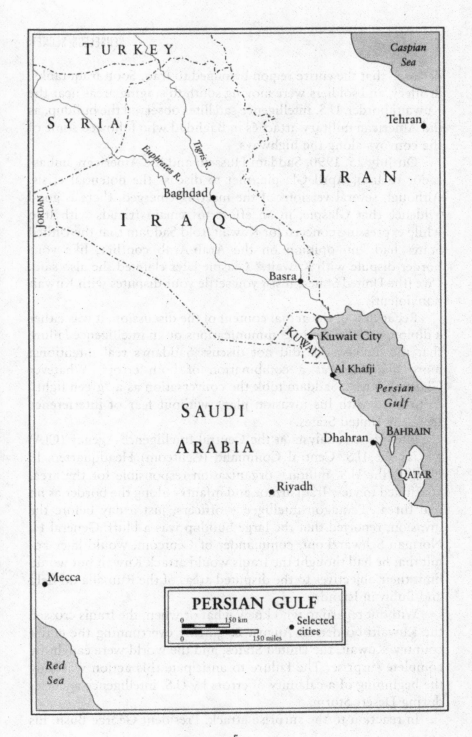

Caspian Sea

TURKEY

SYRIA

Tehran

IRAN

Euphrates R.

Tigris R.

Baghdad

JORDAN

IRAQ

Basra

KUWAIT

Kuwait City

Al Khafji

Persian Gulf

SAUDI

ARABIA

Dhahran

BAHRAIN

QATAR

Riyadh

Mecca

Red Sea

PERSIAN GULF

0   150 km

0   150 miles

• Selected cities

declared that the entire region belonged to Iraq. Soon Iraqi tanks, artillery, and soldiers were moving south to staging areas near the Kuwaiti border. U.S. intelligence satellites observed the buildup, as did American military attachés in Baghdad who followed some of the convoys along the highways.

On July 25, 1990, Saddam Hussein and the American ambassador to Iraq, April Glaspie, met to discuss the potential crisis. Although several versions of the meeting emerged, there is good evidence that Glaspie, in an effort to remain friends with Iraq while expressing concern for Kuwait, told Saddam that the United States had "no opinion on the Arab-Arab conflict, like your border dispute with Kuwait." Glaspie later claimed she also said, "We [the United States] insist you settle your disputes with Kuwait nonviolently."

Regardless of the actual content of the discussion, it was either a diplomatic blunder in communications or an intelligence failure that the ambassador did not discuss Saddam's real intentions; more likely it was a combination of both errors. Whatever Glaspie's intent, Saddam took the conversation as a "green light" to proceed with his invasion plans without fear of interference from the United States.

Intelligence analysts at the Central Intelligence Agency (CIA) and at the U.S. Central Command (Centcom) Headquarters in Florida, the U.S. military organization responsible for the area, continued to view Iraqi armor and infantry along the border as no real threat. Pentagon intelligence officers, just a day before the invasion, reported that the large buildup was a bluff. General H. Norman Schwarzkopf, commander of Centcom, would later admit that he had thought the Iraqis would attack Kuwait but would limit their objectives to the disputed areas of the Rumalia oil field and Bubiyan Island.

Without regard to who knew what or when, the Iraqis crossed the Kuwaiti border on August 2, quickly overrunning the entire country. Kuwait, the United States, and the world were caught by complete surprise. The failure to anticipate this action was only the beginning of a calamity of errors by U.S. intelligence agencies during Desert Storm.

In reaction to the surprise attack, President George Bush, his cabinet, and General Schwarzkopf's Centcom began to plan how to react. While Kuwait would have to be liberated, the immediate response had to be the defense of Saudi Arabia.

Many mistakes that affected the U.S. armed forces during Vietnam and later years were not repeated in Operation Desert Shield/Desert Storm.* Diplomacy was successful in gaining an alliance with Saudi Arabia, and President Bush brilliantly orchestrated the formation of a coalition of countries to combat Saddam. This time the United States would not go it alone.

Desert Storm would directly or indirectly touch nearly every American. With call-ups of reserve and National Guard units from all over the country, millions of Americans soon discovered their doctors, loan officers, and auto mechanics were now in uniform and away from home. Entire communities felt the immediate effects of a nation preparing for war. Yellow ribbons and bumper stickers appeared overnight as World War II–style unity and patriotism swept the country.

Also unlike what occurred during the Vietnam War, the military instituted and maintained tight control of the press, denying media representatives free rein to roam the allied lines, conduct interviews, and take pictures without supervision. The military justified the close control as a means of preventing the Iraqis from gaining useful intelligence. However, the real reason may have been that the senior leaders of the American armed forces were all veterans of Vietnam, and this was one foreign war they did not intend to lose on the front pages and television screens at home.

Within days after the invasion of Kuwait, elements of the 82d Airborne Division began arriving in Saudi Arabia to take up forward defensive positions along its borders with Kuwait and Iraq. The paratroopers were ill prepared to combat Saddam's armored divisions, but they were the most mobile of U.S. forces. Over the weeks and months that followed, other American

---

*The preparatory buildup and defensive stage was known as Desert Shield. The name was changed to Desert Storm when the coalition forces went on the offensive.

personnel, equipment, and supplies began arriving to support a major offensive.

While the U.S. military amassed its forces, intelligence analysts, relying on information gathered by satellite reconnaissance, continued to err. They informed Schwarzkopf of a formidable force of Iraqi infantry and armor occupying Kuwait and digging in along the Saudi border. Based on their information, Schwarzkopf planned his offensive against a force of 600,000 men.

Errors by intelligence personnel were not limited to the Americans during this buildup period. As the allies were about to begin air operations against Iraq, their entire air attack plan was almost compromised. The plan had been provided to the head of the British air force in London, who turned his briefcase and laptop computer, containing the plan, over to his executive officer. A short time later the executive officer went shopping, leaving the materials in his automobile. When he returned, they were gone. Though never confirmed, investigations indicated that the classified materials were stolen by a common thief and did not end up in the hands of the enemy.

As the months passed and more personnel and materials were assembled for the offensive, massive amounts of intelligence were gathered and analyzed. Little of the information was encouraging. Intelligence sources reported that the Iraqi air defenses were even better than those that had defended Hanoi. They also estimated that hundreds of thousands of well-armed soldiers and thousands of the most modern Soviet tanks covered the desert in consecutive belts supported by fire pools of petroleum, millions of land mines, and miles of barbed wire. The U.S. print and electronic media reported that the military had ordered more than 30,000 body bags, now renamed "PAC-2 human remains pouches." Although this number was actually twice the amount of actual orders, 15,000 body bags was a strong indication that the American military was anticipating a difficult foe and a bloody fight.

Even the U.S. commanders who felt the capabilities of the Iraqis were being overestimated planned for casualties in the thousands. Major General Barry McCaffery, who told the secretary of defense that he thought the intelligence figures on the numbers and capabilities of the Iraqis were inflated, still predicted that his 24th Mechanized Infantry Division would sustain 500 to 2,000 casualties. In another instance, a brigade commander known for his taciturn, no-nonsense style of leadership openly wept during a telephone call to his wife back in the States about the numbers of his men who would likely be killed or wounded in the upcoming offensive.

Meanwhile, the buildup continued, but to many of those unaware of the logistics involved in moving corps of soldiers and their equipment, the preparation seemed extremely slow. At the end of four months, cabinet officers and national security advisers in Washington were referring to Schwarzkopf as "General Mc-Clellan"—after the Civil War leader who had incurred Lincoln's ire by being a reluctant warrior. But Schwarzkopf refused to yield to the pressure, partly because of sound strategy on his part and partly because of the intelligence reports about the Iraqi numbers. He held off the offensive until all the units and weapons he wanted were present and prepared.

When Schwarzkopf felt his forces were ready, President Bush gave Saddam until January 15, 1991, to withdraw his troops from Kuwait. Saddam ignored the deadline. On January 17, the coalition forces began their air attacks on Iraq. Few Iraqi planes met the attackers, and their air defenses were mostly ineffective. Around the clock for the next thirty-eight days, the coalition attacked Iraqi government buildings, airfields, and ground units with aircraft and ship-launched missiles.

The first reports out of Baghdad came from news personnel of Cable News Network television, who presented live coverage of the bombing. While Vietnam was the first "television war," Operation Desert Storm certainly brought the use of the medium to a new level of intensity. On CNN, and later on the network channels, viewers sitting in their living-room easy chairs could watch videos of planes taking off from bases in Saudi Arabia and then see the results of their bombing in Baghdad. The military released film footage from gun cameras showing "smart bombs" and missiles flying into the doors of aircraft hangers and down the ventilation shafts of bunkers. It was not until some time after the war ended that the public learned that literally thousands of miles of film footage showing bombing *misses* had not been released.

During the air offensive, interservice rivalries as old as the first use of airplanes in warfare created conflict within the joint force Centcom staff. The air force members were convinced that air power alone could win the war and that the reward for proving its lethal destructive capacity would be increased budget and manpower allocation for their branch. Army commanders wanted the air force to "service" targets that provided a threat to the pending ground offensive. The air force ignored many of the army's tactical air support requests and continued to attack Baghdad and strategic targets. The marines waded into the affray, angry that they were not allowed to control their own aircraft. Only Schwarzkopf, by the force of his personality and the rank on his shoulders, was able to keep the various services focused on national priorities rather than service objectives. As an infantry veteran of Vietnam, Schwarzkopf knew that there could be no victory without foot soldiers occupying land.

While the Iraqis seemed unable to stop or slow the bombing, their army slipped through intelligence detection to provide a surprise on the ground. On January 29, the Iraqi 5th Mechanized Division attacked three locations along the Saudi-Kuwaiti border. Defending marines repulsed one of the enemy columns, but the other two quickly converged and occupied a lightly protected oil-processing complex.

The Saudi village and oil refinery at Al Khafji, both mostly abandoned, were of little military use to either side. Their significance, however, was that they were eight miles inside Saudi Arabia. Two days of bombing attacks by coalition air forces, followed by a counterattack by Saudi Arabia and Qatar armor, were effective, and the allies retook the town. Al Khafji was a costly intelligence failure but ultimately a military success. Several Americans were killed in the fighting, and two others, including an enlisted woman, were taken prisoner. However, nearly an entire enemy division was destroyed, with only 20 percent of the Iraqis making it back across the border. Equally important, the Saudi military had gained much-needed confidence in its ability to fight Saddam's forces.

Two of the principal targets of the air campaign, Saddam Hussein and SCUD missiles, were neither destroyed nor damaged.

Officially the United States did not target Saddam for death, but unofficially every available resource, including new technology brought into the battle for that specific purpose, was aimed at the Iraqi leader. On the opening night of the air campaign, every known Iraqi command bunker location was hit by F-117A Stealth jets delivering 2,000-pound smart bombs. A month later, 5,000-pound monster explosives, GBU-28s, were rushed through production by the air force and Texas Instruments and delivered to the Gulf as super-bunkerbusters. None of the air attacks neutralized Saddam. Although CNN reporters were able to arrange interviews with the Iraqi leader, at no time in the war could American military intelligence pinpoint his location.

A greater failure of the air campaign was the inability of intelligence to locate the Iraqi SCUD arsenal and mobile launchers. Even though the SCUDs were priority targets, and the areas in which they were thought to be located were open spaces with limited overhead cover, there is no conclusive evidence that the "great SCUD chase," as it became known, destroyed a single missile or launcher. American leaders became so frustrated with the failure to find the SCUDs that they committed special teams of the ultrasecret Delta Force* to on-the-ground searches for the missiles. They, too, failed.

The inability to find the SCUDs was more an embarrassment and a diplomatic problem than it was a major sustained threat to the allied forces. Missiles launched by Iraq against Israel created great tension but few casualties as American diplomats struggled to keep the Israelis out of the war. Only one of the far-less-than accurate SCUDs did any major damage to U.S. forces. On the night of February 25, a single SCUD† struck the billets of the 14th

---

*Although the Fort Bragg, North Carolina–based Delta Force has been involved in every American military action since the Vietnam War, the military refuses to "confirm or deny" its existence. A member of the unit is usually referred to as a "member of the Special Operations forces." Its budget and manpower allocations are classified information.

†At the time, U.S. Patriot missiles received great acclaim as being the counter-SCUD, but their ability to destroy SCUDs in flight has been discredited since the war's end.

Quartermaster Detachment in Dhahran, Saudi Arabia. The U.S. Army Reserve detachment's loss of twenty-eight killed and ninety-eight wounded would be the highest casualty figure of any American unit in the war.

During the air campaign, Schwarzkopf was naturally displeased with the intelligence community's inability to locate either Saddam or the SCUDs. While he expressed some satisfaction with his Centcom intelligence staff, he reserved his famous temper for the CIA. Schwarzkopf staff estimates about the enemy, and particularly enemy losses, were constantly in conflict with those of the agency. There was little cooperation on the part of the CIA as it refused to join or support Centcom's Joint Intelligence Center (JIC) and continually reported to President Bush that Schwarzkopf's estimates of damage to the enemy were incorrect. There is also strong evidence that, as the war continued, the agency attempted to distance itself from Schwarzkopf and his staff. Many saw this as the CIA's effort to avoid the blame for intelligence failures in what could be a long, bloody, and possibly unsuccessful war.

Eventually Washington agreed with Schwarzkopf, and before the land battle began the general succeeded in reducing the CIA's influence and preventing the agency from making direct reports to the Washington leadership about the Gulf region. Although CIA staffers continued to provide information, their influence on the war and on its decision makers decreased as the conflict progressed. Ultimately both military and political leaders agreed that the CIA appeared unfamiliar with and unresponsive to the intelligence needs of the wartime commanders.

Initially the lack of information hampered preparation for the ground offensive. Prior to the U.S. air attack against Iraq, reconnaissance overflights, other than by satellites, of Iraq and Kuwait were not conducted, for political reasons. Once the air offensive began, massive amounts of aerial photographs and other data streamed into the Centcom JIC. Thousands of analysts labored over stacks of data as more than 200 tons of raw intelligence "product" was soon assembled in Saudi Arabia alone. So much intelligence was available that Centcom had to contract Saudi bread trucks to haul the data from one place to another. The electronic transfer of the masses of intelligence data so overtaxed the satellite communications system that the United States gave serious consideration to leasing time on Soviet satellites.

Intelligence gathering was not limited to the Gulf theater alone. When Schwarzkopf was considering his "left hook" offensive, around the western flank of Iraqi defenses, he inquired whether tanks and other track vehicles could travel through the wastelands of southern Iraq. Not a single intelligence source could provide an answer. Finally, the information came, not from a spy on a camel in the desert or from sophisticated intelligence technology, but from a team of officers who combed unclassified manuscripts in the Library of Congress. The three-day search revealed old diaries of archaeologists who had carefully recorded data as they crossed the desert looking for antiquities. According to the nearly 100-year-old records of the scientists, the sand was tightly packed and would easily support track- and wheel-vehicle traffic.

On February 21, President Bush issued another demand that Iraq withdraw from Kuwait no later than the 23rd. Schwarzkopf readied his ground forces for an attack if Saddam ignored the warning. By this time, Schwarzkopf and several of his senior subordinates were convinced the Iraqis had been badly mauled in the air campaign, but intelligence sources still maintained that the enemy was a formidable force. Massive casualties of coalition soldiers were anticipated.

The ground attack to liberate Kuwait began on February 24. Immediate resistance across the front was light to nonexistent. The few Iraqi soldiers encountered were anxious to surrender. By the 25th, all coalition units were progressing at a rapid pace with the exception of the U.S. VII Corps. Schwarzkopf exploded in anger at what he considered nonaggressiveness on the part of the corps and threatened to relieve its commander. The VII Corps was proceeding more slowly than the situation warranted because of a lack of intelligence. Where intelligence data was measured in tons in the rear, on the front lines where it would have been more useful, it totaled ounces or did not exist at all.

The Iraqis withdrew in haste from their positions in southern Iraq and Kuwait along the Saudi border, and by February 26 they had evacuated Kuwait City. Except to sabotage most of the Kuwaiti oil-well heads, they did not slow their retreat. By February 27, allied armored and mechanized units were deep into Iraq and discovered that the famed Iraqi elite Republican Guards armored divisions were no more willing to fight than the units along the border had been.

At the end of 100 hours of one-sided combat, President Bush and his advisers decided to stop the carnage. A ceasefire went into effect at 0800 on February 28. On March 2, the final battle of Desert Storm occurred between McCaffery's 24th Division and the Hammurabi Division, which refused to respect the ceasefire. In short order, the 24th destroyed 600 Iraqi vehicles and most of their crews.

Schwarzkopf met with Iraqi generals at Safwan on March 3 to complete the details of the ceasefire agreement. The Iraqis reported they had forty-one coalition captives, including seventeen Americans, which accounted for all the known missing. Schwarzkopf replied to the shocked Iraqi generals that he was holding more than 60,000* of their troops as prisoners of war. Within days, POWs were exchanged, and the American units began their return to the United States or bases in Germany. On June 8, 1991, the largest victory parade since the end of World War II filled the streets of Washington, D.C., as a grateful nation paid homage to its heroes.

American casualties in Desert Shield/Storm numbered 390 dead and 458 wounded. Of the dead, 148 were killed in action. During the entire operation, the United States lost only eighteen M1A1 tanks, two to enemy action, seven to friendly fire, four to antitank mines, and two to onboard fires of unknown origin. Three U.S. crews destroyed their own tanks after mechanical breakdown to prevent their possible capture.

Operation Desert Storm clearly accomplished its primary mission of liberating Kuwait. An added success was the restoration of the reputation of, and appreciation for, the U.S. military at

---

*Schwarzkopf's estimate was conservative. The final count of Iraqi POWs was 85,251.

home and abroad. Yet the victory over Iraq is clouded. Saddam remains in power with a military capable of threatening his neighbors and continuing human rights violations against the country's ethnic minorities.

Meanwhile President Bush, who led the United States during the Gulf War, was not reelected in 1992. Even though many believed that the ghost of Vietnam had finally been put to rest, the newly earned honors and prestige of the U.S. military did not last long. A few months after the election of President Bill Clinton, military personnel were discouraged from wearing their uniforms in the White House. During an official visit to present a White House briefing shortly after Clinton's inauguration, Barry Mc-Caffery, hero of Vietnam and Desert Storm, was snubbed by a minor presidential staffer and informed that he was not welcome there.

Operation Desert Storm, like all military operations, was filled with successes and failures. Initially the high-tech successes and quick victory far overshadowed any failures. But with the passage of time and the opportunity for in-depth study, the incompetencies of the military intelligence community have surfaced as the war's most glaring failure.

Along with being unable to locate Saddam or his SCUD missiles, military intelligence made gross errors in estimating the initial numbers of, and later the amount of damage to, Iraqi equipment and manpower. While Schwarzkopf made his offensive plans based on intelligence estimates of an enemy force numbering 600,000, analysts have since determined that the Iraqi numbers were closer to 225,000. The Defense Intelligence Agency estimated at the end of the war that as many as 100,000 Iraqis had been killed, while other reports placed this number as high as 150,000. More realistic calculations have since determined that between 8,000 and 15,000 were killed, and 25,000 to 50,000 may have been wounded.

Analysis of the numbers of Iraqi tanks and artillery pieces intelligence said were destroyed reveals that these numbers exceed the total numbers of such equipment that ever appeared on the battlefield. The House subcommittee that later investigated the operation stated emphatically that this deficiency in battlefield damage assessment was the most important intelligence oversight of the war. Further detailed findings of the House subcommittee reveal additional errors in intelligence collection, distribution, and analysis that are remarkable in their similarity to, despite technological advances, the intelligence breakdowns consistently suffered by the American military over the past two centuries.

According to the subcommittee report, the national intelligence collection agencies appeared unfamiliar with, or unresponsive to, the intelligence needs of the military commanders at the front. Additionally, the committee found joint service intelligence doctrine, organization, and training lacking. Sharing of information among coalition intelligence agencies was weak; particularly problematic was Saudi intelligence, which was reluctant to share its information with its own armed forces, much less with the United States.

A clear example of an intelligence malfunction during Desert Storm was one that has plagued the military for decades. Despite the fact that intelligence units generated tons of information, intelligence personnel were ineffective in getting it into the hands of the commanders who needed it. This was caused by two primary factors. First, the equipment to disseminate the information did not operate properly, and, second, key intelligence staffs often neglected to pass along information once they had it.

The cornerstone of U.S. intelligence planning for distribution of information to combat units was the Secondary Imagery Dissemination System (SIDS). This system, composed of complex, high-resolution, high-volume photo-transmission devices (similar to fax machines) sends pictures and other information in code. SIDS is a marvelous system on paper; in reality, the machines are unreliable. Of the twelve SIDS deployed to the Gulf, only four operated properly.

Failures in the dissemination of information among the services were best summed up by a Centcom intelligence officer. According to the House subcommittee report, the officer stated, "Intel data could be passed in real-time or near real-time (from Washington) to J-2 (Centcom Intelligence Section) in-theater, but because of lack of common imagery data dissemination systems, the component commands, as well as forward-deployed units, could not always gain timely access to imagery. The Navy had its own system, which could not interface the Army's system, which could not interface with the Marines', which could not always receive data from J-2...."

Logically the air force, which produced most of the intelligence imagery data, would have benefited from more and better intelligence than the other services. Such was not the case. While months of data collection and target selection supported the first few days of the air offensive, once the battle actually began, the intelligence resources could not keep up with the action. The longer the air offensive lasted, the less intelligence the air force had, and most of what it received was late or unusable.

An air force major, assigned as the intelligence officer to one of the combat wings, later explained, "There were actually times when we sent guys out with no imagery at all. They got a map and coordinates to find a target at night. We did continue to get targeting materials, but the coverage was spotty and almost always outdated. We put in our requests, but they got swallowed by a black hole. Of the over 1,000 missions flown by [one of the squadrons], we only got back four imagery responses, and all four were of such poor quality that we couldn't even read the date to check accuracy (or timeliness)."

The ground units also suffered from a lack of intelligence data. Information gathered by the House subcommittee revealed that a brigade in the 82d Airborne Division knew nothing about the Iraqis at its immediate front, much less about secondary enemy defenses. The paratroopers, like American units throughout the front, operated most of the 100-hour offensive "in the dark" about enemy dispositions and capabilities. Officers in the 82d Airborne later claimed to have received more intelligence from the French on their flank than from their own resources.

Lieutenant General Walter Boomer, senior Marine Corps commander in the Gulf theater, stated that the marines were just as unhappy with intelligence as the army was. Boomer also reflected that things had not improved much since his earlier days in combat in Southeast Asia: "I remember being in Vietnam for two tours and never getting a single piece of useful intelligence. It has gotten better, but we still can't get to the company level what they need to do the job."

Many of the problems in disseminating information were caused by the tendency of intelligence personnel to give secrecy precedence over common sense. Quite simply, intelligence personnel tend to hold on to information rather than share it and risk compromising their sources. The House subcommittee summed up the problem: "Some officers wouldn't talk to each other. There was a tendency to sit on information rather than disseminate it." It is interesting to note that many field commanders complained that they received proportionally less information as more intelligence assets and units arrived in the theater.

While collection and dissemination failures plagued Operation Desert Storm, it was the errors in intelligence *analysis* that were the most extreme. In addition to the battle damage estimates that more than doubled the actual enemy losses, the intelligence community was never able to provide an accurate assessment of the morale and will to fight among Iraqi soldiers or of Iraqi chemical, biological, and nuclear capabilities or intentions.

Ultimately Operation Desert Storm was a success, not because of but rather in spite of military intelligence. During the 100-hour ground war, American tank commanders used less than 2 percent of the planned ammunition expenditure. Even though victory cost few American lives, one must wonder how much easier and less bloody the campaign might have been with timely, accurate information.

No conflict of sufficient magnitude has occurred since the Gulf War to determine if the lessons learned there and the recommendations of the House subcommittee have improved the capabilities of the U.S. intelligence community. However, an incident occurring in Somalia in 1993 strongly indicates that military intelligence has made little or no improvement since Desert Storm.

In December 1992, the United States landed marines in Somalia to quell a bloody civil war among bandit clan leaders that had the east African country suffering a famine. This humanitarian aid mission, called Operation Restore Hope, was quickly successful in securing peace and restoring international food deliveries throughout the country.

The marines withdrew the following May, leaving behind only a small detachment of American peacekeepers as part of a United Nations force. As the marines departed, clan leader Mohammed Farah Aidid began an offensive to establish his own outlaw government. One of Aidid's specific orders was to "kill Americans." On August 8, Aidid's forces set off a land mine under a U.S. Military Police vehicle, killing all four soldiers aboard. Two weeks later, six more U.S. soldiers were wounded from ambush.

Since arrival in Somalia, the American military had requested tanks and armored personnel carriers only to be told they would be "too provocative." Washington also felt, based on intelligence, that the threat in Somalia was not sufficient to warrant armored vehicles.

On August 21, a small detachment of the Delta Force, under the guise of Special Operations forces, and 400 rangers were sent to Somalia to find and capture Aidid. Locating the clan leader, however, proved extremely difficult. High-technology radio-intercept equipment failed to pinpoint him, as did overhead reconnaissance. Military intelligence, assisted by the CIA, tried without success to infiltrate a spy into Aidid's organization. Finally, on October 3, military intelligence learned, probably from a paid informant,* that several of Aidid's primary lieutenants were at a meeting at the Olympic Hotel in downtown Mogadishu.

Based on intelligence that Aidid might also be at the meeting, the rangers launched a raid within two hours. Rather than wait for nightfall and the cover of darkness that is the optimum environment for most ranger operations, the soldiers planned to rappel onto the objective from hovering helicopters. A wheeled convoy, coordinated to arrive when the raid was complete, would then take the captured rebel leaders and rangers back to the edge of the city. The ill-planned and undersupported attack might have worked had military intelligence not underestimated the strength of the enemy force. Rather than engaging a handful of bandit

---

*Information on the actual source remains classified.

leaders, fewer than a hundred rangers and Delta Force personnel were soon in combat with a thousand or more well-armed fighters.

The raid originated from the Mogadishu airport, where agents working for Aidid watched the rangers depart and then used the age-old African communications method of drum relays (in this case made of fifty-five-gallon barrels) to warn their compatriots downtown. With the element of surprise lost, two helicopters were quickly shot down by rocket-propelled grenades and small-arms fire. The rangers, following their code of never leaving a comrade behind, rallied to save the survivors and protect the dead. Hundreds of Aidid's forces converged on them.

The lightly armed wheeled convoy trucks bringing American reinforcements were ambushed and stopped at the city's outskirts. Without armor, they were helpless in their attempt to rescue their surrounded comrades.

For nearly twelve hours, the rangers and Special Operations personnel fought the rebels. It was not until nearly 2:00 A.M. that U.S. forces, using U.N. tanks belonging to the Pakistanis and Malaysians—whose intelligence had thought the threat warranted armor—broke through the roadblocks to the surrounded Americans. Within hours, worldwide television carried images of the victorious rebels dragging the corpse of an American through the streets of Mogadishu and displaying a captured American helicopter pilot. The final U.S. toll was 18 dead and 76 wounded. An estimated 300 to 400 Somali rebels and civilians were killed, and 700 to 800 were wounded.

The American aviator was released eleven days later. Two of the dead members of the Special Operations force were posthumously awarded the Medal of Honor, and dozens of rangers and infantrymen were deservedly decorated for bravery.

In the weeks after the disastrous raid, the White House sent more troops to Somalia to pursue Aidid and offered a reward to anyone who would turn in the rebel leader. Then, at the end of October 1993, President Clinton and his advisers in Washington gave up the search for Aidid and ordered the rangers back to their Stateside posts. On December 2, in a diplomatic reversal, the Clinton government agreed to meet with Aidid, providing him

U.S. Air Force transportation to a peace conference of Somalian warring clan leaders. Security for the rebel leader included members of U.S. units who had lost comrades in the October 3 battle attempting to fight their way to rescue the surrounded rangers.

Studies of the ill-fated raid in Mogadishu, as well as most of the military problems in Somalia, directly implicated military intelligence. The failures resulted from a lack of accurate information, inadequate or inefficient technical equipment, and the reluctance of the United States and its allies to exchange information. Collection, distribution, and analysis of intelligence was no better, and possibly worse, in Somalia than it had been in the Gulf War—and, for that matter, every other conflict in which the United States has ever been involved.

★ 2 ★
Beginnings: The American Revolutionary War

The histories of mankind and warfare are indistinguishable. Individuals, families, and clans—and later communities and nations—have needed to expand, inevitably requiring others to defend their living areas, food supplies, and dependents. One of the earliest refinements of such conflict was a recognition by the participants that they could benefit from information. Knowledge about size, capabilities, and intentions of one's enemies became key to survival.

Quite likely the earliest intelligence gatherer was a sentinel posted outside a cave or camp to provide warning of attack. Surely, it would not have taken long for these early warriors to determine the value of sending scouts to evaluate the condition and vulnerability of their potential rivals.

By the time warfare had developed into combat between tribes and nations, intelligence gathering had become an integral part of it. The earliest historical writings noted this importance. According to chapter 16 of the Book of Numbers, God instructed Moses to dispatch a reconnaissance into the land of Canaan before proceeding. The instructions Moses issued to his scouts, although thousands of years old, still provide an excellent guide for the gathering of intelligence: "And Moses sent them to spy out the land of Caanan, and said unto them, 'Get you up this way southward, and go up into the mountain. And see the land, what it is; and the people that dwelleth therein, whether they be strong or weak, few or many; and what the land is that they dwell in, whether it be good or bad; and what cities they be that they dwell in, whether in tents or in strong holds; and what the land is, whether it be fat or lean, whether there be wood therein, or not.'"

Early civilizations in Asia also discovered the importance of intelligence. As early as the fifteenth century B.C., the rulers of the Chinese empire established a network of spies throughout its far-flung territory to report on conspiracies and rebellions. By the fourth century B.C., the Chinese were masters at the art of intelligence, gathering information on both internal and external enemies. About 350 B.C., Chinese General Sun Tzu recorded many intelligence-related maxims, which are still appropriate today, in *The Art of War.*

According to Sun Tzu, "If you know your enemy and your-selves, you need not fear the result of your battles; if you know yourself but you do not know your enemy, for every victory, you will suffer a defeat; if you know neither, you will be defeated." The general astutely added, "Determine the enemy's plans, and you will know which strategy will be successful and which will not."

About the same time Sun Tzu was adding territory to the empire of China in the fourth and third centuries B.C., the city-state of Sparta formed its intelligence and counterintelligence force into an organization named Crypteis. This early spy unit would lend its name many years later to the science of coding and decoding messages, known as cryptography.

Another early purveyor of the importance of military intel-ligence parlayed this knowledge into conquering most of the known world. Alexander the Great created a staff system in the fourth century B.C. that integrated intelligence with operations and administration. In addition to sending agents to spread incorrect information about their own army and scouts to con-duct reconnaissance, Alexander also gathered and analyzed intel-ligence regarding the terrain and the weather.

The arrival of the Christian era brought continuous, albeit slow, advances in the field of military intelligence. Early Romans had no formal intelligence network, but as their empire spread, so

did their informational requirements. By the late first century
A.D., the Romans had instituted intelligence as a branch of the
government and the military. By the end of the third century A.D.,
Flavius Vegetius recorded their strategies in *The Military Institutions of the Romans*. According to Vegetius, "Our spies should be
constantly abroad. We should spare no pains in tampering with
their men, and giving encouragement to deserters. By these means
we may get intelligence of their present or future designs."

Intelligence-gathering and -processing methods made little
further progress following the decline of the Roman empire until
Genghis Khan began his conquests in the thirteenth century. The
Mongolian leader established a cavalry force several thousand
strong who had their pick of mounts and weapons, underwent
arduous training, and swore to sacrifice their lives for their leader.
This elite reconnaissance and intelligence-gathering force would
become the model for future generations of warriors.

From the time of Vegetius until the Mongols, few records exist
concerning military intelligence. That changed in the fourteenth
and fifteenth centuries with the advancement of armaments and
technology and with the expansion of warfare into the recently
discovered New World. By the sixteenth century, military leaders
and observers were publishing their perceptions of the principles
of warfare, stressing the need for extensive, accurate intelligence.

Niccolò Machiavelli wrote in *Discorsi*, published in 1531,
"Nothing is more worthy of the attention of a good general than
the endeavor to penetrate the designs of the enemy."

In his 1747 work *Instructions for His Generals*, Frederick the
Great stated, "One should know one's enemies, their alliances,
their resources and nature of their country, in order to plan a
campaign. Knowledge of the country is to a general what a musket
is to an infantryman and what the rules of arithmetic are to the
geometrician."

Without a doubt, no sitting government or standing military
force was unaware of the importance of intelligence by the time
the first shots of the American Revolution were "heard around the
world" in 1775. Unfortunately, the American colonists who
decided to seek their independence from Great Britain were

without battlefield or at-sea intelligence-gathering and -analyzing apparatus, although they did have a fairly efficient information collection system in place before the beginning of the Revolution. Like the new American nation and its army and navy, a combat intelligence system would have to create itself amidst the war. Although there would be some intelligence successes during the American Revolution, a tradition of military intelligence failures that would haunt the United States for the next 200 years began— failures that would jeopardize lives, resources, and ultimately the country's freedom itself.

Of the many causes that motivated the colonists to seek independence, the Stamp Act of 1765 played a major role. This British legislation required that a tax stamp be purchased and affixed to all legal and commercial papers, newspapers, magazines, pamphlets, and even playing cards and dice. Previous taxation on the colonies had concentrated on various regions or certain products. The Stamp Act, for the first time, imposed levies on all colonists, regardless of location or stature. Inadvertently the Crown provided the tool to unite the colonies in a common cause.

Opponents quickly formed secret societies, or adapted groups from various political and social clubs already in existence, to combat the Stamp Act. One of the larger organizations, the Sons of Liberty, rebelled against the act by rioting, attacking stamp agents, and destroying tax stamps and records. When the British repealed the Stamp Act in 1766, the Liberty Boys, as they were also called, did not disband. Rather, they increased their membership, established liaisons with similar organizations in other colonies, and served as an underground—a prelude to revolution.

The Sons of Liberty gave birth to the more formal and secret Committees of Correspondence in 1772. These committees were active in each of the thirteen colonies, and their interaction was directly responsible for the convening of the First Continental Congress in 1774. The Liberty Boys would continue to operate until the war actually began, when they assimilated into their local militias.

Not everything about the Sons of Liberty and the Committees of Correspondence remained secret, however. British commander General Thomas Gage managed to infiltrate several of the groups with agents who revealed the names of rebel members and, more important, the locations where arms and ammunition were being hoarded. On September 1, 1774, Gage destroyed the rebel arms depot near Cambridge, Massachusetts.

In reaction to the infiltration, a small group of prominent colonists, including Samuel Adams, John Hancock, Dr. Joseph Warren, and Dr. Benjamin Church, formed an intelligence organization called the Mechanics, which met at Boston's Green Dragon Tavern. Although noble in purpose, the Mechanics were a bit naive when it came to safeguarding information. Apparently their only security measure was a request at each meeting that those in attendance swear an oath of secrecy on a Bible.

Unfortunately, the oath on the "good book" was not sufficient. Dr. Church, with a Harvard degree, an English wife, and a tendency to live far beyond his means, sold out to the British early on. As a result, the contents of the secret meetings at the Green Dragon were in the hands of General Gage within twenty-four hours of adjournment.*

In mid-April 1775, Church informed Gage about the rebels' stockpiling of arms and supplies. Gage's order to the commander of the 10th Regiment Foot on April 18 clearly displays the superiority of British intelligence over that of the colonists: "Having received intelligence that a quantity of ammunition, provision, artillery, tents, and small arms have been collected at Concord, for the avowed purpose of raising and supporting a rebellion against His Majesty, you will march the Corps of Grenadiers and Light Infantry, under your command, with the utmost expedition and secrecy to Concord, where you will seize and destroy...all military stores whatever." Gage reinforced this accurate information by including a map of Concord. Each house,

---

*Church's treachery was not discovered until near the end of the war, and then only by the accidental interception of a coded message. He downplayed his involvement and, with no one knowing the depth of his betrayal, received a light jail sentence. It was not until Gage's personal papers, kept under wraps for nearly two centuries, were finally made available to the public that Church's complete complicity was revealed.

barn, and cellar where munitions and supplies were stored was marked.

The Mechanics were not totally unaware of a traitor in their midst. They knew that information from their meetings was reaching the British, but they had no idea how. Anticipating that Gage's troops would soon move on Concord, several of the Green Dragon boys, including Paul Revere, kept a close watch on the British soldiers in Boston to determine if the route would be by sea or by land. Once the famous "two lanterns if by sea" were hung in the North Church steeple, Revere and fellow Mechanic William Dawes set off to warn the Concord Minutemen.

Revere and Dawes soon became separated by a British patrol but rejoined in Lexington, where Revere warned John Hancock, Samuel Adams, and the local militia of the approaching British force. The two riders pushed on toward Concord, accompanied by Dr. Samuel Prescott, whom they met on the road. Near Lincoln, the three confronted the same British patrol that had earlier separated Dawes and Revere. Dawes retreated down the road, while Prescott evaded the patrol by jumping his horse over a rock wall and fleeing through the woods.

Revere, who would be praised in song and story for his famous midnight ride, was captured. Dawes and Prescott continued their warning ride, but Revere was through for the evening. Besides failing to complete his mission, Revere made no effort to hide what he had been doing. He bragged to his captors that from Boston to the place of his capture he had alerted all the colonists of the advancing British forces.

Once alerted, the Minutemen assembled on Lexington Green, then moved to adjacent Buckhorn Tavern when they decided the British were several hours away. They had prepared no fortifications or other defenses. When the British finally arrived the next morning, April 19, 1775, their commander implored the Americans to disperse and return home. Many began to do so, but someone—neither side has ever been able to determine who—fired a shot. The war had begun. In the skirmish, the Minutemen suffered nine killed and eight wounded.

With only two wounded and none killed, the British pressed on to Concord, rightly convinced they had won the battle of

Lexington Green. At Concord, however, they were only partially successful in destroying the rebels' stores and provisions before Minutemen from surrounding villages arrived to outnumber the invaders. After a brief skirmish at North Bridge, the British began a hasty retreat to Boston. The Americans, unhampered by any self-imposed rules of warfare and angry about the losses in Lexington and Concord, began sniping from behind fences, trees, and buildings.

While British losses were heavy, the Americans suffered only three deaths—and these casualties were the result of poor intelligence training. No one had taught the colonists to watch for security flankers put out by retreating professional soldiers. These flankers came up behind three Americans who were preparing to take potshots at the main British force. The rebels paid with their lives for their lack of understanding of their opponent's tactics.

By the time the New Englanders surrounded Boston and its occupying British force during the following weeks, there were ample spies working for each side. Some agents, more interested in money than causes, were in the employment of both the Americans and the British.

The American Revolution was not to be a fight between a united rebel force and a foreign occupier. A free, independent United States was certainly an admirable objective of many of the rebellious colonists. Patriotism and a sense of right were not, however, the primary incentives of many. Wealth, either maintaining it or achieving it, drove many to seek freedom from the British. Other Americans felt their financial well-being lay in remaining loyal to the Crown, while still others simply desired to be left alone, regardless of the government in power. No firm statistics are available, but it is likely that only about one-third of the American colonists actively supported the Revolution. An equal number, known as Tories, sided with the British, while the final third did their best to stay out of the way and remain uninvolved. Regardless of side or loyalty, information was plentiful and cheap. The difficulty, however, was in determining what intelligence was current, applicable, and accurate.

In June 1775, the colonial militia tightened its cordon around

Boston by occupying the narrow peninsula at the end of Charleston Neck. Intelligence reports had recommended that the primary defenses be prepared on Bunker Hill because of its superior elevation. Upon arrival there, the American commander quickly concluded that nearby Breed's Hill, nearer Boston, was a more commanding position. Ignoring orders from higher-ranking commanders who had made a decision based on inaccurate intelligence, the militiamen took action that would typify American military operations for the next two centuries. They dug in on Breed's Hill but referred to the fight that followed as the Battle of Bunker Hill—to keep their senior military and political leaders happy.

The colonists faced a larger intelligence failure than just the recommendation of the wrong hill. Occupying any position on Charleston Neck was fraught with danger. Access by land to both Bunker and Breed's hills was afforded by an extremely narrow passageway from the mainland. If the British had simply decided to seal off this "neck" of land and starve out the rebels, they could have easily achieved victory. Instead, on June 17, 1775, the British attacked from the beach in waves. The dug-in Americans waited until, as ordered by Colonel William Prescott, they "could see the whites of their eyes" and slaughtered the attacking Redcoats.

George Washington learned of the victory at Breed's Hill while in New York on his way to assume command of the newly organized Continental Army, formed by combining the colonial militias on July 2, 1775. Washington joined his troops at Boston and quickly determined that his force was too small to assault the city. General Gage also decided his force was too weak to attack his besiegers. Through the fall and on into 1776 the conflict remained a stalemate. The preponderance of activity was accomplished by spies of both sides who provided a vast amount of information but little true intelligence of any value.

General Washington, commander-in-chief of the rebels and a veteran of the French and Indian War, was well aware of the need for reliable information. However, his staff organization, as dictated by the Continental Congress, did not reflect his appreciation for intelligence. No staff position was provided for an intelligence officer, nor were there units authorized for intelligence production. Ultimately Washington was forced to become his own chief of intelligence.

Neither side could gain an advantage at Boston until the spring of 1776, when the rebels occupied Dorchester Heights and mounted artillery that dominated the city. General William Howe, who had replaced Gage, gathered his troops and sailed out of Boston harbor in hopes of finding better terrain from which to put down the rebellion. Their initial destination was friendly Nova Scotia, but it took no great military expertise to determine that they would soon return and that their objective would most likely be New York.

Unlike Boston, the city of New York was a loyalist stronghold. For the British, New York's central location and many harbors would provide an excellent base from which to split the colonies in two. After capturing the city, they planned to attack north up the Hudson River to meet another British force attacking south-ward from Canada. On July 2, the British landed unopposed on Staten Island. Washington and his army were already occupying the city, but New York was too large and surrounded by too many interconnecting waterways to be easily defended, as the rebels quickly learned. By the conclusion of the battle for New York, Washington would change his entire philosophy on how to fight the war and formally organize the army's intelligence service.

Initially the British at New York attempted to negotiate a peaceful resolution to the rebellion, but the colonists were not interested. With the declaration of independence of the United States from Great Britain on July 4, 1776, the British began plans to end the rebellion by military means.

In early August, General Howe was joined by his brother, Admiral Richard Howe, and 150 ships with infantry reinforce-ments of regular British regiments and Hessian (German) merce-naries. Washington recognized that defending New York would now be all but impossible. Despite his plea that it placed his army at risk, the Continental Congress directed Washington to make a stand.

Both Howes conducted extensive reconnaissance of the Ameri-can positions by land and sea. On August 22, General Howe

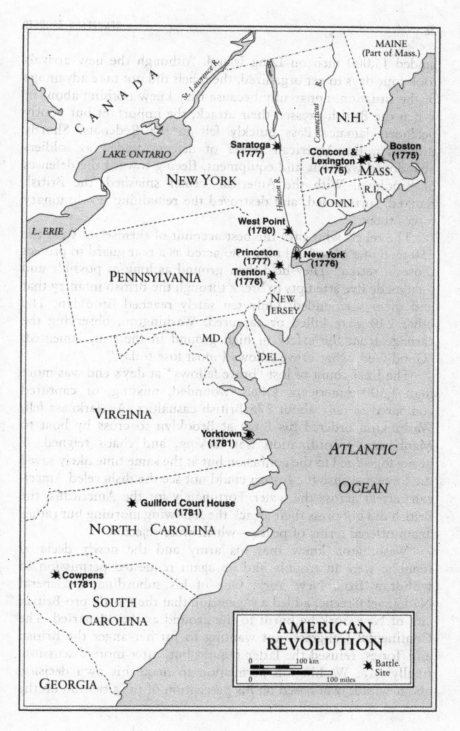

MAINE
(Part of Mass.)

CANADA

St. Lawrence R.

LAKE ONTARIO

NEW YORK

N.H.

Saratoga
(1777)

Concord &
Lexington
(1775)

Boston
(1775)

MASS.

Hudson R.

Connecticut R.

R.I.

CONN.

L. ERIE

West Point
(1780)

Princeton
(1777)

Trenton
(1776)

New York
(1776)

PENNSYLVANIA

NEW
JERSEY

MD.

DEL.

VIRGINIA

Yorktown
(1781)

ATLANTIC

OCEAN

Guilford Court House
(1781)

NORTH   CAROLINA

Cowpens
(1781)

SOUTH

CAROLINA

AMERICAN
REVOLUTION

0   100 km

0   100 miles

★ Battle
   Site

GEORGIA

landed 15,000 men on Long Island. Although the new arrivals
took four days to get organized, the rebels did not take advantage
of the situation, apparently because they knew nothing about it.
When the British pressed their attack, the important but poorly
defended Jamaica Pass quickly fell to the Redcoats. Shortly
thereafter, the American center of defense folded as soldiers
abandoned weapons and equipment, fleeing toward the defenses
of Brooklyn. With the American center smashed, the British
flanked, surrounded, and destroyed the remaining revolutionary
forces there.

The rebels who gave the best account of themselves were the
250 men of a Maryland unit who acted as a rear guard to protect
those in retreat. They held their ground as long as possible and
then made five attempts to break through the British infantry that
had them surrounded. Only ten safely reached Brooklyn. The
other 240 were killed or captured. Washington, observing the
carnage from the safety of high ground in the rear, lamented,
"Good God, what brave fellows I must lose today."

The final count of lost "brave fellows" at day's end was more
than 1,500 Americans killed, wounded, missing, or captured
compared to only about 375 British casualties. As darkness fell,
Washington ordered his force at Brooklyn to cross by boat to
Manhattan. Coordination was lacking, and chaos reigned. A
heavy fog added to the confusion but at the same time likely saved
the force, because the British could not see the disheveled American retreat across the water. Fortunately for the Americans, the
British did not press their attack the following morning but rather
again offered terms of peace—which were rejected.

Washington knew that his army and the newly declared
republic were in trouble and he again requested permission to
withdraw from New York. One of his subordinates, General
Nathanael Greene, added a suggestion that the mostly pro-British
city of New York be burnt to the ground as they departed. The
Continental Congress, not wanting to further anger the British
and Tories, refused the latter request but, after more discussion,
finally gave Washington permission to make his own decision
about withdrawal based on his perception of the situation on the

ground. Washington immediately began planning to evacuate his force from the city.

To facilitate the evacuation, Washington directed Lieutenant Colonel Thomas Knowlton to form a company of volunteers consisting of 130 men and 20 officers to act as scouts and to perform reconnaissance. Knowlton, who had served in a similar organization during the French and Indian War, quickly assembled the unit. By the first of September, with a minimum of additional training, Knowlton's Rangers were scouting the Manhattan shoreline to determine the future actions of the British.*

Washington also directed his subordinate generals to make their own attempts to learn the intentions of the British. To General William Heath, Washington wrote, "As everything, in a manner, depends upon obtaining intelligence of the enemy's motion, I do most earnestly entreat you and General Clinton to exert yourselves to accomplish this most desirable end. Leave no stone unturned, nor do not stick at expense, to bring this to pass...."

After several days with no reliable information reported from either his commanders or his rangers about the enemy's course of action, Washington took one last step in New York in pursuit of intelligence. He summoned Lieutenant Colonel Knowlton and requested the ranger commander solicit a volunteer to cross over the lines into the British sector to act as a spy. He received no immediate response. In colonial America, as well as in most locations around the world at the time, spies were considered the lowest class of any profession. Knowlton's officers thought of themselves as gentlemen, and while they were willing to risk their lives in direct combat or on reconnaissance patrols in uniform, the performance of spy work while disguised as a civilian was repugnant.

---

*Both the current 75th Ranger Regiment and the U.S. Army Intelligence Corps claim descent from Knowlton's Rangers. The latter celebrates the 1776 organization as the date of the "birth of the U.S. Intelligence Corps."

After some delay, one of Knowlton's company commanders stepped forward and accepted the hazardous and distasteful mission. Nathan Hale explained his ungentlemanly behavior in a letter to his friend and fellow captain William Hull, "Every kind of service, necessary to the public good, becomes honorable by being necessary."

Hale was much better known at the time as a scholar rather than a soldier. A native of Coventry, Connecticut, and a graduate of the Yale University class of 1773, he would be one of the first of a long line of Ivy Leaguers to leave their mark, albeit often a black one, on the American intelligence service. Between college and the military, Hale had been a schoolmaster. His primary combat experience before joining Knowlton's Rangers had been to lead a small group of men aboard rowboats to capture a British supply vessel in one of the New York waterways. Even though it was moored next to a large warship, Hale had succeeded in capturing the much-needed supplies.

Hale would prove to be a brave soldier but an extremely foolish spy. From beginning to ignoble end, he and his mission would be inept in every aspect. Neither Knowlton nor Hale apparently considered that the British might also have spies about, so they neglected to create a cover story to explain his absence from his ranger company. In fact, the purpose of his departure was common knowledge. Hale himself was a poor choice for a spy. Taller than average, he stood out in a crowd, particularly since his face had been scarred in an explosion. Even more threatening to the spy's secrecy was his Tory cousin, Samuel Hale, who was an officer on General Howe's staff.

Little is known of Hale's brief time as a spy. It is verifiable that he departed American lines on September 12 dressed in a brown civilian suit and wearing a round-brimmed hat. Taking a circuitous route via Norwalk, Connecticut, to British-held Long Island, Hale claimed to be a schoolteacher and carried his Yale diploma to support the ruse. It is likely that Hale observed the British crossing of the East River and their landing at Manhattan's Kip's Bay on September 15. He probably hoped to determine the British strength and destination before recrossing the lines and reporting to Washington.

Nothing else is known of Hale's actions until the 21st, when the British detained him. No surviving record reveals exactly where or even why Hale was discovered. The consensus is that he was either betrayed or was spotted drawing diagrams of British positions. Whatever the reason for his capture, when Hale readily admitted to being an American officer, Howe ordered the spy to be hanged. The order was carried out the next morning. As an indication of what they thought of spies, the gentlemanly British denied Hale a meeting with a pastor and his request to have a Bible, allowing him only to write two letters, which they destroyed. Hale's only accomplishment was to impress his captors with his stoic bravery and his last words, "I regret I have but one life to lose for my country."*

Hale's positive impression was limited. The British left his body hanging from the gallows for several days as a warning to other possible spies. When finally cut down, he was buried in an unmarked grave.†

Hale's fate would have differed little had he remained with Knowlton. On September 16, Washington ordered the rangers to scout the British as they neared the rebel defenses at Harlem Heights. In performing their reconnaissance, the rangers strayed too near the British and became decisively engaged. Most, including Knowlton, were killed. Knowlton's Rangers ceased to exist.

Washington faced far greater problems than the execution of his first military spy and the destruction of the first military intelligence reconnaissance unit. Howe was pressing the attack, and the main body of Americans was hurriedly evacuating New York. Detachments left behind at Fort Washington and Fort Lee were not able to escape and were quickly captured.

---

*Even Hale's last words may not have been wholly original. As a scholar, Hale was likely familiar with the poems of Joseph Addison, who in 1713 included in *Cato*, "What a pity is it that we can die but once to serve our country."

†Hale was executed and buried in Artillery Park next to the Dove Tavern—near the intersection of Third Avenue and Sixty-sixth Street in today's New York City.

With the fall of New York and the failures of Hale and Knowlton, Washington recognized the obvious need for a better-organized, more secure intelligence service. The general would no longer depend on part-time spies but rather would create a full-time Continental Secret Service. Selected to lead the new organization was Benjamin Tallmadge, a Yale classmate and friend of Nathan Hale. Tallmadge also came from the ranks of the Continental Army, where, noted for his ambition, he had focused his attention on the color of his soldiers' mounts and the cuts of their uniforms rather than on more important matters. Despite his eccentricities, Tallmadge showed a propensity for collecting information from civilians and for recruiting spies. Using available resources—including subordinate spy organizations run by friends and neighbors Robert Townsend, John Bolton, and Abraham Woodhull—and relying on elaborate aliases and coded messages, Tallmadge managed to keep his intelligence-gathering operation secret for the remainder of the war.*

What little information Tallmadge and other sources provided on the movement of the British was of no great benefit to Washington, who continued to be his own intelligence clearinghouse, consolidating information from his infantry regimental commanders and passing along intelligence to them in return. Some regiments, depending on which European army staff model their commander was most familiar with, had their own intelligence officers and staffs. The independent intelligence-gathering efforts of these regimental staffs were not collated at any central location, however, and often placed adjacent units at cross purposes.

Information was extremely valuable in the mobile warfare that followed the battle for New York, but often mobility in itself was

---

*Little proof of successes or failures of the American or Tory spy efforts is available. For obvious reasons, those who spied for the British did their best to prevent the facts from ever being discovered by the victorious Americans. The American spies kept minimal records because of security considerations. The few memoirs later written are self-serving and unsubstantiated. As a result, the "history" of Revolutionary War spies is as much folklore as fact.

the key to the survival of Washington's army. After his withdrawal from the city, Washington avoided direct confrontation with the main British army whenever possible. The general moved his army often and quickly, denying the British current information on their location. When he did stand and fight, it was only when he was forced to do so or when the conditions favored overwhelming success.

Washington's strategy was simple. Because he was constantly short of manpower, arms, ammunition, rations, and equipment while opposing one of the world's strongest and best-equipped forces, he staged a protracted defensive war rather than seek victory on the battlefield. As long as his army existed, so did the United States. What the Americans could not achieve by fighting they could gain by waiting. Sooner or later the British would tire and sail off to face another not-so-elusive enemy. Washington could afford to lose longer than Great Britain could afford to win.*

In the meantime, Washington hoped the approach of cold weather, when armies typically went into winter quarters and awaited spring to resume operations, would give him a reprieve. However, the British followed Washington's retreat out of New York and down through New Jersey. Washington's force was less than 3,500 strong, and, knowing he would need support if the pursuers caught up with him, the general sent word to his second-in-command, General Charles Lee, that his rear guard should join him with all haste. When the rear guard arrived, Lee was not with them. Instead he had become the highest-ranking American officer ever to become a prisoner of war.

Exact details about Lee's capture on December 15, 1776, are hazy, but from existing information it is obvious the blunder was the result of an American intelligence failure to determine the location and intentions of the British. Lee's troops were camped near Morristown, New Jersey, but the general, confident that the

---

*Nearly two hundred years after the Revolutionary War, the world-power United States would face an enemy that used similar tactics in Southeast Asia. Many called Ho Chi Minh "the George Washington of Vietnam."

enemy was nowhere near his force, spent the night three miles outside his lines at White's Tavern. Some accounts claim Lee was at the tavern the evening before to meet a woman and remained the next morning to catch up with correspondence. He did have a small security force, but it was no match for the British cavalry, who may have acted on information about the general's unsecured location.*

Lee proved no great loss. As a result of his capture, his deputy, General John Sullivan, an able leader, assumed command. Sullivan delivered the force to Washington and assisted the rebel commander over the next few weeks as the Continental Army performed two of its more brilliant actions. Although these battles were not pivotal, they built morale and induced enlistments.

On December 26, the first of these actions was Washington's famous crossing of the Delaware River to attack the Hessian garrison at Trenton. With information about the enemy camp and its commander provided by civilian John Honeyman, Washington overran the Hessians, who were sleeping off a Christmas celebration. The Americans suffered no casualties while killing the Hessian commander and twenty-one of his men. Interestingly, Honeyman, neither a formal spy nor paid informer, provided the unsolicited information as a "walk-in," apparently because of a previous friendship with Washington.

After recrossing the Delaware, Washington moved toward his winter quarters at Morristown. Along the way, he surprised a small garrison at Princeton on January 3, 1777, and, for the first time in the war, the rebels achieved two consecutive victories. Howe withdrew his forces to New York, and both armies waited for warmer weather to resume the fight.

The arrival of spring found the British slow in determining a course of action, and it was not until early summer that British forces in Canada, under General John Burgoyne and Colonel

---

*When paroled on April 5, 1778, Lee, escorting a prostitute and reeking of alcohol, rejoined Washington at Valley Forge. Although returned to command, Lee often quarreled with Washington and fought several duels with fellow officers before being dismissed from the army.

Barry St. Leger, continued the campaign down the Hudson River and Lake Champlain to split the colonies. Howe was supposed to attack north but instead sailed south from New York. Washington made great efforts to determine Howe's destination without success. Burgoyne, too, must have wondered where the general and his army had gone as he and St. Leger met defeat at Bennington, Vermont, on August 16 and Fort Stanwix, New York, on August 22. Both battles were marked by a maturing American army that proved valor and discipline were as important as supplies and intelligence.

Washington realized that Howe was bound for the Philadelphia capital. By the time the British landed in Maryland on August 25, Washington was maneuvering his force to block the way to the capital city. Philadelphia was not a place Washington cared to defend, nor did he want to depart from his tactics of using mobile warfare and sidestepping decisive engagements. However, Philadelphia, as the home of the Continental Congress, had to be at least nominally defended.

The Continental Army made its stand at Chad's Ford on Brandywine Creek on September 11. Washington had little intelligence about the approaching British or about the terrain on which he committed his army of 11,000. With no accurate maps of the area, Washington accepted inaccurate information that the creek to his north was too deep for the British to cross. Howe had a better understanding of the battlefield, and within hours he crossed the easily fordable creek with a large force and approached Washington from the rear. Before the rebels were able to break off the engagement, they had suffered nearly 1,300 men killed, captured, or missing.

Washington withdrew toward Philadelphia, leaving a brigade under General Anthony Wayne near Paoli to secure the rear and to harass the advancing British. Wayne was confident he could handle the mission since he was from the region and familiar with its roads and woods. On September 21, Wayne's supposition of invulnerability proved erroneous when he failed to develop intelligence on the location or intentions of his enemy. British troops, under General Charles Gray, approached at night. With flints removed from every musket to ensure a silent attack, the British infantrymen used bayonets to kill, wound, or capture Wayne's entire force while suffering only seven casualties of their own. With his force weakened, Washington gave up plans to defend Philadelphia. Five days later, the British occupied the city and began forming their own defenses around it, clearing remaining rebel units from its approaches. Washington decided an operation similar to Trenton would be tactically sound and important for restoring the morale of his troops and the Continental Congress.

On October 4, the rebels moved against the British at Germantown. For the Americans, the operation was a fiasco. En route to Germantown, one American column became lost and arrived late. A small British scouting force detected the main attack and gave warning, then put up a resilient fight to slow the Americans. Heavy fog caused more problems when two American units became disoriented and briefly fought each other, each believing the other to be the enemy. In the end, the Americans withdrew with nothing accomplished except the capture of General Howe's pet dog, who followed the rebels home. Even the one canine prisoner was soon returned to Howe with a note that the capture had been an accident.

Despite the loss of Philadelphia and the British victories at Brandywine Creek and Germantown, the winter of 1777–78 saw a turn for the better for the infant United States. Under General Horatio Gates, the Americans won a decisive victory at Saratoga on October 17 that ended the threat of the British column from Canada splitting the colonies. Gates, who did not leave his headquarters to lead his troops during the battle, was not the hero of the victory. The battle was won because of the combat leadership of General Benedict Arnold and the maturing soldiers in his command.

The victory at Saratoga, combined with the diplomacy of American representatives in Europe, produced one of the war's significant events. On February 6, 1778, France declared an alliance with the United States, a pivotal action even though it was based on the axiom that "the enemy of our enemy is our friend."

Despite the good news from Saratoga and France, the winter was not an easy one for Washington's army. Food, blankets, clothing—in fact, all necessities—were in short supply. The soldiers who survived the severe winter, however, were hardened and even more dedicated. They also received a boost in military proficiency with the arrival from Europe of Baron Friedrich von Steuben. The Prussian officer, serving as Washington's inspector general, trained the Americans based on lessons he had learned while serving under Frederick the Great in Europe. Von Steuben also shared with Washington and his officers his wisdom on the gathering and use of intelligence.

As a consequence of the American victory at Saratoga, Howe resigned, to be replaced by General Henry Clinton. Clinton arrived in Philadelphia with orders to withdraw to New York so he could transfer part of his command to the West Indies, which were being threatened by France and Spain. Because of the possibility of the French controlling the sea lanes between Phila-delphia and New York, the British were to withdraw by land.

Washington was at his strongest, while the British were weakened and somewhat disgruntled. The best opportunity for a decisive victory for the Americans, and an opportunity to end the war, was at hand.

Unfortunately, it was not to be so; and once again an intelligence failure cost the rebels their victory and prolonged the war. Lacking effective spies, rangers, or other reconnaissance forces, Washington was unable to determine the British routes to New York, even though the choices were few. Because of the poor condition of the roads and bridges, the British infantry was spread out and often separated from artillery and logistical support. In this configuration, the British were as vulnerable as they had ever been during the entire war, but Washington could not locate them.

When Washington's forces finally attacked the British, it was at the wrong place at the wrong time. Rather than destroy small units of the Redcoats, the Continental Army went up against the main body of the British force at Monmouth, New Jersey, on June 28, 1778. Initially the Americans were routed, and only the direct battlefield leadership of Washington rallied the troops to gain a stalemate. Washington planned another attack at daybreak the next morning, but the British withdrew in the night and reached the safety of New York without being detected by American patrols or agents. The last major battle in the north was concluded, but the war would last three more years.

Washington took up positions outside New York but made no offensive plans. His tactics of waiting were working well, and within a year of Saratoga, France and Spain both declared war on England. Washington hoped that final victory might be achieved with a minimum of additional casualties.

While Washington's intelligence agents muddled through attempting to keep up with British force at New York, they failed to provide any warning about the allegiance and plans of Tories and Indians. From July 1 through July 5, the Tory-Indian alliance raided civilian farms and villages throughout Pennsylvania and New York—areas where no regular forces were available and most of the local militias had been called up to join the Continental Army.

Meanwhile, in the southern colonies, the British took the upper hand in practically every encounter. Yet they were unable to destroy the American army, which avoided large-scale combat and conducted mostly partisan raids and harassment of communications lines and logistic centers. Finally, using their mobility by sea and surprise by land, the British captured Savannah, Georgia, on December 29 in the last action of 1778.

From 1779 until the final days of the Revolution, the war was fought in the southern states. Washington and Clinton maneuvered and made hostile gestures toward each other, but combat rarely occurred in the north. With the war between England and France and her allies heating up in Europe, the British began treating America as a secondary battlefield, leaving Clinton too weak to assume the offensive. This development suited Washington, who felt the republic would continue to exist as long as he had an army to lead.

Combat in the southern states turned into a stalemate until Nathanael Greene assumed command of the American forces there. As long as the Americans refused to engage in direct combat, they were successful. When they did attempt to make a stand, as they did at Charleston, South Carolina, in the spring of 1780 and at Camden, South Carolina, later that summer, they failed. By 1781, with Greene in command, the rebel partisans learned to consolidate at weak or unprepared targets and attack quickly and violently. These tactics led to victories at King's Mountain and Cowpens, South Carolina. Greene's force was now strong enough to take on the main body of British forces under command of General Charles Cornwallis at Guilford Court House, North Carolina. Although the British drove the Americans from the battlefield and claimed victory, Cornwallis's army was so weakened it was unable to continue the fight.

No theaterwide intelligence network was ever operational in the southern states. Most information came from family and friends who had access to the British. The most significant intelligence development in the latter stages of the war, however, occurred back in New York in the fall of 1780. It was also the most infamous act of American treason. On September 23, Washington inspected his rebel stronghold at West Point above New York only to find its defenses in disrepair and the commander, General Benedict Arnold, absent. Washington was still at West Point when American patrols detained a civilian with a pass in the name of John Anderson on the road to New York. A search revealed a packet of papers containing the strength and disposition of the Americans at West Point. Washington was amazed to see that the documents were in the handwriting of Arnold. More papers disclosed that Anderson was actually British Major John Andre, not a civilian as his clothes would indicate. Andre, the organizer of Howe's departure party at Philadelphia, a confidant and protégé of Clinton, and an officer marked for success, was arrested as a spy.

The search for Arnold began immediately. However, he was forewarned in time to escape to British lines. Apparently Arnold's plan had been to so weaken the defenses that West Point could easily be defeated. Arnold's treachery, probably motivated by his anger over not being appointed to higher commands after his brilliant victories early in the war, was most likely influenced by his Tory wife, whom he had met and wed in Philadelphia in 1778. There is evidence that he began selling secrets to the British as early as one month after the marriage.

With the execution of Nathan Hale certainly in mind, a board of officers sentenced Andre to death. Washington offered Andre's life in trade for Arnold, but the British responded only with requests for amnesty. Andre was led to the gallows on October 2. When asked if he had any final statement, he replied, "Nothing, but to request you will witness to the world that I die like a brave man." He then personally adjusted the noose, and the execution was carried out.

The Americans made at least one attempt to kidnap the defector but failed. Arnold, later commissioned in the British army, led Redcoats against the Americans during the Virginia campaign.*

Not all the action and intelligence operations of the Revolutionary War occurred on land. Although the American navy was never more than a nuisance to the British, rebel sailors did contribute to defending the newly independent United States. Like their soldier brothers, the American seamen depended much more on bravery and dedication than on adequate weapons and intelligence. The U.S. Navy was never able to launch sufficient ships to operate as a fleet against the British. Only occasionally was it able to engage a single British man-of-war. Generally its targets were merchant vessels.

When American ships were unable to avoid British war vessels, the results were usually disastrous. On March 7, 1778, the Continental frigate *Randolph* was taken under fire by the British ship-of-the-line *Yarmouth*. In less than fifteen minutes, the *Randolph* went to the bottom. Of the American crew of 315, only four survived. Not until the sinking of the *Arizona* at Pearl Harbor would more Americans be lost on a single ship.

One of the greatest American naval victories of the war occurred when John Paul Jones and his *Bonhomme Richard*, with accompanying squadron, attacked a British merchant fleet off the English coast only to encounter two British escort warships. The *Bonhomme Richard* and the British *Serapis* locked into combat for more than three hours. In the confusion of battle, the *Alliance*,

---

*Arnold survived the war, moved to Newfoundland and then on to England where he died in 1801.

one of Jones's sister ships, delivered three broadsides into the *Richard*. More than half of Jones's crew of 300 were killed before the *Serapis* surrendered. The victory was a morale boost to the rebel colonists, but history has made much more of Jones's boast "I have not yet begun to fight" than of the fact that the British merchant fleet escaped during the sea duel and the *Richard* sank shortly after the fight.

Privateers had greater impact, attacking British ships and selling them and their cargoes. Private captains were issued nearly 1,700 "letters of marques," or commissions, to perform what the British thought was "sanctioned piracy." Privateering proved so profitable and volunteers so plentiful that at times it was difficult to find sailors to man warships. The privateers captured more than 600 prizes during the war, which was three times the number captured or destroyed by the Continental Navy.

The tide of the war was turning in favor of the rebels by 1781. The French landed troops to join the Continental forces, and the French navy challenged the British along the coast.

In late August 1781, the Continental Army was strong enough to leave troops surrounding New York while Washington's main force, reinforced by French infantry, marched to Chesapeake Bay to engage the British southern army under Cornwallis. Assisted by the French fleet blockading the seaways, Washington laid siege to the British at Yorktown, Virginia, on September 18. On October 19, Cornwallis, recognizing he could neither achieve victory nor escape the Americans and French, became conveniently ill. He sent his deputy, General O'Hara, marching to the old British tune "The World Turned Upside Down," to surrender in his place. O'Hara attempted to yield his sword to the French commander, who deferred to Washington. The American commander-in-chief, recognizing the slight of the enemy's deputy surrendering rather than the commander, turned and ordered his own deputy to accept the gesture. General Benjamin Lincoln received O'Hara's sword, and the surrender formalities continued.

Although the British garrison in New York never surrendered, and limited fighting continued for more than a year, Yorktown, for all practical purposes, ended the war. Spying continued on both sides, with more money than tangible information exchanging hands. The English Parliament made several efforts to encourage continuance of the war, but the protracted conflict had taken its toll on the enthusiasm of the English people. On September 2, 1783, a definitive document was signed that formally brought the war to conclusion.

Against all odds, the United States of America had won its independence. Freedom had not come cheap. Most reliable sources claim the American casualties were at least 25,000. Others claim double or triple that number. Even accepting the lower figure of 25,000 means that one in eight uniformed soldiers, or one in every hundred Americans, died in the conflict.

Just how many lives could have been saved with timely, accurate intelligence is impossible to calculate. What is known is that during the Revolution progress in military intelligence was paid for in the same coin as it would be in future wars—the blood and lives of young Americans.

★ 3 ★

The Second War for Independence: The War of 1812

With the close of the Revolutionary War, Americans set aside thoughts of maintaining a military force and developing intelligence organizations. The War Department, established in 1789, consisted of Secretary Henry Knox and one clerk. Nothing in its specific duties, as authorized by Congress, made any reference to military intelligence. To gain any information whatsoever about possible foreign enemies, Knox and his "staff" had to rely on reports from State Department representatives stationed overseas and on newspaper and magazine articles from around the world.

England and other foreign governments did not take intelligence so lightly. In the late eighteenth century, European powers had informants in the U.S. Senate, in the army, and on President Washington's personal staff. Most of this information went to the highest bidder without pretense of ideology. Americans seemed fairly oblivious to this espionage within their government, and it was not until near the end of the century that the country passed any laws against spying within its borders. Ironically, it was not America's past enemies that finally caused congressional action, but rather its most powerful Revolutionary War ally. Concern about the number of French immigrants brought about the Alien and Sedition Acts of 1798, which provided broad definitions of espionage and crimes against the nation and included legal

47

procedures to prosecute spies and agents. The law's definitions,
however, were so broad they proved useless and were allowed to
expire in 1781.

Most foreign espionage in the immediate post-Revolution
years involved economic intelligence, because the U.S. Army was
extremely small and the U.S. Navy virtually nonexistent. The
primary focus of the American military forces of the period was
exploration of the frontier. Several military expeditions during the
first decade of the nineteenth century explored the riches of the
western territories. Their primary mission was to produce maps,
gather basic intelligence on the animal and plant life, and determine the friendliness or hostility of the Indians who occupied the
lands. In 1804, President Thomas Jefferson dispatched a "journey
of discovery" expedition under the command of Meriwether
Lewis to the lands west of the Mississippi. Lewis, a former
Virginia neighbor and personal staff member of the president,
selected his own companions. He invited William Clark, a fellow
frontier officer who had impressed him years earlier, to share the
command of the expedition.

Lewis and Clark and their company of thirty-two men departed St. Louis, Missouri, on May 14, 1804. Following the
Missouri to what they thought was its source, they then crossed
the Rocky Mountains, made their way by horseback to the
Columbia River, and followed its course to the Pacific Ocean.
After wintering near what is now Astoria, Oregon, they retraced
their route with several side trips and returned to St. Louis on
September 23, 1806. The expedition lost only one man, a victim of
a ruptured appendix.

Leadership of the two army officers, the discipline of their
subordinates, and a specific mission from the president to gather
information without seeking personal fortune played key roles in
the success of the Lewis and Clark expedition. The explorers'
journals provided significant information on the terrain as well as
on the new varieties of plants and animals inhabiting the western
territory. Maps they made were invaluable to future expeditions.
Also noteworthy was the use of indigenous personnel, such as the
Shoshone woman Sacajawea, as guides and support. The friend-

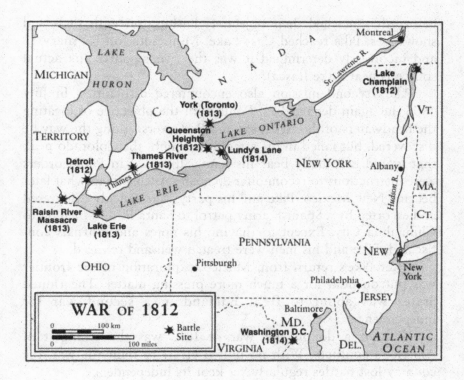

ships the explorers formed with the native population would pay great dividends during later national expansion.

Not all of the early explorations were as successful in gathering intelligence. During the summer of 1805, career army officer Zebulon M. Pike, under orders from Commanding General of the Army James Wilkinson,* went in search of the source of the Mississippi River. Not departing from St. Louis until August 9, Pike and his twenty men encountered the hazards of winter long

---

*Wilkinson was an American military intelligence failure in himself. In 1787, he was recruited as a spy by Spain and received an annual salary from that country for the information he provided. Although Wilkinson, as the commander of the entire U.S. Army, was the highest-ranking American military officer ever to sell out, neither Pike nor his missions were apparently anything other than legitimate.

before they reached their objective. Pushing on with sleds and snowshoes, Pike reached Cass Lake, Minnesota, on February 12 and incorrectly determined it was the river's source (its actual source is near Lake Itasca).

Pike's second mission also encountered difficulties. In July 1806, he again departed St. Louis with the objective of locating the headwaters of the Arkansas and Red rivers. Along the way he discovered, but failed in his attempt to climb, the Colorado peak that would eventually bear his name. Included in Pike's orders were instructions to reconnoiter Spanish settlements in what later became New Mexico. Pike and his party were quickly discovered and escorted by a Spanish army patrol to Santa Fe and then on to Chihuahua City. Except for having his notes and journals confiscated, Pike and his men were treated well and released.

After Pike's return from Mexico, exploration of the frontier was put on hold for a much more pressing matter. The United States was about to fight England in a second war for independence.

Without a doubt, the War of 1812 was the strangest of America's conflicts. With no united effort to fight the war, the country lost battles regularly yet kept its independence.

In no other conflict in U.S. history has the country been less prepared for war. The regular army had fewer than 10,000 soldiers led by poorly trained officers. The U.S. Navy had not twenty ships. In the midst of this state of unpreparedness, the resource most lacking was military intelligence. No intelligence network was in place, nor was there any information on file that would assist in planning the war's operations. The Americans had no maps or terrain studies of neighboring Canada, where British troops were stationed. Neither did they have any accurate estimates of the number of troops and ships the British would dedicate to the war. Although some information had been gathered by Lewis and Clark and Pike, no one knew which side the Indians might support in the conflict.

The only development remotely related to intelligence preparedness was the formation of six companies of regular army rangers on January 2, 1812. However, these companies were fighting units rather than reconnaissance scouts, and there is no record that they, or the eleven similar units formed over the next three years, made any significant intelligence contributions to the war.

Despite these weaknesses and intelligence voids, President James Madison asked Congress to declare war on Britain. The justification for war, according to the president, was the interference in trade by the British, their impressment of American sailors, and their encouragement of the Indians in the Northwest Territories to raid American settlements. On June 18, by a vote far from unanimous (seventy-nine to forty-nine in the House and nineteen to thirteen in the Senate), Congress declared war. In just one of the war's many oddities, the British agreed to many of the demands two days before the declarations of hostilities, but by the time the news reached the United States, the conflict was already raging.

Anticipating the declaration of war, the army moved troops toward Canada to be in position to attack as soon as Congress authorized the conflict. Instead of massing the army and attacking a communications center such as Montreal, the plan was for a three-pronged assault into Canada from Detroit, the Niagara River, and Lake Champlain.

General William Hull, in charge of the western portion of the attack, warned his superiors in Washington that the invasion was ill advised and that neither his soldiers nor supplies were adequate for such a mission. With his concerns ignored, Hull and his army of only 1,500 troops departed Dayton, Ohio, for Detroit on May 25, 1812. His army's logistic reserve, as well as his personal trunks and papers, sailed aboard an American ship that was to navigate the Maumee River and safely pass the British fleet on Lake Erie since war had not yet been declared. Trekking through an uncharted wilderness, Hull had not yet reached Detroit when notified on July 2 that war had begun. Unknown to Hull, his British adversaries had learned about the war's beginnings two days earlier and seized his supply ship, discovering his trunks containing a detailed plan of his attack and a complete by-name list of his officers and men.

A careful, experienced soldier, Hull kept reconnaissance parties to the front and flanks of his advancing army and dispatched a spy into Canada at Fort Maulden to determine the British strength and armaments. These actions were successful but did not help, because by the time he reached Detroit and pushed on into Canada, the British force under General Issac Brock was well prepared to repel the invasion. Although the Americans outnumbered Brock's force—composed of British regulars, Canadian militia, and Indians—the intelligence from Hull's captured baggage ensured the initial British victory.

Hull remained at a disadvantage after the first fight because Brock used deception and misinformation to fool the Americans into believing his troops were professional soldiers. Brock allowed the Americans to capture messages that exaggerated the British strength, and he dressed Canadian militiamen in the red coats of regulars so it would appear he had a more experienced army. He also planted rumors that he would allow his Indian allies to massacre the survivors of the next battle.

The American commander, unsure if he would be reinforced and unaware that what little information he had about his enemy was inaccurate, was greatly concerned about the capture and massacre of his force and the 800 citizens of Detroit. Hull surrendered to the British on August 16, drawing criticism from his superiors and common citizens alike for yielding a defensive position to a force that was at best equal to his own in size. Some critics noted that Hull's daughter and her two children were in Detroit and that he possibly surrendered to guarantee their safety with the British captors. Actually, the surrender by Hull and the loss of the entire Northwest to the British was simply the result of superior gathering and processing of intelligence by the victors. Hull never had sufficient accurate information about his enemy to make a plan, let alone conduct an attack or a defense.

The other two avenues of American advance fared no better. At Niagara there was confusion as to just which American commander was responsible for the offensive. Months passed with neither side prepared or motivated to fight. Finally, on October 11, American General Stephen Van Rensselaer decided to cross the river at Queenston. When Van Rensselaer's troops arrived at their boats, they discovered that a deserting officer had stolen one boat and the oars to all the others and rowed to the Canadian side. The next day, with new oars, the Americans tried again. Although the troops were inexperienced, Van Rensselaer attempted a difficult night attack. Unknown, or ignored, by the Americans was the fact that a 275-foot cliff rose on the Canadian side. The noisy attackers alerted the British force, who rained musket and cannon fire on them. A few managed to swim back across the river to safety, many died by the enemy's fire or by drowning, and the remainder were captured.

Lake Champlain proved to be another failure, albeit mostly a bloodless one. In November, regular troops and militia departed Plattsburgh, New York, under the command of General Henry Dearborn. The regular soldiers crossed into Canada and fought a brief skirmish at the Lacolle River, capturing a blockhouse but allowing the British occupiers to escape in the dark. In the ensuing confusion, the Americans engaged each other, resulting in wounds to several. Dearborn ordered his militia forward to reinforce the regulars, but the New York state militiamen refused to advance into Canada because their enlistment did not require them to operate outside their state. All the American general could do was to retreat to winter quarters in Plattsburgh.

The year 1812 ended with the American offensive thwarted and all three attacks on Canada failures. Unprepared, poorly led, and operating with little or no intelligence, Americans were paying the consequences in blood and lives. The second year of the war would bring more failure and finally, with a maturing American armed force, a few victories. Fortunately for the Americans, the British, because of their huge commitment to the war in Europe against Napoleon, assumed a defensive posture in North America and did not exploit their advantage gained in the initial battles.

Success, however, was not soon to come in 1813. The year's first action occurred in the Northwest, where Americans were now under the command of General James Winchester. With about 1,200 Kentucky militiamen, Winchester, in the dead of winter, advanced to Maumee Rapids in southeast Michigan and established a fortified camp. He then dispatched half of his command to Frenchtown to free American settlers being held by a small detachment of Canadian militiamen and to secure much-needed supplies. After a brief fight, the Americans occupied Frenchtown only to be threatened by British forces from nearby Malden.

Winchester and a column of 300 American reinforcements arrived at Frenchtown about the same time as did 1,400 British soldiers and Indians. Winchester, operating with no intelligence on his enemy, made the mistake of fighting instead of withdrawing. Outnumbered and without artillery, he compounded his error by preparing his defenses on the British side of the Raisin River rather than using the water as a natural barrier. Moreover, as he later admitted, he did not specifically order pickets or patrols, believing such procedures were routine. Before daylight on the morning of January 21, the British attacked and overran the Americans, killing 100, wounding fifty, and capturing the rest.

In the surrender agreement, Winchester gained a promise of fair treatment for his captured command. But shortly after the British marched the ambulatory prisoners away, the Indians assaulted the fifty or so wounded Americans left with the medics at Frenchtown. In a drunken orgy, the Indians tortured and killed all the Americans. Ultimately the only accomplishment of the first engagement of 1813 was to provide the Americans in the Northwest with a rallying cry of "Remember River Raisin."

A few months later on March 3, 1813, Congress authorized the president to designate eight army topographical engineers and appropriate assistants "to make such surveys, and exhibit such delineations of these as a commanding general shall direct; to make plans of all military positions and of their respective vicinities, indicating the various roads, river, creeks, ravines, hills, woods, and villages to be found therein; to accompany all reconnoitering parties sent out to obtain intelligence of the movements of the enemy or of his position; to make sketches of their route, accompanied by written notes of everything worthy of observation thereon...."

An act of congressional legislation and the actual hiring and use of topographical engineers who could provide accurate information to field commanders were two different things, but it was a major development in American intelligence capabilities. For the first time in American military intelligence history, a group of officers and men other than normal foot or cavalry reconnaissance were responsible for gathering information.

In the spring of 1813, the Americans resumed their offensive against Canada to regain the Northwest Territories lost by Hull. The key was to control the Great Lakes, because transporting men and supplies across water would prove much more efficient than traveling overland through the uncharted forests. To gain command of the lakes, the Americans attacked the port of York, near present-day Toronto, to destroy the ships that controlled Lake Ontario. On April 27, 1,700 troops under former frontier explorer Zebulon Pike attacked and overran the British garrison at York, killing 150 and capturing twice that number.

American casualties were light until, near the end of the battle, an extensive British powder magazine exploded, showering the victors with shot and shell. More than 300 Americans were injured, including Pike, who was killed when a large stone from the magazine wall struck him in the forehead. The surviving Americans, angered by their unnecessary losses from the explosion and the discovery of scalps taken by the Indian allies of the British, looted and burned portions of the town, including the Parliament Buildings of Upper Canada.

A more important victory occurred on Lake Erie on September 10. Commander Oliver H. Perry and a flotilla of nine ships attacked the British squadron and, after a furious battle, sank or captured the entire fleet. Perry fought with ships handmade from timber procured from the lake's shores and with vessels previously captured from the British. His crews included teenage sailors and freed blacks. One hundred Kentucky sharpshooters brought the firepower of infantry to the decks of the fighting ships. At battle's end, the Americans controlled Lake Erie from shore to shore. Perry penned a brief message on the back of an old envelope informing his commander, "We have met the enemy and they are ours."

Perry's victory had nothing to do with intelligence resources. His calmness under fire, the bravery of his crews, and the accuracy of his Kentucky riflemen carried the day. Perry was honored throughout the country as the war's first hero. Congress, to show its appreciation, voted Perry and his men three months' additional pay.

The more seasoned American army moved overland to exploit Perry's victory on Lake Erie. Without their Great Lakes fleet, the British, under General Henry Procter, and their Indian allies, led by the famed war chief Tecumseh, abandoned Detroit and withdrew into Canada. Procter, thinking the Americans would not pursue, progressed at a leisurely pace. General William H. Harrison did not hesitate to do so, however. At the Thames River on October 5, the Americans caught up with the British and after a brief firefight captured 600 soldiers. Only the Indians, fighting for their survival as a people, offered any real resistance, and that ended with the death of Tecumseh. The defeat of Procter and the demise of Tecumseh dissolved the British-Indian alliance in the Northwest, and the region returned to U.S. control for the remainder of the war.

The Americans were not so successful, however, in their actions on the Niagara front during 1813. Their failures were generally the result of poor military intelligence. The campaign started well enough with the capture in May of Fort George on the Canadian side of the Niagara River. This victory caused the British to withdraw deeper into Canada to other garrisons along the Niagara frontier. When the Americans failed to pursue the retreating force, the British regrouped and counterattacked. At Stoney Creek the British used the password secured from a prisoner to neutralize American sentries and surprised the garrison, capturing two general officers.

To counter the loss at Stoney Creek, American Lieutenant Colonel Charles Boerstler and a force of 500 planned to attack a small British outpost near Fort George. Laura Secord, a young pioneer settler, became a Canadian national heroine when she learned of the American plans and walked twenty miles to warn the British garrison. With the knowledge of Boerstler's plans, the British dispatched their Indian allies under command of French-Canadian James FitzGibbon to attack the approaching Americans. FitzGibbon ambushed the numerically superior Americans and used the threat of an Indian massacre to convince the survivors to surrender. Along with Boerstler's surrender went the Americans' hope of holding the line along the Niagara. By winter the entire region was back in British hands.

Meanwhile, the American navy was mostly ineffectual as a fighting force and impotent to provide intelligence for U.S. sea or land forces. On June 1, 1813, the commander of the H.M.S. *Shannon* challenged the U.S.S. *Chesapeake* to come out of the blockaded Boston harbor to engage in a one-on-one fight. Captain James Lawrence probably could have escaped the blockade, as had several other U.S. frigates, but he nonetheless accepted the challenge. Although the *Shannon* and *Chesapeake* were about equal in size and number of guns, the British ship was manned by an experienced crew of expert gunners, while aboard the American ship was an inexperienced crew led by newly assigned officers. After a brief, bloody fight, many of the *Chesapeake*'s crew, including Lawrence, were dead, and the ship fell into the hands of the British. Again, the only American accomplishment was memorable fighting words. Lawrence's last command was, "Don't give up the ship."

Several battles did go in the favor of Americans. The U.S.S. *Constitution* defeated the H.M.S. *Guerrière* on August 19, 1812, and the H.M.S. *Java* on December 29, 1812. On October 25, 1812, the *United States* was victorious against the *Macedonian*. American privateers also captured hundreds of merchant vessels. However, none of these actions made the slightest impact on the overall conduct or results of the war. By the end of 1813, the American navy was either at the bottom of the sea or rotting at docks in blockaded ports. The powerful British navy continued to rule the oceans.

The American land forces had matured during the first two years of the war. Yet, even though the U.S. Army was becoming professional under the leadership of experienced, competent officers, its abilities to gather and use military intelligence improved little, which put it at a distinct disadvantage in 1814. The British defeated Napoleon in Europe that year and refocused their military might on the war with the United States. When the British dispatched an additional 15,000 troops to North America, the war quickly changed. American strategy shifted from offensives into Canada to defenses of its own territory and cities.

During the summer of 1814, Americans under General Winfield Scott managed a final brief offensive across the Niagara to win a victory at Chippewa on July 5 and battle to a hard-fought draw at Lundy's Lane on July 25. A victory by the American fleet on Lake Champlain in September stopped the British invasion of the United States in the north, but a lack of intelligence allowed a surprise British invasion from the sea along Chesapeake Bay. Without accurate knowledge of where the British would come ashore, the Americans were too scattered to be effective when they finally determined that the enemy's objective was Washington, D.C. The Americans attempted a defense of the capital at Bladensburg, Maryland, but failed. A short time later the British occupied Washington and, in what they claimed was retribution for the burning of the Parliament Buildings in York, put the Capitol, the president's quarters, and other public buildings to the torch.

Despite the increasing success of their military in America and on the surrounding seas, the British were tired of war and the expenditures it required. The Americans, equally exhausted by the conflict, were aware that more defeats would likely follow. Late in 1814, the British and Americans met in Ghent, Belgium, and, with Russian representatives acting as mediators, agreed to end the war. The final terms simply reverted everything, including borders, back to the way it had been at the beginning of hostilities without addressing the root issues of the war, such as impressment of sailors and blockage of trade.

Official records list 2,260 Americans killed and another two to three times that number dying from accidents and disease. The wounded numbered 4,505.

The war's final disaster was oddly an American victory. Although the Treaty of Ghent was signed on December 24, 1814, word of the peace did not reach New Orleans in time to avert one last battle. Andrew Jackson, commanding a strangely mixed army of American regulars, militiamen, blacks, and privateers—and supported by the fleet of sometime pirate Jean Laffite—lured

8,000 invading British troops through swampy terrain to his defensive positions.

From behind makeshift barriers of cotton bales, Jackson's force won a decisive, but meaningless, victory. More than 1,500 British soldiers fell to the fire of the defenders of New Orleans, 291 of them dying. The Americans had fewer than sixty casualties, thirteen of them deaths. The only outcome of the war's last major battle and the Americans' greatest victory, aside from the loss of life, was the furthering of Andrew Jackson's political ambitions.

★ 4 ★
Expansionism: The Mexican War

The ratification of the Treaty of Ghent on February 17, 1815, brought about a quick demobilization of the American army and navy. Discharged soldiers and sailors, hailed and honored during the war, returned to their peacetime roles. Enlisted men who remained in the military suffered abuse from civilians who saw them as loathsome and incapable of finding other employment. The officer corps, although tolerated as gentlemen, endured much of the same contempt.

Although operating with few personnel and limited funds, the U.S. military made strides in developing intelligence capabilities. The most significant military intelligence development of the War of 1812 had been the authorization of topographical engineer officers by Congress in 1813. The postwar reductions saw the engineers' numbers reduced, but what they lost in quantity, they gained in status. In 1818, the topographical engineers became a "bureau" under the chief of engineers and subsequently, on July 5, 1838, became the separate Corps of Topographical Engineers.

The focus of the infant intelligence-gathering community was two-pronged. In looking to expansion of the United States, the topographical engineers participated in the exploration of the western frontier. In regard to defense, the military sent representatives to Europe to attend military schools and to observe military operations.

Postwar exploration of the West focused on the same missions as before the conflict—to gather data about the terrain, wildlife, plants, and inhabitants, and to prepare accurate maps. As with previous explorations, the results were mixed.

Topographical engineer Major Stephen H. Long, who had begun his career as an explorer with a series of short ventures into the upper Mississippi River Valley, led the first postwar expeditions. Between 1816 and 1818, Long had visited areas adjacent to the river in Arkansas, Missouri, Iowa, Illinois, Minnesota, and Wisconsin as he inspected established frontier army forts and examined the terrain for locations of future installations. Long's reports, generally unremarkable, also included information on the area's natural resources.

His enthusiasm for exploration whetted, Long persuaded the War Department to provide men and supplies for a trek to the Rocky Mountains. Long's scientific expedition of 1819 traversed the Missouri River to the present site of Omaha and then followed the Platte and South Platte rivers to the Rockies. His group managed to climb Pike's Peak in Colorado but was unable to locate the Red River.

Long made one last expedition in 1823 to search for the origins of the Minnesota River and to inspect the northern boundary of the United States at Lake Superior. More interested in seeing what was over the next horizon than in fulfilling the scientific or intelligence responsibilities of his missions, Long formed faulty conclusions. He described the Great Plains as "the Great American Desert," and his reports of inhospitable climate and seemingly unarable land slowed the immigration to this region that would eventually become known as the nation's "breadbasket."

The next major expedition to the West set out from Fort Osage, Missouri, on May 1, 1832. In the lead of a party of 110 men was West Point graduate Benjamin L. E. de Bonneville. Although Bonneville, on leave of absence from the military, described the purpose of his unofficial exploration as information gathering, both he and his eastern financial backers knew his real mission was to determine the value of a commercial fur-trading venture along the Green River in the Rocky Mountains.

Bonneville did not return to Missouri until late in the summer of 1835, more than three years after his departure, bringing back no new discoveries, maps, or useful intelligence. The expedition had been gone so long that the army dropped Bonneville from its rolls and considered the expedition lost. Bonneville and his adventures in the West would probably have been soon forgotten had they not been glorified in the writings of Washington Irving. In 1837, Irving wrote "The Adventures of Captain Bonneville, U.S.A.," which transformed a failed commercial venture into a heroic expedition of discovery.

More significant expeditions into the West were led by army officer John C. Fremont, who earned the title of "the Pathfinder" on his merits rather than from the pen of a novelist.* Commissioned a second lieutenant in the Topographical Corps in 1838, Fremont engaged famed frontiersman Kit Carson as a scout and, on his first expedition in 1842, reached the South Pass of the Continental Divide, charting the most favorable route to the Pacific Northwest.

Fremont returned from this first expedition only long enough to make his reports and refit for a more ambitious second journey. In 1843–44, Fremont and his party crossed the Rocky Mountains to visit Oregon's Fort Vancouver, then traversed the Cascades into Nevada and conducted a winter crossing of the mountains into California. Fremont followed a southern route back to St. Louis, where he soon produced the first scientific map of the West. Fremont set out again in 1845, but events along the Texas-Mexico border would change his mission from one of exploration to one of war.

Along with the explorations of the West, military intelligence advanced after the War of 1812 by assigning army and navy officers to attend European military schools and to observe foreign military maneuvers and conflicts. On April 20, 1815, Secretary of War James Monroe selected two Corps of Engineers

---

*Fremont's marriage in 1841 to the daughter of influential U.S. Senator Thomas Hart Benton likely influenced the young Fremont's selection to lead an expedition west. Regardless of how he gained his command, Fremont proved to be more than capable.

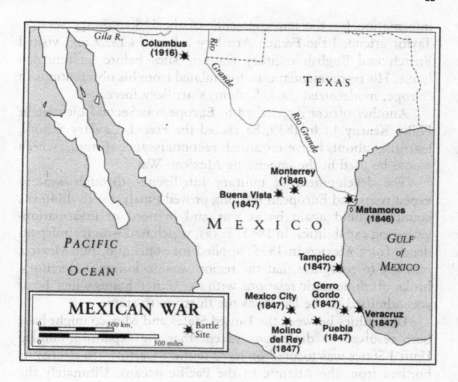

officers, Major William McRee and Captain Sylvanus Thayer,* to sail to Europe. Their orders stated in part, "In consideration of the advantages the United States may derive, by the increased experience and scientific improvement of its officers—the President is pleased to afford you an opportunity for professional improvement....The military schools, work shops and arsenals, and canals and harbors will claim our particular attention."

In 1828, First Lieutenant Daniel Taylor of the American Artillery School at Fortress Monroe went to France "to collect

---

*When Thayer returned from Europe in 1817, he became the Superintendent of the U.S. Military Academy, where he remained for the next sixteen years. A major influence on the development of West Point, Thayer passed along to the academy's cadets, the country's future military leaders, the lessons he had learned about gaining information in noncombat settings.

information for the improvement" of the U.S. military service. Taylor attended the French Artillery School in 1829 and visited French and English military training sites before he returned home. His recommendations, formulated from his observations in Europe, modernized the U.S. Army's artillery force.

Another officer dispatched to Europe was Second Lieutenant Philip Kearny Jr. In 1839, he visited the French Cavalry School, learning about horse-mounted reconnaissance forces, which would be used in the impending Mexican War.

The development of military intelligence through western expeditions and European training proved timely, for by 1846 the country would again be at war and in need of information-gathering capabilities. In 1845, Texas, which had won its independence from Mexico in 1836, applied for statehood, but Mexico, refusing to recognize that the region was no longer its territory, broke off diplomatic relations with the United States when Texas was admitted to the Union as the thirty-sixth state.

Difficulties between the United States and Mexico might have been resolved by diplomacy except that the expansion-minded United States was focused on its "Manifest Destiny" to stretch its borders from the Atlantic to the Pacific oceans. Ultimately the primary dispute between Mexico and the United States was the exact location of the Texas border. Mexico claimed the Nueces River, while Texas and the United States put the border much farther to the southwest along the Rio Grande.

Despite the tensions and anticipated warfare with Mexico, there was no military plan of action or intelligence-gathering priority. Information was so scarce that American commanders did not know whether the roads in southern Texas and northern Mexico would accommodate their supply wagons. The only intelligence information on file about the region was the forty-year-old reports of the Zebulon Pike expedition.

Total U.S. Army strength at the time was about 5,300. This force, spread out over more than 100 posts, camps, and stations, had several regiments so fragmented that they had never trained or drilled as units. Although small, the army had strong West Point officers, and its arms, especially artillery, were superior. The requirement for intelligence personnel continued to be ignored, however, and no formal organization or manpower was dedicated to the gathering and processing of information. Commanders still had to act as their own intelligence officers.

Intelligence capabilities, once the war with Mexico actually began, developed only after the loss of American lives. In March 1846, President James Polk ordered Major General Zachary Taylor to proceed from Corpus Christi, cross the Nueces River, and move to defend the Rio Grande. Although Taylor had been anticipating the order for months, he did not order a route reconnaissance, nor did he plan how the army would advance. Taylor, who did not believe any information he did not personally observe, refused to employ native Texans as scouts to lead his army, even though local officials encouraged him to do so.

After a difficult trek across the mesquite thickets of southern Texas, Taylor neared the Rio Grande in late April. Initially the Mexicans withdrew rather than fight, but finally a skirmish between cavalry patrols allowed Taylor to inform President Polk that American blood had been spilled. After some creative maneuvering to gain support, Polk succeeded in getting Congress to sanction the war officially on May 13, 1846. Reaction across the United States was positive, and volunteers streamed forward to enlarge the army and join the fight.

Meanwhile Taylor, although outnumbered, moved his force to the Rio Grande and built a camp on the Texas side of the river opposite Matamoros. Within easy range of Mexican artillery, the camp received more than 2,700 shells in five days. Despite the bombardment, Taylor was able to maneuver outside the installation and win decisive battles over the Mexicans at nearby Palo Alto on May 8 and at Rasaca de la Palma on May 9. On May 18, Taylor crossed the Rio Grande and entered Matamoros to find that the Mexicans and their artillery had withdrawn.

In addition to the mistake of building their fort within range of Mexican artillery, the Americans also suffered from enemy propaganda that weakened their army. Taylor's force was nearly 50 percent immigrants, about half of whom were Irish. Mexico, predominately Catholic, claimed the war to be against the church and promised the immigrants 320 acres of quality farm land if they would desert. More than 200 Irish Catholics accepted the offer and even formed a "regiment" to fight against their former comrades.

Taylor remained in Matamoros during the early summer of 1846 to receive replacements for the deserters and to train the arriving volunteer units. On July 6, he marched west along the Rio Grande and on the 14th captured Camargo, where his lack of attention to field sanitation rivaled his failures to develop and use intelligence properly. Although the importance of cleanliness, waste disposal, and disease prevention was common knowledge among nineteenth-century military commanders, Taylor either was not aware of or, more likely, did not enforce, proper field sanitation. As a result his army at Camargo suffered measles, dysentery, and malignant fevers. As many as one-fourth to one-half of some units became medical casualties. By the time Taylor ordered his army southwest toward the major northern Mexican city of Monterrey, his soldiers were calling Camargo "the Yawning Graveyard."

With little advance reconnaissance and without knowing the type or depth of Monterrey's defenses, Taylor divided his army into two columns and attacked. After a four-day frontal assault on the city's defenses, Taylor weakened his opponent enough for the Mexican commander to request terms of surrender. Taylor allowed the enemy forces to withdraw under the condition they leave their stores and ammunition behind.

While Taylor planned and conducted his invasion of the interior of Mexico, two major events that would profoundly affect the war were in progress in Washington, D.C. First, before shots of the war were ever fired, members of the U.S. War and State departments began negotiations with former Mexican president Antonio Lopez de Santa Anna, who was in political exile in Cuba. When Congress declared war, Santa Anna convinced American diplomats and President Polk that if allowed to return to Mexico, he would bring the hostilities to a peaceful conclusion.

On August 16, Santa Anna, under escort of the U.S. Navy, landed at Veracruz. By September 14, he had assumed command of the Mexican army—and was already planning the defense against the invading Americans from the north. It is doubtful that Santa Anna's motives ever included negotiating a peace. More likely, his plans were always to dupe the American officials into assisting his homecoming.*

The second major event affecting the war caused a more direct disaster for the Americans. Since the war's beginning, the army's senior officer, General Winfield Scott, had been lobbying President Polk to allow him to leave Washington and lead from the field. Polk finally agreed to Scott's proposal of a "second front" consisting of a landing at Veracruz and an offensive against Mexico City.

To conduct the offensive against the Mexican capital, Scott needed many of the troops currently assigned to Taylor in northern Mexico. Not surprisingly, Taylor was extremely unhappy with the proposed loss of regiments to Scott and the decreased importance of his area of operations. In January 1847, Scott wrote Taylor ordering him to transfer the bulk of his soldiers to support the new front. Included in the letter were the complete strategy and plans for conducting the remainder of the war.

Scott dispatched instructions for the transfer of forces and his battle plans by two messengers carrying identical letters to ensure the orders reached their destination. In charge of one of the messages was West Point graduate Second Lieutenant John Alexander Rickey. Accompanied by a small escort, Rickey made camp outside the village of Villa Gran on January 13. That evening he was murdered when he went alone into town to purchase supplies. Scott's letter outlining American plans and locations of troops, taken from Rickey's body, was shortly in the hands of Santa Anna. Compounding the loss of information was the fact that it was several days before the Americans were aware a copy of the message was missing. The duplicate had arrived safely, and American units were already moving from Taylor's to Scott's command.

---

*The return of the former president was not necessarily a blunder on the part of the Americans. Santa Anna, who had massacred the defenders of the Alamo, had let an inferior force defeat and capture him in 1836 at San Jacinto, providing Texas with its claim to independence. Santa Anna's past and future would prove him a much better politician than a soldier.

Taylor regrouped and moved farther into Mexico to occupy Saltillo and Victoria. With the transfer of troops to Scott, Taylor was left at the end of a long supply route with only 5,000 soldiers, many of whom were replacements untested in battle. Santa Anna, realizing Taylor's weakness and knowing his location from the intercepted letter, gathered a force of 20,000 and moved north. With his intelligence edge over the Americans, Santa Anna anticipated he could destroy Taylor's weakened army and then turn to meet and defeat Scott's force before it was totally prepared for battle. The better-informed Mexican general was almost successful.

At Buena Vista Ranch outside Saltillo, Santa Anna attacked. In the war's only major battle where they were the defenders rather than the attackers, the Americans were outnumbered four to one. So many of the untested volunteer units ran from the battle on its first day, February 22, that Santa Anna sent a messenger asking Taylor if he wanted to surrender. Taylor replied that he did not care to do so, rallied his men, and called upon his regular army artillery commander, Captain Braxton Bragg, to "double-shot your guns and give 'em hell." Bragg did, and by the evening of the 23rd the Mexicans had had enough and withdrew. Only the advantageous use of terrain and his artillery had saved Taylor and his army. Once again, well-led, brave American soldiers had prevailed in spite of an intelligence failure.*

While Taylor was winning the last fight in the north, Scott was preparing his offensive in the south, and other American commanders were taking the war to the Mexicans in another theater. On June 14, 1846, American civilians at Sonoma, north of San Francisco, overthrew the small Mexican garrison and declared California a republic. John Fremont, in California with a party of sixty on his third exploration expedition to the West, claimed the new California Republic for the United States on July 7 when he learned that the United States and Mexico were at war.

---

*The fame Taylor gained from his victories propelled him into politics and the presidency in 1848. His instructions to his artillery commander, misquoted as "A little more grape [shot], Captain Bragg," added to his image and the war's folklore.

Meanwhile, back at Fort Leavenworth, Kansas, Colonel Stephen W. Kearny, commanding only 1,700 troops, was ordered to proceed to New Mexico to capture Santa Fe. Kearny and his "Army of the West" met little resistance and occupied Santa Fe on August 18, 1846. Along the way the difficult terrain and hot weather caused more hardship than did the Mexicans. Nonetheless, Kearny was an experienced leader who understood the importance of intelligence. Whether moving or in camp, Kearny assigned front and flank scouts to spy the land. They daily brought in military prisoners and civilian farmers and shepherds for questioning.

At the end of September, Kearny departed for California to join Fremont and U.S. Navy forces to put down a rebellion by those opposed to U.S. occupation. Kearny again faced more hardship from the southwestern desert and the elements than from combat itself. After a series of small fights, including one at the San Gabriel River where Kearny enlisted U.S. Navy sailors from offshore ships to fight as infantry, California came under the U.S. flag. By the end of 1846, all of the territory that the United States had gone to war to gain was in possession of its armed forces. The only remaining opposition was the Mexican army, and General Scott was soon to end that challenge.

Scott's plan to conduct the largest amphibious assault in U.S. history at the port of Veracruz required a staging area nearer than the Texas coast. He secured such a place—not by means of combat, diplomacy, or American espionage, but rather as a "gift" from an amateur spy. Ann McClarmonde Chase, an Irish-born British citizen married to U.S. Consul Franklin Chase, lived with her husband at the port of Tampico, Mexico. She remained there as a British citizen when her diplomat husband returned to the United States at the outbreak of hostilities. Chase made maps of the Tampico harbor and its defenses and gathered information about troop movements in the area—all of which she then had smuggled out of the port by British sailors, who delivered the information to the American fleet blockading the coastline.

Chase also began a campaign of disinformation, soon convincing the Mexicans that a force of 30,000 Americans was about to invade the port. Not ready to counter such a strong invasion, the Mexican garrison evacuated. A few days later, on November 14, American warships sailed into the harbor to find no opposition and the U.S. flag flying from Chase's rooftop.

Scott assembled his invasion force during the winter of 1846–47 at Tampico and nearby Lobos Island in the Gulf of Mexico. His objective was to seize Veracruz as early in the spring as possible and advance inland from the coastal lowlands before the arrival of summer and the yellow fever season. After logistical nightmares of delayed soldiers and supplies, Scott finally had a force of 11,000, only half the number he had planned for the invasion.

On March 9, Scott's force landed a few miles outside of Veracruz. Despite the vulnerability of the Americans on the beach, the Mexican commander withdrew his troops into the defenses of the city rather than fight. A twenty-day artillery* battle followed with the Mexican garrison surrendering on the 29th.

Scott, losing only thirteen killed and fifty-five wounded, was anxious to move west. He faced delays of several weeks, however, when his supply wagons, arriving unassembled to save shipping space, had to be put together. He had a problem, too, finding enough draft horses, which he had planned to purchase locally, because many of the ranchers hid their animals to keep them from the "gringos." Rather than hold his entire army along the yellow fever–infested coastline, Scott began to dispatch his force inland in fragments as wagons and horses became available.

Santa Anna, meanwhile, had reorganized after his Buena Vista defeat and, using the captured document outlining American plans to move against Mexico City, had prepared his first line of defense at the mountain passes near the small town of Cerro Gordo, sixty miles northwest of Veracruz. By the time the battle

---

*Another indication of the lack of intelligence preparation prior to the war, or perhaps more proof that profit outweighs preparedness, was the origin of some of the Mexican guns. Mexico's best artillery at Veracruz consisted of heavy cannons cast in a Hudson River foundry just across the river from West Point and sold to the Mexicans shortly before the war began.

began, the 9,000 American attackers faced 13,000 Mexican defenders. U.S. horse-mounted reconnaissance prevented an initial ambush by the Mexicans, and the American commander realized that a frontal assault would be disastrous.

Scott summoned his chief of engineers, Captain Robert E. Lee, to reconnoiter the terrain to find a flanking route through the rugged mountains. Lee,* accompanied by two lieutenants who would also go on to Civil War fame—George B. McClellan and P.G.T. Beauregard—found such a route, enabling Scott to win a decisive victory on April 17–18. The American forces killed or wounded 1,200 Mexicans while sustaining only 431 casualties themselves.

Both Scott and Santa Anna followed the battle of Cerro Gordo with psychological warfare. Scott destroyed the weapons he captured but released the Mexican prisoners with the hope that they would spread the word of their good care and encourage other soldiers to surrender in future battles. Actually, Scott had little choice, as he had hardly food enough to feed his own troops. Santa Anna responded with a proclamation offering cash and land to any Americans coming over to his side.

Within a month of the victory at Cerro Gordo, the Americans moved across the mountains into the important city of Puebla, where Scott, delaying in order to accept reinforcements and to prepare for the offensive against Mexico City, faced a new problem. Scott's advance had been across rugged terrain that he had neither maps of nor information about, except the terrain reconnaissance done by his engineers and limited intelligence provided by cavalry. Although he now knew the area behind him, Scott did not have enough manpower to secure the supply route back to Veracruz from Mexican army patrols and bands of local bandits. The solution to his security problems was the formation of what would become known as the Mexican Spy Company.

---

*Lee's career would have ended at the conclusion of his reconnaissance at Cerro Gordo if an American infantryman's aim had been accurate. The nervous sentry, mistaking Lee for a Mexican as he recrossed the lines, opened fire at close range. A bullet passed between Lee's ribs and arm, leaving a hole in his uniform jacket.

Neither Scott nor any other American commander yet had a full-time intelligence officer on his staff. Scott had acted as his own intelligence chief early in the offensive, but by the time his army reached Puebla he had turned the responsibility over to his inspector general, Colonel Ethan Allen Hitchcock. A graduate and former staff member of West Point who read philosophy and dabbled in alchemy and Eastern mysticism, Hitchcock sought outlaws from the Mexican government rather than organize intelligence units within the regular American army. Initially Hitchcock recruited only a half-dozen bandits for scouting and spying missions, but the force rapidly increased to more than a hundred. Although this "spy company" was officially led by an American officer, its real head was Manuel Dominguez, a bandit gang leader who supposedly held a grudge against the Mexican army because an officer had robbed him when he was an honest weaver before becoming an outlaw.*

Whatever Dominguez's motivation, he and his bandits performed their duties well. Their knowledge of the mountain trails and water sources was invaluable to the advancing Americans. The bandits' experience with other outlaw bands also provided security along the long supply lines back to Veracruz. One method employed by Dominguez to gain the support of other bandits was to put them on his payroll at two dollars a day. When all other recruitment means failed, Dominguez and Hitchcock enlisted civilian prisoners they released from Mexican jails in liberated towns and villages.

A part of Scott's preparations for the assault on Mexico City was to send members of the Mexican Spy Company across the battle lines to mingle with the population in the capital in order to determine defenses and morale of the defenders. Although information about the exact contributions of the agents of the Mexican

---

*Typical of many intelligence-gathering operations, fact is difficult to separate from fiction. Some accounts identify the company's American leader as a captain from Virginia named Spooner; others do not list a commander at all. Dominguez's name appears differently in several accounts; some list his first name as Juan. Still other sources claim the spy company had over 200 members.

Spy Company is sketchy at best, they had enough impact that Santa Anna made several overtures to encourage them to change sides and turn against the Americans. Apparently none of them did.*

There is no doubt that the spy company was of assistance in the final assault on Mexico City, and Scott needed all the help he could get. Cutting short his stay at Puebla, Scott resumed his offensive with a force inferior in numbers to his Mexican foes because the United States citizenry was tiring of the war and literary figures, journalists, and politicians were turning against it.

Scott's army may have been inferior in size, but it was far superior to the Mexicans in every other aspect. Outnumbered more than three to one, the 9,000 Americans defeated the Mexicans at Contreras and Churubusco, six miles south of Mexico City, on August 20, 1847. Scott exploited his advantage with unrelenting attacks, often made without benefit of reconnaissance. This tactic was at times costly. At Molino del Rey, the Mexicans lured the Americans into a trap by spreading the story that a church bell foundry was being used to cast cannons. In the ensuing attack on September 8 against the heavily fortified foundry, the Americans suffered nearly 800 casualties to find, after their hard-won victory, only church bells, and not cannons, were being produced in the otherwise unimportant objective.

By September 12, when Scott's army attacked Chapultepec, a fortified hill guarding the entrance to Mexico City, the Mexican army was reduced to employing military cadets as young as

---

*The Americans compensated the Mexican Spy Company members poorly for their loyalty. At the end of the war, Dominguez and sixty-one of his followers, accompanied by thirty family members, were evacuated to New Orleans so they would not be punished by the Mexican government. Other than transport and some rations, the bandits received little else. As late as October 1848, Dominguez was still lobbying Washington for support of his command. The secretary of war asserted in a November 1 letter that the spy company agents had been paid well while in service but "are not [currently] in the service of the United States and cannot be paid or clothed." The secretary did offer the bandits transport back to Mexico but reported that Dominguez "did not accept this offer."

thirteen to fight the invaders. Chapultepec fell, and two days later the Americans dashed across the causeways into the Mexican capital. Santa Anna escaped but was unable to assemble another army. That left no one in charge to surrender the remnants to Scott.

On February 2, 1848, the United States and Mexico signed the Treaty of Guadalupe Hidalgo. In exchange for $15 million, Mexico ceded 522,568 square miles of territory to the United States, including Texas, California, and areas of the future states of New Mexico, Arizona, Nevada, Utah, Colorado, and bits of surrounding territories.

Of course, the price was not in money alone. Of the 116,000 Americans who served in Mexico, 13,000 died.

Nonetheless, the U.S. military had learned much in its first war fought almost completely on foreign soil. The army had perfected the use of artillery and improved the management and use of long supply lines. Leaders also recognized the importance of maintaining civilian support during an ongoing war. Finally, the military had learned or relearned various methods for collecting and using intelligence.

Some of these lessons, particularly concerning artillery and logistics, would become military doctrine. Other lessons, especially those involving military intelligence, would be forgotten or laid aside before the ink on the peace treaty was dry.

5

Brother Against Brother: The Civil War

Following the Treaty of Guadalupe Hildago, signed on February 2, 1848, the army quickly mustered out the volunteers who had joined to fight in the Mexican War, reducing its authorized numbers to a skeletal size. While discharged veterans rejoined the civilian ranks, who were pouring into the regions formerly held by Mexico to seek their fortunes, a small number of officers and regiments remained on active duty at remote posts at low pay and with little chance for advancement. What little had been learned about the gathering and use of military intelligence in the Mexican War was lost or forgotten in the redistribution of the soldier population.

The only important development in military intelligence during the next decade was the formation of a special military commission to visit Europe and study the advances in military tactics and logistics developed during the Crimean War. Jefferson Davis, secretary of war, established the commission in April 1855 and selected army officers Major A. Mordecai of the Ordnance Corps and Major Richard Delafield and Captain George B. McClellan of the Corps of Engineers as its first members. The commission's lengthy orders included instructions to investigate supply distribution, field medical care, arms and munitions, fortifications, and the possibility of employing camels as a means of transportation.

For nearly a year the three officers visited the principal western European powers as well as Russia. Their detailed reports revealed an amazing amount of access to a wide variety of information. Some of the lessons learned by the commission were implemented by the U.S. Army; others were at least studied by its officers. Generally the reports focused on information for use within the army itself, but they also contained massive intelligence about the European armies. Commission members seem to have wandered about Europe realizing that what they were seeing and learning was of tremendous importance but without having any clear idea about what to do with the information. Unfortunately, neither the commission members nor the army itself had yet grasped the importance of military intelligence in planning and conducting field operations. Actually, little time remained for conjecture. The United States' most costly war was about to sweep across the country to pit American against American and brother against brother.

Intelligence failures preceded the actual beginnings of the hostilities. The Civil War's first breakdown in information involved a cast of characters who would play prominent roles in the years that followed. On October 16, 1859, the fanatical abolitionist John Brown led a surprise raid against the unprepared U.S. arsenal at Harpers Ferry in hopes of sparking a slave rebellion. U.S. Army Colonel Robert E. Lee and his assistant, Lieutenant J. E. B. Stuart, accompanied by a company of U.S. Marines under the command of Lieutenant Israel Greene, were sent from Washington to capture Brown and his supporters. By the 18th the marines had put down the insurrection and arrested Brown, who would soon face the gallows.

Brown's raid did not trigger the American Civil War. Rather, the conflict was inevitable from the time of the Revolutionary War. Even though the North and South—divided by geographical and political differences, which were compounded by slavery and states' rights issues—had long been on a collision course, neither side had made any great efforts to prepare militarily.

The majority of the American people did not believe that the differences would lead to bloodshed. Even when South Carolina seceded from the Union in December 1860, and other states followed its lead in the ensuing months, many remained unconvinced that war was near. The newly formed Confederate States of

America thought that they had met their objectives by seceding and forming their own country. In the North, many people, including political and military leaders, believed that a blockade of the Confederacy supported by diplomacy would peacefully return the Southern states to the fold. When the war actually began with the fall of Fort Sumter, South Carolina, on April 14, 1861, no one foresaw the length and brutality of the conflict.

The initial months of the Civil War bore a distinct similarity to the American Revolution. Both sides spoke the same language, both were familiar with the terrain on which the war would be fought, and a large segment of the population, mostly in the border states, was unsure of which side to support. The Southern rebels, like their colonial forefathers, did not have to defeat their opponents. As long as their army was in the field, the Confederacy existed. For the United States, victory and preserving the Union required an offensive against the rebels to destroy their armed forces. The similarities extended to the navies. Just as Great Britain had controlled the waterways to the American coast, the U.S. Navy was strong enough to hinder Southern shipping.

Without a doubt, no other American conflict has been romanticized more than the Civil War, and military intelligence is glorified as much as, or more than, any other aspect of it. Stories of gallant men and women stealing information at the dining tables of presidents and from the camps of generals dominate the autobiographies of spies, tales better suited to the stage than to history books.

Other stories about "the" Secret Service of the North and South add to the myth but not to the facts. While spies and various secret services did exist on both sides, neither had a centralized organization responsible for its national intelligence. Despite this lack, great strides in the development of American military intelligence were made during the Civil War. As in previous wars, commanders gathered information on their own by means immediately available to them: cavalry reconnaissance, prisoner interrogation, and the other side's newspapers. Victories were certainly won by better-informed commanders, but in most cases, especially with generals like Lee and Grant, the winner was usually simply the "better" commander, regardless of information. Of course, the

commander who had the larger number of better-armed and
-equipped men was also at an advantage. Regardless of the fanfare
and myth making, the fact remains that not a single major Civil
War battle was won or lost strictly because of intelligence or the
lack of it.

For three months after the fall of Fort Sumter, neither side
made any significant hostile moves. This delay allowed both the
North and the South to prepare their armies and to begin
organizing a military intelligence system.

While not as organized, powerful, or successful as the participants' written accounts suggest, the Civil War did spawn some of
America's first formal national military intelligence organizations.
The earliest, and perhaps best known, was Pinkerton's National
Detective Agency. Allan Pinkerton, fleeing Scotland where he had
become involved in violent political reform movements in 1842,
had emigrated to Chicago and become a policeman. During his
off-duty hours, Pinkerton was a dedicated abolitionist active in
the Underground Railway that smuggled escaped slaves to free
territory. By 1849, he had been appointed the city's first detective.
A few years later he established a private practice focusing on
railroad security with the trademark of a vigilant open eye
accompanied by the slogan "We Never Sleep."

Pinkerton came to national attention in January 1861 while
working for the Philadelphia, Wilmington & Baltimore Railroad
to provide security for President-elect Abraham Lincoln's journey
to the capital for his inauguration. In Baltimore, Pinkerton
discovered and thwarted a conspiracy to assassinate the newly
elected president.

After the fall of Fort Sumter, Pinkerton wrote Lincoln to offer
his agency to Union service. Although Pinkerton and Lincoln met
in Washington in April, nothing came from their discussions. In
May the commander of the Army of the Ohio, General George
McClellan, who had met Pinkerton while both were working for
the Illinois Central Railroad, hired the detective. In July, Mc-
Clellan was promoted to lead the Army of the Potomac, and
Pinkerton and his detectives joined the command.

McClellan's primary use of "the Pinkertons" was in determining Confederate troop strength and unit identifications. The

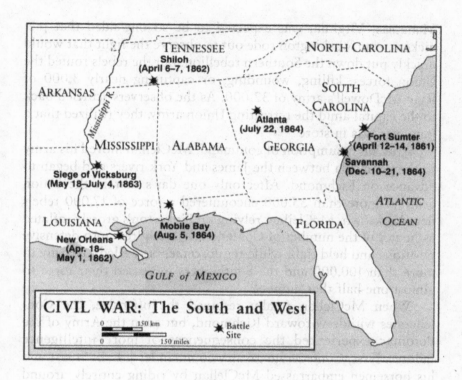

CIVIL WAR: The South and West

civilian detectives—including Pinkerton himself, who assumed the rank and alias of Major E. J. Allen—were woefully inadequate. Pinkerton possessed no military experience and apparently was unable to understand or process the information provided by his detectives and military scouts. He consistently overestimated by two to four times the size of the rebel army opposing the Army of the Potomac. McClellan, a reluctant warrior at best, used the inflated enemy troop estimates as further rationale not to fight.

Pinkerton did have some success in establishing agents in Richmond and in breaking up a Confederate spy ring in Washington. There is no evidence, however, of this intrigue actually making any impact on the combat forces in the field. All in all, Pinkerton proved to be a much better policeman than an intelligence officer.

McClellan had gained command of the Army of the Potomac after the Union loss at the First Battle of Bull Run. The clash at

Manassas, Virginia, was expected to be so one-sided that pic-
nickers from Washington rode out to observe the fight that would
quickly put down the Southern rebellion. But the rebels routed the
Union forces, killing, wounding, or capturing nearly 3,000 of
Irvin McDowell's army of 32,000. As the observers scurried back
to the capital amid the retreating Union army, they realized that a
long war was in store.

After his assumption of command, McClellan moved his army
to the peninsula between the James and York rivers and began to
advance on Richmond. After only one day's march, the Union
army of more than 85,000 encountered a force of 17,000 rebels
near Yorktown. McClellan, relying on Pinkerton's grossly inflated
estimates of the number of Confederates, withdrew into defensive
positions and held tight while reinforcements swelled his army to
more than 100,000 and the Southerners increased their force to
almost one-half that number.

When McClellan finally resumed the offensive, the Confederates withdrew toward Richmond, but soon the Army of the
Potomac experienced the consequences of more intelligence
failures. First, Confederate cavalry commander J. E. B. Stuart and
his horsemen embarrassed McClellan by riding entirely around
the 100,000-man Union force stealing horses and stores and
scouting the army's strength and positions.

Even though there were accurate maps of the area, and many
of the Union soldiers were familiar with the Virginia peninsula
region, neither Pinkerton nor anyone else informed McClellan
that the Warwick River was not fordable by foot soldiers or
mounted cavalry. Because of this lack of intelligence, the Union
army was forced to slow its attack in order to build bridges to
cross the water obstacle. In the following days, Pinkerton convinced his commander that the Confederate force was actually
larger than his own, even though McClellan's army was twice the
size of the Southern enemy. In a series of unremarkable battles,
fought by a reluctant McClellan, the Army of the Potomac arrived
within six miles of the Confederate capital. There, in late June
1862, they were stopped by the new commander of the Army of
Northern Virginia, General Robert E. Lee, at the Battle of Seven
Pines.

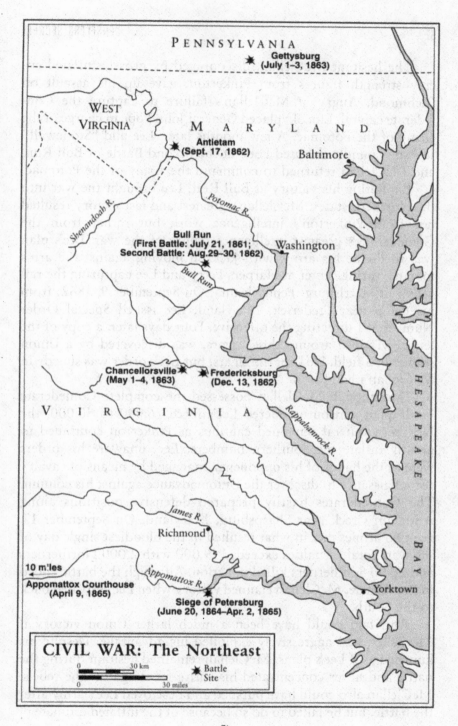

PENNSYLVANIA

★ Gettysburg
(July 1–3, 1863)

WEST
VIRGINIA

M A R Y L A N D

★ Antietam
(Sept. 17, 1862)

Baltimore

Shenandoah R.

Potomac R.

Bull Run
(First Battle: July 21, 1861;
Second Battle: Aug.29–30, 1862)

Washington ●

★

Bull Run

C
H
E
S
A
P
E
A
K
E

Chancellorsville
(May 1–4, 1863)

★ ★ Fredericksburg
(Dec. 13, 1862)

V I R G I N I A

Rappahannock R.

James R.

Richmond ●

10 miles

Appomattox R.

B
A
Y

Appomattox Courthouse
(April 9, 1865)

Siege of Petersburg
(June 20, 1864–Apr. 2, 1865)

Yorktown ●

CIVIL WAR: The Northeast

0   30 km

★ Battle
Site

0   30 miles

The hesitant McClellan, discouraged by grossly inflated enemy strength figures from Pinkerton, gave up his assault on Richmond. Angry at McClellan's failure to capture the Confederate capital, Lincoln placed General John Pope in charge of the Army of the Potomac. A few months later, Lee and "Stonewall" Jackson soundly defeated Pope at the Second Battle of Bull Run, and McClellan returned to command the Army of the Potomac.

Exploiting his victory at Bull Run, Lee brought the war into the Northern states. McClellan's greatest and last victory resulted not from Pinkerton's intelligence work but rather from the Confederacy's greatest intelligence failure of the war. Lee's plan was to divide his army, with Jackson moving against the arms manufacturing center at Harpers Ferry and Lee capturing the rail center at Harrisburg, Pennsylvania. On September 9, 1862, from his camp near Frederick, Maryland, Lee issued Special Order Number 191 directing the offensive. Four days later, a copy of the letter, wrapped around three cigars, was discovered by a Union soldier in a field. He kept the cigars, but Lee's order was shortly in McClellan's hands.

Even though McClellan possessed the complete Confederate battle plan and outnumbered Lee's force 76,000 to 40,000, the Northern general remained cautious as Pinkerton continued to grossly inflate the Southern numbers. Lee, unaware his orders were in the hands of his opponents, managed by means of cavalry reconnaissance to discover the Union advance against his column. The Confederates hastily prepared defensive positions along Antietam Creek near Sharpsburg, Maryland. On September 17, the two armies met in what resulted in the bloodiest single day of the war. Total casualties exceeded 19,000 with 2,000 Northerners and 2,700 Southerners killed in action. Although the battle ended in a stalemate, McClellan claimed victory when Lee retreated back to the South.

Antietam could have been a much larger Union victory if McClellan had aggressively exploited his advantage. Despite his knowledge of Lee's plans, McClellan remained hesitant during the battle and never concentrated his entire force against the rebels. McClellan also could have pursued and destroyed Lee's army after the battle, but he failed to do so because of the inflated estimate of

Confederate strength. Even though he allowed Lee to escape, the victory at Sharpsburg tremendously lifted the morale of the Union, and, more important, it paid huge diplomatic benefits. Several European countries, including Great Britain, were on the verge of recognizing the new Confederate States of America and providing financial and military aid. The Union victory caused them to reevaluate the future of the Confederacy and to withhold their support.

Lincoln was happy with the victory at Antietam, using it as a springboard to issue the Emancipation Proclamation* on September 22. But the president was unhappy with his general. Lincoln replaced the reluctant McClellan with Ambrose E. Burnside on November 5. Pinkerton and his detective force departed the Army of the Potomac with McClellan, never again to be involved in military intelligence. For the remainder of the war, Pinkerton and his agency worked for the War Department investigating fraud and claims against the government.

Pinkerton's intelligence operations were of little if any value to the Union army in the field. His most lasting, and perhaps only, impact on military intelligence was simply "being there." Despite his failures and later inflation of his own importance, Pinkerton could honestly lay claim to being in charge of the first organized national intelligence collection agency in the U.S. Army.

There is no record dating from the time of Pinkerton's actual service to McClellan of any official title for his organization. Although he often referred to his "National Detective Agency," his official reports were on stationery headed by the titles "Headquarters, City Guard" and "Headquarters, Army of the Potomac." It was not until twenty years after the war that Pinkerton, in his autobiography, labeled his unit the U.S. Secret Service.

Pinkerton was not the only person to claim to head the Union's Secret Service. War Department Provost Marshal Lafayette C.

---

*The Emancipation Proclamation was a political act, freeing slaves only in rebel-held territory where Lincoln had no real authority. It did not mention slaves in the North or in Union-held regions. The majority of America's slaves were not liberated until two years later with the passage of the Thirteenth Amendment in January 1865.

Baker led a staff of detectives and investigators from February 1862 until February 1866. Baker's office stationery was embossed with "National Detective Police Department," although at various times he referred to his organization as the Bureau of Secret Service, the National Detective Police, and, most commonly, the National Detective Bureau. Not until the war had been over for two years did Baker claim the title of U.S. Secret Service for his agency.

Whatever the designation, Baker accomplished little beyond a personal undercover visit to Richmond. His "spy" organization did expose a few rebel agents in Washington, but his primary mission was the investigation of fraud and graft among government staffs and the various manufacturers and suppliers who were profiteering from their war efforts. Baker and his bureau's accomplishments were so few that neither he nor his organization is mentioned in the War Department's official report on the conflict. The nearest Baker came to any actual military intelligence activity was in his role as the commander of the First District of Columbia Cavalry, or "Baker's Rangers." This cavalry unit, which did not include his detective staff, was so obscure that even Baker in his highly fictionalized autobiography made no boast of its accomplishments.

While Baker and Pinkerton played the role of early performers in the drama of military intelligence, both were far better actors than intelligence practitioners, for the only people who acclaimed their services were themselves in their own writings. Their postwar claims of heading a nonexistent U.S. Secret Service are strictly fiction, as neither ever had a "national" role in military intelligence.

When Pinkerton and his detectives departed with McClellan, the Army of the Potomac was left with a single intelligence officer. Twenty-six-year-old John C. Babcock, who had been hired by Pinkerton after his agency assumed its intelligence role, remained behind. An architect before the war, Babcock had primarily served as a map maker while working for Pinkerton.

McClellan's replacement, General Ambrose Burnside, was as bold as his predecessor had been reluctant, but there is no evidence that Burnside paid any attention to Babcock's intelligence advice or made any attempt to replace the Pinkertons. On December 13, 1862, Burnside and his army crossed the Rappahannock River and attacked the combined forces of Lee and Jackson at Fredericksburg. Burnside conducted no cavalry reconnaissance, nor did he attempt to infiltrate spies into the Confederate lines to learn their strength and disposition. Instead he ordered his army of 106,000 up the hills of Marye's Heights into the strength of 73,000 rebels and their supporting artillery. At day's end the Union counted 12,700 casualties. The rebels, who still held their position, had suffered 5,300 dead, wounded, and missing.

Another intelligence asset Burnside failed to use at Fredericksburg had been employed by other Union commanders with various degrees of success. Several balloonists, or aeronauts as they preferred to be called, offered their services to the Union at the outbreak of hostilities. Balloons, used for military reconnaissance in Europe as early as 1794, had been proposed but not tried by the U.S. Army during the Florida Seminole Indian campaign and at Veracruz in the Mexican War. After the fall of Fort Sumter, Major Hartman Bache, the chief of the War Department's Bureau of Topographical Engineers, assumed the responsibility of investigating the possibilities of balloon reconnaissance. Bache was assisted by Captain Amiel W. Whipple, who was on General Irvin McDowell's Department of Northeast Virginia staff performing topographical duty.

The first official balloon launched for the army was a demonstration flight by James Allen on June 9, 1861, in Washington. Allen's practice flight proved successful, but when he attempted to launch actual reconnaissance missions the next month at Falls Church, Virginia, high winds destroyed both of his balloons before they could become airborne. A friend and mentor of Allen, John Wise, attempted to employ a balloon in support of McDowell's fight at the First Battle of Bull Run, but the craft was damaged en route to the battlefield. Wise is often referred to as the "father of American ballooning" because of his early experiments and a book he wrote on the subject. He did manage to launch another craft successfully on July 24, 1861. The tethered balloon's observer was able to spot and report several rebel cavalry and artillery units to the south of Arlington, Virginia. Two days later

Wise's balloon, with no one aboard, was accidentally released and had to be shot down by Union troops to prevent its floating into rebel hands. Captain Whipple was so critical of Wise's loss of the balloon that the aeronaut resigned.

With Allen and Wise no longer in the balloon business, another early aeronaut came to the forefront. Thaddeus S. C. Lowe, a twenty-eight-year-old New Hampshire native, had already made quite an impression with balloon demonstrations in Washington. On June 18, Lowe ascended above the city and reported his observations by telegraph using a wire suspended to the ground. The telegraph message went to the War Department, which relayed it to the White House. It reported, "Sir: This point of observation commands an area nearly fifty miles in diameter. The city, with its girdle of encampments, presents a superb scene. I have pleasure in sending you this first dispatch ever telegraphed from an aerial station.... T.S.C. Lowe." Lowe followed his demonstration with several more flights during the next few days over Arlington and Falls Church that yielded intelligence on Confederate positions. President Lincoln was so impressed that he recommended to the army's commander, General Winfield Scott, that Lowe be employed full time.

Scott was not enamored with balloons or balloonists, and it was not until August that Lowe was formally hired as a civilian employee of the Bureau of Topographical Engineers for the Army of the Potomac. On September 24, Lowe took to the air aboard the balloon *Union* and directed artillery fire against Confederate positions at Falls Church. Over the next weeks, Lowe, who called himself "chief aeronaut," constructed additional balloons until his fleet numbered eight and hired a staff of nine, including James Allen.

The only other balloon activity in the Union army at the time was conducted by John La Mountain in support of Benjamin F. Butler, commanding general of the Department of Virginia at Fortress Monroe. La Mountain began his flights on July 25, 1861, and made several ascents to locate rebel forces threatening Butler's defenses of the fort. La Mountain became the first aeronaut to conduct balloon missions over water by taking off from the deck of a transport ship when on August 10, accompanied by Butler, he made a night ascent from the tugboat *Adriatic*. The following month La Mountain and his balloon transferred to McClellan's army, where he became subordinate to Lowe. La Mountain preferred free-flight reconnaissance missions, while Lowe believed tethered flights were superior. These differences, along with petty jealousies on the part of both men, led to a bitter feud that eventually resulted in La Mountain's dismissal from the service on February 9, 1862.

Lowe's balloons were made of double-layered sections of tan raw silk known as pongee. The balloon envelope was enclosed in a rope netting tied to the observer's basket. To make the balloon lighter than air, Lowe filled it with hydrogen gas, which was produced by pouring sulfuric acid on iron filings in a wagon-mounted gas generator.

Fully inflated, the larger balloons were several stories in height. Although some of Lowe's balloons reached an altitude of more than 5,000 feet, the normal operating height varied from 450 to 2,000 feet. Because he did not support free-flight, Lowe conducted most of his ascents with the balloon tethered to the ground. When aeronauts did undertake free-flight missions, they controlled altitude by jettisoning ballast and returned to the ground by releasing gas from the envelope. Normally only one person manned the balloon, but on occasion an additional observer went along. A few commanders went aloft with Lowe or members of his staff to gain their own view of the battlefield. General Fitz-John Porter, a division commander, made dozens of flights; once his balloon broke free from its tether, and he was nearly captured by the rebels before a friendly wind blew him back to safety.

The Confederates also made limited attempts to field a balloon force during the war, but, due to a shortage of silk and limited gas-producing assets, they made little progress. In May 1862, Confederate Captain E. P. Bryan constructed a balloon from varnished cotton cloth and inflated it with hot air from a pine and turpentine fire. Near Yorktown, he got his balloon airborne and signaled his observations to the ground with semaphores.

A short time later, during the Seven Days Battle, the Confederates sewed together another balloon at Richmond, filled it with gas from the local light company, and moved it to the front tethered to a railroad engine. After a single ascent for reconnaissance, the balloon broke free and floated into Union hands. Although the balloon's service to the South was unremarkable, it nevertheless joined the "magnolia myths" of the Confederacy. According to legend, the balloon was made of "the last silk dresses in Richmond," which had been sacrificed to the Southern cause by the local ladies.

While there were certainly some reconnaissance successes with the balloons—their mere presence requiring the rebels to hide their camps and movements from aerial observations—they were abandoned a full two years before the conclusion of the war. The reasons for the demise of the Federal Balloon Corps were the amount of support they required and the personality of "Professor" Lowe. Movement of the balloons, gas generators, and other equipment required a large number of wagons and attached enlisted men. This cumbersome column of wagons had difficulty keeping up with the advancing army. Because of its tremendous logistical burden, the balloon corps transferred from branch to branch of the army in an attempt to find the best fit. In its short duration, the balloon corps served under the Topographic Engineers, the Quartermaster Corps, and finally the Corps of Engineers.

Lowe, although an able aeronaut, remained a civilian during his service, and the fact that he was not in uniform certainly affected the way the Union officers related to him and treated the information he gathered. Officers willing to go along on flights with Lowe seem to have had a satisfactory opinion of the balloonist, but on the whole the military officers saw Lowe as a highly paid civilian not worth his wages of ten dollars a day. There is also some evidence that "Professor" Lowe, more than a bit pompous, tended to pad his expense accounts to the point of embezzlement. Lowe resigned in May 1863, after his pay was cut to six dollars a day. James Allen briefly replaced Lowe, but the following month the balloon corps disbanded altogether.

Despite the demise of the balloon corps and the earlier exit of the Pinkertons, the Union army was not without an intelligence organization. In January 1863, General Joseph Hooker, Burnside's replacement after the disaster at Fredericksburg, appointed Colonel George H. Sharpe as his deputy provost marshal with the added duty of reestablishing an intelligence organization for the Army of the Potomac. Sharpe, assisted by John Babcock and Captain John McEntee, quickly formed the Bureau of Military Information, which would serve the U.S. Army until the end of the conflict. The Bureau of Military Information was the most professional intelligence organization on either side during the war. Sharpe oversaw the collection of information from a multitude of sources, including cavalry, prisoners of war, civilians, and communications intercepts.

Sharpe's and Hooker's first big test produced some success but ended in a battlefield failure. In April and May of 1863, operating on information about Confederate dispositions reported by Sharpe, Hooker moved to envelop Lee's force at Fredericksburg by means of a flanking movement. With an advantage of 118,000 Union soldiers to 60,000 Confederate troops, Hooker was successful initially, but Lee and Jackson countered the Union flanking movement with one of their own. The resulting battle at Chancellorsville, Virginia, May 1–4, produced a rebel victory with more than 17,000 Union casualties compared to fewer than 13,000 for the Confederates.

While he gained a victory at Chancellorsville, Lee also suffered a great loss. On May 2, Jackson and a few staff members rode beyond the rebel lines in an attempt to discover the intentions of the Federals. Returning from this intelligence-gathering mission, his party was mistaken by Confederate pickets for the enemy. Jackson was wounded in the left arm, which had to be amputated. During convalescence, he developed pneumonia and died on May 10.

Despite the loss of Jackson, Lee was confident enough after the victory at Chancellorsville to undertake another invasion of the North. Hooker followed the advancing rebels northward using a parallel route. Lincoln, still looking for a general who could defeat Lee, replaced Hooker with General Gordon Meade on June 28. Within a week, Meade delivered the decisive Union victory at Gettysburg.

Sharpe's Bureau of Military Intelligence remained intact under the new commander and provided Meade information through reconnaissance and agent reports on Confederate strength and maneuvers as the battle developed. However, the outcome of the Battle of Gettysburg was influenced far more by Confederate intelligence failures than Union information successes.

Confederate and Union cavalry sparred in several engagements during Lee's move northward as civilian spies and opportunists on both sides reported movements and locations of the armies. On July 1, General John Buford's Union cavalry division, on a reconnaissance forward of the main Federal force, encountered a rebel unit advancing on Gettysburg to "liberate" a warehouse of shoes rumored to be stored there. Buford, recognizing the importance of the crossroads, dismounted his horsemen to hold the rebels until infantry reinforcements could arrive. By the end of the day, both Lee and Meade were moving their entire forces toward the small southern Pennsylvania town, which neither side had intended to be the objective. The battle lines had been drawn more by chance than tactical or terrain intelligence.

As the battle progressed, Lee's cavalry, under the famous J.E.B. Stuart, was out of contact on another reconnaissance. The Confederates probably could have won the battle had they been more aggressive, or had they had more information the first day of the fight. Meade left his flank at Round Top and the Devil's Den lightly protected, and if Lee had capitalized on the weakness he could have rolled up the entire Union force. However, Lee was forced to fight most of the battle with almost no information about the Union dispositions.

Relying on an army that had never failed him in battle rather than on adequate intelligence, Lee sent his force across a mile-wide open field* into Meade's strength on high ground. By the end

---

*The Gettysburg battlefield has been preserved much as it was on that bloody day in 1863. Members of the "Lee was the greatest American general" club will quickly change their minds as they walk across the open area between Confederate and Union lines. The inevitability of Southern defeat in such an attack is obvious even to the newest student of military tactics. The only surprise is that any rebels survived the charge.

of July 3, more than 28,000 of Lee's army of 75,000 were casualties. The rebel dead numbered nearly 4,000. Of the Union force of 88,000, more than 23,000, including 3,100 killed, were casualties. Lee and his survivors struggled through a rainstorm back to the South, never again to invade the North.

After Gettysburg, Sharpe broadened his intelligence responsibilities to include providing information to General William S. Rosecrans and his Army of the Cumberland. In March 1864, Sharpe and the bureau joined General U. S. Grant when he assumed his new role as commander of the Union army. Babcock remained with Meade, who stepped down to a lesser role.

The Bureau of Military Information continued to support Grant until the end of the war. While Sharpe and his men provided useful information, there is no evidence that their intelligence input had any great impact on particular battles or campaigns. Surely they accomplished some objectives, or the Union commanders would not have kept them on duty. However, no Union commander under whom they served mentioned the bureau in his memoirs—an indication of their relative unimportance. More damning is the fact that the Bureau of Military Intelligence was disbanded at the end of the war, its personnel and budget authorization not retained in the peacetime military.

Confederate intelligence efforts in the Civil War are generally credited as being superior to those of the Union, but a look below the surface reveals that the South was equally inept in the information business. Although the Confederates were well known for surprise attacks against unwarned and unprepared Union forces at such battles as Shiloh, Second Bull Run, and Front Royal, their successes were more the result of superior generalship than of good intelligence.

At no time during the war did the Confederacy have a centralized intelligence organization. Commanders in gray, like their counterparts in blue, had to rely on their own intelligence sources. The Confederates officially recorded little about intelligence, and most of those scarce documents were destroyed when Richmond fell so they would not end up in the hands of Union authorities.

What is known is that the Confederate Signal Bureau was

established within the Adjutant and Inspector General Office of the War Department at Richmond in May 1862. It was headed by Yale graduate Colonel William Norris, a Baltimore businessman, lawyer, and secessionist who devised a communication system using semaphores while serving under General John Magruder during the Peninsular Campaign.

The primary responsibility of the Signal Bureau was to oversee the operations of the Confederate Army Signal Corps, which included telegraph, semaphore, and courier communications. Norris was also responsible for secure courier communications with rebel agents in the North and abroad. This branch, referred to as the Signal and Secret Service Bureau, must certainly have collected information, but little if any of it ever reached field commanders.

Norris's personal papers were destroyed in a fire in 1890. One other veteran of the Signal and Secret Service Bureau wrote of his experiences, recording a brief and sketchy account in 1903 that alluded to successes but gave no specific details or examples. No other documentation by bureau participants has ever surfaced.

The only Confederate field commander to organize an intelligence service beyond the standard assigned cavalry and signal units was General Braxton Bragg, commander of the Confederate Army of Tennessee. In June 1862, Bragg directed Colonel J. Stoddard Johnston to organize a unit of scouts to gather information in Tennessee and Kentucky. The unit had little success until it transferred to the command of General Benjamin F. Cheatham. In April 1863, Cheatham placed fellow Tennessee native Captain Henry B. Shaw in charge.

Shaw was a veteran of both military scouting and civilian spying missions in the same region for Generals Nathan Bedford Forrest and Joseph Wheeler. He recruited forty-five men capable of individual spying in civilian attire and of conducting limited cavalry reconnaissance as a unit. Because Shaw used the pseudonym of E. C. Coleman, his unit became known as "Coleman's Scouts" as they provided information to a series of Confederate commanders throughout Tennessee and later monitored Sherman's march to the sea through Georgia. Despite some success by Coleman's Scouts in reporting Union locations, most of the time the rebel army was too weak to take advantage of the information. Shaw, or "Coleman," was captured after a brief skirmish in November 1863, and Captain Alexander Gregg (or Greig) led the scouts for the remainder of the war.

Without a doubt the greatest intelligence advantage of Confederate commanders in the field, at least early in the war, lay in their cavalry forces. J.E.B. Stuart's 150-mile ride around the entire Army of the Potomac as it advanced on Richmond was the high point of early Confederate cavalry supremacy. More important was Stuart's ability, which failed him only at Gettysburg, to monitor enemy movements just before and during actual combat to allow Lee to maneuver his force advantageously. Other Confederate cavalrymen conducted raids to destroy enemy supplies and disrupt Union logistic lines while also gathering information. General Nathan Forrest was successful in Tennessee, while General J. H. Morgan gained fame on his raid through southern Indiana and Ohio in the summer of 1863. John "the Gray Ghost" Mosby's raids behind Union lines were so famous they resulted in songs and poems at the time and provided the basis for a television series nearly a century later.

It was not until 1863 that Union cavalry could match the efforts of Forrest and Morgan. In April of that year, Colonel B. H. Grierson and his 6th Illinois Cavalry raided Mississippi, destroying lines of communications and creating a diversion that assisted Grant's capture of Vicksburg. By 1864, the Union cavalry was a match for, if not better than, the rebel horsemen. In May of that year, Union cavalry commander General Philip Sheridan raided the Richmond area and fought an engagement at Yellow Tavern in which J.E.B. Stuart was killed by a Union infantryman.* By the

---

*Cavalry clashes and raids were common during the war, but the horse was more a means of transportation than any assistance in fighting. Cavalrymen did not usually carry sabers, and medical reports rarely mention injuries or death delivered by a sword. Cavalrymen, as useful as they might be for reconnaissance, have never in any war received much respect from the infantry. A statement commonly made by Civil War infantrymen of both sides was that "you would never see a dead cavalryman."

last year of the war, the Union cavalry was providing information on Confederate movements to prevent the advantageous surprise attacks that had characterized earlier rebel offensives.

As the war progressed, both the North and the South looked for advantages in improved weaponry—such as refinements in small arms, artillery, and explosives—and in intelligence-gathering techniques. In addition to the use of lighter-than-air balloons, both sides employed new developments in signaling and in the telegraph.

Both the Union and the Confederacy tried alphabetic signaling from buildings, towers, or hills through a "wig-wag" system employing red and white flags called semaphores. With the aid of telescopes, the distance that information could be relayed was restricted only by line of sight. The disadvantage was, of course, that the enemy could also monitor the signals. Even with the use of cipher systems, commanders on neither side considered out-going semaphore messages secure. Nor could they be sure incoming messages were valid, because both sides sent out misinformation to confuse possible interceptors. As a result, semaphores were rarely used for important messages and were even more rarely believed. For example, Union signalmen at Fredericksburg intercepted messages about Lee's departure from his defenses, but General Hooker discounted the information as a hoax and did not take advantage.

A much more useful means of communications available to commanders of both sides was the telegraph—Samuel Morse's invention that was almost thirty years old. The telegraph, in limited use in European conflicts during the previous decade, came of age in the war between the North and South with its networks criss-crossing both the Union and the Confederacy. Even before the beginning of the war Union agents began monitoring telegraph messages to gather information about secessionists.

The U.S. Army Signal Corps, formed in early 1861, provided tactical telegraph communications in the field until October, when the Military Telegraph Service was established as a civilian organization in the Quartermaster Corps. Its leader, Anson Stager, formerly the general superintendent of the Western Union Telegraph Company, supervised strategic communications between field headquarters and the War Department, which took control of all telegraph facilities in the North and occupied South on February 25, 1862. The telegraph office in the War Department building next to the White House became an information center, and by late 1862 President Lincoln often visited there to receive current situation updates. In this capacity, the Military Telegraph Service "war room" become the forerunner of the national command and control center in use today.

In the South, Major William Norris's Signal and Secret Service Bureau was responsible for all telegraph activities. Although the civilian telegraph network was not nationalized to support the war effort, Confederate commanders did use the system and commandeered portions of it at will.

Both sides successfully tapped into enemy telegraph lines to gather intelligence and to transmit false information. However, these activities produced limited results because of counter-measures by the other side. Most messages, especially those of any military importance, were encrypted; although these rather rudimentary codes were often broken, they usually provided sufficient delay to make the acquired information less useful. Another countertapping method, once a leak was detected, was to send large amounts of false information to be intercepted. However, tapping a line to send false information rarely worked because each telegraph operator's sending style, or "fist," was distinctive and recognizable by other telegraph operators.

Another intelligence resource, especially valuable to the South, was the other side's newspapers. Reporters, called special correspondents, accompanied units and submitted stories and drawings of life in camp and on the battlefield. They often included battle maps with their stories as well as lists of those killed, wounded, or missing in action. Units and commanders were frequently identified, and on occasion newspapers printed troop strengths and movement plans. The major daily newspapers devoted as much as one-third of their space to war news.

Confederate leaders learned of the intelligence value of Union newspapers early in the war, and Norris's Signal and Secret Service Bureau was given the responsibility of gathering Northern newspapers. Washington and Baltimore dailies were in the hands of

President Jefferson Davis and his staff within twenty-four hours of publication. New York and Philadelphia papers were in Richmond within two days or less. Commanders in the field, as well as frontline pickets, often informally traded newspapers with the other side. Confederate commanders also frequently instructed their cavalry and scouts to secure Union newspapers.

U.S. Army commanders, quickly spotting the intelligence compromises in their newspapers, attempted to reduce the military information they contained and to stop the exchange of dailies with the enemy. General Joe Hooker, during his brief command of the Army of the Potomac, required reporters to place their names on news releases rather than just sign them "special correspondent" as was the trend of the time. General William T. Sherman went as far as to label newspaper reporters as rebel spies. When told three journalists had been killed by a cannon shot while observing a battle, Sherman replied, "Good! Now we will have news from hell before breakfast." Union efforts to censor military news were never effective. Every effort to limit news from the front met with arguments from politicians and the public about "freedom of the press."

Southern newspapers, in contrast, were not as useful to Union commanders, for several reasons. Only about 5 percent of America's newsprint was produced in the South at the time, so the number and size of newspapers were limited. Also, in the less-populated South, fewer men were available to report the war when they were needed to fight it. Finally, the Confederate government was more stringent in its censorship efforts, and Southern editors were more cooperative in keeping potential intelligence from the enemy.

While newspapers were a source of information, they, like other means of military intelligence, had no great impact in the overall scheme of the war. No battle was won or lost because of a news story. The primary reason newspapers played no greater intelligence role than they did was that commanders quickly learned that just because something was in print did not necessarily mean it was true—or that it contained even the bare bones of veracity.

Most of the Civil War and all of its decisive battles were fought on land. The navies of both sides, however, did play an important supporting role on the inland rivers and surroundings seas. American sailors and marines—U.S.A. and C.S.A. alike—also suffered from intelligence failures as did their land-bound brothers.

After the fall of Fort Sumter, Lincoln ordered a blockade of the South that stayed in place until the war was over. Lincoln erred, however, when he failed to order U.S. Navy ships and property to evacuate Confederate ports so they would not be confiscated by the rebels. On April 20, the Confederates seized the navy yard at Norfolk, Virginia, obtaining dry-dock facilities and hundreds of cannons. Before being overrun, the U.S. Navy personnel at the yard scuttled several of the ships in port, but the Southerners were able to raise the frigate *Merrimac* and later rebuild it as the C.S.A. ironclad *Virginia*.

Most U.S. Navy intelligence activities during the war were focused on gathering information about Confederate coastal and river defenses. This information was delivered directly to commanders in the field as well as transferred to a temporary advisory group formed to assist Secretary of the Navy Gideon Wells in his decision making. Union navy agents also operated in Europe to prevent, or at least report, the acquisition of warships by the rebels.

The U.S. Navy and Army conducted joint operations on the rivers and costal waterways. They coordinated capture of forts at Fort Henry, Vicksburg, New Orleans, Fort Fisher, and Charleston. Most of these operations were successful not because of any great amount of intelligence but because of the overwhelming superiority of Union naval and land forces.

Despite the vastly superior number of Northern ships, the U.S. Navy did suffer losses directly attributable to intelligence failures. On September 8, 1863, four Union gunboats escorted 4,000 soldiers under the command of General William B. Franklin from New Orleans to Texas. At Sabine Pass, a Confederate garrison of only forty-two men used fake cannons made from logs to trick the Union boats into the sights of the five real guns hidden behind earthworks at what the defenders had boldly dubbed Fort Griffin. Although rebel Lieutenant Richard Dowling had compatible ammunition for only four of his cannons, his gunners were extremely accurate against the unprepared Federal gunboats. At day's end, two of the Union boats were at the bottom of the Gulf of Mexico, 350 sailors and soldiers were Dowling's prisoners, and the remainder of the invasion fleet was in full retreat.

The U.S. Navy proved much more successful in its August 5, 1864, attack against Mobile Bay, but a proper reconnaissance of the harbor's mine defenses would have made victory less costly. Admiral David G. Farragut, commander of the Union naval forces, staked his claim to fame when he ordered, "Damn the torpedoes [mines]! Full speed ahead." His rhetoric overshadowed the fact that during the attack the U.S.S. *Tecumseh* struck a mine and sank in minutes, killing ninety of the 114-man crew.

On both land and sea, military intelligence has been one of the most romanticized aspects of the conflict. No greater myths about the Civil War have filtered into history than those of female spies on both sides. According to many accounts, women espionage agents, whether acquaintance or household worker, spied on presidents and generals to provide information on unit strengths, locations, and intentions. Confederate sympathizers Rose Greenhow and Belle Boyd and Union agents Elizabeth Van Lew and Mary Elizabeth Bowser, among others, receive credit for passing along secrets that changed the course of several battles, including First Bull Run and Front Royal. As interesting as these romantic myths might be, they are almost entirely fiction.

Most of what is known about the women spies comes from their memoirs written after the war. One of these, the biography of Emma Edmonds, appears to be such a fabrication that doubts arise about whether Edmonds existed at all beyond the pen of her biographer. The only substantiation for any of the women spy adventures is Lafayette Baker's self-congratulatory claim, in his autobiography, that he broke up Greenhow's spy network. No official record, or any other reliable source, supports the spy stories. The American Civil War would not be the first American conflict where spies and intelligence operatives told a much better story than they actually produced.

Of all the advances, both real and mythical, in military intelligence during the Civil War, the only one that remained in place after the war would play a great role in the Indian Wars of the next three decades. In 1864, General S. R. Curtis, commanding general of the Department of Kansas, organized a unit of Pawnee Indian scouts to support his field operations. Frank North, a veteran frontiersman who had lived with the Indians, commanded the Pawnee Scout Company, which would eventually number 200.

Curtis originally used the scouts to counter roving bands of Sioux Indians, who were on the warpath against whites regardless of the color of their uniforms. He also used the scouts to patrol along the Kansas River to detect rebel advances. When the Confederates did attack later in the year, an early warning provided by the Pawnees gave Curtis the advantage he needed to defeat them.

The Pawnee scouts remained on the rolls of the U.S. Army after the war and provided security along the Union Pacific Railroad right-of-way until April 19, 1877, when they were no longer needed. The lessons learned from the use of the Pawnee scouts would hold true in future use of indigenous forces in intelligence work. When employed in their natural capacity as inhabitants of the plains, they performed well. Problems only occurred when overzealous commanders attempted to remake the Indian scouts into "garrison" soldiers.

The Civil War changed America's way of conducting warfare. Civil War soldiers were the first to fight under a unified command structure, to use repeating firearms, to employ railroads and submarines, and to use trench warfare. It was the first "total war" where the entire resources of both sides were dedicated to the conflict. The primary result was the preservation of the Union. The cost from battle and disease was 620,000 dead soldiers—360,000 Union and 260,000 Confederate.

★ 6 ★

Combat on the Plains: The Indian Wars

At the time of Lee's surrender at Appomattox Court House in April 1865, the United States had more than a million men in uniform armed with modern, sophisticated weapons. A year later, only 30,000 were still on the active rolls. By the 1870s, the number of active duty U.S. Army soldiers, including officers, dropped to 27,000. Discounting men in the stockade, those in the hospital, deserters, and others absent from duty, as few as 19,000 were present for duty at any one time to make up the 430 company-sized units assigned to more than 200 military installations across the United States.

The U.S. Navy was in even worse condition. Hundreds of ships and thousands of sailors were decommissioned and discharged with the arrival of peace. Shortly after the war, the navy's budget was so reduced that the service had to mothball or sell its steam-driven ironclads and return the few remaining ships to sail power.

Officers faced demotions in rank earned on Civil War battlefields and slowdowns in future promotions. Food, quarters, and other necessaries were of poor quality and often in short supply. So little ammunition was available for practice that few soldiers were real marksmen.

Although wartime advances in military intelligence had been shelved with the arrival of peace, others were made in the postconflict years. In February 1870, a congressional resolution directed the secretary of war to "provide for taking meteorological observations at military stations in the interior of the Continent and at other points in the states and territories, and for giving notice on the northern lakes and on the sea-coast by magnetic telegraph and marine signalling of the approach and force of storms."

The following year the Corps of Engineers began a topographic survey of all the lands west of the 100th meridian, which bisects the United States from central North Dakota south through the plains states and central Texas. First Lieutenant George H. Wheeler was selected to lead the survey, which he expanded to include geological, zoological, and ethnological information. Wheeler, eventually promoted to major, devoted his entire career to conducting the survey and publishing its results. He released his findings in increments between 1875 and 1889 in seven primary volumes, one supplementary volume, and two atlases—one topographical and one geological.

Intelligence efforts outside the United States also resumed after the war. Because military leaders from the principal European countries had visited the United States during the Civil War to accompany both the Union and Confederate armies as observers, these countries welcomed U.S. Army officers to observe their operations. In the summer of 1870, General Philip Sheridan made the first such postwar visit, accompanying the Germans during their siege of Paris in the Franco-Prussian War. Sheridan's writings, read widely by the military as well as the general population, noted how German and French procedures and systems could be used to solve current U.S. military problems. Unfortunately, Sheridan did not address the German general staff's proficiency in planning and battle execution nor its effective intelligence system.

Other officers, including Commanding General of the U.S. Army General William T. Sherman, also made tours of Europe. In June 1875, General Emory Upton* requested permission from Secretary of War William W. Belknap to make the most ambitious

---

*General Upton earned his rank at the Battle of Spotsylvania when he was only twenty-five years of age. After the Civil War, he created the revised system of drill for the infantry that was adopted in 1867. He then served a tour as the commandant of cadets at West Point.

foreign visit yet, including Asia as well as Europe. Belknap approved enthusiastically and instructed Upton to proceed to Japan, China, and India on his way to the Continnent. According to Upton's memoir of the journey, Belknap directed him to "examine and report upon the organization, tactics, discipline, and maneuvers of the armies along the route mentioned, and in the special examination of the schools of instruction of officers in strategy, grand tactics, applied tactics, and higher duties in the art of war, and the collection and compilation of such other information as might generally be expected to be of utility to the Government."

Upton also received orders from General Sherman, who obviously had the collection of intelligence in mind when he told Upton to focus on countries about which the United States knew little, such as Persia, Bokhara, Afghanistan, and Turkestan. He also ordered Upton to take a close look at India to determine how the small number of British troops there could govern and control a country of more than 200 million people.

Upton was accompanied by Major G. A. Forsyth of the 9th Cavalry and Captain J. P. Sanger of the 1st Artillery. The three officers spent nineteen months observing the Orient and Europe. A year later, with the help of his companions, Upton published his report. Upton's foreign observations eventually motivated him to undertake a detailed study of the history of American military organization because he believed the United States had consistently failed to develop any realistic military policy in war or peace.*

Meanwhile, on the home front the purchase of Alaska from Russia in 1867 led to several expeditions to the polar region, with various results. Lieutenant P. H. Ray of the 8th Infantry suc-

___

*Upton suffered from a brain ailment and committed suicide on March 15, 1881, before he had completed his study of military policy. Few read or heeded the message in the writings he did complete until 1901, when Secretary of War Elihu Root based many military reforms on Upton's study. Root arranged for the publication of Upton's *The Military Policy of the United States*—a document still studied by military officers.

cessfully conducted scientific observations in the vicinity of Point Barrow from 1881 to 1883 without any mishaps.

An expedition under Lieutenant Adolphus W. Greely during the same period was not as fortunate. Greely and a party of twenty-four sailed from Newfoundland in July 1881 and established a base camp on the eastern shore of Ellesmere Island at Franklin Bay. Greely's party conducted wide reconnaissance of the area and compiled meteorological, oceanographic, and geophysical studies, but severe weather prevented resupply ships from reaching Greely's camp during the summers of 1882 and 1883. In the spring of 1884, the group, nearly out of supplies, made its way south, linking up with navy rescue ships in June. Only Greely and five of his men survived.

Visits to other countries and explorations of newly acquired territory were but a small part of post–Civil War military activity. The army focused on pacifying or combating the Indians of the plains and far West. During the first half of the century following the American Revolutionary War, most conflicts with the Indians involved local militias supported by armed civilians. The whites, with their superior weapons, defeated the Indians, but on occasion their inexperience and failure to gather or use proper intelligence resulted in disaster. On August 20, 1794, along the Maumee River in northwestern Ohio, 183 militiamen in the command of General Josiah Harmer were killed by an Indian ambush. A year later, 3,000 militiamen under the command of General Arthur St. Clair returned to punish the Indians who had attacked Harmer's expedition. St. Clair failed to post proper security and to conduct sufficient patrols to locate his enemy, allowing the Indians to overrun his unwarned, encamped army and kill 630 soldiers—the largest number of deaths suffered by any American military unit in warfare with the Native Americans.

In the southern United States, militiamen and the regular army defeated the Creeks through the excellent leadership of General Andrew Jackson. However, the whites fought two wars during 1817–18 and 1835–42 against the Seminoles in Florida without ever totally removing them from their Everglades strongholds.

The last major Indian uprising in the eastern United States occurred during the late summer of 1862 when 400 Santee Sioux warriors, led by Little Crow, killed more than 500 white settlers, including women and children, in the area of New Ulm, Minnesota. The Sioux, angry about their poor treatment on the reservation, took advantage of the call-up of the local manpower for the Civil War. They burned and destroyed several farms and villages before a militia force of 1,700 arrived to combat them. Most of Little Crow's force surrendered, believing they would be allowed to return to their reservation. Instead, 303 were sentenced to be executed. Ultimately all but thirty-eight received a reprieve— their hanging remaining the largest mass execution in U.S. history. The remainder of the tribe was moved from their homeland to a reservation in the Dakotas.

After the Civil War, a westward migration of Americans began, and settlers soon learned that Stephen Long's writings about a Great American Desert were false. The only thing separating the settlers from rich plains farmland and the even richer Western mountain mineral deposits was the indigenous people.

The westward expansion transferred the responsibility of dealing with the Indians from the local militias to the regular U.S. Army. The post–Civil War policy was to place Indians on reservations near their old hunting grounds rather than relocate tribes great distances from their original homelands. With free movement for hunting restricted, the Indians became wards of the government, which provided food and other supplies. This system had little chance of success because of wholesale corruption and mismanagement by the U.S. government agents appointed to administer the reservations.

What followed was "the Indian Wars," actions by the U.S. military against the Indians from 1865 to 1891. During the twenty-six-year Indian Wars, so designated to credit individual participation and authorize battle streamers, the army conducted twelve official campaigns. "Campaigns" was, in fact, a more accurate label than "wars" for the clashes between the U.S. Army and the various western Indian tribes. Most combat occurred in relatively limited geographical areas between small forces on both sides. Congress never declared war, as such, on the Indians, nor did the Indians ever surrender in mass as a defeated "nation."

Both sides were guilty of brutality, extending the war to non-combatants.

On November 28, 1864, militiamen of the 3rd Colorado Cavalry under the command of Colonel John M. Chivington attacked a poorly armed village of Cheyennes at Sand Creek and killed 200. George Custer and his cavalry victimized the same tribe on the Washita River on November 27, 1868, and killed another 103 villagers.

Although certain individuals and some government officials supported the belief that "the only good Indian is a dead Indian," neither the U.S. Army nor the government had a policy of genocide against the Native Americans. Much of the fighting occurred when the Indians left their reservations and murdered defenseless settlers. The military pursued to force the renegade Indians back to their reservations.

Whatever the correct label—war, battle, or campaign—and regardless of the rights and wrongs of the reservation system, the period of the Indian Wars was a difficult, bloody one for the U.S. Army. Individual soldiers and leaders continued to serve their regiments and their country bravely, but their ranks, unfortunately, would suffer the same casualties and hardships resulting from intelligence failures as had their predecessors.

The first great defeat of the U.S. Army by the Indians in the West occurred as a result of arrogance as well as poor military intelligence. One of the earliest missions of the U.S. Army in the region was to secure the Bozeman Trail against bands of Sioux warriors for the safe passage of wagon trains. Colonel Henry B. Carrington, methodically building a line of forts along the trail, was so slow and deliberate in his actions that the Indians were able to force the Americans into a defensive posture. Captain William J. Fetterman did not appreciate his commander's lack of aggressiveness and boasted that with eighty men he could defeat the entire Sioux Nation.

On December 21, 1866, Fetterman got the chance to prove his brash claim when he was ordered to rescue a woodcutting party under attack by Crazy Horse and his Oglala Sioux near Fort Kearny. Fetterman's command was composed of himself, forty-nine infantrymen, twenty-seven cavalrymen, a captain, and two civilian observers—exactly eighty, the number on which Fetterman had made his boasts. Although his orders were only to save the woodcutters, Fetterman ignored instructions and chased the small party of Sioux into the Peno Valley of the Sulliant Hills. With no advance guard or scouts, Fetterman charged into an ambush of nearly 2,000 warriors. In minutes Fetterman and all of his men, the group that "could defeat the entire Sioux Nation," were dead, their bodies stripped naked and mutilated.

Humiliated by "the Fetterman Massacre," the army took measures to ensure that it did not happen again. Breechloaders replaced muzzle loading rifles, and drills emphasized pickets and patroling. Soldiers soon had the opportunity to test their effectiveness. On August 1, 1867, they rescued hay cutters under attack near Fort C. F. Smith, an action that became known as the Hayfield Fight, and on August 2 they reinforced woodcutters near Fort Kearny who were defending themselves behind overturned wagons, in the Wagon Box Fight. In both skirmishes, despite the Indians' vast numerical superiority, the soldiers were victorious because they had early warning from sentries and were able to use their weapons and defenses to their advantage.

Another positive aspect of Indian War intelligence was the expansion of the Pawnee Scout Company formed during the Civil War. The army also recruited other indigenous scouts with promises of money, weapons, and the opportunity to fight long-time enemies from other tribes. White civilians, particularly those who had lived with the Indians, also hired on as scouts, guides, and interpreters.

In 1868, General Sheridan planned an aggressive winter campaign against the Cheyenne and Sioux tribes. He authorized Major George A. Forsyth, who had risen in rank from private to brevet brigadier general during the Civil War, to organize a group of civilian scouts to conduct a forward reconnaissance of villages and travel routes. Forsyth recruited fifty frontiersmen who welcomed the opportunity to be paid a dollar a day to fight Indians, as most of them had been doing for free since their arrival in the West. In August, they rode out on their mission, using tactics and maneuvers more similar to their adversaries' than to the regular army's.

Forsyth's Scouts should have been an excellent innovation in gathering military intelligence on the elusive Indians. However, proving that even good ideas in military intelligence can lead to failure, the scouts met disaster at the Arickaree Fork of Republican River in eastern Colorado on September 17, 1868. A force of at least 600—and possibly 1,000—Cheyenne Dog Soldiers (an elite tribal society of fighters) and Sioux warriors led by Roman Nose surrounded the scouts, who during an eight-day siege on a sandy island in the middle of the stream* had little more than their dead horses for protection. Finally, a column of black soldiers of the 10th Cavalry rescued Forsyth and the surviving half of his scouts. Forsyth was wounded, as was the concept of a frontiersman scout company.

For the next several years, the Cheyennes and Sioux limited their activities to small raids from their reservations until the discovery of gold in the Black Hills brought a large number of whites onto what the Indians considered sacred ground. This incursion, in combination with poor treatment from the government agents and the encouragement of warrior chiefs like Sitting Bull and Crazy Horse, caused many Indians to leave their reservations. By 1875, the Northern Cheyennes and the Oglala, Hunkpapa, and Miniconjou Sioux had returned to their home hunting grounds. Other smaller factions of the Sioux, including Santee survivors of the 1862 Minnesota wars, who had been relocated to the western reservations, joined the camps.

On January 31, 1876, the U.S. government, acting on recommendations of politicians and Indian agents, ordered all the Indians back to their reservations with the threat that those who failed to obey would be considered hostile and hunted down by the U.S. Army. The Indians ignored the ultimatum. With no desire to return to reservation life, many were more than ready to fight. Also, because the winter was extremely severe, those Indians who

---

*Following the battle, the previously unnamed bit of land became Beecher's Island in honor of Lieutenant Frederick Beecher, Forsyth's second-in-command, who was killed in the fight. He was a nephew of writer Harriet Beecher Stowe.

might have wanted to follow the order would have had great difficulty in doing so.

The army launched several expeditions despite information from local frontiersmen about the harsh weather. Custer and his 7th Cavalry set out from Fort Lincoln only to be turned back by heavy snow. Colonel Joseph J. Reynolds and a force of 300 were able to penetrate the Powder River country of northern Wyoming and attack a village of Oglala Sioux and Cheyennes, but they were repulsed by the combination of the cold and a strong Indian defense. When he returned to Fort Fetterman, Reynolds faced charges for his failure to defeat the village. Reynolds appealed directly to General Sheridan, stating, "These winter campaigns in these latitudes should be prohibited." He concluded that the one month on the plains during the winter had taught him "more than any five years" of his life. Sheridan ordered the charges dismissed and postponed further operations until warmer weather.

The arrival of spring brought a much more ambitious campaign plan. Sheridan ordered a three-pronged attack involving more than 2,500 soldiers. General George Crook advanced north from Fort Fetterman; General John Gibbon moved east from Fort Ellis, Montana; and General Alfred Terry, along with Custer, moved west from Fort Lincoln. The three columns, accompanied by Crow and Shoshone scouts, had intelligence reports from reservation officials that estimated the total hostile Indian force at about 500 to 800 warriors armed with old muskets or bows and arrows. Rapid-firing Gatling guns were available for the expeditions, but three commanders, including Custer, left them back in garrison, assured by their intelligence that they would not be needed against the poorly armed Indians.

On June 17, as Crook's column of 1,000 camped on Rosebud Creek, scouts provided an early warning of an attack by the Sioux and Cheyennes. Even so, the soldiers were barely able to defend themselves in the six-hour fight that followed. Crook immediately recognized that the Indians, who usually fought in haphazard individual efforts, were better organized this time, and they were armed with repeating rifles. Crook's command retreated from the Rosebud to care for their wounded, bury their dead, and secure resupplies, a delay that prevented their keeping up with the other columns. Because Crook did not inform the other two columns of what he now knew about the Indians' numbers, organized attacks, and repeating rifles, the information proved useless. The units that needed it most were left uninformed.

A few days later, Terry and Gibbon met at the mouth of the Rosebud and made plans to continue the advance despite the unexplained absence of Crook's column. Based on a discovery by Major Marcus A. Reno of a recently traveled, mile-wide network of trails, the commanders concluded that there must be a major encampment at what the Sioux called Greasy Grass along the Little Big Horn River in southern Montana. They planned an enveloping maneuver against the Indians.

On June 22, Custer—in command of 600 cavalrymen, 40 Indian scouts, and 20 civilian traders and packers—moved up the Rosebud toward the Little Big Horn while Gibbons and Terry paralleled him along the Yellowstone River. Their plan called for the column making the first contact to drive the Indians into the other half of the pincers; in the event of no contact en route, the two commands would attack the camp on June 26. Although the commanders knew neither the exact location of the enemy nor the numbers of warriors they might face, the plan seemed reasonable based on the typical Indian tactic of using hit-and-run to avoid decisive combat.

By the evening of June 24, Custer was camped near the Little Big Horn Valley, where his Indian scouts reported having observed the enemy camp, which was nearer than expected and occupied by a much larger force than anticipated. Despite a personal reconnaissance the next morning from a vantage point called Crow's Nest that allowed him to see part of the enemy camp, Custer disccunted, or ignored, his scouts' warnings about the numbers of Indians along the Little Big Horn.

Custer, who had earned general's stars during the Civil War by making snap decisions, decided not to wait for the other column before he attacked. As a veteran of many campaigns in which he had chased elusive Indians for weeks, he did not want to allow his quarry to run away. At least in his mind, Custer was about to teach the Sioux a few things about warfare. By noon of the 25th, Custer had divided his regiment into three columns to cut off escape routes and moved against the enemy camp. Reno advanced on the south bank of the Little Big Horn, Custer on the north. Captain Frederick Benteen, leading the other cavalrymen, followed Reno.

Several miles away from the Indian camp, Reno engaged a small band of Sioux and pursued. Within minutes, Indian reinforcements arrived, and Reno had to retreat to the high ground on the north side of the river. Benteen, who had received a courier message to join Custer, also crossed to the north side of the river but made it only as far as Reno's position before being stopped by the Indians. The two officers combined their force of 368 and dug in to repel their attackers.

Shortly after Reno and Benteen joined forces, they heard sounds of a battle nearer the Indian camp along Custer's route of advance. Heavily engaged themselves, they could not move to support Custer. The Indians continued their attack on Reno and Benteen for the rest of the day and briefly on the morning of the 26th before withdrawing when Terry's and Gibbon's columns arrived. Within the small hilltop defensive position of Reno and Benteen lay 57 dead and 52 wounded cavalrymen. Later in the day, Gibbon's troopers found the remains of Custer and more than 200 of his men. There were no survivors.

Historians and students of military history have relentlessly scrutinized the Battle of the Little Big Horn to find the exact cause of the disaster. Some experts criticize Custer for attacking a day early; some fault Reno for failing to reinforce Custer; others blame the prone-to-jamming rifles carried by the cavalrymen. None of these arguments provide the complete reason for the demise of the 7th Cavalry. Primarily, Custer and his command died because of the failure of military intelligence. Instead of the 500 to 800 poorly armed and poorly led warriors that they expected, they faced more than 3,000 well-armed Indians operating as the most cohesive Native American force ever massed in the American West.

Many advances within the U.S. Army have occurred as the result of disasters following intelligence failures, and "Custer's Last Stand" certainly created change. Congress, previously reluctant to budget additional funds for the military, authorized an increase in strength of 2,500 troops and funds to have repeating rifles replace the breechloaders. Investigation into the reservations and their government agents led to improvements in the system.

As the Sioux and Cheyenne drifted from the Little Big Horn in small groups, the military pursued, with cavalry commanders Colonels Ranald S. Mackenzie and Nelson A. Miles pushing hard to punish Custer's vanquishers. Over the next year, the cavalry won several small battles, and by 1878 most of the Indians who had been at Little Big Horn were either dead or back on their reservations. A band of 200 Sioux, including Sitting Bull, hid in Canada until July 19, 1881, when they recrossed the border to surrender. The Sioux would never again unite into an effective fighting force.

Most of the other U.S. Army intelligence failures with the Indians centered on the soldiers' inability to locate their adversaries. Small bands of Indians went on the warpath, killed or captured settlers, and then eluded the pursuing cavalry. Typical was the Modoc War in southern Oregon and northern California. A band of about sixty Modoc Indian families under the leadership of Captain Jack refused to be removed from their homeland to a reservation. Over the next several years, Captain Jack and as few as fifty warriors managed to resist both the cavalry and groups of armed white settlers. On April 11, 1873, Captain Jack killed General Edward R. Canby, the only fatality of a general during the Indian Wars, during a peace negotiation and then escaped.

The army brought in artillery to dislodge the Modocs from their rocky northern California lava bed retreats. At one time more than 500 soldiers were in pursuit, but even on the run the Modocs were lethal to soldiers without proper security. On April 26, a patrol of sixty-four soldiers and twelve Indian scouts stopped for a lunch break and posted no security. A mere twenty-two Modocs, under the leadership of Scarface Charley, sneaked up on the relaxing soldiers and killed twenty-five, including all five officers, and wounded another sixteen. The massacre might have been complete, but Scarface Charley withdrew his warriors, shouting to the reeling soldiers, "All you fellows that ain't dead had better go home. We don't want to kill you all in one day."

Despite the successes against the army, the Indians faced food and water shortages in the lava beds, and by May the Modocs had

divided into groups of several families each to survive. Some
groups were killed, others captured, a few surrendered on their
own. All survivors were sent to their reservation. On June 3,
Captain Jack was captured, and he and three of his fellow leaders
were tried and hanged for the killing of Canby.

An even more telling example of the inability of military
intelligence to assist the army in pursuing Indians occurred during
the Nez Perce War of 1877. The Nez Perce were "nonreservation"
Indians allowed to live in their own territory in the Wallowa Valley
of Oregon. They remained peaceful until white settlers en-
croached on their lands. When the Nez Perce killed several
settlers, the army arrived to punish the Indians only to find that
the entire tribe had begun a cross-country move to Canada. Over
the next three months, under the leadership of Chief Joseph, the
Nez Perce traveled more than 1,000 miles across the Bitterroot
Mountains, through the future site of Yellowstone Park, and then
north toward Canada.

The Nez Perce consistently outdistanced their pursuers, who
were never able to determine where the Indians were located or
where they were going. When the soldiers were able to close in on
the fleeing Indians, the outnumbered warriors engaged the cavalrymen from ambush and escaped. Ultimately the Nez Perce
retreat ended when Colonel Nelson A. Miles surrounded the
Indians' encampment just short of the Canadian border on
September 30. After a six-day siege, Chief Joseph surrendered and
made an eloquent speech, concluding, "From where the sun now
stands I will fight no more forever." The tribe was punished by not
being allowed to return home to the Wallowa Valley.*

The ultimate failure of large U.S. cavalry forces to locate and
defeat small bands of renegade Indians occurred in the lengthy
campaign against the Apaches in Arizona and New Mexico from
1861 to 1886. Apache leaders Cochise, Victorio, Mangas Colo-
radas, and Geronimo led small groups—from many clans, which
had frequently fought each other—who raided and killed isolated

---

*Miles and other army officers so admired the leadership of Chief
Joseph and the bravery of his warriors that they later supported returning
the Nez Perce to their homeland, but the request was never approved.

ranchers and settlers in the southwestern United States and northern Mexico.

The difficulty for the cavalry, whose mission was to force the Indians back to their reservations, was not in winning face-to-face engagements against a greatly outnumbered enemy but rather in finding the renegades. Success in actually catching the bands occurred only when Apache scouts from less warlike clans assisted the cavalry. Without these scouts, efforts proved futile. Captain Henry W. Lawton acted on orders from Nelson Miles—now commander of U.S. troops in the Southwest—not to use Apache scouts and as a result spent most of the summer of 1886 pursuing a group of fewer than forty Apaches led by Geronimo.* Lawton chased the Indians for more than 2,000 miles and never once got within rifle range of them.

Before the Indian Wars officially concluded, one last uprising took place. On the Pine Ridge Reservation in South Dakota a "ghost dance" movement that supposedly would resurrect dead warriors and bring back the buffalo herds divided the various factions of the Sioux subtribes. Sitting Bull, who had lived peacefully on the reservation for more than a decade since his return from Canada—when not performing as a part of Buffalo Bill's Wild West Show—supported the ghost dance movement and was killed by reservation policemen when they tried to arrest him on December 15, 1890.

About 350 other believers in the ghost dance, under the leadership of Big Foot, separated themselves from the rest of the tribe and established a camp near Wounded Knee Creek. General Miles, again the commander called in to put down the uprising, sent soldiers of the 7th Cavalry, supported by four howitzers, to

---

*Geronimo was never actually captured. By August, the Apache leader and his small band were hungry and exhausted. A single army officer, Lieutenant Charles Gatewood, accompanied by two Indian scouts, entered Geronimo's camp and talked him into returning to Fort Bowie, Arizona, and surrendering to Miles. Geronimo and his followers were exiled to Florida for several years before being transferred to a reservation near Fort Sill, Oklahoma, where the old warrior lived to the age of eighty before dying in 1909.

surround the camp on December 30. When the soldiers attempted to disarm the Indians, gunfire erupted. In a short time, 153 Indians, including Big Foot, were dead. Although later unofficial estimates would inflate this number to 300 or even 350 and label Wounded Knee a massacre perpetrated by the 7th Cavalry in revenge for Little Big Horn, an official inquiry exonerated the commander of the 7th, noting that twenty-five of his soldiers had been killed and thirty-nine wounded in the fight.

The inglorious battle at Wounded Knee concluded more than three centuries of warfare between the whites and the Native Americans. Once numbering more than a million, the Indians were reduced to about 240,000 living on 187 reservations that occupied slightly more than 180,000 square miles of land. The U.S. Army had learned many lessons in the guerrilla-style fighting but unfortunately, because of the absence of usable military intelligence, often it was the same lesson repeated over and over.

Even though the Indian Wars had dominated the U.S. military's actions for a third of a century, the most important intelligence developments of the period had nothing to do with the campaigns on the plains: in 1882, the navy formed its Office of Intelligence; in 1885, the army established the Military Information Division.

The U.S. Navy spent the post–Civil War period virtually in mothballs, ignored in funding as the military budget went for the army's efforts against the Indians. The few officers and crews in the active fleet at the time did, however, make some commendable efforts to gather and process intelligence. Solitary steamers cruised waterways around the world, creating maps and gathering scientific and strategic data. As early as 1869, Commander Thomas O. Selfridge Jr. was searching for a possible canal route across Central America.

Still other navy officers made visits to European sea powers to observe their improvements in weapons, engines, and armor plating. By 1876, the year Custer made his last stand at Little Big Horn, American naval officers reported to Washington that the United States was far behind in all aspects of shipbuilding and weapons manufacture. While European navies had modernized their fleets to steam-powered, steel-hulled, and armor-clad ships armed with breechloading rifled guns, the U.S. Navy was still outfitted with wooden sailing ships equipped with smooth-bore, muzzle-loading cannons.

Despite the little interest shown by Congress and the public in naval matters, U.S. Navy officers did their best to stay current with world developments. On October 9, 1873, fifteen officers assigned to the Naval Academy at Annapolis established a society "for the purpose of discussing matters of professional interest." A year later, the U.S. Naval Institute published its first issue of *Proceedings*, a professional journal aimed at "the advancement of professional, literary, and scientific knowledge in the Navy." While only implied, the development of intelligence, especially with regard to new technology, was also a part of the institute's charter.

The American political leadership finally began to share the concerns of the navy when Chile fought against Bolivia and Peru in the War of the Pacific from 1879 to 1883. During naval engagements, both sides used European-built iron-hulled vessels sold to them as obsolete surplus. Even these castoffs were far superior to any ship in the U.S. Navy. Politicians belatedly recognized that with a weak fleet the United States could neither protect its coastal cities nor enforce the Monroe Doctrine in opposing extension of European control or influence in the Western Hemisphere.

After nearly two decades of being ignored, the navy became the center of attention. In 1881, President Chester A. Arthur demanded an immediate modernization of the navy, stating, "I cannot too strongly urge upon you my conviction that every consideration of national safety, economy, and honor imperatively demands a thorough rehabilitation of our navy."

Amid the modernization activities of the fleet, the formation of the first permanent information-gathering service organization received little notice, but it was an important step in future intelligence operations. On March 23, 1882, Secretary of the Navy William H. Hunt issued General Order 292, which established the Office of Intelligence as a part of the Bureau of Navigation.

Within a few months, Lieutenant Theodorus B. M. Mason became the first chief of the agency now known as the Office of

Naval Intelligence (ONI). Commodore John G. Walker, chief of the Bureau of Navigation, defined Mason's duties and later reflected, "The Office of Naval Intelligence was established in order that the Navy Department might be supplied with the most accurate information as to the progress of naval science, and the condition and resources of foreign navies."

Mason, who had spent much time at sea and in Europe observing foreign navies, was well qualified to head the ONI. With a staff of more than a dozen ambitious junior officers, the ONI began collecting and analyzing foreign technical publications and other printed sources on the navies of the world. Each U.S. Navy ship captain appointed an intelligence officer for his vessel, usually the senior marine officer aboard. By 1887, these officers had cameras and photographic equipment to record foreign ships, ports, and land defenses. The ONI also received massive amounts of information from "naval attachés" assigned to American embassies around the world.

During the 1880s buildup, the U.S. Navy had no specific threat on which to focus, so its intelligence agents secured information from all available sources. Rather than being tactical or strategic in nature, most information focused on warship building and armaments technology.

Meanwhile, army leaders, despite the information failures during the Indian Wars, seemed happy, or at least complacent, with their lack of intelligence organization. It was not until October 1885 that the Adjutant General of the Army, Brigadier General R. C. Dunn, formed the Military Information Division (MID).* Its mission was to collect military data for the War Department and the Army at large. This data collecting, much like the ONI's, focused on foreign military capabilities and technological advances in arms and equipment.

The MID, however, did not enjoy the same support the ONI received. Initially a staff of one officer, Major William J. Volkmar,

---

*A popular story within the intelligence community is that Dunn established the MID after being unable to provide Secretary of War William C. Endicott with information about a foreign military power. No official records or writings by the participants support this account.

and one civilian clerk mostly filed information from officers visiting other countries and from newspapers and periodicals. Besides minimal staffing, another detriment and indication of its perceived lack of importance was MID's assignment subordinate to the Reservations Division of the Miscellaneous Branch of the Office of the Adjutant General.

Volkmar, who took his job seriously, found his efforts hampered by a succession of political appointee civilian clerks who had few qualifications for and little interest in military intelligence. However, that changed on September 22, 1888, when Congress authorized a budget for permanent military attachés. Secretary of War Endicott spelled out the duties in a document dated March 2, 1889, which directed attachés to "examine into and report upon all matters of a military or technical character that may be of interest and value to any branch of the War Department and to the service at large. Keep informed through the Legation, public press and such other channels as your official position may secure for you from foreign governments. Examine the military libraries, bookstores, and publishers lists in order to give early notice of any new or important publications or inventions or improvements in arms, or in any branch of the service; also give notice of such drawings, plans, etc., which may be of importance and within your power to procure."

The MID files grew rapidly and had more than 30,000 pieces of information on record by 1892. Five years later, the office had eleven officers and dozens of clerks and messengers. By the end of the decade, the MID reported directly to the adjutant general, and its director carried the title of assistant adjutant general.

As the nineteenth century neared an end, the United States for the first time had viable peacetime intelligence organizations on duty, gathering information to assist in readiness for the next conflict. Neither the ONI nor the MID had long to wait before putting its capabilities to work.

★ 7 ★

Remembering the *Maine:* The Spanish-American War

The smoke had barely cleared from the Indian battles on the plains before the United States engaged in a war that neither Americans nor their Spanish adversaries really wanted to fight. Even so, for the first time in U.S. military history, an intelligence network was in place at the war's beginning to prevent unnecessary bloodshed. Unfortunately, the network failed to accomplish what many believe it could and should have.

Before the American Civil War, Southerners had encouraged the acquisition of Cuba as a slave state to balance the number of western territories admitted to the Union as "free." Annexation hopes dwindled after Appomattox, and instead of perceiving the island as a potential state, many Americans began to see the Spanish colony only ninety miles from U.S. shores as a threat.

By the close of the nineteenth century, several factors merged to thrust the United States into a war on the side of Cuban rebels who had been fighting Spain for twenty years. Intensified by the onset of the 1895 depression and by the increased Spanish mistreatment of the Cubans, the rebellion had brought instability to an area where American businessmen owned sugar, cattle, and shipping industries. Fanning the flames of the crisis was the circulation rivalry between two of America's most powerful newspaper publishers, William Randolph Hearst of the *New York*

American and Joseph Pulitzer of the *New York World.* Hearst and Pulitzer, vying to publish the latest and most sensational news from Cuba, printed "yellow journalism" stories that exaggerated the Cubans' mistreatment at the hands of the Spanish and encouraged U.S. intervention.

Hearst sent the famed western artist Frederic Remington to Havana to sketch and report on rebel activities. After several days, Remington telegrammed his boss, "Everything is quiet, there is no trouble. There will be no war. I wish to return." Hearst, who would later deny the exchange took place, supposedly sent the telegraphic response, "Please remain. You furnish the pictures and I'll furnish the war."

Despite expansionists and journalists, President William McKinley convinced Spain in November 1897 to grant Cuba limited self-government within the Spanish empire. The compromise satisfied no one. Cuban rebels continued their fight, and pro-Spanish forces in Havana rioted in protest.

To show support for the compromise and provide protection for any American endangered by the rioting, the modern twenty-four-gun battleship U.S.S. *Maine* arrived in Havana on January 25, 1898. Tensions on both sides increased until February 15, when they reached a crescendo with the sinking of the battleship. The *Maine,* sitting calmly in the harbor, suddenly and without warning exploded and quickly sank, killing two officers and 266 enlisted crewmen.

American and Spanish officials alike initially believed that the explosion resulted from spontaneous combustion of the ship's coal dust, as had happened on other ships. Several high-ranking naval officers disagreed, however, claiming coal dust explosions were impossible aboard modern warships—even though their own records clearly showed otherwise. The most vocal of these officers, who were obviously interested in protecting themselves and the safety records of their ships, was the admiral in charge of procuring the coal. Rear Admiral Royal B. Bradford, chief of the Bureau of Equipment, assured anyone in the press who would listen—and there were plenty who did—that the coal his bureau had supplied the *Maine* was of the highest quality.

An official investigation continued for more than a month as witnesses, including Bradford, testified to protect their own interests rather than reveal the truth. The *Maine*'s captain, Charles D. Sigsbee, and several of his officers presented testimony about the ship's strict internal security and safety procedures and their belief that the explosion was an external torpedo, mine, or bomb.

During the official inquiry, Hearst, Pulitzer, and other American publishers more than doubled their newspaper circulation with inflated and falsified accounts of eyewitnesses who reported seeing the bomb that blew up the *Maine*. Long before the official inquiry rendered its findings, the American public had decided that the Spanish were guilty of sinking the ship, and "Remember the *Maine*" became the slogan of 1898, both on the lips of U.S. citizens and on the front pages of their newspapers. Although it did not appear in print and rarely made its way into history books, verbally "To hell with Spain!" usually followed.

The naval court of inquiry agreed on March 28. The *Maine*, according to the navy, had been sunk by an external, submerged mine of unknown origin that had detonated the ship's powder magazines. Navy Captain William T. Sampson, chief of the inquiry, announced that the effects of the blast "could have been produced only by...a mine situated under the bottom of the ship."*

President McKinley tried again to solve the problem peacefully, including offering to buy Cuba from Spain. None of McKinley's efforts proved successful, and, giving into public pressure to "remember the *Maine*," the United States declared war on Spain on April 21, 1898.

---

*In 1911, the *Maine* was raised from the harbor floor and yielded the remains of sixty-five seamen, who were interred at Arlington National Cemetery with the ship's mast as a monument. A navy board of inspection, reexamining the wreck of the *Maine* before it was towed to sea and again sunk, disagreed with the original inquiry's fixing of the explosion's location but confirmed that its cause was an external mine. In 1976, Rear Admiral Hyman G. Rickover investigated the incident once again. His findings, now generally accepted, were that spontaneous combustion in a coal bin caused an internal explosion.

From a planning standpoint, the United States was generally prepared for a war with Spain. In 1896, the Office of Naval Intelligence, in coordination with the Naval War College, had begun gathering information and formulating plans for just such a contingency. The basic plan called for a naval blockade of the Spanish Caribbean possessions— Cuba and Puerto Rico—and a follow-up land operation to capture Havana. Simultaneously, the navy would launch another operation against Manila to capture the Philippine Islands, which were the primary Spanish possession in the Pacific Ocean. The Military Intelligence Division, with no organized planning section, did not officially help with the war plan. However, since the MID and ONI were both located in the State-War-Navy Building next to the White House, the army intelligence officers, who had been gathering information about Spanish troops in the Caribbean for several years, did provide some input. Within days of the declaration of war, the ONI plan for the conflict against Spain was placed in action.

Unfortunately, the MID's most important contribution was ignored. Early in 1898, MID chief Colonel Arthur L. Wagner briefed President McKinley that a summer invasion of Cuba would be disastrous because of yellow fever and other tropical diseases. The president seemed to favor Wagner's recommendation to delay the attack, until Secretary of War Russell A. Alger, fearing the navy would take the glory and resulting appropriations, demanded an immediate army land campaign. McKinley, swayed by his secretary of war, ordered the land attack to proceed.

Even though Secretary of War Alger dismissed him from the MID after the meeting,* Colonel Wagner did make one last contribution to intelligence gathering in Cuba. Wagner selected Andrew Summers Rowan, a West Point graduate who had previously served as an attaché in Cuba and in the MID Mapping Division, for an expedition to determine the size and strength of Cuban and Spanish forces on the island. Rowan's mission was to infiltrate Cuba to find rebel General Calixto Garcia Iniquez, who

---

*Alger was so angry at Colonel Wagner that he told him that future promotions would be blocked.

would brief him on Spanish troop location and strength and on the current status of the Cuban insurgents. Rowan sailed in an open boat from Jamaica to Cuba and landed on the Cuban coast on April 24. He then crossed swamps and jungles to reach Garcia and other rebel leaders who provided information and current maps.

Rowan returned to the United States by the end of May with intelligence useful in planning the land invasion of the island. He was immediately welcomed to a cabinet meeting as a hero, and his exploits were reported in the newspapers, where Cuba stories still guaranteed high circulation. The widely distributed and read "A Message to Garcia," an essay penned by author Elbert Hubbard, further enhanced Rowan's reputation and his Cuban adventures, even though his actual "spying" operations differed vastly from those in the celebrated story. Rowan was not in eminent danger during his Cuban journey, because he visited only areas firmly in the hands of the rebels. In fact, several American journalists regularly visited Garcia using the same route as Rowan.

The land invasion had to wait, though, as the United States first turned its attention to the Spanish navy, in both the Caribbean and the Pacific. In fact, the war's first action occurred on the other side of the globe. Commodore George Dewey, in command of the Asiatic Squadron of seven ships, received an alert on February 25 to resupply his fleet at Hong Kong in readiness for an attack on the Philippines in the event of the outbreak of hostilities.

Dewey had information about the Spanish fleet's armaments and manpower at Manila but none about Manila Bay itself, or the islands in general, because the navy provided no maps of the area. The commodore purchased several from mapmakers in Hong Kong and then sent one of his officers disguised as a civilian traveler to question seamen arriving from the Philippines about what they had seen.

On April 25, the Asiatic Fleet received a cable about the declaration of war against Spain, and two days later Oscar F. Williams, the American consul in Manila, arrived in Hong Kong to tell Dewey that the Spanish fleet had left Manila and repositioned at Subic Bay. Dewey immediately weighed anchor, sailing toward Subic to follow orders that directed him to "proceed at once to Philippine Islands. Commence operations...against Spanish Fleet. You must capture vessels or destroy."

Dewey, confident he had ample intelligence about the Philippine Spanish fleet, sailed into Subic Bay on April 30 only to find the waters empty. The Spanish fleet under Admiral Patricio Montojo y Pasaron had returned to Manila because shore batteries at Subic were unable to assist in the harbor's defense.

Dewey's intelligence about the strength of the Spanish fleet was as incorrect as that about its location, but this error worked in his favor. Assuming the Spanish fleet was formidable, Dewey planned a dangerous night attack through an entrance to Manila Bay that he could only hope was not mined, since he had no accurate intelligence available on the possibility.

Dewey would later write that word in Hong Kong was that his fleet was sailing to certain destruction, adding that wagers were being offered with no one willing to put money on the Americans even at long odds. Actually, the Spanish capabilities were vastly overrated. Their lightly armed, deteriorating ships had poorly trained, unenthusiastic crews. Admiral Montojo, aware that a successful defense was all but impossible, took measures to protect his men by anchoring his fleet in shallow waters at Cavite Navy Yard, where their superstructures would be above the waterline even after they sank.

With a firepower advantage of three to one, Dewey sailed into Manila Bay in the early morning darkness of May 1. Within hours the Americans destroyed the Spanish fleet, killing 167 and wounding 214. Dewey's undamaged ships had only six men slightly wounded. The single American fatality was a victim of heat prostration in the engine room of the U.S.S. *McCulloh.*

A small party of marines went ashore to raise the first American flag on Spanish soil, but Dewey had too few men to secure the islands. All he could do was blockade Manila Bay and wait. It would be two months before sufficient American forces arrived to completely take over the Philippines.

The destruction of the Spanish fleet in Manila Bay ended the war in the Far East. However, another Spanish fleet stood between the United States and its capture of the Cuban mainland. This fleet of four armored cruisers and three destroyers, under command of

Admiral Pascual Cervera y Topete, sailed from the Atlantic Cape
Verde Islands on April 29. The ONI, ordered to monitor the fleet,
could not determine its destination or condition. Planners in
Washington could only assume Cervera's ships were well armed
and stocked with sufficient coal, relief supplies, and ammunition
for the Spanish soldiers in Cuba. Panic reigned along the East
Coast when newspapers reported Cervera was at sea. The army
land force assembled in Tampa for the invasion of Cuba could not
embark for fear Cervera would sink the transports en route to
Cuba.

For nearly a month, the navy and the American public fear-
fully speculated about Cervera's location and destination. Initially
navy intelligence was sure the Spanish fleet was bound for Puerto
Rico, and the American North Atlantic Fleet, under the command
of Captain William T. Sampson, sailed in pursuit. By mid-May
Sampson realized Cervera was not coming and returned to Key
West to refuel his ships. On May 19, the navy decided the Spanish
fleet was bound for either Cienfuegos or Havana and dispatched
the Flying Squadron of Commodore Winfield Scott Schley to
pursue.

It was as if the Keystone Kops had gone to sea, and Schley and
Sampson were the stars. Sampson sailed from Key West to patrol
the Nicholas Channel entry to Havana while Schley positioned his
squadron off Cienfuegos in the belief that Cervera was already at
anchor in the hidden harbor. On May 23, Sampson informed
Schley that Cuban rebels reported Cervera was at Santiago, but
Schley remained convinced he was at Cienfuegos. Captain Charles
Sigsbee was back at sea in command of the auxiliary cruiser *St.
Paul* after the *Maine* inquiry. On patrol off Santiago, he reported
sighting "absolutely nothing of the Spanish fleet."*

Not until May 28 did the U.S. Navy finally discover Cervera
and his fleet at anchor at Santiago, where they had been since May

---

*Rather than being cashiered for his loss of the *Maine* and his failure
to spot the Spanish fleet entering Santiago harbor, Sigsbee remained in
the navy and, amazingly, was assigned as the chief of the Office of Naval
Intelligence in 1900.

19—and then only as a result of an army telegraph operator monitoring Spanish wire traffic. Schley and the Flying Squadron were the first to reach Santiago and confirm the presence of the Spanish fleet. A few days later, Sampson took charge of the harbor blockade. Sampson, who had been no more successful than Schley in finding Cervera, still managed to write that Schley's failure to find the Spanish admiral was "reprehensible."

The U.S. Navy made several armed reconnaissances up the narrow channel leading to Santiago harbor, but heavy shore guns stopped their progress. By June 2, the naval war was at a stalemate, with Sampson unable to penetrate the harbor and Cervera unable and unwilling to attempt a breakout. Not much can be said for the Spanish ships that had eluded the ONI and the U.S. Navy, delayed the army land invasion of Cuba, and by their mere existence terrorized the East Coast. Reputation was the fleet's only asset. Cervera commanded the last remnants of the former-world-power Spanish navy, which now consisted of old, leaky, and almost unseaworthy ships with nearly empty coal bunkers. Cervera's sailors were poorly trained, his guns outdated, and his ammunition in short supply. The only thing more amazing than the Spanish fleet's evasion of the U.S. Navy was that Cervera's ships were able to stay afloat for the transatlantic voyage.

With the Spanish fleet neutralized, the land forces could embark. The military objective for both the army and the navy was now Santiago and Cervera's ships. Once they were destroyed, the Spanish army at other Cuban locations, with no means of support or resupply, would have to surrender.

While the navy had career professionals to fight the sea war aboard ships acquired during the recent twenty-year buildup, the prewar army had fewer than 30,000 soldiers, most of whom were spread across a string of western forts. Within days after the declaration of war, President McKinley issued orders to raise an army of 125,000 men. More than a million men responded. For once the army could afford to be selective, and it accepted only one in five who applied to enlist.

Volunteers for Cuba came from all professions and social statuses. Theodore Roosevelt secured a commission as the second-in-command of the Rough Riders; Buffalo Bill Cody volunteered to deliver 30,000 Indian fighters; reformed outlaw Frank James offered to form a company of his old gang; a band of Sioux Indians volunteered; several eastern university athletic teams enlisted en masse; future movie star Tom Mix joined the artillery; and multimillionaire John Jacob Astor obtained a commission as a lieutenant colonel. Famous journalists came forward, too. Remington, who provided drawings while his boss delivered the war, was joined by Stephen Crane and Richard Harding Davis. William Randolph Hearst made a brief appearance to observe the invasion from aboard his private yacht.

On June 14, the U.S. Army V Corps, composed of 17,000 soldiers, departed Tampa under the command of Major General William T. Shafter, an officer weighing more than 300 pounds. Shafter was an unusual choice to lead an army in hot tropical warfare, but then his army was equally unusual.

Shafter and Sampson met on June 22 to coordinate their attack on Santiago. Either service rivalry between the soldier and sailor provided a convenient misunderstanding or the two commanders simply miscommunicated, with each basically believing the other agreed to support his own plan for the attack. Shafter left the meeting thinking his objective was the entire city of Santiago, while Sampson thought that the army agreed to assault and capture the heavy gun batteries protecting the harbor channel.

The American invasion force landed at Daiquiri and Siboney near Santiago on June 22, its plan of attack dictated by the mountainous terrain and few available roads and trails. After landing, the Americans would march directly inland on the only two routes available to capture the heights above Santiago. Shafter, limited by exhaustion and illness from his obesity, later admitted that there was little attempt at any grand strategy or tactics.

Although Shafter complained later about the lack of information provided him about the enemy, leadership was as much to blame for his problems as was any intelligence failure. Receiving inaccurate news that the Spanish were reinforcing Santiago, Shafter hurried his attack and began the assault on the city on July 1. Unwisely, he sent his best infantry division of 6,600 men to attack a stone blockhouse defended by 550 Spaniards at the fortified village of El Caney. The village was four miles northeast of Santiago and could easily have been isolated by a small blocking force rather than the direct attack that resulted in a great loss of life. More important, the insignificant El Caney siphoned off more than a third of the U.S. forces that should have been used in the main attack.

The primary objectives of the assault on Santiago were two hills, San Juan and Kettle, which overlooked the city and dominated the terrain. Shafter ordered a frontal attack at those points, sending the bulk of his command forward and keeping no reserve except nearly half of his artillery—an amazing tactic, since military doctrine stated that artillery should always be committed and never kept in reserve.

Despite poor planning and worse execution, the Americans had a ten-to-one advantage in manpower. Unfortunately, the Spaniards on San Juan and Kettle hills were good marksmen, and the frontal-attacking Americans made easy targets. As the first American units advanced along a narrow road straight up the hills, the Spanish turned them back in disarray. Volunteer units, such as the 71st New York, broke and ran in retreat. The famous Rough Riders and Teddy Roosevelt had to be supported by black soldiers of the 10th Cavalry.*

---

*The Rough Riders received far more newspaper ink than their exploits deserved because Roosevelt was a great publicity agent and attacked any negative press about the regiment or himself with a vengeance. He made no effort to correct the newspaper reports of his brave cavalry charge up San Juan Hill, when, in fact, the Rough Riders were dismounted and pinned down during most of the fight for Kettle Hill, not San Juan. Although five black cavalrymen were awarded the Medal of Honor for their valor in coming to the support of the Rough Riders, in his later writings Roosevelt emphasized the poor fighting ability of the 10th Cavalry. The Rough Riders were "good copy" but talked a much better fight than they delivered. A captain in the regiment, William O. "Bucky" O'Neil, a real cowboy and former sheriff from Prescott, Arizona, believed officers should not take cover in battle but rather lead from the open. When advised in the midst of the fight to "get down," O'Neil replied, "The Spanish bullet isn't made that will kill me." Seconds later O'Neil was proved wrong as a bullet tore through his head.

During the final phases of the fight, Shafter was not present, having been incapacitated by the heat and his weight. A lieutenant on his staff acted as his spokesman and gave orders to colonels and generals.

The American army advanced with little information about the enemy occupying the hilltops. One attempt to gather intelligence was the use of an observation balloon. At the beginning of the Spanish-American War the U.S. Army had one balloon in active service. Although thirty years had passed since balloons were last used in combat, the design of the army's single balloon was unchanged from that of Professor Lowe's in the Civil War, except that the telegraph wire to the ground was now replaced by a telephone line. The balloon and its support wagons, under the command of Lieutenant Colonel Joseph E. Maxfield, had been assigned to the Signal Corps at Fort Logan, Colorado, when the *Maine* was sunk. Maxfield and his balloon were immediately ordered to Sandy Hook, New Jersey, to provide early warning of the feared Spanish fleet of Cervera.

When Schley found Cervera in Santiago, Maxfield and the balloon were sent to Tampa and arrived in time to join the V Corps. At Siboney, Maxfield was initially able to assist the army planners by making ascents and producing maps of what he observed. Both the Cuban rebel commander and the V Corps engineer went on flights with Maxfield on June 30 to see the terrain leading to San Juan and Kettle hills.

During the actual attack on July 1, Maxfield followed the advancing troops in his balloon. Airborne directly above the center of the American attack, Maxwell and his balloon drew the fire of Spanish artillery, which then rained down on the infantry soldiers on the ground below. The balloon was shot down, but Maxfield was unhurt. Although never confirmed, several stories later circulated among the ground troops that Spanish fire alone did not shoot down the balloon that served as a Spanish aiming point. Even Roosevelt, who found nearly everything about the war "bully," later wrote that the balloon was "worse than useless."

By the end of the day, the Americans were in full command of the heights overlooking Santiago and effectively had the city under siege. The costs had been heavy. Fully 10 percent of Shafter's V Corps were dead (216) or wounded (1,318). About the same number of Spaniards had died, but their number of wounded was only 310.

Sampson was none too happy when he discovered that the army had taken the heights above the city but had failed to neutralize the guns dominating the harbor entrance. Shafter correctly believed the city itself was too heavily defended for a land assault and recommended that Sampson attack from the sea. The discussion between the two rival service commanders became quite heated. Shafter told Sampson that the army had suffered great casualties and now it was the navy's turn. Sampson argued that he would willingly risk his men but could not afford to risk his ships. The three sides at Santiago—the U.S. Army, the U.S. Navy, and the Spanish—remained at a stalemate for several days. Before the American commanders could decide whether to attack by sea or land, the Spanish made the decision for them.

On the morning of July 3, the Spanish fleet, on orders from the governor general of Cuba, made an effort to break the blockade and escape to the open sea. The breakout attempt caught the Americans by surprise, and in the battle's early phases the *Brooklyn* and the *Texas* nearly collided. Some of the Spanish ships probably would have escaped had they scattered instead of following each other in line along the coast.

Within four hours, the entire Spanish fleet was at the bottom of the sea. Had the American marksmanship been better, the battle would not have lasted that long. Of more than 1,300 shots fired, only forty-two found their targets. Most of the American ships were in more danger from friendly fire than from the enemy because the Spanish gunners were even less accurate. Only one American was killed and one wounded, while the Spanish suffered 323 dead, 151 wounded, and 1,800, including Cervera, taken prisoner by the rescuing American ships.

Sampson's report on the one-sided battle began, "The fleet under my command offers the nation as a Fourth of July present the whole of Cervera's fleet." He did not add "such as it was" but did take full credit for the victory—although he was not present during the bulk of the fighting. Shortly before Cervera attempted his breakout, Sampson had sailed up the coast for a meeting with Shafter, leaving Schley in command of the American fleet for most of the fight.

Cut off by sea and land, Santiago surrendered on July 17. A week later, Major General Nelson A. Miles led a land force to capture Puerto Rico with minimum casualties. The Spanish government, realizing it could not reinforce or resupply troops in Cuba and the Philippines, initiated peace negotiations through the French ambassador in Washington. Hostilities ended on August 12, and the peace treaty was signed in Paris on December 10. Under the accords, the United States gained possession of Cuba, Puerto Rico, Guam, and the Philippines.

The Spanish American War lasted only three months. More than 2,500 Americans, most of them from the army,* died. Only 365 of these were battle casualties; the rest were victims of disease contracted by fighting the war during the hot season. About 1,500 were wounded, most of them in the charge up the hills above Santiago.

Despite the inept search for the Spanish fleet, the U.S. Navy was the definite victor over both the enemy and its rival, the U.S. Army. The navy had achieved victories at Manila and Santiago with minimal losses of men or ships, the result of its buildup over the past twenty years and, of course, the weakness of the Spanish navy. The American political leadership and public were appreciative of the navy's accomplishments in the war.

This was not the case with the U.S. Army. Secretary of War Alger received justifiable criticism for the large number of casualties from disease and for Shafter's loss of 10 percent of his force in the battles for San Juan and Kettle hills. Critics also claimed Alger caused delays in the delivery of medical supplies and military equipment, and they charged him with providing contaminated beef to American troops.

------

*The navy, which faced little opposition and did not have to contend with the land-born diseases, lost eighteen killed and sixty-seven wounded (excluding those killed before the war aboard the *Maine*). Of the dead, only one was a commissioned officer. Ensign Worth Bagley died on May 11, 1898, in a skirmish in the harbor at Cardenas, Cuba.

A presidential board of inquiry found Alger and the War Department negligent in not being prepared for the conflict. Three of the major witnesses at the hearing in 1900 were Shafter, who had been in command of ground troops in Cuba; Miles, who had been in charge of the Puerto Rico invasion; and Major General Wesley Merritt, who had led the first soldiers ashore on the Philippines. Each testified that he had received insufficient information on his area of operations. Frontline commanders had not received what little information the Military Intelligence Division had gathered.

Regardless of who, or what, was to blame for the intelligence failures and casualties, the brief Spanish-American War vaulted the United States into the role of a world player, if not a world power. America was now a colonial force with holdings in the Caribbean and the Far East. Along with these responsibilities came new rivalries with European and Asian countries, such as Germany and Japan, which would cause problems in future years.

Other problems outlived the war itself. Originally many American planners had seen the conflict as a means of liberating and then annexing Cuba. Instead the United States granted the island its independence in 1902, albeit with American businessmen remaining firmly entrenched.

The Philippines, captured primarily as a bargaining chip in negotiations, remained an American possession. Instead of a valuable prize briefly held, the Philippines became a long-term burden for the United States as Filipino rebels, pleased with the American defeat of the Spanish, nonetheless demanded independence instead of occupation. By February 1899, American forces were in active combat with Filipino guerrillas led by General Emilio Aguinaldo. The Filipino Insurrection, fought with questionable tactics by both sides, resulted in American units pacifying the cities while the guerrillas controlled rural villages and the countryside.

The Military Intelligence Division, not anticipating land action in the Philippines during or after the Spanish American War, had neither files nor an intelligence network to assist U.S. Army counterguerrilla efforts. Like other U.S. commanders without central War Department intelligence support, General Elwell S.

Otis, the American military governor of the Philippines, formed his own information-gathering organizations. Otis organized the Bureau of Insurgent Records as a part of his Manila headquarters early in 1899, placing Lieutenant Colonel Joseph T. Dickman in charge. Captain Ralph Van Deman, a former member of the MID, assisted Dickman and eventually became one of the key players in the development of U.S. military intelligence.

Initially the small bureau began by maintaining files on individual guerrillas, but by December 1899 it was recruiting agents, securing and preparing maps, and producing tactical intelligence and counterintelligence. The bureau established communication and liaison with each of the 450 U.S. military outposts spread throughout the islands. This enlarged organization was placed under the Philippine Headquarters Adjutant General Office and renamed the Military Intelligence Division. Although the Philippine MID shared the same name as the Washington office, it remained a separate entity until the two were combined in June 1902, after most of the hostilities on the islands were over.

The Philippine MID performed fairly well, but providing information about a small, mobile guerrilla force proved difficult. Most combat was between small units, and the longer the conflict lasted, the nastier these actions became. Both sides regularly tortured prisoners for information or revenge. Many American casualties resulted from murder in "pacified city" back streets and alleys.

Military intelligence did play a key role in the capture of the guerrilla leader Aguinaldo, which weakened the insurrection. Soldiers under command of Colonel Frederick Funston detained one of Aguinaldo's messengers. The Americans later claimed they merely questioned the courier, while the Filipinos claimed they severely tortured him. Whichever account is accurate, the messenger revealed Aguinaldo's location. Funston, fluent in Spanish from his service with the rebels in Cuba, gathered a force of ninety soldiers and a few Filipino guides. Disguised as prisoners and guards, Funston and his men entered Aguinaldo's camp on February 4, 1901, surprising the security force and capturing the guerrilla leader. Funston, an instant hero in the Philippines and in the States, was immediately promoted to brigadier general and awarded the Medal of Honor for his capture of Aguinaldo, which ended a large portion, but not all, of the rebel activity.

Fierce Muslim warriors of the Moro tribe, who fought with long curved knives called bolos and subjected prisoners to lengthy torture sessions, continued their resistance against the Americans.* Even though the United States offered to provide electricity and other modern conveniences to their villages, the Moros apparently preferred dying for a glorious afterlife to enjoying a better lifestyle in this one.

The tribe continued to attack isolated American units. In the fall of 1901, the Moros surprised Company C of the 9th Infantry Regiment in the village of Balangiga on the southern end of Samar Island, killing forty-five—many only after gruesome torture.

Americans reacted to the massacre of C Company as they had to Custer's Last Stand on the Little Big Horn—with shock and outrage. Retribution by the U.S. Army was immediate. The American commander on Samar Island, Brigadier General Jacob Smith, according to later testimony, verbally ordered his soldiers and an attached brigade of marines to take no prisoners. Smith, a veteran of both the Civil War and the Indian Wars, clarified his order to the marine commander, Major Littleton Waller, stating, "I wish you to kill and burn. The more you kill and burn the better you will please me. I want all persons killed who are capable of bearing arms in actual hostilities against the United States."

Waller asked Smith how old the general thought a person had to be to bear arms and thereby be considered an enemy. Smith responded, "Ten years."

---

*The Moros believed that when they died in combat they were guaranteed a place in paradise and that the number of women awaiting them in their afterlife harem depended on how many infidel enemies they killed. So fanatical were the Moros that American soldiers had to fire several shots from their standard-issue army .38 caliber handguns to stop a charging warrior. As a result, a more powerful .45 caliber pistol designed by John M. Browning replaced the .38 and remained the standard army sidearm for more than half a century.

When Smith later recorded his verbal orders into official writing, he was a bit less direct, but their intent was still obvious. Smith wrote, "Short, severe wars are the most humane in the end. No civilized war, however civilized, can be carried out on a humane basis. Create in the minds of all the people a burning desire for the war to cease; a desire or longing so intense, so personal...that it will impel them to devote themselves in earnest to bringing about a state of real peace."

Neither Major Waller nor any of the army commanders on the island completely followed Smith's orders, but the intensity of the conflict definitely increased. In December 1901, Waller led a patrol into the interior of Samar, where without maps he had to depend on Filipino guides. The marines and their guides became lost, and eleven died of starvation and fatigue before the unit found its way back. Waller held an unofficial "drumhead" court-martial, executing one guide for each marine lost.*

By April 1902, successful operations had brought about the surrender of most surviving bands of Moros and other guerrillas. While flare-ups did occur in the following years, open warfare in the Philippines ceased when on July 4, 1902, President Theodore Roosevelt declared the war ended. More than 4,200 Americans died during the insurrection, with half that many more wounded. Officials estimated guerrilla losses at 20,000 killed and as many as ten times that number of civilians dead from disease, famine, and direct combat.

Performance of the army and military intelligence in the Philippines heightened rising concern in Washington about the organization of the War Department. As a result of several postwar investigations and studies the Army General Staff Corps

---

*Press accounts of what the newspapers called "the rape of Samar" resulted in the court-martials of both Waller and Smith. Waller was charged with murder, while Smith was accused of "conduct to the prejudice of good order and military discipline." Smith was convicted, but the sixty-two-year-old general was allowed to retire from active service at his current rank with full pension and benefits. Waller was acquitted of all charges, returned to active duty, and was eventually promoted to major general.

was founded in 1903. The general staff had the mission of providing a clear chain of command from the president, as commander-in-chief, through the secretary of war to the military forces. To achieve its objectives, the general staff assigned officers to prepare war plans and make policy recommendations at the national level.

Three divisions made up the new Army General Staff Corps. The First Division, headed by the adjutant general, was responsible for administration, training, and mobilization. The Second Division* was responsible for military information, including gathering intelligence, assigning military attachés, and maintaining reference documents—all of these functions assumed by the Military Intelligence Division, which coexisted as a part of the new intelligence organization. Third Division responsibilities included war planning, staff officer training, and operating the newly established Army War College in Washington, D.C.

The primary mission of the Second Division in its initial years was to provide the Third Division with information for war planning. To expedite the delivery of timely information, the Second Division moved from its quarters near the White House to the War College at what would later become Fort McNair in the southeastern portion of the District of Columbia. This organization worked fairly well until 1908 when the Third Division chief requested that the army chief of staff, General Franklin Bell, place the Second Division directly under Third Division control, arguing that the small amount of intelligence gathered by the Second Division could be handled by a few low-paid clerks as easily as by the high-salaried officers who were currently performing the mission. Bell, who had not been impressed with American intelligence during the war in the Philippines, agreed with the Third Division chief.

When the Second Division's status as a separate branch ended, its manpower and budget were reduced or redistributed. The few

---

*Some sources incorrectly credit the "2" in "G-2" and other intelligence organizations as having originated with the formation of the "Second" Division. This is not correct. The term "G-2" was not adopted until World War I.

officers who remained with MID, which was retained as a "committee" of the war college, had little knowledge about intelligence, and until World War I, nearly a decade later, the U.S. Army was virtually without an intelligence organization.

Unlike MID, the Office of Naval Intelligence, as well as the navy as a whole, came out of the Spanish-American War with its prestige and budget intact. While the navy and the Marine Corps assisted in the Philippine Insurrection and later deployed to the Far East and the Caribbean in police actions, the ONI focused on future enemies, both within and external to the United States.

Upon assuming the position of chief of ONI in February 1900, Captain Charles Sigsbee, former commander of the *Maine*, instituted massive security changes in the office. Some of these were prudent, such as adding locks to file cabinets, while others, such as needless cross-checks, were simply bureaucratic.

Sigsbee also ordered an immediate navy-wide investigation into the loyalty of its enlisted men, particularly targeting sailors with German surnames. The security checks had sailors strip to their underwear to reveal any pro-German tattoos. Other than being highly detrimental to morale, Sigsbee's great German spy hunt proved fruitless.

Although Sigsbee's suspicions about his men were misguided, his belief that Germany could be a future threat was sound. The U.S. Navy had almost clashed with Germany in the Pacific over Manila and Samoa, and the Germans threatened the Monroe Doctrine by attempting to establish colonies in the Caribbean and South America. Over the next decade, the ONI would collect information and prepare a plan for going to war against Germany. A system of color codes for war plans provided the contingency's name of War Plan Black.

Sigsbee's replacement, Captain Seaton Schroeder, continued refinement of War Plan Black and also focused the ONI's interest on Japan, now a Pacific power after its defeat of Russia in 1905. The ONI's concerns were justified. Many Japanese were extremely unhappy with the United States because what they considered an unfavorable peace treaty ending the war with Russia had been negotiated by President Roosevelt. Others were angry about the racism Americans exhibited against Japanese immigrants to the

West Coast. By 1912, the ONI had completed War Plan Orange for conducting a conflict against Japan. Over the next few years, the ONI continued to gather information about Japan and to update its war plans.

Overall, U.S. military intelligence seemed briefly to be headed in a productive direction. In 1912, the Joint Army and Navy Board was formed to promote interservice cooperation in war planning. In 1913, the American press revealed the mission of the board. At about the same time, increased racial discrimination against Japanese immigrants on the West Coast was causing unrest in U.S.-Japanese relations. Newly elected President Woodrow Wilson, striving to keep his campaign promise of peace, suspended the Joint Board. The President's action, convincing the military and its civilian leadership that Wilson was against war planning, led to reduced manpower and money for the Office of Naval Intelligence. By the end of the year, the ONI had declined to an agency responsible only for collecting and storing technological information.

★ 8 ★
Over There: The First World War

The cutbacks in the Military Information Division and the Office of Naval Intelligence could not have come at a more inopportune time. Conflict in Europe was escalating into what became the First World War, and trouble was brewing along the Mexican border. Facing the greatest external threat since its fight for independence, the United States once again was without viable military intelligence assets.

Initially the United States, and particularly its businessmen, viewed the war in Europe as a financial opportunity rather than a military conflict. Profits could be made by trading with both sides, and Americans were much happier making money than considering that they might soon be involved in overseas combat, especially since many were unsure which side they should favor in the war. England pushed for the United States to join the Allies, while Germany lobbied for continued American neutrality. The British and German overt and covert propaganda efforts greatly taxed the abilities of the American military and law enforcement officials to control them.

In addition to a growing concern about the European war, Americans found themselves faced with a more immediate military threat from Mexico. No available intelligence network prepared to deal with Europe also meant that no intelligence agents or organizations were in place for Mexico, a country with a long history of government instability.

In 1913, Francisco Madero, president of Mexico by virtue of

his revolution against longtime dictator Porfirio Diaz, was murdered by army general Victoriano Huerta. President Woodrow Wilson, an admirer of Madero, refused to recognize the Huerta government and openly sided with former Madero supporters who united under Venustiano Carranza to fight Huerta. Wilson dispatched cavalry units to patrol the Mexican border and to protect American interests from cross-border raids by bandits. To prevent shipments of arms to Huerta's army, Wilson authorized the U.S. occupation of the Mexican port of Vera Cruz. Huerta saw the occupation as an act of war but was powerless to do anything about it. Late in 1914, Carranza occupied Mexico City and forced Huerta to leave the country.

Carranza was in power but not in control of his country. Rebel leaders Francisco (Pancho) Villa in northern Mexico and Emiliano Zapata in the south demanded government reforms, and when Carranza refused to deliver, they resumed warfare. President Wilson, glad to see Huerta deposed, supported the Carranza government by allowing arms shipments to his forces and halting export of supplies to the rebels. By late 1915, Carranza was well entrenched in Mexico City, and early in 1916 Carranza's forces had gained sufficient control to encourage American mining companies, who had abandoned their claims during the revolution, to return to Mexico.

Throughout this complex series of events, Pancho Villa's fortunes as a rebel leader had risen and fallen depending on who was in power. At times he led a bandit gang of less than a dozen, and at other times he led an army, complete with artillery support, that numbered in the many thousands. Villa's status waned with Carranza's successes. Although uneducated, Villa understood the politics of revolution. The bandit general correctly determined that one enemy all Mexicans could unite against was the United States—and he began to get the Americans further involved in the conflict.

On January 9, 1916, seventeen Americans and twenty Mexicans, who composed the management and administrative personnel of the Cusi Mining Company, boarded a train in El Paso and headed south. The next day, outside of Chihuahua City at the cattle-loading station of Santa Ysabel, Villistas under command of

Colonel Pablo Lopez stopped the train, robbed the Mexican miners, and shot the Americans—all the while shouting, "Viva Villa." One American survived by playing dead amid the bodies of his countrymen. The "Santa Ysabel Massacre" angered President Wilson and the American public, but, by promising swift justice Carranza convinced the United States to take no action.

Villa had failed to get the "gringos" involved in the conflict by murdering Americans in Mexico; so now he took the war across the border. On March 9, Villa personally led 500 mounted men to attack Columbus, New Mexico. Villa's raid came as a complete surprise, beginning late at night when the residents were asleep. The Villistas took over the town, killing five guests, including a Sunday school teacher, who were staying at the local hotel.

Villa had not anticipated the quick reaction by the well-trained 13th Cavalry, stationed outside Columbus at Fort Furlong, which sent the bandits running back to Mexico. Sixty of Villa's men were left behind either dead or captured, and in the running fight to the border, cavalry troops killed seventy-five more bandits. Total cavalry losses, in town and during the pursuit, were eighteen. In numbers of casualties, the raid on Columbus was a defeat for Villa. Overall, however, it was a success because it accomplished Villa's objective. President Wilson responded to the attack on Columbus by ordering Brigadier General John J. "Black Jack" Pershing to lead a 15,000-man punitive expedition into Mexico to capture Villa.

Initial orders from Washington to the U.S. Army headquarters at San Antonio on March 10 were specific. The telegram stated, "President has directed that an armed force be sent into Mexico with the sole object of capturing Villa and preventing further raids by his band, with scrupulous regard to the sovereignty of Mexico." By the time the message reached Pershing, leaders in Washington realized that giving orders to capture one man was setting up the expedition for failure. Before they could amend the order to include Villa's band, rather than just the outlaw himself, American newspapers were already printing the initial order. As far as the press and the American public were concerned, Villa was the objective. If he was not brought in, dead or alive, the expedition would be a failure.

General Pershing established his headquarters at Columbus on March 14 and immediately deployed columns of cavalry across the border to pursue Villa. The soldiers, although well trained, had to proceed with a severe lack of information. Villa and his "army" were basically a guerrilla force who did not wear uniforms and easily blended in with the civilian population, making it difficult for American soldiers to identify the enemy. More critical was the lack of reliable maps of the region because much of northern Mexico was uncharted. The advantage went to the Villistas, who had operated in the area for years. To compensate, the Americans hired local guides, whose loyalties were often in question, and relied on American civilians who had lived in the area before the revolution. Pershing also recruited veteran Apache scouts who had pursed Geronimo in the same region.

With no assistance from the dormant Military Information Division in Washington, cavalry regiments of the expedition had to produce their own intelligence, and reconnaissance patrolling was generally the only means available. Occasionally troops supplemented their knowledge by questioning local inhabitants. Nearly every cavalry unit had one or more soldiers who spoke Spanish, but information obtained from locals often proved inaccurate, if not deliberately falsified to aid the Villistas.

Pershing was without an intelligence officer until he appointed Major James A. Ryan. Ryan, who spoke Spanish, had been assigned to the 13th Cavalry at Columbus and was familiar with Mexico and the Mexicans. Ryan was assisted by Captains William O. Reed and Nicholas W. Campanole, both of the 6th Cavalry, who were also fluent in Spanish.

Campanole employed several Mexicans, whom he referred to as "agents" or "messengers" in his written reports. The agents claimed they had penetrated Villa's army and visited his camps. Even if these claims were true, and there is no substantiation that they were, Pershing received the information too late to affect any action. The expedition's intelligence officers did send telegrams and written reports to the remnants of the MID at the Operations Division. Records show that an officer at the War College was detailed to read the reports, few of which were filed or kept, but there is no evidence that anything was done in reaction to them.

The expedition did enjoy the benefits of two significant innovations that had immediate effect on intelligence and overall military operations. The first was trucks and motorcars, which the expedition used to transport supplies and to carry messages. In addition, the expedition conducted a few motor patrols. The newly fielded motor transports, prone to mechanical breakdown and of limited use on the poor road system in Mexico, nonetheless proved useful.

One of the most successful motorized operations was a supply mission that unintentionally turned into a combat operation. In May, Pershing ordered his aide, Lieutenant George S. Patton, to take three Dodge cars and several soldiers to a nearby ranch to buy grain for the cavalry. Before returning, Patton decided to drive by another ranch where Villistas had been previously spotted. As they drove through the hacienda gate, three mounted men opened fire. Patton, who would become famous for his ivory-handled pistols and his exploits in World War II, drew his revolver and shot one of the riders out of the saddle. In the ensuing firefight, the other two Mexicans were killed, including one of Villa's high-ranking subordinates, General Julio Cardenas. Patton returned to Pershing's headquarters with the bodies of the three bandits tied to the hoods of the automobiles.

The second innovation that benefited the expedition also marked the United States' first use of airplanes against hostile forces. Congress had authorized aircraft for the military in 1907, and the army had purchased its first airplane two years later, but leaders had not been sure what to do with it and thus had assigned the plane to the Signal Corps, which was responsible for scientific development. The first pilot, Lieutenant Benjamin D. Foulois, was instructed to learn how to fly and to "keep out of trouble."

By 1916, the 1st Aero Squadron, Aviation Section, Signal Corps had eight aircraft with appropriate officers and maintenance crews. On March 12, the squadron was ordered to Columbus to support Pershing's expedition. He assigned the aero squadron to provide aerial reconnaissance, photo mapping, and courier services. On March 15, aviators flew their first mission. During the next few weeks, the airplanes delivered some photographs, but none of the air missions found any Villistas. After only a few reconnaissance missions, Pershing limited the planes to courier duty. By April 20, following only one month of operation and numerous breakdowns and accidents, not a single airplane was operational.

The failure of the 1st Aero Squadron did not come about because of pilot error or misuse by Pershing, but rather as a result of the design of the planes themselves. Practically worn out when they arrived in New Mexico, the planes were neither powerful nor strong enough to survive the harsh northern Mexico conditions. Replacement planes that arrived near the end of the expedition were more powerful, but they had propeller problems and could not operate in areas of high altitude, such as the hills where the Villistas commonly hid.

Pershing's instructions to give "scrupulous regard to the sovereignty of Mexico" proved as difficult to heed as Villa was to find. Without intelligence about Mexican federal army locations, the American cavalry frequently encountered the federalists, who felt more kinship with Villa's bandits than with the gringo invaders from north of the border. Usually the encounters were bloodless, but on June 21, soldiers of the 10th Cavalry engaged in a heavy firefight with federal troops who would not allow them to enter the village of Carrizal. It was never determined who fired first, but at the end of the day twelve Americans were dead and eleven wounded. Mexican losses were estimated at four times that number.

The information void affected not only the frontline troops but also National Guard units activated from the Midwest and the Atlantic coast to provide security along the border while the regular army pursued Villa. In one instance, a National Guard unit en route to the border by train was delayed by a broken rail near San Antonio. The guardsmen quickly disembarked from their rail cars and established a defensive perimeter to repel an immediate attack, not realizing they were still well inside the United States and hundreds of miles from the nearest Villistas.

The expedition continued to pursue Villa futilely for the remainder of 1916. President Wilson, yielding to public pressure to get out of Mexico and to focus on the Great War across the Atlantic Ocean, he finally ordered the expedition to return home.

Cavalry operations during the punitive expedition were marked by hardship, diligence, and bravery on the part of the officers and troopers in the field. Columns of U.S. Cavalry penetrating more than 300 miles into the interior of Mexico were the last American soldiers ordered to "live off the land" without supply lines to the rear. In every encounter with the bandits, the cavalrymen were victorious. Villa, however, remained elusive, apparently never even within firing range of his American pursuers. When the last American cavalryman crossed the border back into the United States on February 5, 1917, Villa was still loose in the hills of Mexico.* Even though the expedition had been labeled a failure because Villa remained at large, the military had learned a great deal about the new technology of warfare, and leaders had gained experience that would be beneficial in the rapidly approaching war in Europe.

While the expedition had been unsuccessfully pursuing Villa in Mexico, the conflict in Europe had escalated. Along the western front in 1916, the French and Germans sustained more than a million casualties with no significant gains by either side. On July 1, at the Battle of the Somme, the British sustained 60,000 casualties including 19,000 dead in a single day of fighting. Europeans on both sides were losing an entire generation of young men in the muddy trenches of France.

Meanwhile, President Wilson won reelection in 1916 on the platform of neutrality and with the slogan "He kept us out of war." American businessmen continued to sell weapons, munitions, and other war materials to Great Britain, Russia, and other Allies. Germany, which had a worldwide intelligence network in operation before the war began, had already instituted a campaign of subversion and sabotage within the United States.

German efforts against the United States were multifaceted. They included the puchase of important strategic raw materials,

---

*Villa's fortunes and the size of his army continued to rise and fall with revolutionary developments in Mexico. In 1923, he was assassinated by a rival Mexican faction while riding in an automobile. To date, Villa is the last foreign enemy to lead a ground attack against the United States mainland.

such as carbolic acid and chlorine, to prevent their shipment to the Allies and also the encouragement of labor unrest at major manufacturing plants. When these efforts did not slow the exports across the Atlantic, German agents took a more direct approach. The most spectacular incident occurred on July 30, 1916, when more than two million pounds of munitions bound for Russia exploded on Black Tom Island near the Statue of Liberty in New York harbor. A similar explosion, never definitely proven to be the result of German agents, occurred on April 10, 1917, at the Hercules Power Company at Eddystone, Pennsylvania, with the loss of 112 lives.

German propagandists provided news releases to the American press and published German- and English-language newspapers encouraging American isolationism and neutrality. They also targeted emigrants to the United States from countries with long-term dislike for the English, such as the Irish and Indians.

The British did not sit idly by as the Germans worked at influencing American opinion. In addition to attempting to persuade the United States to enter the war on the side of the Allies, the British provided intelligence in the absence of viable American agents to counter German sabotage.

To compound the weakness of having no meaningful intelligence or counterintelligence organization, the United States had failed to enact specific laws against German intrigue. Finally, after two years of German espionage and terrorism, Congress passed the Espionage Act of 1917, which provided strong punishment for acts of violence and made it illegal to interfere with American neutrality laws.

A year later, Congress added the Sedition Act, which made it illegal during wartime to "utter, print, write, or publish any disloyal, profane, scurrilous, or abusive language" concerning the flag, the government, or the armed forces. By the end of the Great War, more than 1,500 people were prosecuted under these acts.*

---

*The Sedition Act of 1918 was repealed in 1921. The Espionage Act of 1917 remains in force as amended in 1940 and 1970 to clarify offenses and to fix penalties. According to the amended act, the general definition of espionage is action that presents a "clear and present danger" to national security.

Most, however, were charged for verbal or written statements against the war, and few, if any, of the cases made any impact on actual military or diplomatic operations.

Competition between German and British agents to accomplish their aims in the United States was brought to the forefront on May 7, 1915, when a German submarine sank the British liner *Lusitania*. Of the 1,200 civilian passengers killed, 128 were U.S. citizens. Angry Americans demanded the United States declare war on Germany, but the Germans launched an immediate propaganda campaign, including the inaccurate claim that the *Lusitania* was carrying war supplies to England.

The sinking of the *Lusitania* pushed the United States to the brink of war, but the tradition of American noninterference in Europe, combined with German propaganda efforts, maintained American neutrality. More and more citizens were siding with the Allies and encouraging U.S. involvement, feeling kinship with Great Britain and sympathy for a longtime friend, France. The British tipped the scales when they provided America with information about still another incident of German espionage. Germany, long interested in expanding its colonial empire into the Western Hemisphere, had over many years dispatched envoys and agents into Mexico. Since the turn of the century, German agents in Mexico had encouraged anti-American sentiments among both revolutionists and those in power in Mexico City while supplying arms and ammunition to the various Mexican factions.

On January 16, 1917, German Foreign Minister Arthur Zimmermann sent an encrypted message to his representative in Mexico, Heinrich J. F. von Eckardt, instructing him to approach the Mexican authorities with an alliance proposal. Zimmermann's telegram suggested that, once the United States was involved in the war, Germany and Mexico could join forces. The reward for Mexico would be Texas, New Mexico, Arizona, and the other western U.S. territory lost as a result of the Mexican War. British intelligence intercepted the "Zimmermann Telegram," deciphered it, and on February 24 turned it over to the U.S. government, which then released it to the press. Although Mexico, still burdened with internal strife, did not respond to the proposal, Zimmermann was forced from office—not for the contents of the telegram but because it had fallen into the wrong hands. Americans increased their demand for war against Germany.

Public opinion, resulting from the publication of the Zimmermann Telegram and the sinking of three American merchant ships by German U-boats in March, forced President Wilson to set aside his neutrality stance. On April 6, 1917, Wilson asked Congress to declare war on Germany and the Central Powers.

The United States was a late entry into the war, now in its third year with total casualties for both sides already in the millions. Amazingly, despite years of forewarning, the U.S. military intelligence community was unprepared. The entire U.S. Army intelligence department consisted of one man, and the Office of Naval Intelligence was little better off. Once again the United States would enter a war, and send soldiers and sailors into combat, without possessing the bare necessities of military intelligence.

The one person assigned to army military intelligence at the beginning of the war was Major Ralph Van Deman. Van Deman graduated from Harvard and later earned degrees in both law and medicine. Commissioned in 1891, he served in successive infantry and intelligence positions, remaining a soldier and never practicing either law or medicine. During the Spanish-American War, he was assigned to the MID in Washington. In 1901, he became an intelligence officer in the Philippines. After he returned to the United States, Van Deman commanded an infantry company and then spent a brief assignment at the General Staff Second Division in 1907, followed by alternating intelligence and infantry assignments in the Far East and the United States.

Van Deman was one of the army's most experienced intelligence officers and greatest supporters of an organized military information system when he was assigned to the general staff in 1915. For two years, Van Deman lobbied military and civilian leaders to reestablish an intelligence service, but it was not until the declaration of war against the Central Powers that Van Deman finally received permission on May 3, 1917, to form the Military Intelligence Section (MIS). This was the first instance of the army identifying a department as "intelligence" rather than as "information."

Initially Van Deman was given three officers and two clerks for the MIS, but within eighteen months his section had grown to a staff of more than 1,700. Van Deman modeled the MIS on the British intelligence organization design of two major branches. The Positive Branch was responsible for gathering information about the Central Powers, and the Negative Branch for preventing the enemy from securing information about the United States. From its inception, the Negative Branch occupied most of Van Deman's attention and claimed most of MIS's assets. This emphasis left direct tactical information responsibilities to the front-line forces in Europe, while strategic information about the Central Powers came from British and French sources.

Van Deman would serve in military intelligence in one aspect or another for the next twenty-five years, including during World War II. His organizational skills and persistence in maintaining a military intelligence organization earned him the title "father of military intelligence" that is still associated with his name today. His accomplishments as the head of the U.S. Army's MIS during the Great War, however, centered more on establishing and organizing the service than on producing information that affected the war's fighting forces.

One of Van Deman's early achievements was the establishment of a cryptology unit. Van Deman recruited Herbert Osborn Yardley, a State Department employee with a knack for code breaking, to set up the first formal foreign communications intelligence-gathering organization in the United States. Yardley, commissioned as an army lieutenant, formed a staff of 151 officers, code breakers, and clerks capable of reading more than fifty different American and foreign shorthand systems and of detecting invisible ink messages. Similar cryptology units in Europe were referred to as "Black Chambers," and Yardley soon adopted this unofficial but intrigue-laden title for his organization.

Yardley and the Black Chamber managed to break the diplomatic codes of several countries, including current allies such as Japan. Historically, however, the Black Chamber has received far more credit for viable output than it deserves. Its most publicized accomplishment was deciphering a letter found in suspected

German spy Lothar Witzke's luggage when he was captured at Nogales, Arizona on January 18, 1918. The contents of the letter outlined Witzke's mission in the United States and provided prime evidence in his conviction as a German agent.*

The Office of Naval Intelligence also grew in size and responsibility with the declaration of war against the Central Powers. With the creation of the position of chief of naval operations early in the conflict, the ONI transferred from the Bureau of Navigation to the Office of Operations to assist in war planning. The ONI was little prepared to gather positive information of benefit to American ships at sea and left the majority of that area of intelligence to the British and French. What little positive intelligence the ONI did gather came from agents disguised as businessmen, miners, and agricultural workers in South America and the Far East, where they often worked with the various navy attachés. Their adventures were marked by intrigue and large expense accounts, but no evidence exists that indicates they provided any information that directly affected the war itself.

Like the MIS, the ONI was far more involved with domestic counterintelligence and countersubversion than positive intelligence gathering at or near the battle sites. The ONI filled its rapidly increasing number of intelligence positions with reservists and volunteers. ONI agents proved to be overzealous and prone to "find" a spy behind every tree or wall. Honest citizens who spoke German or merely "looked German" were hounded from their jobs by the ONI. When they could not find "subversive" Germans, ONI agents turned their suspicions on Jews, labor union members, and pacifists.

The American Protective League assisted the MIS and the ONI in their domestic counterintelligence efforts. Headed by Albert M. Briggs, it was organized as a part of the Justice's Department

---

* Witzke, although a minor actor at best in the espionage game, was the only spy sentenced to death during World War I by the United States. His death sentence was commuted to life imprisonment by President Wilson, and in 1923, after only five years in prison, Witzke was released to return to Germany.

Bureau of Investigation, the forerunner of the Federal Bureau of Investigation (FBI). The American Protective League was without a doubt the most amateurish—and the grossest violator of civil rights—of any Great War organization. This unpaid auxiliary quickly grew to a force of a quarter million avid spy hunters. League members sought out German sympathizers, labor leaders, draft dodgers, and anyone else they considered anti-American— or anti–Protective League. Illegal searches, arrests, and wiretaps were but a few of their tools of counterintelligence. By war's end, the American Protective League had conducted more than six million investigations. Not one produced a confirmed German spy.

Spies, counterintelligence, and espionage were of great interest to the American public, and such intelligence work began to take on an aura of respectability that attracted prominent American businessmen. All claimed to want to do their part in the war effort, and some even specified that their business success made them good candidates for "intelligence." None mentioned, but many outsiders noted, that working for Van Deman and MIS in Washington was certainly better duty than being an infantryman in the muddy trenches of France. The ONI was also overrun with big businessmen seeking navy commissions. Again, Washington had its advantages over a ship's bridge in the icy, U-boat-filled northern Atlantic.

Many of these volunteers for both the MIS and the ONI were Ivy Leaguers. Van Deman signed up several of his fellow Harvard graduates; Yale alumni also made themselves readily available. By the end of World War I, Ivy Leaguers dominated the U.S. military intelligence community—a domination that would continue for decades to come. Unfortunately, many of the eastern elites would prove more competent in the boardroom than in uniform.

The lingering effects of the Ivy Leaguers on military intelligence were both positive and negative. On the plus side was the legitimacy they lent the profession, but on the negative side they displayed an arrogant elitism that they transferred to the intelligence community. For many of the Ivy Leaguers, military intelligence was a "grand game" rather than the actuality and finality of the battlefield.

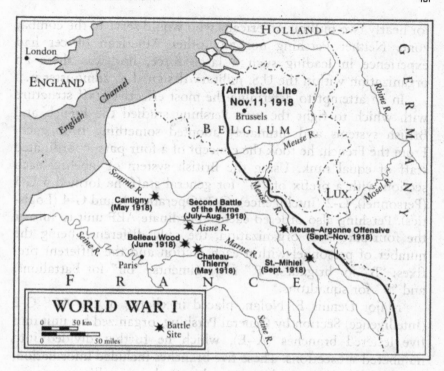

In Europe, the U.S. Army and Navy were facing the most formidable foe in their history. Despite all the ongoing MIS and ONI intrigue and adventure in the States, combat units entered the war without adequate intelligence or intelligence assets.

The American Expeditionary Force (AEF) headquarters, commanded by Black Jack Pershing, landed in France with a staff of 200 within weeks of the declaration of war. On June 26, 1917, doughboys* of the 1st Infantry Division arrived, leading the way

---

*The term "doughboys" dates from the Mexican War, when adobe dust covered infantry soldiers plodding along dry roads in Mexico. Mounted troops called the foot soldiers "adobies," which evolved to "dobies" and ultimately became "doughboys." It was not a popular term among the senior military leadership, but the press and the enlisted soldiers seemed comfortable with it. At one time in the Great War, there was a move to call the American soldiers "sammies" for Uncle Sam, but it did not stick.

for nearly two million Americans who would serve in the combat zone. Neither Pershing nor any other American officer had experience in leading such a large force, nor was there an organization within the U.S. military designed to administer it.

In an attempt to determine the most effective staff structure with which to fight the war, Pershing studied the French and British systems and ultimately adopted something from each. From the French, he took the concept of a four-part, coordinated staff of equal rank. Using the British system of labeling each section with a prefix of "G" for general staff, he formed a G-1 (Personnel), G-2 (Intelligence), G-3 (Operations), and G-4 (Logistics). Pershing also ordered each subordinate AEF unit to mirror the four-part staff organization, the only difference being the number of personnel within each section and the different prefixes: "B" for brigades, "R" for regiments, "Bn" for battalions, and "S" for squadrons.*

Major Dennis E. Nolan, placed in charge of the AEF G-2 (Intelligence) Section by General Pershing, organized his unit into five lettered branches (A–E), which he further divided into numbered subsections. These five branches included information, secret service, topography, censorship, and the intelligence corps. Components of the G-2 quickly assembled information on the enemy, weather, and terrain in the AEF area of operations. For the first time in American military history, consistent postings of the enemy order of battle, along with maps showing the front line and the estimated location of enemy units, were available to the operations branch and to the commander.

One of the more innovative G-2 subsections was the Radio Intelligence Section (RIS). Wireless communications had added a new dimension to warfare as well as providing another source for the gathering and compromise of information. RIS, the predecessor organization of today's Army Security Agency, controlled and

---

*This letter designation system evolved over the years to "G" for staffs at or above division level and "S" for staffs below it. The "J" prefix was later adopted for joint service staffs. In each of these staffs, the "2" was, and is, the intelligence section.

enforced U.S. codes and ciphers and monitored and examined those of the enemy.

To monitor enemy message traffic, RIS established liaison with other Allied resources and maintained a team of crypt-analysts at each army headquarters and at five intercept and eight direction-finding stations. The section did intercept some important messages, but by the time it deciphered the contents and forwarded them to frontline units, the information was often no longer valid. However, some effective artillery attacks on enemy positions, and in one instance early warning of the formation of a new German unit for a major offensive, did result from RIS intercepts.

In fulfilling its mission of monitoring American communicators' proper use of codes and ciphers, RIS recorded that the AEF was extremely vulnerable to signal intercepts. The doughboys were not fond of codes or adept in their use. Major Frank Moorman, RIS chief, later wrote, "There certainly never existed on the Western Front a force more negligent in the use of their own code than was the American Army." With no outside assistance, Moorman's radio intercept operators were able to assemble the entire friendly order of battle for the attack on the St. Mihiel salient in August of 1918 by monitoring their own American wireless traffic.

The AEF's intelligence organization was better, or at least more innovative, than any groups had been in previous American conflicts. For the first time, there was an adequate, in-place, coordinated intelligence organization that reached from frontline battalions all the way back through the chain of command to the senior military headquarters. The nature of World War I itself was responsible in part for these advances in intelligence organization and performance. The front line was long, and, by the time the Americans arrived, warfare was extremely static. Trench operations had replaced mobility, and surprise proved difficult for either side to attain. Maps were more available and accurate than they had been in any previous American conflict.

The cornerstone of World War I army intelligence was information produced at the battalion level. Battalion S-2s gathered information directly for their commanders' use as well as for passing along to higher headquarters for overall evaluation and dissemination. One lieutenant was authorized at the battalion staff level, assisted by a scout group of up to thirty noncommissioned officers and enlisted men. The missions of the S-2's scouts included operating observation posts during daytime and listening posts at night to provide early warning of attack. Scouts also went on patrols beyond friendly front lines to determine enemy dispositions. One of the most common techniques intelligence officers employed to secure information about enemy strengths and intentions was prisoner-snatch operations. Night patrols, armed with grenades, pistols, and trench knives that had long blades and brass-knuckle handles, penetrated enemy defensive positions and engaged in hand-to-hand combat in order to capture live prisoners to be brought back for questioning.

While the AEF had the best-organized intelligence network in the history of the U.S. Army, it was far from a perfect system. At times it could not even attain marginal effectiveness. Inexperienced intelligence officers had no official doctrine or manuals to guide their performance. Patrols were not always well planned, and there was the constant danger that members of a snatch mission would be taken prisoner themselves. The most valuable asset of World War I intelligence, especially at battalion level, was personnel assigned from combat units. For the scouts to be successful, they needed to possess a thorough knowledge of friendly and enemy organization, tactics, and combat psychology.

Pershing's G-2 staff used aerial reconnaissance, but like most aspects of the AEF, the American air corps was less than prepared for combat at the beginning of the war. When the AEF arrived in France, the entire American aerial fleet had 15 airplanes, all of inferior quality to the Allied and Central Powers planes that filled the skies. Modern airplanes were not available from American manufacturers and the war would end before U.S. production could meet the AEF's demand for aircraft. Congress was forced to authorize the purchase of French and British airplanes.

It was not until April 15, 1918, that the first American aerial reconnaissance flew over enemy lines. During their first weeks, the reconnaissance flights relied on the visual observations of the air crew. The Americans, however, soon adopted the British method of aerial photography. Pilots and observers experimented with many different cameras, mounts, and photography methods before they eventually devised techniques that would remain standard for the U.S. Air Corps through World War II.

The AEF received little or no intelligence assistance from Van Deman and his Military Intelligence Section back in Washington. Pershing had little confidence in the bureaucratic senior headquarters and wanted as little "help" from the War Department's general staff as possible. Major Dennis E. Nolan, as head of the AEF G-2 (Intelligence) Section, shared Pershing's desire for no interference from Washington and, because of previous contact, cared little for Van Deman personally or professionally.

Not surprisingly, one of the few joint ventures between Nolan and Van Deman hardly proved a success. In August 1917, Nolan proposed a Corps of Intelligence Police (CIP), a counter-intelligence unit to detect treason, sedition, and subversive activity and to detect and prevent enemy espionage and sabotage. To man the CIP, Nolan requested Van Deman recruit fifty sergeants. Nolan stated that minimal requirements were that the NCOs be trustworthy, have investigative experience, and be fluent in French. Van Deman turned to three of the largest private detective agencies in the country for assistance, repeating Nolan's requirements. The response he received was, "There ain't no such animal."

The initial recruits were an unusual mix of Americans and Europeans who had immigrated to the United States for various reasons, including a deposed Belgian nobleman, a Russian train robber, a French murderer, and a Foreign Legion deserter. This motley crew was shipped to Europe, and the CIP was formally organized on August 13, 1917. When Nolan attempted to secure schooling at the French intelligence center for his sergeants, initial security checks revealed the murderer, the train robber, and not one but five deserters from the French army, who had fled to the United States. Nineteen more CIP members had enlisted under assumed names because of criminal pasts or other suspicious reasons.

In spite of its shaky beginnings, the CIP grew to a force of 400. CIP agents investigated a few acts of espionage and assisted in keeping unauthorized people out of sensitive areas. They were better known to the doughboys, however, as investigators of criminal acts by soldiers, such as black marketing, and therefore gained little acceptance. An indication that the Corps of Intelligence Police accomplished little if anything is that its records were classified and later destroyed—a classic means of covering up failures that is still standard practice in the intelligence community.

Pershing and the AEF faced far worse problems than just intelligence when they arrived in France. America's entrance into the war did not immediately swing the advantage to the Allies. Revolution in Russia had toppled the czar, and the new government withdrew its forces from the war. The British and the French, desperate for manpower, wanted to use the American soldiers as replacements in their own divisions rather than have them fight as cohesive units. A few doughboy units were initially plugged into frontline Allied positions, but Pershing continued to demand that the AEF participate in the war as one self-contained army. When Pershing prevailed, there was still the problem of where to commit the doughboys at the front. The British were dug in along the northern part of the battle line nearest the channel and their resupply links to England. French forces were defending Paris and, because of national pride, refused to let any other country's forces defend their capital. By default, the AEF moved to the southern Lorraine front, which encompassed the area from Verdun to the Swiss border.

One of the reasons the Allies had opposed the AEF fighting as units, rather than replacements, was their lack of confidence in the Americans' fighting ability. Volunteers not long off farms and city streets filled the ranks of the AEF, and neither the officer corps nor career enlisted men had adequate combat experience. Nevertheless, on October 20, 1917, the 1st Infantry Division, the initial U.S. unit committed to the front lines, was assigned a quiet area in the French sector under overall command of a French general. The French were so dubious about the Americans that they interspersed the 1st Division's units among their own battalions rather than have the Americans occupy a continuous sector.

The Germans, sharing the perception that the AEF was a weak force, moved to take advantage at the first opportunity. On April

20, 1918, doughboys of the 26th Infantry Division, with little intelligence on the area or the enemy on the other side of the trenches, relieved French troops at Seicheprey. After nightfall the Germans laid down a rolling artillery barrage and followed it with an infantry assault. The surprised, unprepared Americans were quickly overrun, losing 179 men captured and more than 300 killed or wounded. The Germans held the village for most of the next day before the French returned to drive them out. By that time, Germans were dropping pictures of the captured Americans and their positions onto the French and English lines from airplanes. German radio broadcasts also beamed the news to the Allies that the Americans could not fight.

Pershing, both concerned and angry about the American defeat at Seicheprey, convinced his superiors in Paris that the AEF needed an immediate opportunity to prove itself to the Allies and the Germans, as well as to bolster sagging morale back home. Pershing received the mission of pushing back the German penetration around the village of Cantigny, and he chose the 1st Infantry Division to lead the way. It took nearly a month of preparation and extensive artillery barrages before the "Big Red One" made its attack on May 28. With intelligence limited on both sides of "no man's land," men rather than information decided the battle's outcome. At the end of the day, the Americans held the former German salient, and the next day they repulsed an enemy counterattack.

The Allies now believed that the Americans could fight; the Germans were not yet convinced. They soon would be, however, when they continued their spring offensive by moving against the French at Chateau-Thierry along the Marne River. When the French line weakened, the U.S. 2nd and 3rd Infantry Divisions reinforced their allies on May 31 and blunted the German attack.

During the first week of June, Pershing sent the 4th Marine Brigade, composed of the 5th and 6th Marine Regiments, to drive the Germans out of the heavily fortified Bois de Belleau. Although the marines were the most combat-ready units in the AEF, Pershing had committed less experienced army units to the first fights, apparently wanting any glory to go to his own service rather than the Marine Corps. While the army was being bloodied in its first weeks of combat, the marines had been held in the rear to guard supply depots and other administrative sites.

By June 6, Pershing realized there was glory and bloodshed enough for all, and the marines attacked, with little information about their adversary, at what would become known in American history as the Battle of Belleau Wood. It took weeks of close combat—typified more by grenades and bayonets than techniques of modern warfare—but in the end, at a cost of 4,677 killed or wounded, Belleau Wood belonged to the U.S. Marine Corps.

On July 15, American troops again beat back a German attack at Chateau-Thierry. Three days later, American and French soldiers defeated the German advance at the Second Battle of the Marne. In August, the British, French, and Americans began a general offensive throughout France, and the entire German army began to retreat. Divisions of the AEF defeated the Germans at St. Mihiel in September and continued the attack into the Argonne Forest in October. The Allies were now winning the war, not, however, because of good or adequate intelligence but rather due to superior numbers of forces, supplies, and weapons.

Vice Admiral William S. Sims, commander of all U.S. naval forces in the combat zone, shared Pershing's lack of intelligence information assistance from Washington. Forced to form his own intelligence organization at his London headquarters, Sims placed Commander John V. Babcock in charge of what essentially was an ONI "forward." In reality, Babcock's organization generated little intelligence on its own but rather relied on information from the British.

The primary responsibilities of Sims's forces were convoy escort, mine laying, and antisubmarine warfare. One of the navy's largest operations of the war incorporated two of these missions. During the summer of 1918, the U.S. Navy laid a 240-mile-long mine field across open seas from Norway to Scotland. The British, after studying the possibilities of such a barrier, had decided it was impractical; nonetheless, the Americans proceeded and completed the task on September 20. The objective of the more than 70,000 mines was to pen the German U-boats in the North Sea. In spite of the huge expense in dollars and manpower, the U-boats quickly breached the mine barrier and did not allow it to slow their operations. The navy eventually claimed that the mines "possibly" sank as many as six U-boats, but no records of either the United States or Germany confirm a single U-boat sinking as a result of the mines.

By November 1918, German forces were in retreat across Europe, and Allied commanders were planning an offensive into the German heartland if necessary. It appeared that the German military would fight indefinitely, but the German people, near starvation from the British blockade, rioted in the streets and demanded peace. On November 6, German government officials approached the French and proposed an end of hostilities. At 11:00 in the morning of November 11, an armistice went into effect.

Nearly nine million were dead and twenty-one million wounded. Europe had sustained more casualties in the four years of the Great War than it had in all the conflicts of the previous century. A war-weary world celebrated peace, but military leaders on both sides recognized that little had been resolved and that the battles of the Great War would recur some time in the future. The "war to end all wars" would fail to live up to its billing.

While Europe was in ruins, the United States had become more of a world power. Europeans downplayed the American role in the conflict, but Americans were convinced the doughboys had won the war. The truth, of course, lay somewhere in between. Whatever the outcome, the cost had been great. Official U.S. casualties, mostly incurred by the infantry in the trenches of the western front, numbered 116,516 dead and 234,428 wounded.

The armistice of November 11 did not mean that all American servicemen would immediately return home to victory parades. Unfinished business in Russia resulted in U.S. forces being committed to a thoroughly confusing and pointless military operation. The original purpose seemed reasonable enough. Vast stores of arms and supplies sent to Russia by the Allies were still on the docks at Vladivostok in Siberia, and the Allies now feared the newly empowered Bolsheviks would sell them to the Germans. Also, at Archangel, in northern Russia, thousands of Czechoslovaks, who had been prisoners of the Russians, wanted to return home and join the Allies in hopes of forming their own country.

Their only route out of Russia was to the west by railroad to Vladivostok.

Against the advice of his cabinet, President Wilson, on the basis of information supplied by the British, made the decision to send American troops to assist the British and French in Siberia and northern Russia. Neither the MID nor the ONI provided any intelligence to assist the president in his decision, and on-site intelligence by the American forces in Siberia and northern Russia would not be sufficient to assist commanders to accomplish their missions.

The American Expeditionary Force, Siberia (AEFS), composed of 9,000 soldiers from the 27th and 31st Infantry Regiments and support units transferred from the Philippines, arrived in Vladivostok in August 1918. In command of the expedition was Major General William S. Graves, assisted by a general staff. Major David P. Barrows, the AEFS's G-2, had an intelligence staff, also from the Philippines, of five officers and fifty-one enlisted men, as well as a detachment from the Washington office of MID. Barrows and the AEFS's chief of staff, Lieutenant Colonel O. P. Robinson, did not get along well. In addition to their basic personality conflict, Robinson did not believe that Barrows and his staff understood the mission or what intelligence to gather. It is likely, considering the confusing circumstances in Siberia, that Robinson was not all that sure himself, but since colonels outrank majors, Barrows remained mostly ineffective. Graves shared the views of his chief of staff and expressed in his reports that his intelligence staff was not meeting his needs.

Meanwhile, the American Expeditionary Force, Northern Russia, composed of about 5,000 men of the 339th Infantry and support units, deployed from France via England to Archangel, arriving in September 1918. Under command of the British, the Americans did not have a separate general staff until the arrival of Brigadier General Wilde P. Richardson in March 1919. Richardson appointed Captain W. N. Thomas as his G-2, but the Americans withdrew two months later before Thomas could have any impact.

On March 31, 1920, well over a year after the conclusion of World War I, the last soldiers of the AEFS withdrew from

Vladivostok. During more than eighteen months of operations, the Americans in Siberia and Northern Russia fought Russian factions, bitter cold, and unmitigated confusion in a futile attempt to offer some stability to the postrevolutionary country. The final American death count was 139, and U.S. accomplishments totaled zero with the exception of leaving the Bolsheviks with a long-term dislike for the interfering Americans.

An after-action report written by the AEF staff noted, "The entire affair was manifestly conceived in an atmosphere of inaccurate intelligence information."

General Graves presented the best summary of the Russian expedition in his memoirs, published in 1931. Graves wrote, "I was in command of United States troops sent to Siberia and I must admit, I do not know what the United States was trying to accomplish by military intervention."

While it had made great mistakes during the war, particularly in its vigilantism in pursuing suspected anti-Americans at home, military intelligence as a whole had made advances. In earlier wars, military intelligence organizations had been formed during combat and disbanded with the peace, but World War I left behind permanent U.S. intelligence organizations at several levels. The Military Intelligence Division remained a formal part of the War Department general staff, and intelligence officers and staffs continued as permanent parts of all army organization down to division level. The Office of Naval Intelligence had achieved a similar level of permanence and importance in the navy.

World War II: The Pacific Theater

The United States' ability to mobilize for war is exceeded only by its ability to dismantle what it has created as soon as peace prevails. Both the Military Intelligence Division and the Office of Naval Intelligence survived the post–Great War demobilization, but only as skeletons of their wartime structures. The remaining intelligence personnel tried to determine the purpose of their peacetime missions and the tasks necessary to accomplish them as the army and navy—and branches within the services—competed for a share of the limited budget and for personnel allocations.

The MID maintained its status as a separate division of the War Department until 1921, when General Pershing became the army chief of staff. Pershing reorganized the general staff into the same "G-staff" structure that he had used in the AEF in France. Because Congress limited the number of generals, Pershing found himself with only four brigadiers to fill five G-staff director positions. Pershing chose to assign the only colonel as the head of G-2 intelligence, which absorbed the MID's personnel and responsibilities.

Following the general staff model, subordinate army corps and area commands designated officers to serve as their G-2s, or assistant chiefs of staff for military intelligence, while lower-level commands designated staff intelligence officers as S-2s. Although the War Department published a series of manuals and guides outlining intelligence functions and procedures, the documents neither clearly defined the duties of these intelligence officers and their staffs nor made clear the relationship between subordinate intelligence officers and the War Department G-2.

Despite the chaos of reorganization, the War Department did continue its efforts in foreign intelligence collection. Military attachés in embassies overseas and intelligence officers assigned to U.S. units in Hawaii and the Philippines focused on Japan, which, despite its status as a Great War ally, still presented the greatest future threat. When Germany reemerged as a military power in the 1930s, the intelligence service also made that country a priority.

However, army intelligence personnel focused far more on domestic rather than foreign "enemies" during the years immediately after World War I. MID investigated labor unrest, the rise of socialism, the influence of the Soviets in America, and other instances of "un-American activity." This work by army intelligence—amateurish at best and heavy-handed at worst—included unsuccessful attempts to infiltrate agents into suspected subversive organizations and the commitment of federal troops to break up public gatherings. Neither President Warren Harding nor the general public approved of the army's efforts, so MID, ordered to cease and desist, neglected domestic counterintelligence, both valid and invalid, from the mid-1920s until a short time before the United States entered World War II.

The advancements in aerial reconnaissance during the postwar period should have been extremely beneficial to the intelligence community, but rivalries and turf battles limited progress. Because the airplane had proven to be an effective reconnaissance platform from which to gather visual and photographic intelligence, the MID created an Air Section in 1926 to advance aerial reconnaissance and photography technology. In February of that year, air attachés were assigned to major embassies in Europe to monitor aeronautical advances. About the same time, the army's Air Service, which had been the AEF's air arm in France, gained a more independent status as the Army Air Corps and formed its own Intelligence Office (initially called the Information Office), with basically the same duties as the MID Air Section. The two offices fought over resources and responsibilities as they duplicated efforts and competed for advancements.

The number of naval intelligence personnel was also dras-
tically reduced after the armistice. In the eight months following
the end of the war, the ONI shrank from a staff of 306 officers to
only 42. Despite these cutbacks, the ONI continued to focus its
efforts on Japan and specifically on Japanese fortification of the
Pacific island groups—the Carolines, Marshalls, and Marianas—
seized from Germany during the Great War.

The overall increase in the militarism of the Japanese, and
their invasion of Manchuria in 1931, reinforced ONI's intelligence
priorities. Additional naval attachés assigned to Tokyo attempted
to gather information and to establish indigenous secret intelligence networks but had little success.

When the army and navy recognized that current methods
were not producing adequate information on Japan and were not
likely to improve, both services turned to new and innovative
means to develop intelligence data. Their resulting work in
communications intercepts and cryptanalysis over the next two
decades would produce one of the greatest intelligence successes of
World War II.

With assistance from now–civilian government employee Herbert Yardley, the army led the way in intercepting and decoding
Japanese messages. Yardley's Black Chamber, renamed the Cipher
Bureau after its move to New York in 1919, broke the diplomatic
and military codes of at least twenty countries, including those of
Japan, which provided U.S. negotiators extremely useful information about Japan's bargaining position during the 1921 disarma-
ment conference.

Only a limited group of officers and diplomats knew about
Yardley's and the Cipher Bureau's successes. No one in navy
intelligence was privy to the information, but ONI had its own
operations to intercept and read Japan's message traffic. In late
1920, ONI agents broke into the Japanese consulate office in New
York City and photographed the code books.* Determining how

---

*ONI agents placed the stolen information in a red notebook, and as
a result the materials were called "the Red Book." Some accounts
indicate the ONI employed prostitutes and other criminal elements to
accomplish the procurement of the Red Book; even if true, this is not the
type of information recorded in official histories.

the codes worked took extensive time and required several other break-ins before the navy was finally able to read Japanese naval and other communications in 1929.

The year 1929 also brought increased difficulties to the military intelligence agencies practicing communications intercept and cryptanalysis. When President Herbert Hoover assumed his office in March, he appointed Henry L. Simpson as secretary of state. Informed of the existence of Yardley's Cipher Bureau, Simpson angrily ordered it be immediately closed because he believed it was neither legal nor proper. Years later he would explain his actions to his biographer simply: "Gentlemen do not read each other's mail."

Simpson's order not only directly concluded operations of the Cipher Bureau but also had an indirect impact on ONI efforts. When the Black Chamber was closed, Yardley placed his personal financial self-interest ahead of the importance of national security, taking with him two large boxes of sensitive documents. In 1931, Yardley published the story of the Cipher Bureau's activities in *The American Black Chamber*. The book sold well in the United States but even better in Japan, where the Japanese were interested in, and angry about, Yardley's description of how their codes were broken. Evidence later revealed that Yardley embezzled government funds allocated to the Black Chamber and that he sold secret information to the Japanese just prior to the release of his book. Yardley's revelations had governments around the world, including Japan, rushing to change their codes and methods of transmitting classified messages.

Yardley was not prosecuted for compromising the secrets of the Black Chamber primarily because, even though the Cipher Bureau was out of business, the army and the navy were still in the business of "reading other people's mail." About the same time Simpson was closing the Bureau, the army formed the Signal Intelligence Service (SIS) under the leadership of William F. Friedman, a civilian and recent graduate of Cornell University. The SIS was not a part of MID but rather was subordinate to the Signal Corps. On the navy side, the Office of Naval Communications (ONC) worked with, and at times in competition against, the ONI in similar code-breaking efforts.

The Japanese changed all of their codes and developed a machine cipher system, which they fielded in 1931. It took four years for the ONC to reproduce the Japanese cipher system into what they called "the Red Machine." The SIS, during this time, operated in isolation from the ONC and ONI and concentrated its limited personnel on various Japanese codes still in use at lower military and government levels.

In 1939, the Japanese introduced a much more complex code system that the Americans labeled Purple. The navy and army worked independently for months with no progress in solving the new Purple crypto system. Purple's Japanese inventors were convinced the system was impossible to break, and by 1940 American intelligence analysts were beginning to agree. Finally the navy code breakers, now operating under the designation of OP-20-G, went to SIS to suggest a collaboration, which resulted in the SIS concentrating all its efforts on Purple while OP-20-G assumed all other cryptanalysis duties.

Friedman and his staff made little progress on solving the Purple mystery until finally, in 1940, Harry L. Clark determined that instead of using rotors to vary the electrical connections that changed plain-text messages to cipher, as the Red Machine and most other code devices did, Purple operated on a system of telephone stepping switches. This initial breakthrough opened the way for decoding Purple, and by August the SIS had assembled its own version of the Japanese alphabetical typewriter code machine, which worked although it was apt to emit sparks and loud noises.

Japan's most secret messages could now be read by the Americans—but not with the ease or accuracy that some later reports would indicate. The Purple Machine did not intercept Japanese transmissions and immediately present a printout in understandable English. First, the Americans had to intercept a message through traditional means. This was not always an easy task, because the Japanese frequently changed their transmission wavelengths, causing U.S. interceptors to spend hours searching for the new frequencies. Once they had captured the message, they had to feed it into the Purple Machine, which then produced the content in Japanese. Then authorized Japanese linguists, always few in numbers because of the reluctance to trust Japanese-Americans, had to translate the message. The translation process itself was complex because the same word can have several different meanings depending upon context. Compounding the difficulty, the Japanese transmitters sometimes erred and sent the wrong word altogether. In addition to translation problems with Purple, the intercept system was often "too successful," producing far more information than decoders could handle in a timely manner. The Japanese further compounded the situation by still sending message traffic on the old Red system. And finally, defying all code-deciphering technology, the Japanese sent many messages, particularly the most sensitive, by secure courier rather than electronically.

Regardless of its complexities, Purple was easily the most significant intelligence success to that point. Purple began deciphering intercepted Japanese messages on September 25, 1940—the most opportune of times. On September 27, Japan, along with Germany and Italy, signed the Tripartite Pact forming the Tokyo-Berlin-Rome Axis.

Despite the collaboration between the army and the navy to break the Purple system, the relationship between the services remained competitive. Bureaucratic squabbling about intelligence responsibilities continued within each service, especially the navy. The ONI won few of its fights with the Office of Naval Communications and lost all its responsibilities except domestic counterintelligence and internal security.

The various agencies associated with intelligence within the army and the navy seemed at odds about responsibilities and assets. J. Edgar Hoover and his Federal Bureau of Investigation added to the confusion, believing that all domestic intelligence was in their charter. As a result, the intelligence officers shared little information with each other or with war planners.

President Franklin Roosevelt, acutely aware of the lack of coordinated analysis of the tremendous amount of information flowing into Washington, was particularly concerned with the rapidly expanding war in Europe, which had begun in 1939 with Germany's invasion of Poland. Roosevelt dispatched William "Wild Bill" Donovan, a Columbia University graduate and Wall

Street lawyer who had received the Medal of Honor during the Great War, to England to make contact with various Allied intelligence services and to determine Britain's ability to fight the Axis successfully. Donovan became convinced that the United States would soon be in the war and that intelligence would be a key to victory.

Upon his return from Europe, Donovan proposed that Roosevelt create a central agency to control all foreign information. On July 11, 1941, Roosevelt authorized the Office of the Coordinator of Information (COI) with Donovan at its head. By the end of the year, the COI had a growing staff of 600 and a budget of $10 million. What it did not have, however, was the support of the service intelligence organizations or of the FBI's Hoover. While it was making advancements in collating intelligence and in reducing redundancy, the COI, serving as the "central agency for intelligence," amazingly did not receive any information about Purple. Donovan and his staff went about their business without a clue about the existence of the code-breaking system, which was generating tremendous amounts of information about Japanese war plans. For the COI, this information would remain useless secrets.

The secrecy surrounding the Purple system would continue. Intelligence agencies have always been inherently reluctant to pass on information they gather because, quite reasonably, the more people aware of the secrets, the greater the chance for compromise. Information is power, which decreases in proportion to the amount of information shared. However, at times a secondary factor enters the picture, and it is that intelligence personnel have ordinary human foibles. Rivalries and jealousies between different intelligence agencies and individuals on occasion take precedence over what is in the best overall interest of the country. Supporting these conflicts is the primary rule of distribution, which says that intelligence should be available only on a "need to know" basis. The information originator thus makes the decision about who has the "need to know," and this determination often proves to be beyond the intelligence operator's capabilities or good judgment.

The intelligence gleaned from Purple is a classic example of limited access to information leading to disaster. In December

1941, Purple information was restricted to only the president, the secretaries of state, war, and navy, and a select group of military officers and White House staff. Field commanders, including those in Hawaii and the Philippines, were not considered as having a "need to know," nor were they even aware that the codebreaking system existed.

While Purple provided a select few Americans with excellent information about Japanese activities, most U.S. intelligence about the European war came from the English, who also had a "need to know" policy, which often failed to include their American cousins. As a result of budget and personnel reductions, as well as the intense rivalries among American agencies, intelligence organizations by 1940, other than Purple, were gathering little critical information on potential aggressors against the United States. General George Marshall, chief of staff of the U.S. Army, would later sum up the situation this way: "Prior to World War II, our foreign intelligence was little more than what a military attaché could learn at dinner, more or less over the coffee cups."

The United States retained its neutrality as the two-year-old war expanded. Americans, sympathetic to both the British and the Chinese, nonetheless resisted being pulled into another overseas conflict. As in the early stages of the Great War, American businessmen sold arms and supplies to Britain and France. While it did curtail exports of armaments and war resources to the Axis, the United States did little in the way of its own military preparedness.

In the Pacific, the Japanese had been increasing their sphere of influence for nearly a century, and in the 1930s their military began territorial acquisition to gain raw materials to end their dependence on other nations. After acquiring resource-rich Chinese Manchuria in 1931 and continuing their attack farther into China in 1937, the Japanese began planning to conquer all of eastern Asia. American merchants continued to sell scrap metals and other strategic materials to the Japanese until July 1941, when President Roosevelt placed an embargo on exports to Japan and froze Japanese financial assets and credit in the United States. Roosevelt's action, although belated, confirmed the Japanese belief that the only country with had the ability to impede their conquest of Asia and the Pacific was the United States.

The Japanese had anticipated that they might someday go to war with the United States since late in the nineteenth century. From those early days, they had included a surprise attack against the American fleet at Pearl Harbor in their plans, and, in fact, during the 1920s and 1930s, their advanced military schools presented an attack on Hawaii as one of the basic planning exercises. Operating under the bushido code of samurai warriors, which taught that surprise attacks were honorable and that death before surrender was preferable, the Japanese military had previously initiated war against an unsuspecting enemy when they attacked the Chinese in 1895 and the Russians in 1904.

In late 1940, Admiral Isoroku Yamamoto began finalizing plans for an attack on Pearl Harbor. In January 1941, the American ambassador to Japan learned about these plans from the Peruvian embassy in Tokyo. However, Washington paid little attention to the information, because military intelligence officers claimed that Hawaii was beyond both the interests and the capabilities of the Japanese. More important, they discounted the reports because the waters of Pearl Harbor were too shallow for the principal Japanese weapons of aerial- or submarine-launched torpedoes.

What the Americans did not know was that Yamamoto had studied the British attack on the Italian navy at Taranto, where on November 11, 1940, a mere twenty-one British airplanes armed with torpedoes had sunk three Italian battleships. Using information on the battle, Yamamoto worked with Japanese industry to produce a shallow-running torpedo. By summer, the new torpedo was ready, and the Japanese government approved Yamamoto's plan to attack the American fleet.

In September, the Japanese military sent a message to its agents in Honolulu instructing them to regularly report the number and types of ships at Pearl Harbor. Purple operators intercepted this message and the responses to it over the next two months. Military intelligence in Washington interpreted these messages as either plans for sabotage or only an exercise to train

Japanese foreign agents. Not a single source suggested that the requested information might be for air attack planning.

By November, tensions between the United States and Japan had reached the point where even the most obtuse intelligence and operations staffs anticipated hostilities. America's leaders were aware that war was imminent, but no one seemed to know when, where, or how it would begin. By the end of the month, special Tokyo envoys negotiating in Washington had failed to achieve their economic, trade, and diplomatic demands. On November 19, Tokyo sent a message to its embassies around the world advising them that because communication might soon be cut off they should prepare to destroy code books and classified documents. The message contained a list of code words that would be broadcast on regular Tokyo shortwave radio in the event secure communications were interrupted. Included in the codes, which Purple intercepted, was the phrase "east wind rain,"* meaning U.S.-Japan relations were in danger and warfare was imminent.

On November 1 and again on December 1, American intelligence noted complete changes in the radio call signs and frequencies of the Japanese navy. Once American intercept stations were able to reestablish monitoring by determining the new frequencies and call signs, they realized that there was no communications traffic from or to the Japanese carrier fleet. After a continued search, intelligence officers finally decided that the Japanese carriers had switched to frequencies that they employed only in their home waters outside the range of U.S. signal interception.

Despite the inability of American intelligence to determine the exact intentions of the Japanese, the mounting information called for some action to be taken. On November 24, the navy sent its

---

*Some reports claim that Tokyo sent the "east wind rain" message by shortwave radio a day or more before the attack. There is no proof of this, and it would have made little sense. The "winds codes" were for use in the event secure communications were interrupted, and this did not occur until after the bombing of Pearl Harbor. There simply never was any reason for the Japanese to initiate the codes.

Pacific and Far East Fleet commanders a "war warning" including an alert of a possible attack by Japan "in any direction including attack on Philippines or Guam." A second message two days later added the warning of a possible "amphibious expedition against the Philippines, Thai or Kra Peninsula or possibly Borneo." The army sent similar messages to its Pacific commanders, but in Hawaii the only perceived threat was sabotage, not direct attack. Aircraft were concentrated, in some cases wing to wing, so ground sentries could easily guard them. The navy increased its air and sea patrols to the south but left the skies and seas north of the islands unattended.

By late November, Admiral Yamamoto had finalized his attack plan for December 7 (December 8 across the international date line in Tokyo), selecting a Sunday because Japanese agents in Honolulu reported it was the day that the most ships were typically at anchor at Pearl Harbor. Yamamoto's fleet of six carriers, more than 400 aircraft, a screening force of nine destroyers, and other support ships assembled at Hitokappu Bay in the Kurile Islands in northern Japan on November 22. Four days later, the fleet sailed eastward under the cover of fog and stormy seas. On December 3, the fleet reached a point 900 miles north of Midway Island and changed course to the southeast. Yamamoto's orders were for the fleet to turn back if detected and to attack only if it could achieve surprise. The admiral was confident his fleet would not be discovered because twice in October he had dispatched naval officers aboard civilian liners that sailed from Yokohama to Honolulu, and none of them had spotted a single ship or aircraft along this seldom-used northern route.

In Washington, intelligence analysts were receiving intercepts from Purple locations and interpreting a fourteen-part message from Tokyo to their negotiators. The first thirteen parts indicated a breakdown in negotiations, but there was no threat of immediate hostilities. It was not until the early morning hours of the 7th that a navy intercept station near Seattle received the fourteenth part of the message and relayed it to Washington. Navy Purple operators broke the message into Japanese plain text, but no one on duty was capable of converting the message to English, so it was transferred to the army for translation.

The fourteenth part of the message instructed the Japanese Ambassador to deliver an ultimatum to the U.S. secretary of state at 1:00 P.M. Washington time—7:30 A.M. in Hawaii. The fourteenth portion said in part, "The Japanese government regrets to have to notify the American Government that in view of the attitude of the American Government it cannot but consider that it is impossible to reach an agreement through further negotiations."

It was obvious to the military personnel that the message was a declaration of war. The emphasis on delivery at 1:00 P.M. Washington time was a strong indication that an attack against American possessions or ships would take place about the same time. Duty officers in the War and Navy Departments scrambled to notify their superiors, who on a lazy Sunday morning were at church, on the golf course, or still in bed. It was 11:00 A.M. Washington time before Army Chief of Staff George C. Marshall could prepare an alert to his forces in Hawaii and the Philippines. Dedicated army circuits to Hawaii were busy, so the signal duty officer sent the complex coded message via Western Union, a transmission that took sixty-two minutes and reached the Honolulu Western Union office at 7:33 A.M. Hawaiian time.

At 3:42 A.M. local time on the morning of December 7, the minesweeper U.S.S. *Condor* reported spotting a periscope in restricted waters just outside Pearl Harbor. At 6:30 A.M., the U.S.S. *Antares* spotted a suspicious submerged object in the same area. Ten minutes later, the destroyer U.S.S. *Ward* opened fire on an unidentified submarine and reported the contact to its naval headquarters.

At 6:00 A.M. Hawaiian time, the Japanese fleet reached its launch point 275 miles due north of Pearl Harbor. A half hour later, the flagship *Akagi* raised a carefully preserved signal banner used to begin the attack against the Russians in 1904. Within fifteen minutes, the fleet launched 191 torpedo, dive, and high-level bombers and their accompanying fighter aircraft.

At 7:02 A.M., radar operators of the army's 515th Signal

Aircraft Warning Service on the north side of Oahu reported a large number of blips on their screens indicating approaching aircraft. The signalmen's headquarters told them that either they were incorrect or the blips signaled an early arrival of planes expected from the U.S. mainland.

At 7:53 A.M. the first wave of Japanese aircraft neared Pearl Harbor. Commander Fuchida Mitsuo, operational leader of the attack, shouted the code word, "Tora, tora, tora!" into his mouthpiece, announcing that the mission had achieved complete surprise. At 8:25 A.M., the attackers withdrew to their carriers, and a second wave of 170 planes arrived at 8:40 A.M. to continue the almost uncontested attack on ships, airfields, and aircraft on the ground. By the time the last Japanese airplane returned to its carrier, eighteen U.S. ships were either at the bottom of the harbor or badly damaged. This included four battleships sunk and four more nearly so. The army and navy had 164 aircraft destroyed and 124 more damaged—most hit on the ground. Of the few American planes that did manage to get into the air during the attack, at least four were shot down by "friendly" fire. American casualties totaled 2,403 dead and 1,178 wounded. In less than two hours, the United States had sustained its largest naval defeat and its worst intelligence failure in history.

Japan lost only twenty-nine planes and five midget submarines, but its most significant losses were missed opportunities to inflict even more damage. American aircraft carriers, unbeknownst to the Japanese, were at sea on a training mission rather than in port at the time of the attack. Yamamoto, believing the first two waves had been an overwhelming success, elected not to send in a planned third attack of more than 100 planes and thus passed up the chance to destroy American oil storage tanks, the dry-dock ship repair facilities, and the submarine pens.

But the complete and total destruction of the Americans had not been the attackers' objective. The Japanese had incorrectly assumed that crippling the U.S. Pacific Fleet would cause the isolationist Americans to sue immediately for peace. Japan would then be left alone to continue its domination of Asia and the Pacific without an outside threat. Unwittingly Japan had pursued the one course of action that would unite public opinion in the

United States and bring the country into the war against the Axis. The only nation with the resources to defeat Japan now had the resolve to do so as well.

Within seconds of the first attack, the naval air station on Ford Island near the destroyed "battleship row" had broadcast the message, "Air raid, Pearl Harbor. This is not a drill." In a space of only a few minutes, the word of the attack traveled around the world by radio, telephone, and telegraph. Message traffic in Honolulu, however, was not quite so fast. General Marshall's warning about the fourteenth part of the Japanese message was hand carried in the middle of the air attack from Western Union to Fort Shafter just east of Pearl Harbor for decoding. The deciphered information did not reach the army commander of Hawaii, Lieutenant General Walter C. Short, until 3:00 P.M., more than seven hours after the attack began.

All Americans—political, military, and intelligence leaders as well as the public—were surprised and outraged by the "sneak" attack, even though the full extent of the damage at Pearl Harbor would not be made public "for security reasons" until months after the raid. While horrified by the Japanese treachery, many Americans were equally confused about how the military could be caught so unaware. That the Japanese could secretly plan and successfully conduct such a long-range attack seemed incomprehensible, but even more incredible was that no one provided a warning.*

Official investigations of the attack on Pearl Harbor undertaken both during and after the war either directly or indirectly place the blame on a failure of the U.S. intelligence community, and accurately so. Yet neither the head of MID, ONI, or COI nor

---

*No other single incident in World War II has produced more books, articles, and discussion than the bombing of Pearl Harbor. Americans were, and continue to be, so amazed that a successful surprise attack could be made on Hawaii that they have rationalized many excuses. Some writers have gone so far as to accuse Winston Churchill and Franklin Roosevelt of conspiring to allow the attack in order to get America into the war. As with most conspiracy theories, conjecture and titillation exceed facts or evidence.

any other military or political leader in Washington lost his job or was punished in any way. Ironically, however, high-level field commanders—such as Short, the army commander in Hawaii and Admiral Husband E. Kimmel, navy commander of the Pacific Fleet, who were not in the intelligence loop and not deemed important enough to "need to know"—were relieved of commands and forced out of the service for their failure to be prepared.

The fleet at Pearl Harbor was still ablaze when the second major American intelligence failure of World War II occurred. Although war with Japan had been anticipated for months before the surprise attack on Hawaii, most American leaders had believed that the conflict would begin in the Philippines. In fact, when Secretary of the Navy Frank Knox read the message informing him of the attack on Pearl Harbor he exclaimed, "My God, this can't be true, this must mean the Philippines."

Knox was wrong, but only by happenstance. The Japanese had planned a second, simultaneous attack on American airfields on the island of Luzon, where efforts to build a bomber and fighter force had been ongoing for more than six months. But bad weather at their launch bases on Formosa caused a delay—which should have given Americans time to prepare.

Reports reached the Philippines about the attack on Hawaii within seven minutes after the first bombs and torpedoes fell. Yet, more than nine hours later, fifty-four delayed Japanese bombers and accompanying fighter escorts caught the entire American air fleet on the ground at Clark Field outside Manila. In minutes, the Japanese destroyed 100 U.S. Army Air Corps planes—seventeen of which were B-17s, the most advanced bombers in the U.S. inventory. Only four U.S. fighters made it into the air, and all were shot down. The Japanese lost a total of seven planes.

The disaster in the Philippines never received the scrutiny of Pearl Harbor, nor were the responsible intelligence officers and field commanders disciplined, even though they had had ample alert time to pursue defensive measures. Indecision and arrogance allowed the Japanese to attack almost unopposed.

Immediately after he received the warning from Pearl Harbor,

Major General Lewis H. Brereton, the U.S. air commander in the Philippines, wanted to launch a preemptive strike on Japanese airfields on Formosa. He requested permission from his senior headquarters but was forced by protocol to deal with the Philippine Command chief of staff, Major General Richard K. Sutherland, who did not have, and would not assume, the authority to approve the strike. General Douglas MacArthur, the U.S. commander-in-chief in the Philippines, unwilling to authorize the strike or unaware of the total situation, did nothing, perhaps because he did not trust his own intelligence sources. Brereton, on his own, finally ordered his planes into the air to disperse the fleet and to conduct reconnaissance. After finding nothing, and still without approval to attack Formosa, the airplanes returned to Clark Field. They were in the process of refueling when the Japanese attacked.

Exact details of why the U.S. air fleet in the Philippines was not prepared for an attack nine hours after Pearl Harbor remain a well-guarded secret. No report or memoirs from any of the principal officers or their staffs have ever satisfactorily clarified the reasons behind the disaster in the Philippines. Some files were destroyed before the islands fell to Japanese land forces, and other records either never existed or were disguised as classified information. MacArthur, who would eventually rise to a status equal almost to royalty, refused to have his decisions or conduct questioned by anyone, including the president.

The intelligence failures that resulted in the sinking of much of the Pacific Fleet in Pearl Harbor and the destruction of the air fleet on the ground in the Philippines left the western Pacific and Southeast Asia defenseless against Japanese aggression. In a matter of weeks after Pearl Harbor, Japan captured the U.S. Pacific islands of Guam and Wake as well as most of Southeast Asia, including Thailand. With no chance of U.S. naval support, Great Britain surrendered Singapore to the Japanese on February 8 in the worst military defeat in its history. By August 1942, the Japanese empire stretched northeast to the Alaskan Aleutian Islands, west to Burma, and south to the Netherlands East Indies (now Indonesia).

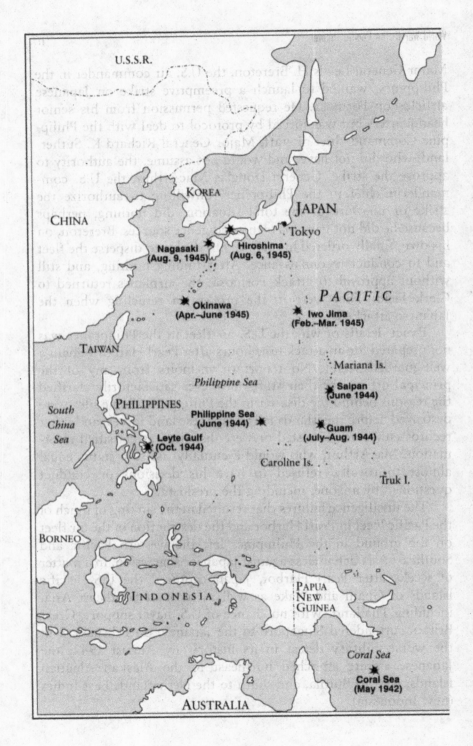

U.S.S.R.

KOREA

CHINA

JAPAN

Tokyo

Nagasaki
(Aug. 9, 1945)

Hiroshima
(Aug. 6, 1945)

PACIFIC

Okinawa
(Apr.–June 1945)

Iwo Jima
(Feb.–Mar. 1945)

TAIWAN

Mariana Is.

Philippine Sea

Saipan
(June 1944)

South
China
Sea

PHILIPPINES

Philippine Sea
(June 1944)

Guam
(July–Aug. 1944)

Leyte Gulf
(Oct. 1944)

Caroline Is.

Truk I.

BORNEO

INDONESIA

PAPUA
NEW
GUINEA

Coral Sea

Coral Sea
(May 1942)

AUSTRALIA

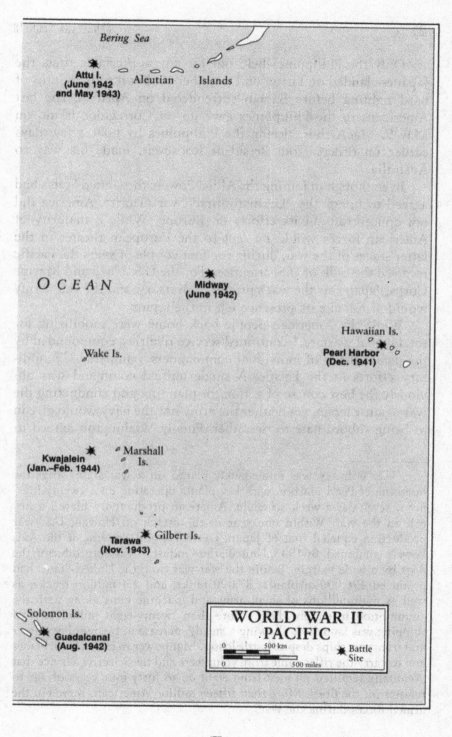

Bering Sea

Attu I.
(June 1942
and May 1943)

Aleutian   Islands

OCEAN

Midway
(June 1942)

Hawaiian Is.

Wake Is.

Pearl Harbor
(Dec. 1941)

Kwajalein
(Jan.–Feb. 1944)

Marshall
Is.

Tarawa
(Nov. 1943)

Gilbert Is.

Solomon Is.

Guadalcanal
(Aug. 1942)

**WORLD WAR II
PACIFIC**

0   500 km

0   500 miles

★ Battle
Site

Only the Philippines held out for any appreciable time. the Japanese landed on Luzon on December 10, but it took months of hard fighting before Bataan surrendered on April 9. The last Americans in the Philippines gave up on Corregidor Island on May 9. MacArthur, fleeing the Philippines by boat a few days earlier on orders from President Roosevelt, made his way to Australia.

Even though in joining the Allied Powers the United States had agreed to honor the "Germany first" war priority, America did not concentrate all its efforts on Europe. While a majority of American forces would be sent to the European theater in the latter stages of the war, during the first couple of years the Pacific received the bulk of U.S. attention. For the U.S. Navy and Marine Corps, Japan was the war's primary adversary, and the U.S. Army would also make its presence felt in the region.

While the American people back home were mobilizing for total global warfare,* continued service rivalries, compounded by the personalities of individual commanders, hampered U.S. military efforts in the Pacific. A single unified command was obviously the best course of action for planning and conducting the war against Japan, yet neither the army nor the navy would give in to being subordinate to the other. Finally Washington agreed to

---

*U.S. industry was immediately placed on a war status after the bombing of Pearl Harbor, with key plants operating on a twenty-four-hour, seven-day-a-week schedule. American productivity played a key role in the war. Within one year of the attack on Hawaii, U.S. war production equaled that of Japan, Germany, and the rest of the Axis Powers combined. By 1943, United States industry was outproducing the Axis by a wide margin. Before the war was over, the United States had produced 296,000 airplanes, 87,000 tanks, and 2.4 million trucks, as well as multimillions of small arms and machine guns along with the ammunition to supply them. More than twenty-eight millon tons of shipping was launched, allowing a steady increase in the number of war and transport ships despite battle losses. Manpower to crew the airplanes and to carry the rifles came from volunteers and the Selective Service that eventually required all men from eighteen to forty-four years of age to register for the draft. More than fifteen million Americans served in the armed forces during the war.

two separate commands divided by the 159th longitude line. Admiral Chester W. Nimitz led the navy command, which was sectioned into North, Central, and South Pacific Ocean Areas. MacArthur had his own South-West Pacific Command, based in Australia, which included the Philippines, the Netherlands East Indies, Borneo, and New Guinea.

Fortunately Nimitz and MacArthur got along fairly well, at least professionally, and cooperated in planning their operations while at the same time competing for assets. They agreed that there were ample Japanese for both of them to fight.

Even united, Americans entered the Pacific war in a vacuum of information about the enemy and the terrain. Intelligence was so scarce about many of the Japanese-occupied islands that requests went out across the United States for anyone who had made prewar visits to these places to send pictures, postcards, and any other materials of use to Washington. Missionaries and merchant seamen were particularly good sources. Unofficially this means of gathering intelligence was known as the "Aunt Minnie" system because much of the information received was pictures of "Aunt Minnie" at the boat dock in Manila or "Aunt Minnie" standing beside a palm tree in New Guinea. The primary map source for many of the islands was not the intelligence services or the Corps of Engineers but rather the National Geographic Society, which provided maps and articles it had published in its monthly magazine.

With the exception of Purple, neither the army nor navy in the Pacific depended upon intelligence from the various Washington agencies. The prewar conflicts within the navy about ONI's organization and functions had left senior officers with little confidence in its abilities. During the war, the ONI's minimal contribution remained mostly in domestic counterintelligence, and no fewer than seven different directors headed the organization as it became known as a "dumping ground" for incompetent senior intelligence officers.

The MID had more respect from the army's leadership but shared the ONI's lack of true intelligence responsibilities. Most of MID's work remained within the continental United States, with major command G-2s responsible for overseas combat intelligence. Counter-Intelligence Corps and Signal Intelligence Service detachments were decentralized and worked directly for these G-2s.

Donovan's COI became the Office of Strategic Services (OSS) on June 13, 1942, under the newly formed Joint Chiefs of Staff. Charged with providing a centralized command for intelligence, propaganda, sabotage, subversion, and other clandestine activities, the OSS was to perform these functions for both the European and the Pacific theaters.

MacArthur, as the senior army commander in the Pacific, refused OSS support in his area of operations, ostensibly because he could not wait for OSS agents to arrive from the States. MacArthur also claimed that it would be inefficient for the OSS to direct intelligence efforts in the Pacific from Washington headquarters. However, MacArthur had opposed the formation of the OSS from the beginning, and he did not like the idea of relinquishing any part of his command to an outside agency. The OSS would eventually conduct some operations in Southeast Asia, China, and Korea outside MacArthur's area of operations, but it was never otherwise involved in the Pacific theater.

In July 1942, MacArthur directed his G-2, Major General Charles A. Willoughby, to form a command intelligence organization, the Allied Intelligence Bureau (AIB), as a joint U.S.-Australian unit headquartered in Melbourne. Unlike Europe, where the United States could slowly enter the conflict, the war in the Pacific was a shooting affair from the beginning. MacArthur faced fighting in a little-known part of the world against an enemy who differed greatly from Americans in language and fighting style.

MacArthur also formed other intelligence organizations on his own rather than depend on Washington assets. In September 1942, he organized the Allied Translator and Interpreter Section (ATIS), composed mostly of Americans of Japanese descent, who interrogated prisoners and translated captured documents. Willoughby later praised the ATIS as "possibly the most important intelligence agency in the war."

Accurate geographic information about his wide area of operations was so sparse that MacArthur formed the Allied

Geographical Agency (AGA). The AGA gathered available maps and produced new ones when they were otherwise unavailable. They also printed hundreds of different handbooks to inform ground commanders and troops about the terrain on which they were to fight.

While the United States mobilized at home for war and organized for combat in the forward areas, Japan continued its conquest of the Pacific at a rate that astonished even the Japanese planners. With the fall of Burma, Japanese forces threatened India, and their victory in the Netherlands East Indies and the following bombing missions against Darwin had the Australians fearing invasion. The massive Japanese empire had, however, reached its zenith, and the tides of fortune in the Pacific for Japan were about to change. Unfortunately, failures of intelligence would continue to plague the American forces.

On April 18, 1942, sixteen B-25 bombers, led by Lieutenant Colonel Jimmy Doolittle, made the first air strike against Japan. Taking off from a carrier, the "Doolittle Raid" did little physical damage, but it boosted sagging American morale and alarmed the Japanese, whose leaders had assured them that they were safe from Allied bombs. Considered a success, the raid nonetheless suffered from intelligence failures. Doolittle had planned to launch his night attack when the carrier force was 500 miles from the mainland, a plan based on intelligence that indicated how far out the Japanese picket ships patrolled. But the intelligence was incorrect. When Japanese pickets detected the carrier force 650 miles off shore, Doolittle had to take off hours earlier than planned, causing a daytime rather than a nighttime attack.

This early takeoff also resulted in the sixteen bombers being unable to reach their planned landing fields in China, because the extended miles required more fuel than the planes could carry. Four bombers crashed near their assigned landing fields while one plane diverted to land safely at Soviet Vladivostok. The remaining eleven crews were forced to bail out of their fuel-depleted planes, causing the deaths of five airmen. The Japanese captured eight surviving aviators and executed three as war criminals; another died of disease in captivity.

Under the circumstances, and considering the psychological

success of the mission, nine deaths from a crew of eighty is amazingly low. While the estimate of Japanese picket boat range had been an intelligence failure, a far greater information error occurred in neglecting to consider Japanese reprisals against the Chinese in occupied areas of China. For their collaboration in providing landing fields for the American planes and for helping the downed flyers escape, more than 25,000 Chinese died in executions.

The Doolittle Raid did nothing to stop the Japanese offensive toward Australia. American combat commanders, unable to depend on intelligence from other sources, continued to rely on the oldest and most proven means of gathering information: visual reconnaissance. The military conducted aerial scouting, and Australian coast watchers, remaining on occupied and remote islands near sea lanes, provided accurate and timely information about Japanese activities.

Early in May 1942, a U.S. observation plane over the Coral Sea spotted a large Japanese armada sent to secure Japan's hold on New Guinea and the Solomon Islands and to block American supply routes to Australia. U.S. carriers and support ships sailed immediately to intercept the Japanese fleet. When they neared, both launched their carrier planes. From May 4 to 8, aircraft of each force fought each other and attacked opposing ships, resulting in history's first naval battle during which no enemy ships were within gun range or had visual contact.

The Battle of the Coral Sea was a clear victory for neither side. Americans lost the carrier *Lexington*, an oiler, and a destroyer, and the carrier *Yorktown* was seriously damaged. The Japanese lost a small carrier, a destroyer, and several support vessels and sustained damage to another small carrier. However, the most important result of the Battle of the Coral Sea was not total losses but rather the fact that for the first time the Allies had stopped a Japanese advance.

Although it was a setback for the Japanese, their offensive goals did not cease with the Battle of the Coral Sea. Instead they continued planning to expand their empire eastward by conducting a diversionary attack on the Aleutian Islands while concentrating their main force against Midway—only 1,100 miles northwest of Hawaii. In addition to capturing Midway, Japan hoped to destroy a major portion of the remaining U.S. fleet in the battle.

American code breakers intercepted the first plans for the Japanese Midway offensive during the Battle of the Coral Sea. At the time, they could decode only about one-third of the Japanese messages using Purple, or other systems, and the process often took as long as a week. Decoders could not decipher the most important portions of the messages, but they could determine that code letters "AO" stood for the diversionary attack location and "AF" for the primary objective. From references to bad weather and bare terrain, the intelligence analysts were reasonably sure that "AO" was the Aleutians, but "AF" remained a mystery.

Admiral Nimitz believed that "AF" was Midway, but he needed confirmation. Joseph Rochefort and Lieutenant Commander Jasper Holmes, navy intelligence division personnel at Pacific Command headquarters in Hawaii, devised a plan to confirm "AF." Holmes, aware that Midway had no source of fresh water other than an evaporation and recondensing system, arranged for Midway to broadcast in a low-grade cipher that there was trouble with the water system. A short time later American code breakers intercepted a Japanese message reporting, "AF is short of water."

Operating on the best and most detailed intelligence of the Pacific campaign, Nimitz ordered a small task force of five cruisers and ten destroyers under Rear Admiral Robert A. Theobald to intercept the Aleutian diversionary attack. Nimitz then assembled four carriers—including the patched-up *Yorktown*—escort ships, and a submarine force to sail toward Midway. The victory that followed was a direct result of an intelligence success and, as even Nimitz would later admit, a bit of luck as well.

On June 4, Japanese carrier aircraft launched bombing runs against Midway not knowing the U.S. fleet was nearby. American torpedo planes attacked the Japanese carriers, but the outdated planes and their ineffective torpedoes did little damage. One U.S. squadron lost all of its planes and twenty-nine of its thirty crewmen. Japanese commanders, now aware of the American naval presence, began reloading their planes, replacing bombs meant for Midway with torpedoes to attack combat ships. In a stroke of luck that rivaled the intelligence coup, more U.S. carrier attack planes arrived while most of the Japanese aircraft were still changing armament and being refueled on their carrier decks. By the end of the battle, four Japanese carriers (of only nine in their entire fleet) and more than 300 of their planes were at the bottom of the Pacific.

What remained of the Japanese fleet retreated toward their homeland. The first great U.S. victory of World War II had been achieved only six months after the disaster at Pearl Harbor. Although victorious, the United States suffered heavy losses. The *Yorktown,* not as lucky as she had been in the Coral Sea, was sunk by a Japanese submarine on June 6. Other losses included a destroyer and 147 airplanes.

While successful against the Japanese primary attack at Midway, the navy did not handle the diversionary attack nearly as well. Admiral Theobald had little confidence in naval intelligence, including information gained from Purple. Instead of placing his task force in position to counter an attack on the far western Aleutians, he decided on his own that the Japanese target would be closer to the Alaskan mainland at Dutch Harbor. As a result, the Japanese invasion fleet attacked the islands of Attu and Kiska* with little resistance on June 6 and 7. Theobald, unaware that the Japanese had occupied the islands, did nothing until the small detachment of weather observers at Kiska failed to report for three days. He then sent an aircraft on an overflight that discovered the Japanese force preparing defenses on the island.

The Battle of Midway and the Japanese occupation of the Aleutians had a great impact on future use of Purple and other code-breaking methods. On June 7, only days after Midway, the *Chicago Tribune* ran an article under the banner headline NAVY HAD WORD OF JAP PLAN TO STRIKE AT SEA. The story, picked up by

---

*Attu and Kiska are so remote that remains of Japanese and American fighting positions, as well as expended ammunition and battlefield "junk," still litter the tundra. The islands remain some of the least-disturbed World War II battlefields.

several other metropolitan dailies across the United States, reported that the United States had learned in advance the Japanese order of battle and plan for attack on Midway. Investigation revealed that *Tribune* reporter Stanley Johnson had filed the story after returning from observing the battle as an authorized journalist aboard the *Lexington,* where he had been shown the complete Purple intelligence intercepts.

Johnson, investigated under the Espionage Act, was never brought to trial for fear of more information being revealed. The *Tribune*'s publisher, also investigated, received only a verbal chastisement from Congress, while within the intelligence community there was fear that the entire code-breaking system had been compromised. Fortunately this was not the case, because the Japanese arrogantly refused to believe their codes could be broken and maintained that the American presence at Midway had been the result of chance rather than good intelligence.

While the *Tribune* article had little impact in Japan, it caused great change within the U.S. intelligence community. Access to Purple information was further limited, with even fewer personnel, including field commanders, allowed to have a "need to know."

With the defeat of the Japanese at Midway, the Allies changed from a defensive to an offensive posture, intending to recapture Japanese-held territories by attacking their empire from two sides. On the southern flank the Americans would advance through New Guinea and New Britain; on the east they would concentrate on Wake Island, the Marshalls, and the Gilberts.

The Japanese, although still reeling from their defeat at Midway, were not entirely finished with offensive actions of their own. In July, they landed forces on Guadalcanal in the southern Solomons and began preparing an airfield to interdict U.S. shipping lanes to Australia. On August 7, the Americans launched their first amphibious operation of the war and successfully captured the unfinished airfield. For the next six months, marines fought the original Japanese garrison as well as reinforcements landed by barge at night. This initial ground action in the dense, disease-laden tropical jungle against suicidal soldiers who rarely surrendered typified the remainder of the Pacific war.

While the landing on Guadalcanal went fairly well, the navy escorts off the beach and in the straits surrounding the beachhead were not as fortunate. Their gunfire protected the marines on the beach, but they paid a high price to deliver their support. Intelligence personnel had little information about the location and strength of the Japanese naval capabilities, and what they did know, they did not communicate to the U.S. Navy task force commander. Bad weather kept most reconnaissance aircraft grounded, so the Americans were unaware of an enemy fleet buildup until the Japanese attacked without warning early in the morning of August 8. Over the next two days, the U.S. Navy suffered a severe defeat in the Battle of Savo Island, losing four cruisers and one destroyer, along with 1,270 sailors. One additional cruiser and two destroyers were badly damaged, and 709 men were wounded. Japanese losses were negligible.

Five more lesser naval battles occurred during the battle for Guadalcanal, with mixed results. In each case, when the Americans properly used their reconnaissance capabilities to determine Japanese locations and strengths, they were successful; when they did not, they came out second best.

By the end of 1943, the U.S. Pacific offensive was progressing well through a leapfrog campaign wherein Americans bypassed many Japanese strongholds, leaving the intact Japanese garrisons without secure resupply lines. The American navy had achieved a degree of superiority on and under the sea and in the air, but Japan continued to fight with vigilance and gave up no spot of land easily. The difficult task of the marines and army infantrymen was to neutralize the critical islands along the route to Japan. Unfortunately, failures in intelligence made their difficult jobs even more hazardous.

Even the few American military intelligence successes were marred by the inability to maintain security. On April 18, 1943, American P-38s from Guadalcanal's Henderson Field shot down a plane en route to Bougainville in the Solomon Islands carrying Admiral Isoroku Yamamoto as a result of Purple's interception of his flight plans.

Yamamoto's death, planned and executed to perfection, still had the potential for a major intelligence consequence. The

Americans attempted to cover their intercept of Yamamoto's schedule initially by claiming to be unaware of the admiral's death and later by crediting the intercept to a coast watcher's report from along the aircraft's route. This story apparently satisfied the Japanese, who continued to assume their codes were unbreakable. Meanwhile, the real story of Yamamoto's assassination was the principal gossip in offices and cocktail parties in Washington and across the United States. In order to eliminate a single Japanese leader, the American military had risked the compromise of the war's best intelligence-gathering system.

In addition to successes, 1943 also brought more overt intelligence failures in the Pacific. The Americans believed it important to remove enemy forces from Alaska, although the area was of little tactical or strategic importance to either side. On May 11, more than 11,000 soldiers of the U.S. Army's 7th Infantry Division—trained, equipped, and clothed for jungle warfare in the Pacific—landed on the Aleutian Island of Attu. It took weeks of fighting the icy, wet elements, as well as the Japanese, to secure the island. A few remaining Japanese made a final surprise suicide attack that carried them through the infantry lines and into the rear, where they slaughtered the patients and staff of an American aid station. Of the total Japanese garrison on Attu of more than 2,400, only twenty-nine survived. American battle casualties were 549 killed and 1,148 wounded; trench foot, frostbite, and exposure disabled an additional 2,100.

With Attu secured, the Americans concentrated on the last Japanese stronghold in the Aleutians at Kiska Island, where American intelligence reported an enemy force larger and better supported than the troops on Attu. Having learned their lesson about the "fight to the last man" tactics of the Japanese in the Aleutians, the Allies assembled a massive force of 34,000 soldiers, supported by an armada of three battleships, two cruisers, nineteen destroyers, and twenty-six other vessels. Air support came from 118 bombers and sixty fighters.

On the morning of August 15, preceded by a massive bombardment from sea and air, the invasion force landed on the Kiska beach. For four days infantrymen pushed inland. Their only contact occurred when units became lost in the fog and engaged each other. In the confusion, twenty-four Americans were killed and fifty wounded before it became apparent the Japanese were no longer on the island. Kiska's only inhabitants were three pet dogs left behind by the Japanese force of 5,183 men who had withdrawn undetected on July 28. Needless casualties had been caused by still another American intelligence failure, which had also expended limited resources and diverted combat forces needed elsewhere.

In the central Pacific, the marines of the newly formed V Amphibious Corps assaulted the islands of Makin and Apamama of the Tarawa Atoll in the Gilberts and secured them readily. But on Betio, the third Gilbert objective, the marines encountered the 5,000-strong Japanese elite Special Naval Landing Force, who were dug into concrete and log bunkers that protected them against the preparatory aerial and sea firing.

On the morning of November 20, the marines embarked from their ships aboard amphibious tractors and landing craft. The first wave made it to the beach, but the outgoing tide stranded the following marine landing craft on a coral reef hundreds of yards from the shore. Japanese machine gunners and marksmen zeroed in on the men wading to shore in chest-deep waters.

The failure of military intelligence to provide information about underwater obstacles and accurate tide tables at Tarawa proved costly. The marines lost 990 killed and more than 2,300 wounded, the highest proportional daily casualty rate in Marine Corps history. Only seventeen of the Japanese defenders survived. These numbers become even more appalling given that the attack may not have been necessary at all. Several of the marine generals opposed the attack as planned by the navy and supported by military intelligence. They believed the island was of no tactical or strategic value and could be bypassed.

Major General Holland M. Smith, commander of the marines at Tarawa, later recorded in his biography his response when asked if the attack was worth it. Smith wrote, "My answer is unqualified: No. Tarawa should have been bypassed. Its capture— a mission executed by marines under direct orders from the high command—was a terrible waste of life and effort." Smith did not directly link the number of casualties with the intelligence failure about the location of the reef but surely must have had it in mind when he added, "The futile sacrifice of marines on that strategically useless coral strand makes me as sad today as it did then."

In the southwest Pacific, army ground commanders also suffered from intelligence failures and became so frustrated with the sparse information about the enemy and terrain that they formed a special unit on their own to gather intelligence. In November 1943, 6th Army commander Lieutenant General Walter Krueger organized the Alamo Scouts and assigned their training and deployment to the 6th Army G-2. More than 300 men, organized into six-man teams, were inserted into enemy-held areas by seaplanes, submarines, and PT boats to perform reconnaissance. In January 1945, the scouts performed their most successful mission by gathering information about a Japanese prisoner of war camp on Luzon that resulted in a successful rescue of Allied prisoners.

In 1944, the American island-hopping campaign closed in on the Japanese home islands. In February, marines and soldiers of the 7th Infantry Division, transferred from the Aleutians to the tropics, captured Kwajalein and Eniwetok in the Marshall Islands; in June they leapfrogged another thousand miles to attack the Marianas. Bitter fighting on land and at sea continued, with Japanese holding out to the last man or hiding in the jungle rather than surrendering.* Americans could still rapidly replace planes, ships, and arms of all sorts, while the Japanese had reached the limits of their resources. With the capture of Saipan, American B-29s were within striking range of the Japanese home islands. Japan's chances for victory were long past, but the Japanese fought on.

The Pacific battles of 1944 were characterized by an increased number of participants, a greater number of casualties, and no

---

*The last Japanese soldier, at least to date, to surrender did not emerge from the jungle until nearly three decades after the war. In 1972, Corporal Yokoi Shoichi of the 38th Infantry Regiment came out of hiding from the jungle of interior Guam. He still carried his rifle, although its wooden stock had rotted away.

improvement in ground intelligence about the island objectives. Saipan alone cost the Americans 3,426 killed and 13,099 wounded. Japan lost more than 26,000 dead.

There is no evidence that the Japanese ever broke the American code system, but they did take advantage of information intercepted "in the clear" and from other sources. Soldiers and marines preparing to hit the beach at Eniwetok listened to radio broadcasts of Tokyo Rose announcing their battle plans and telling the Americans to prepare to die.

Many lapses in U.S. security went undetected by the Japanese, but on occasion they did make use of information they managed to gather. American submarines, despite inferior torpedoes, continued their superiority over their adversaries, and had certain intelligence not been compromised, the U.S. submarine service would have undoubtedly lost fewer than the fifty-two subs it did. That intelligence failure involved U.S. Congressman Andrew Jackson May, who as a member of the House Military Affairs Committee visited the Pacific theater, where he received many intelligence and operations briefings. On his return, May held a press conference and stated that American submarines had a high survivability because Japanese depth charges were fused to explode at too shallow a depth. Soon enemy depth charges were rearmed to explode at a more effective depth of 250 feet. Vice Admiral Charles A. Lockwood, commander of the U.S. submarine fleet in the Pacific, later estimated that May's revelation cost the navy as many as ten submarines and 800 crewmen.

Other events that did not involve direct contact with the Japanese also hurt the Americans in the Pacific. On December 18, 1944, a typhoon struck U.S. Navy Task Force 38 off the Philippines. Weather forecasters were aware of the storm but failed to predict its track accurately. The American fleet, directed to sail out of the anticipated path of the storm, instead went straight into it, losing 146 planes destroyed on deck or overboard from the storm-tossed carriers. Three destroyers, including the Pearl Harbor survivor U.S.S. *Monaghan,* sank along with most of their crews.

The losses in Task Force 38 were but a small part of the total number of casualties involved in MacArthur's promise to "return" to the Philippines. To save the Philippines, MacArthur very nearly destroyed them. Of the island's prewar population of 800,000, more than 100,000 died during the liberation. Approximately 350,000 Japanese were killed, with American losses totaling more than 10,000 dead and 36,500 wounded.

By 1945, with Japan practically defenseless from American bombing, the defenders of the final atolls leading to the home islands intensified their efforts. On Iwo Jima in March, the Japanese killed or wounded more than 30 percent of the 25,000 U.S. attackers. Japanese deaths totaled 21,000. For the first time in the Pacific War, U.S. casualties exceeded the Japanese death count.

Okinawa, only 350 miles from the home islands, proved even more costly during the attack in April. Kamikaze, or suicide planes, first used in the Philippines, sank thirty American ships and damaged 350 more. At sea and on land, U.S. casualties at Okinawa exceeded 50,000. Enemy dead numbered more than 110,000, including Japanese civilian residents of the islands who committed suicide along with their soldier defenders.

The fall of Okinawa provided a clear path for invasion of the Japanese home islands. With the surrender of Germany in May, all Allied strength concentrated on Japan. American planners estimated that a protracted battle to merely gain a beachhead on the Japanese mainland would produce more than a million Allied casualties. Since 1942, the Allies had proclaimed that they would accept only an unconditional surrender, which the proud Japanese envisioned as making them a slave colony of the West. Although some of the Japanese leaders were rumored to support suing for peace regardless of the conditions, others demanded a fight to the death.

While intelligence had been a weakness of American operations throughout the Pacific war, the industrial might and superior technology of the United States had produced victory after victory, and it seems only appropriate that a technological advance finally brought an end to the war. In July 1945, the top secret Manhattan Project, experimenting since 1942 with an explosive designed around splitting the atom, detonated the first successful A-bomb at a New Mexico test range.

The Allies issued an ultimatum for Japan to surrender or face destruction. When the Japanese ignored the message, a B-29 named *Enola Gay* dropped an atomic bomb on Hiroshima on August 6, 1945, destroying five square miles of the city and nearly 70,000 of its inhabitants. On August 9, the U.S. dropped a second superbomb on Nagasaki, killing at least 20,000 more. On August 14, Japan surrendered unconditionally.

Celebration of victory in the United States obscured the war's last great intelligence failure. On July 26, the U.S.S. *Indianapolis* delivered the atomic bomb detonation devices from the United States to the forward airfield on Tinian in the Mariana Islands.* After unloading its sensitive cargo, the *Indianapolis* sailed for Leyte to join Task Force 95, which was training for the invasion of Japan. Naval intelligence was aware that an enemy submarine had been spotted along the *Indianapolis*'s proposed route, but no one informed the ship. Late on the 29th, just east of the Philippines, the Japanese submarine I58 torpedoed the *Indianapolis*, blowing off the ship's bow and destroying the vessel's power plant, which eliminated its ability to transmit an SOS. Shortly after midnight, only twelve minutes after the first torpedo struck, the *Indianapolis* went down.

Of the original 1,197 crewmen, approximately 900 survived the sinking. Despite the fact that the *Indianapolis* sank so quickly that lifeboats with their emergency containers of water and food were not launched, these survivors were optimistic they would be rescued because the ship would be reported overdue the next day, when it was scheduled to join Task Force 95. However, because of a collage of blunders, including confusion caused by the various coding and classifications requirements, TF 95 disregarded the message to expect the *Indianapolis*. The next day, Purple intercepted a message from the Japanese submarine I58 to its headquarters claiming the sinking of an American battleship, but military intelligence analysts ignored the report as an exaggeration and did not report the intercept.

---

*Neither the captain of the *Indianapolis* nor any of his crew had any knowledge of the cargo, because they were considered not to have a "need to know."

With no one aware that the *Indianapolis* was missing, it was more than four days later before a passing navy plane spotted the survivors. Only 316 were still alive. More than 500 survivors of the sinking had become victims of thirst and the hundreds of sharks that filled the waters. The total death count of the *Indianapolis* was 881, making it the greatest disaster of a ship at sea in the history of the U.S. Navy.

The impact on the war if the Japanese submarine I58 had spotted the *Indianapolis* a few days earlier, before it had delivered its cargo to Tinian, would have been immense. No other A-bombs besides the two aboard had yet been built, and it would have taken months to construct another device. Instead, the *Indianapolis* became a minor footnote in the Pacific war as the last ship to be sunk by the Japanese. The incident also closed out a long and infamous history of repeated failures in the Pacific by military intelligence that had begun at Pearl Harbor.

★ 10 ★

World War II: The European Theater

In the Pacific theater, Americans were in combat from the first day of the war. By contrast, the United States' entry into the European theater allowed for a period of preparation. The British and Soviets had been battling the Nazis since 1939, and by the time of Pearl Harbor, the Allies were beginning to stop the German advance. When the United States joined the war, the Allies began plans for liberating Germany's conquests and taking the war to the Nazi heartland.

The Allies' initial plan called for a buildup of forces for a cross-channel invasion of Europe from Great Britain within a year. While the Russians held the eastern front, the Americans, British, and other Allies would push into France. After much debate, however, the Allies postponed the plan for an invasion of occupied Europe—which they were not yet strong enough to pursue—in favor of more immediate action. This decision placated the Russians, who were pressing for a "second front" to relieve pressure on their forces, as well as the American public, who expected their military to began fighting immediately. Too, the British wanted American support as soon as possible for an offensive at the outer edges of Germany's expansion rather than a delayed attack against their strength. The Allies finally decided to launch Operation Torch against the Axis in North Africa.

Allied intelligence was well established by the time the United States entered the war, and the British freely shared information with the Americans. Where information had been sparse to nonexistent about the remote islands in the Pacific, a great deal of data was available about North Africa and Europe, including maps, terrain studies, and detailed weather information.

As with the Pacific, neither the ONI nor MID had any great impact on the war in Europe. The neglected ONI concentrated on counterintelligence operations within the continental United States. Its most successful domestic operation stretched ethical bounds and later drew much criticism. To secure the New York waterfront, the ONI approached Charles "Lucky" Luciano and other mob leaders for assistance. Luciano and his cronies were rewarded for their cooperation by having jail sentences commuted and pending charges dropped.*

Ultimately, the only significant ONI contribution to the European and Atlantic theater was the establishment of the Advanced Naval Intelligence School in New York. Its students were trained in operational or tactical intelligence before assuming fleet G-2 positions against the Axis in North Africa.

MID also focused on internal intelligence matters, leaving overseas operations decentralized, with no single army agency or unit responsible for European theater intelligence. Field command G-2s headed army combat intelligence in North Africa and Europe with responsibilities filtering down through similar offices at corps and division level and on to S-2s at regiments and battalions. These G-2s and S-2s had intermittent support from detachments of the Counter-Intelligence Corps, formally the Corps of Intelligence Police, while units of the Signal Intelligence Service also assisted on occasion.

The Office of Strategic Services became the most famous American intelligence organization. Unwelcome in the Pacific theater, the OSS was extremely active in North Africa and Europe. No other aspect of World War II has been the subject of more books or movies than the OSS. Some of this notoriety is deserved; some is not. Much of its fame is a direct result of the organization's

---

*Luciano and friends had no difficulty in preventing damage to the docks because by the time they began their cooperation there were no German agents in the area to provide a threat.

own promotion of its many intriguing "cloak and dagger" tales from the war. The primary impetus behind the OSS publicity was the organization's members themselves. The OSS, like its predecessor Office of the Coordinator of Information, was filled with Ivy League graduates and elites from the East Coast publishing, business, and industry worlds. If nothing else, these OSS men were extremely literate, and stories by and about them have filled the store shelves since the war, making the OSS the most public of any of America's secret organizations of any period.

Whether manned by "brilliant amateurs" or "bumbling amateurs"—both labels are frequently applied—the OSS did have operatives who were indeed amateurs. Some were brave, some brilliant, some inept. Most were happy to be members of an elite organization, and more than a few were even happier to be part of an organization composed of the elite.

The mission of the OSS, like that of the Coordinator of Information before it, included coordinating national intelligence, conducting propaganda activities, and executing special operations. Although the cloak and dagger activities in the actual war zone have received far more attention, the greatest OSS contributions to the war efforts were made by its Research and Analysis Branch (R&A). The R&A researched printed matter, technical reports, and business information to assess how food supplies and manpower resources were affecting Germany's ability to continue the war.

Other branches of the OSS contributed direct support to battlefield operations. The Secret Intelligence Branch operated a network of agents throughout occupied Europe who provided information on weapons development as well as target locations and defensive concentrations. OSS agents of the Special Operations Branch, assisted by resistance groups and other recruits, also attempted to disrupt German transportation and logistics behind the lines. OSS agents operated only from the highest army or army group headquarters, and it was unusual for a division G-2 ever to be in contact with them.

While there is no doubt that the OSS did contribute strategic intelligence of use to Washington, it had little impact on frontline combat. A postwar study by the European Theater of Operations

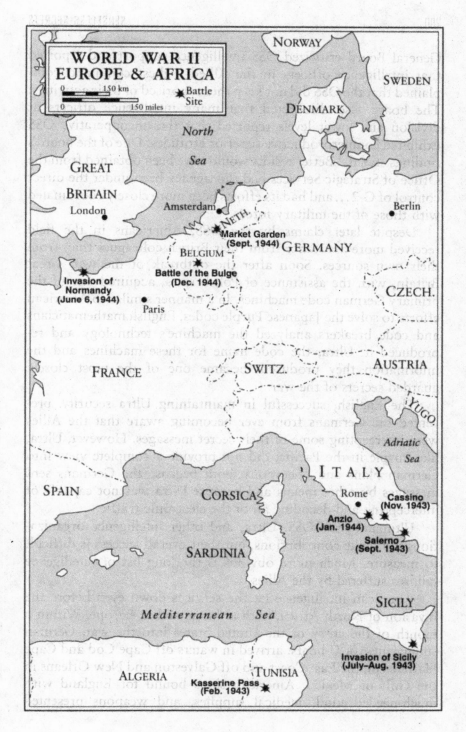

WORLD WAR II
EUROPE & AFRICA

0 — 150 km
0 — 150 miles

★ Battle Site

NORWAY

SWEDEN

DENMARK

North Sea

GREAT BRITAIN

London

Amsterdam

NETH.

Berlin

Market Garden (Sept. 1944)

GERMANY

BELGIUM

Battle of the Bulge (Dec. 1944)

Invasion of Normandy (June 6, 1944)

Paris

CZECH.

FRANCE

SWITZ.

AUSTRIA

YUGO.

SPAIN

CORSICA

ITALY

Adriatic Sea

Rome

Cassino (Nov. 1943)

Anzio (Jan. 1944)

SARDINIA

Salerno (Sept. 1943)

Mediterranean Sea

SICILY

Invasion of Sicily (July–Aug. 1943)

ALGERIA

Kasserine Pass (Feb. 1943)

TUNISIA

199

General Board criticized OSS intelligence support and reported that intelligence officers in the Allied highest command complained that the OSS did not keep them apprised of their activities. The board also discovered that many intelligence officers at division and lower levels reported that the uncooperative OSS exhibited counterproductive superior attitudes. One of the board's findings stated, "Better results would have been obtained from the Office of Strategic Services had this agency been under the direct control of G-2 . . . and had its efforts been more closely coordinated with those of the military forces."

Despite later claims by the OSS, Americans in the field received more assistance from their British colleagues than from their own sources. Soon after the outbreak of the war, Great Britain, with the assistance of Polish spies, acquired one of the primary German code machines. In a manner similar to American efforts to solve the Japanese Purple codes, English mathematicians and code breakers analyzed the machine's technology and reproduced it. Ultra, the code name for these machines and the information they produced, became one of the most closely guarded secrets of the war.

The English, successful in maintaining Ultra security, prevented the Germans from ever becoming aware that the Allies were intercepting some of their secret messages. However, Ultra, like Purple in the Pacific, did not provide a complete view into German plans and operations, both because the Germans sent messages by other means and because Ultra was not capable of intercepting and decoding all of the electronic traffic.

Ultimately, the OSS, Ultra, and other intelligence organizations did make contributions, but their overall success is difficult to measure. Much more obvious is the long list of intelligence failures suffered by the Allies.

American intelligence let the services down even before the invasion of North Africa, both at home and in Europe. Within a month of the entry of the United States into the war, German submarines, or U-boats, arrived in waters off Cape Cod and Cape Hatteras on the East Coast and off Galveston and New Orleans in the Gulf of Mexico. American ships bound for England with much-needed food, medical supplies, and weapons presented lucrative targets for the U-boats. Although the British had devised a convoy system with armed escorts to secure merchant ships from submarine attack, American intelligence and operations personnel discounted the process as a waste of ships and manpower. They soon discovered the error of this assumption.

Protection of American merchant shipping was the responsibility of the U.S. Navy, but its entire antisubmarine defense at the beginning of the war consisted of two dozen World War I–vintage boats. As a result, German submarines were sinking one American merchant vessel a day and often as many as three. During the first year of American participation in the war, the U-boats sank more than 500 U.S. ships, totaling more than 2.5 million tons, even though the limited U-boat fleet never had more than twelve submarines in American waters at any one time. Unmolested by the unprepared American antisubmarine capabilities and protected by the U.S. reluctance to use the convoy system, U-boats crept to within a mile of the shore in broad daylight. At night they used shore lights to provide illumination to aim their torpedoes.

Because the Germans had changed their codes prior to their U-boats staking the American shoreline, the British had to break the new ciphers, a process that took months. In the meantime, the Germans had broken the Royal Navy's code system and at least a portion of the U.S. Navy's.

Technology again came to America's rescue when its intelligence fell short. Improved radar and the invention of the underwater detection device known as sonar assisted in tracking the U-boats. Through employing these advances, finally adopting the convoy system, adding escort ships, and using long-range reconnaissance and attack aircraft for protection, the Americans and their allies by mid-1943 began sinking the U-boats faster than Germany could replace them.

Intelligence failures also occurred on the European mainland preceding the invasion of North Africa. On August 19, 1942, a Canadian-British force landed at Dieppe, France, an action later described as too large for a raid and too small for an invasion. Officially, the operation's mission was to test new Allied weapons and the strength of Germany's costal defense system. Unofficially, the raid, or reconnaissance in force, was a political move in response to Russian and American demands for the opening of a "second front."

Forty-two Americans of the U.S. 1st Ranger Battalion, under the command of Captain Roy Murray, accompanied the Canadian-British force. The rangers played a minor role in the battle, and their casualties were few compared to those of their allies. However, the United States press reported the rangers' participation as larger and more heroic than it actually was to please an American public desperate for some good war news.

Prior to the raid, Allied intelligence officers remained confident that they had all the information necessary for a successful operation, including extensive basic intelligence on the topography of the area, first-hand information from several of the planners who had visited the region during prewar holidays, current information about German fortifications from aerial reconnaissance photographs, and reports from English agents and the French underground. In contrast to what they did during many future battles, the Allied intelligence staff freely shared their information with the operational forces, providing a forty-eight-page book containing maps and an intelligence estimate of the enemy situation.

The Dieppe plan looked extremely good on paper. On the beaches and in the skies of France, it was a completely different story. The invasion force of 252 ships, sixty-nine air squadrons, and 6,086 men planned for a predawn attack against eight separate targets. As the attack force sailed toward Dieppe, it encountered a German coastal convoy, which British naval intelligence had been aware of but had not informed anyone else about.

On landing, the Allied attackers discovered an alerted German defense force protected by unreported concrete roadblocks and a ten-foot-high sea wall topped by barbed wire that prevented Allied tanks from getting off the beach. German machine gun positions, hidden in cliff caves and bunkers and undetected by aerial photographs and agents, raked the exposed attackers. German fighters joined the battle, engaging the Allied air cover and strafing the attackers. Few of the raiders survived the beaches of Dieppe. Allied dead, wounded, and captured totaled 4,384, and in the air the Allies lost 106 planes.

With the unsuccessful raid at Dieppe behind them, the Allies' focus turned to North Africa. The British, fighting Italian forces in Somaliland, Ethiopia, and Libya since 1940, had successfully defended Egypt and the Suez Canal. In early 1941, Germany dispatched General Erwin Rommel and his Afrika Korps to North Africa. Clever tactics in the use of his tank units earned Rommel thee name "the Desert Fox" as he penetrated British lines and moved to within 200 miles of the Suez Canal at El Alamein by May 1942. In August, Rommel continued his attack, but the British stopped the Afrika Korps at Alam el Halfa and then counterattacked in October to drive Rommel back into Tunisia. About the same time, the Russians defeated the Germans at the Battle of Stalingrad. Germany's string of victories dating back to its 1939 invasion of Poland had come to an end on two fronts.

While the British pursued Rommel in Tunisia, the Americans made their entry into the North Africa fight. On November 8, 1942, U.S. Army Operation Torch units landed in Morocco, Algeria, and Tunisia against limited resistance from Vichy French forces aligned with Germany. Within days, the Vichy forces changed sides and joined the Allies.

The Americans hoped to advance rapidly across Tunisia to cut off the Axis troops from their Mediterranean supply lines. Lack of experience in the desert and rain that turned the sand into sticky mud slowed their advances. By the time the Americans reached the western border of Tunisia, the Germans had received reinforcements and were dug in for battle. General Dwight D. Eisenhower, commander of all American forces in North Africa, ordered Major General Lloyd Fredendall's 39,000-man II Corps to prepare defenses at Kasserine Pass and to plan on resuming the attack when the rainy season ended in two months.

In their initial battles, the Americans made a poor impression on the veteran British desert soldiers, who began referring to them as "our Italians." The Germans held an even lower opinion of the Americans. When the Germans captured and interrogated Americans shortly after their arrival in Tunisia, they learned that their new Allied enemy had inadequate training, low morale, and poor leadership.

In addition, Americans possessed inferior equipment. Of the

two types of tanks available for combat, one mounted a single 37-mm gun whose shells merely bounced off the larger, more heavily armored German tanks. The other American tank, the Sherman, mounted a 75-mm gun capable of penetrating German armor, but everyone, including the enemy, knew that the thinly armored Sherman used gasoline rather than diesel, making it extremely likely to explode into a ball of fire when hit. The American tankers sarcastically called their Shermans "Ronsons" after a popular brand of cigarette lighter.

Counterintelligence measures among the U.S. tank corps were as weak as the Shermans' armor plate. Constant chattering on unsecure radio nets often revealed strengths, locations, and plans to German signal interceptors.

General Fredendall commanded the II Corps from an underground bunker in a remote canyon eighty miles behind the front line. He positioned his troops by studying a map rather than by making ground reconnaissances. The hilly terrain he selected isolated units and prevented their mutual support. Many of the American units, anticipating going back on the offensive, did not dig in or make other defensive preparations.

In February, British intelligence reported Ultra intercepts to the Americans that indicated the Germans were preparing for an attack, but Eisenhower and his intelligence staff discounted the information. They did reposition some of the II Corps forces; however, they misinterpreted the intelligence available and actually weakened the defenses at the German main attack points.

Early in the morning of February 14, 1943, the Germans attacked across the American front.* Despite the intercepted messages, the frontline troops had received no warning, and, as the Germans pushed through their lines, many U.S. troops streamed to the rear in an unorganized rout while others, unable to flee, were either killed or captured. Rommel's attack did not

---

*Fredendall was not present during the initial stages of the attack against his corps. Ironically, he was away visiting the ruins of another army's defeat at Carthage, which had fallen to the Romans in 146 B.C.

slow for a week. By February 27, more than 3,000 Americans were dead or wounded and 4,000 more were the prisoners of the Germans.

Kasserine Pass embarrassed the U.S. Army. However, with the state of its training and leadership, it is doubtful if the army could have won the battle even with adequate and properly analyzed intelligence. The losses, though, might not have been so great. Still, the battle did have its positive points. While Rommel advanced against the Americans, British Field Marshal Bernard Montgomery gained an advantage to the south and east. Eisenhower quickly replaced Fredendall with George Patton, a veteran of the Mexican Punitive Expedition and the Great War. Another soon-to-be military hero, Omar N. Bradley, arrived from the States to assist Eisenhower.

Montgomery's advantage, combined with the new U.S. leadership and reinforcements, put the Germans back on the defensive by March. On April 7, U.S. and British units converged at Gafsa and effectively encircled the Axis forces in Tunis. The Allied navies, in the meantime, had taken control of the Mediterranean to remove any avenue of German escape or resupply. On May 12, more than 250,000 Germans and Italians surrendered. The war in North Africa concluded, providing the Allies secure bases from which to launch an invasion of southern Europe.

While the American ground forces conducted Operation Torch in North Africa, the American air force joined the British in a sustained bombing campaign against Germany. Before the war, some aviation experts had become so enamored with long-range bombers that they believed air power alone could win wars by destroying an enemy's cities and industry, and thus his will and ability to fight. Germany had attempted this approach with extensive bombing of London and major English cities in the early months of the war, but the British had remained resilient and eventually produced enough fighters to shoot down the Luftwaffe bombers in the Battle of Britain. By May 1941, the British had stopped the German air assault on their territory.

Although air power did not defeat the British, the Allies attempted the same strategy against the German homeland. By

1942, British bombers were relentlessly pounding German cities. On May 30 alone, 900 British planes attacked the city of Cologne. The United States joined the bombing campaign against Germany in 1942, and the attack continued almost around the clock until war's end.

Identifying potential bombing targets was the responsibility of the Army Air Forces Intelligence Division, the A-2, which based most of its target selection on aerial reconnaissance photographs. Disagreements between the A-2 and the army's G-2 were frequent as the two groups quarreled over whether air power should respond to tactical ground needs or assist in the strategic bombing of Germany.

Allied bomber losses over Germany were considerable. On August 17, 1943, the U.S. 8th Air Force launched 376 bombers against the ball-bearing plants of Schweinfurt and aircraft production facilities at Regensburg and Wiener Neustadt. German ground antiaircraft batteries and fighter planes downed sixty of the bombers, killing or capturing their 600 crew members. Fifty more of the bombers made it back to their home bases but would never fly again. Twice that many more planes were grounded for weeks because of the damage they suffered. In October, the 8th Air Force again attacked the same targets with 300 bombers, only to lose another sixty planes and their crews. While the raids destroyed the downtown area of Schweinfurt, the ball-bearing plants did not receive enough damage to slow production.

Not until the Allies designed fighter escorts with enough range to protect the bombers all the way to their targets and back did losses reach more acceptable numbers. By the end of the war, Allied bombers and their fighter escorts ranged virtually unopposed over all of Germany, almost completely destroying Dresden and Hamburg in early 1945. Total German civilian casualties from Allied bombing by the end of the war numbered more than 300,000 dead and 780,000 injured; millions of the survivors were left homeless. Despite the tremendous resources dedicated to it, the Allied strategic bombing of Germany ultimately was no more successful than the Luftwaffe's attack on Great Britain. German morale failed to crack. More important, until the last months of the war, when ground forces were sweeping across the Third Reich, German war production actually increased.*

While most of the Allied air forces concentrated on the strategic bombing, tactical air cover and the delivery of airborne units and resupplies were also Air Corps missions. Allied fighters gained air superiority over the Germans in North Africa shortly after the invasion and generally sustained this throughout the war.

With Operation Torch a success and strategic bombing of Germany in progress, the Allies next turned their might against southern Italy in an effort to force the Italians out of the war. On July 10, 1943, seven American and British divisions landed on Sicily. The beach landing went smoothly, but a preinvasion drop of American and British paratroopers and glider-borne infantry behind the lines produced a disaster. Not informed of the airborne operation for security reasons, the invasion-force ships off shore shot down several of the paratrooper transports. Unanticipated fierce winds scattered the remainder of the jumpers and glider troops all across the southern part of the island.

The Italians on Sicily offered little resistance, but the German defenders fought doggedly as the British under Montgomery and the Americans under Patton attacked on two axes toward Messina, competing to be first to the port city. Patton won the race by a few hours, but poor planning and a lack of intelligence on German intentions and capabilities denied the Allies a great victory on Sicily. Believing the Germans would stand and fight at Messina, the Allies planned no contingencies to block the narrow strait between the island and the mainland. By the time Patton reached the port on August 17, more than 100,000 Axis troops, along with their weapons and 10,000 vehicles, had escaped to the Italian mainland.

---

*Much of Germany's nonmilitary production also remained operational throughout the war. During the week that Hitler committed suicide in his underground bunker and the Soviets occupied Berlin, all but one of the city's dozen breweries remained in operation, making and marketing their beer.

The greatest impact of the Allied invasion of Sicily was the Italian replacement of dictator Benito Mussolini with a government that wanted peace with the Allies. Due to a series of diplomatic errors, however, negotiations were not completed until the first week of September—a delay that allowed Germany to reinforce and take control of much of the country.

On September 3, the British landed on the toe of Italy at Reggio Calabria and met little opposition as they moved up the coastline. Five days later, the Americans, underestimating the German ground defenses and air support, assaulted the beaches of Salerno only to be driven back almost into the sea. The landing of tanks and the diversion of air assets from other missions to support the attack saved the invasion. On September 16, the British and American forces converged to push toward Naples, which fell on October 1.

Eisenhower expected to capture Rome by November 1, but neither he nor his intelligence staff completely understood the rugged terrain between Naples and the Eternal City. The treacherous mountains and a vigorous German defense halted the Allies at Cassino at the beginning of 1944. To relieve the stalemate and to speed the advance on Rome, the Allies made another amphibious attack at Anzio, thirty miles south of Rome in the German rear. Landing almost unopposed on January 22, the Allies from Anzio could have quickly made their way into Rome, but they delayed to consolidate and to gather intelligence on the unknown German strength and positions. Before the Allies resumed the attack, the Germans sent in reserves to surround them on the small beachhead.

The Allies made several efforts to get off the Anzio beach, but even elite units famed for their fighting abilities and intelligence skills failed. On the night of January 29, the 1st and 2nd Ranger Battalions led the 3d Infantry Division off the beachhead to attack and secure Cisterna. Lacking intelligence on German locations, the rangers advanced along a flooded irrigation canal in a valley leading to the village and were caught in one of the most devastating ambushes in American military history. German tanks, artillery, and machine guns lining the valley fired point-blank into the rangers. The 4th Ranger Battalion, from its reserve position in the rear, attempted to reinforce its comrades but was turned back with 50 percent casualties, including the deaths of all of its company commanders. Of the 767 original rangers who advanced toward Cisterna, only six returned.

Meanwhile, near Cassino, the Americans were faring no better. With little intelligence and a poor plan, the 36th Infantry Division of the Texas National Guard attempted to cross the Rapido River on January 17, attacking directly into well-dug-in Germans. The attack quickly broke down, and the Texans barely escaped annihilation. The 36th Division's attack made such a poor impression on the Germans that they reported the battle merely as an increase in enemy patrol activities in their sector.

To assist in the breakout from Anzio and to end the stalemate to the south, the Allies began diverting more and more bomber sorties from the German heartland to attack Axis supply lines and troop concentrations in Italy. Convinced by intelligence that the historic Benedictine abbey on Monte Cassino harbored German artillery observers and other military forces, the Allies bombed the monastery to rubble on March 15. The abbey had been empty—with hills all around, the Germans had not needed the monastery and, because of its historical value, had not occupied it.

After more than four months the Allies, continuing their bombings and reinforcing Anzio with more and more combat divisions, finally broke out from the beachhead and, on May 25, linked up with the forces advancing from Cassino. On June 4, Rome fell to the Allies, but the war in Italy was far from over. Once again, most of the Germans escaped, enabling them to defend northern Italy, which they did not surrender until May 2, 1945, after the fall of Berlin.

Before the occupation of Rome, the Allies were already planning and preparing for the cross-channel invasion of Europe. During this preparation phase, the Americans made fatal intelligence errors while training for the future battle. To prepare for their landing on Utah Beach, the U.S. Army VII Corps practiced amphibious landings at Slapton Sands, a shoreline in western England that resembled Normandy.

After a series of limited practices, the VII Corps planned a full-scale rehearsal, Exercise Tiger, for April 28 with all facets of the trial run designed to replicate the actual operation as much as possible, including using the same embarkation ports that would be employed in the actual invasion. The planners, however, failed to consider the enemy capabilities during the rehearsal.

When Operation Tiger forces sailed from their ports on April 26 in preparation for a daylight landing on the morning of the 28th, the only protection they had for their lightly armed landing craft were two small, antiquated British escort vessels, one of which had to return to port for repairs. That left only one escort ship to protect the amphibious force from German E-boats, the extremely mobile torpedo vessels that regularly patrolled the British islands and the channel.

Shortly after midnight on the 28th, other British patrol boats spotted a flotilla of E-boats in the vicinity of the Tiger training area. They informed the convoy's remaining escort, but no one related the information to the Americans. At 1:30 A.M., nine E-boats attacked the landing craft of the U.S. 4th Infantry Division, sinking two boats and damaging another. In the confusion, several of the other American landing craft fired at friendly vessels, adding to the casualty list. Hundreds of men, untrained in how to inflate or wear their life preservers properly, were thrown into the freezing waters. By daylight, 946 Americans were dead or missing.

More than twenty of the missing were officers with complete knowledge of the Normandy invasion plans. For a time the Allies feared E-boats might have picked up one or more men alive, compromising the biggest secret of the war. All of the bodies were eventually recovered, however, and the invasion plans continued on schedule.

The Allies immediately classified all information related to Operation Tiger and its needless casualties. The official reasons given for the increased security were the protection of the secrecy of the Normandy invasion and the prevention of a rift in British-American relations that could be caused if the failure of the English to provide sufficient convoy security were known. For obvious reasons, all concerned, except possibly the relatives of the dead soldiers, were relieved to have the truth hidden behind classified covers, where it stayed for more than thirty years.

Details of one of the largest intelligence and operational disasters of the war were not made public until the late 1980s.

While Operation Tiger by design became a little-known aspect of World War II, the invasion for which it was preparing would become the best known of the conflict. Operation Overlord, with Eisenhower in command, was originally planned for May 1944, when weather conditions would be best for landings. Due to shortages in shipping and a last-minute increase in the invasion force numbers, the Allies postponed "D-Day" until June 5. Bad weather caused another delay, but in the darkness of the early morning of June 6 three airborne divisions parachuted several miles inland. A few hours later, the landing force of five combat divisions, supported by more than 2,000 ships and 11,000 aircraft, landed along sixty miles of beach at Normandy.

The Germans had anticipated such an attack for more than two years and had instituted an unrivaled defense preparation. While the attack itself was no surprise, the location was. For once, Allied intelligence had maintained security, and the Germans had to guess the point of attack rather than base their actions on hard information. Only two sites met the requirements for a large-scale invasion: Calais and Normandy. The Germans decided that Calais, at the narrowest part of the English Channel, would be the landing area. They guessed wrong.

Operation Overlord began with the intelligence success of gaining surprise and concluded with the combat success of gaining a foothold on the European continent. In between, however, Normandy contained many of the same intelligence failures that plagued the Allies during the entire war. The OSS conducted extensive preinvasion coordination with the French Resistance to identify German units. The OSS, always concerned with publicity, arranged for a special movie production unit under famed Hollywood director John Ford to film the invasion. In addition, Allied aerial reconnaissance produced more than 85,000 photographs of the Normandy area that 1,700 photo interpreters studied to locate the German defenses. Weather officers analyzed the ocean currents, tide tables, and historical weather trends to provide information about the channel crossing, the landing sites, and the inland parachutist and glider drop sites.

Despite all of this preparation, few of the invading units at the five landing sites and the multiple interior drop zones found the terrain, or the enemy, to be what they expected. Disoriented pilots dropped airborne troops in the wrong areas, and unpredicted winds further dispersed the paratroopers. Some of the airborne soldiers landed in German-held villages or on top of enemy units in field camps; still others fell into swamps and canals, which caused the heavy-laden paratroopers to drown. Amazingly, the airborne operation fiasco, a failure by every planning standard, ended as a success. The drop was so unorganized, and the paratroopers so widespread, that the Germans, as confused as the invaders, could not estimate the number of airborne troops or their locations. As a result, the Germans diverted several units from reinforcing the beach attack to defend against the unknown number of airborne troopers.

In order to maintain the attack's surprise, air and naval bombardment of the assault sites preceded the landing by only a few hours. For the protection of the parent vessels from shore fire, the landing craft were launched more than twelve miles from the beaches, causing a two-hour journey through heavy seas that left many of the infantrymen violently seasick. Many also were near exhaustion from bailing water from breaking waves that threatened to sink their landing crafts. Lack of information on the wave conditions near the beach also resulted in twenty-seven of thirty-two amphibious Sherman tanks sinking far from shore.

The Allies found German resistance at four of the Normandy beach sites light, but at the fifth, code-named Omaha, the U.S. troops met heavy fire and were barely able to sustain the beachhead. Most of the Americans hitting the beach at Omaha were members of the famed 1st Infantry Division—the Big Red One. Briefed by intelligence officers to expect poorly organized coastal defenses, the infantrymen met instead veterans of the German 352d Division.

These same intelligence officers had informed the Omaha Beach invaders that their primary resistance would come from a heavy artillery battery positioned on a prominent cliff, Pointe du Hoc, just west of the beach, from where German guns would be able to rake the beach and its approaches. To neutralize Pointe du

Hoc, a task force made up of elements of the 2d and 5th Ranger battalions, under command of Lieutenant Colonel Earl Rudder, had to scale the 200-foot cliffs. As the rangers climbed and clawed their way up the sheer rocks, they encountered German machine gunners and infantrymen hurling hand grenades. When the rangers took their objective, they found not the German artillery reported by intelligence but rather only infantrymen whose weapons did not have the range to do any appreciable damage to the Omaha Beach invaders. Of the 355 rangers who had started up the cliff, 197 were casualties.

The Americans barely held the beach at Normandy, and several times during the first day commanders considering withdrawing from "Bloody Omaha." So tenuous was the Utah Beach foothold that the confident German defenders diverted more of their reserves to combat the other four landing sites. Finally, with the leadership of a few and the bravery of many, small groups of American infantrymen slowly made their way forward off the beach. By day's end, the Allies were slowly pushing the Germans back as follow-on landings began. Along the beach and in the surf lay more than 2,000 American casualties.

Once the Germans determined that Normandy was not a diversionary attack, as they had first thought, reserve units from across France began to reinforce, but the Allies had gained a foothold that the Germans could not dislodge.* At the same time, the Allies were unable to push inland for any appreciable distance. A full six weeks after the invasion, the Allied beachhead remained only sixty miles long and five to fifteen miles deep. The Allies were stalemated not only by tough defenders but also by the terrain.

---

*The initial defense and reinforcement of the Normandy beachhead were delayed not only because German intelligence did not anticipate it would be the invasion location but also because the area commander, General Erwin Rommel, reassigned to France after his defeat in North Africa, was absent on leave back to Germany. Also, during the first hours of the battle, reinforcements were not committed because Hitler's aides were afraid to awake the late-sleeping Fuhrer to seek his permission for their movement.

Hedgerows were so thick that neither foot soldiers nor armored tanks could penetrate them. Sunken roads paralleling most of the hedgerows provided natural cover for defenders. The only areas free of hedgerows were networks of marshes, bogs, and swamps that swallowed up both men and machines.

The planners had not considered how to breach the hedgerows or cross the marshes. Despite the fact that many of the hedgerows were more than a thousand years old, and the marshes even older, neither American military intelligence nor the various OSS operatives had noted the obstacles in their reports. Intelligence had again failed, and once again technology and ingenuity arrived to save the day. The Air Corps delivered a new weapon called napalm to burn out the dug-in defenders, and a sergeant welded steel stakes from the German beach defenses onto the front of tanks. These giant pitchforks gouged gaps in the hedgerows for passage of foot soldiers and vehicles.

In August, Patton's 3d Army came ashore to assist in the breakout, and by midmonth the Germans were in general retreat across France. The Allies liberated Paris on August 25 and Antwerp on September 4 before halting to allow their supply lines to catch up. Meanwhile, planners turned their sights toward the Rhine River and the German heartland.

The Allies were confident that the war was almost over—by the end of the year, they calculated. The collapse of the German army seemed imminent with replacement men, equipment, and especially fuel in short supply. The Supreme Headquarters Allied Expeditionary Forces (SHAEF) intelligence section, believing that German resistance was nearly finished, issued an intelligence summary on August 26 stating, "The August battles have done it and the enemy in the west has had it. Two and a half months of bitter fighting have brought the end of the war in Europe within sight, almost within reach."

A week later the SHAEF G-2 was even more definite in its end-of-the-war prediction. On September 2, the G-2 reported, "Organized resistance under control of the German High Command is unlikely to continue beyond 1 December 1944."

The next day, the G-2 section of one of SHAEF's subordinate units issued an intelligence estimate supporting this prediction.

According to the 1st U.S. Army, political upheaval in Germany, which would end the war, would occur within the next thirty to sixty days.

To take advantage of the intelligence estimates of the deterioration of Germany's ability to continue the war, Field Marshal Montgomery* proposed a bold airborne operation of three divisions, two American and one British, to seize seven bridges from Eindhoven to Arnhem in Holland. Once the bridges were secure, the British 2d Army would sweep ninety miles from Antwerp to the Rhine River and cross at Arnhem. The Allies, then having outflanked the remaining German units in the low countries, would have easy access to the center of Germany via the relatively flat western part of the country.

The plan approved, Montgomery began Operation Market Garden on September 17 with more than 20,000 paratroopers jumping to secure the Holland bridges. Lieutenant General Sir Frederick Browning, commander of the airborne forces, remarked before the drop that the attack might be going "one bridge too far." Events over the next few days would prove Browning correct and the Allied intelligence estimates about Germany's rapid decline woefully incorrect.

The most significant intelligence failure of Market Garden was the gross underestimation of enemy strength. Evidence from Ultra intercepts and aerial reconnaissance had indicated the possibility of several German armor units in the vicinity of Arnhem, but Montgomery and his intelligence staff had discounted the reports. On September 13, the 1st Airborne Corps Intelligence Summary reported that only a few infantry reserves and no more than fifty to a hundred tanks were in the area. The

---

*Montgomery, not known for bold or risky operations, may have made his proposal for the airborne operations based on the incorrect intelligence that it would be an easy offensive. Recent changes in the Allied order of battle had eroded the vain field marshal's power. With approval of the plan, Montgomery would gain three airborne divisions and an operation supply priority. A successful flanking movement, the first invasion of German soil, and a race to Berlin could do nothing but add to the fame of the egotistical Englishman.

British 2d Army intelligence section reported on September 16 that aerial reconnaissance of the area showed no tanks and that the chance of enemy armor in the vicinity of Arnhem was highly unlikely.

Intelligence reports by other Market Garden units echoed this estimate of limited enemy resistance. Intelligence officers claimed there were no more than 2,000 enemy troops at any concentration in Holland. Attacking ground units were told that the enemy was supported by few, if any, tanks.

The actual operation of getting the three airborne divisions on the ground by parachute and glider was the most effective air assault of the war. Few accidental injuries were sustained, and most of the invaders reached the correct landing zones with units intact. It was only after they got on the ground that their troubles began.

In planning the invasion, Market Garden intelligence officers made no attempt to contact the Dutch government-in-exile in London, which maintained communications with the under-ground in Holland. Information about the terrain for glider landings and for cross-country trafficability was readily available from the Dutch if they had asked; they did not. Thus, many of the airborne units, particularly the glider troops, were deliberately dropped miles from their targets when perfectly suitable sites were available within yards of their assigned bridges. As a result, by the time the paratroopers marched to their objectives, the Germans had reinforced their defenses.

Difficult terrain and too many unanticipated enemy troops made for a disaster at the landing zones and bridge sites. Instead of just one bridge being too far, the Allies found all of the bridges to be death traps. The British 1st Airborne Division landed in the midst of the veteran 9th and 10th SS Panzer Divisions. The U.S. 82d and 101st Airborne Divisions also encountered heavy resistance at their drop zones and bridge sites.

The Germans responded rapidly to the air assault by pouring reinforcements across the Rhine from reserve units in Germany. It was not difficult for the German commander to determine where to position his forces. In a gross breach of security, an American officer aboard one of the gliders that was shot down during the opening moments of the invasion carried a complete battle plan for the operation. The Allied plans for Market Garden were in the hands of the German commander two hours later.

To the south, Allied ground troops, who were to attack along a corridor to link up with the airborne assaults, were faring no better. Restricted to roadways by boggy terrain and multiple canals, they encountered German artillery and armor from both sides. Their attack, which was supposed to race to the bridges, became a slow plod compounded by unpredicted fog and rain that reduced Allied air support. Without the ground reinforcements linking up as planned at Arnhem by the third day, the American airborne divisions barely held a narrow corridor through which they and the British could withdraw southward. Some did escape, but by the end of the operation, more than 17,000 Allied soldiers were killed, wounded, or captured. Arnhem would not be liberated until April 15, 1945—less than a month before the war was over.

The intelligence estimates of a quick conclusion of the war in 1944 had been proven grossly incorrect. SHAEF and Montgomery's intelligence officers attempted to cover their errors by claiming that the Germans received advanced warning of the attack from a double agent, but neither German army records nor postwar interviews with the surviving enemy commanders lend any creditability to the Allied intelligence claims.

Market Garden expended men and supplies needed for the final attack on the German homeland, delaying the final push until the Allies could replenish resources. By December 1944, Eisenhower, as the Supreme Allied Commander, was ready to continue the straightforward strategy directed by the Anglo-American Chiefs of Staff: "Undertake operations aimed at the heart of Germany and the destruction of her armed forces." Across Belgium, Luxembourg, and France, the Allies had been closing on the German border. By early December, the 21st Army Group had driven the Germans from Maas, the 1st and 9th U.S. Armies had won the Battle of the Hurtgen Forest east of Aachen, and Patton's 3d Army had liberated Metz. All along the front, the Allies continued to resupply and reinforce in preparation for the invasion of Germany. Unfortunately, the Germans did not idly

wait to be attacked, and American military intelligence soon had
still another opportunity to fail.

Ultra code breakers and aerial reconnaissance detected a
German buildup in late November and reported the possibility of
a counteroffensive. Allied intelligence discounted the reports on
the basis of contradictory information they had gathered about
German troop strengths and supplies. On December 12, the 12th
U.S. Army Group in the Ardennes Forest of Belgium and Luxembourg issued a lengthy intelligence summary outlining the
enemy weaknesses and presenting an optimistic outlook for a
quick victory when the offensive resumed. The summary stated in
part, "It is now certain that attrition is steadily sapping the
strength of German forces on the Western Front and that the crust
of defenses is thinner, more brittle and more vulnerable than it
appears on our G-2 maps or to the troops in the line."

To the north, the British 21st Army Group was even more
optimistic of Allied superiority in the area. The group commander
wrote on December 16, "The enemy is at present fighting a
defensive campaign on all fronts; his situation is such that he
cannot stage major offensive operations. Furthermore, at all costs
he has not the transport or the petrol that would be necessary for
mobile operations....The enemy is in a bad way; he has had a
tremendous battering and has lost heavily in men and
equipment."

Despite these reports by Allied G-2s and commanders, the
Germans managed to concentrate 250,000 men, 1,900 artillery
pieces, and 1,000 tanks without detection by Allied military
intelligence. This vast counteroffensive force lay in wait for two
weeks until rain and cloud cover grounded Allied air support. On
the morning of December 16, the Germans struck across an
eighty-mile front in the Ardennes against five American divisions.
Two of these divisions were "fresh off the boat" from the States
with no battle experience, while another was refitting from hard
combat in the Battle of the Hurtgen Forest.

The German Ardennes offensive, personally planned by Hitler,
committed the last of Germany's manpower and fuel reserves to
the battle. Hitler's objective was to make a lightning-bolt drive to
Antwerp through 100 miles of Allied lines, a move he hoped

would allow him to sue for some type of peace with Great Britain and the United States so he could then concentrate his forces on the advancing Soviets. Hitler's generals had little confidence in the plan but vigorously executed it once the attack began.

Neither the "great game"–playing OSS agents, who, according to their own later writings, had penetrated virtually every aspect of the German military and government, nor any other intelligence operation detected the forthcoming counteroffensive. Surprise was complete.

The green U.S. units yielded rapidly, with more than 7,000 soldiers surrendering during the first day of the fight. More experienced units fought back valiantly, surrendering ground bloody foot by bloody foot. While it is true that some American units performed poorly, overall the totally surprised and outnumbered GIs did well for themselves, forcing the Germans to take a week to gain objectives they expected to occupy the first day.

During the initial hours of the attack, Allied intelligence officers refused to believe the German action was a major counteroffensive, labeling the attack as only a reconnaissance in force or a minor spoiling attack. By day two, the size of the attack was obvious even to military intelligence, and Allied commanders poured reinforcements into the Ardennes to stop the "bulge" in their lines. The 82d and 101st Airborne Divisions, still recovering from Operation Market Garden, were rushed by open truck in freezing weather to shore up the front lines. At Bastogne and St. Vith, the two largest towns in the Ardennes, the Americans made their stand and, by Christmas, stopped the counteroffensive. About the same time, the clouds cleared, allowing air resupply to resume and Allied bombers to join the fight. Patton's 3d Army, having made a ninety-degree turn from its advance toward Germany, arrived with tanks and infantry.

It took until the end of January 1945 to drive the Germans back to their preoffensive positions. The Battle of the Bulge concluded as the largest single land battle ever fought by the United States, with more than twenty-nine divisions and 650,000 troops committed. The 79,000 casualties in the Ardennes accounted for about 10 percent of the total suffered by the United States in all theaters of World War II. A monument erected at

Bastogne after the war notes, "Seldom has more American blood been spilled in the course of a single battle." The Germans lost 100,000 men and expended the last of their ground reserve units, equipment, and fuel.

In early 1945, the Allies crossed the Rhine into Germany and advanced toward Berlin. With much hard fighting, city after city fell, and the Allies liberated concentration camps to expose the mass execution of Jews and other "undesirables."* By April, the Allies had Berlin surrounded, and on the 30th Hitler committed suicide. On May 7, the chief of staff of the German armed forces, Colonel General Alfred Jodl, signed an unconditional surrender. The Allies declared May 8 as Victory in Europe Day (V-E Day).

Victory over the Axis Powers in Europe and the Pacific was costly. American World War II losses totaled 294,000 dead and 671,000 wounded. The "Good War," as it would later be known, took more lives and caused more destruction around the world than any other conflict in history. More than seventeen million military personnel lost their lives, and nearly double that number of civilians died directly from combat or indirectly from famine.

---

*How much Allied intelligence knew about the German death camps and the "final solution" has never been revealed. Given the level of penetration claimed by OSS and other agents, and the availability of aerial photography, the Allies must have had some information. The reasons why they made no effort to bomb railways into the camps or to liberate the prisoners earlier remain classified or missing from the history of World War II.

★ 11 ★

The Unknown War: Korea

At the end of World War II, the United States had the strongest navy and air force in the world and a land army rivaled only by that of the Soviet Union. As the only nation possessing "the Bomb," the United States was alone among world powers—and Americans assumed it would stay there because, as the Manhattan Project staff and high-ranking intelligence advisers assured President Harry Truman, it would easily take the "backward" Russians twenty years to develop their own atomic device. Truman began a demobilization plan that quickly reduced the size of the military establishment. Personnel were discharged; ships, planes, and tanks mothballed or scrapped; and budgets cut.

Especially hard hit in the reductions were all aspects of intelligence. While Roosevelt was still the president and before the war ended, Bill Donovan had proposed that he continue the OSS in peacetime as a nucleus of a permanent, centralized national intelligence organization. This recommendation was not popular with military leaders. First, they believed intelligence should remain a part of the uniformed services rather than become a separate agency working directly for the president. Second, they generally disliked the "elitism" and its superior attitude of the OSS. Hoover at the FBI also opposed Donovan's idea, because it would downgrade the importance of his bureau and, more important, lessen his own personal power.

Roosevelt was seriously considering a postwar OSS when the press learned about the proposal in February 1945. Several of the country's major newspapers carried editorials condemning the formation of what they called an "American Gestapo." When Roosevelt died a few weeks later, Truman had too much to learn, and too many decisions to make, to worry about the OSS.

One of Truman's first budget-cutting actions following the surrender of Japan was to sign an executive order terminating the OSS effective October 1, 1945. He transferred the OSS Research and Analysis Branch to the State Department with directions to "take the lead in developing a comprehensive and coordinated foreign intelligence program." Truman transferred other OSS personnel and responsibilities to the army. Donovan, relieved from active duty, returned to his prewar law practice.

In the euphoria of victory, Truman, as well as many other Americans, believed a postwar period of world peace would endure, with the United Nations resolving any conflicts that did arise. However, it did not take long after the U.N. began operations in January 1946, for such optimists to realize that World War II had merely been a single step in the Soviet Union's master plans to promote communism and eventually to dominate the world. The Americans learned in late 1945 and early 1946 that joint Allied control of occupied territories could not succeed. Political maneuvering kept the Soviets out of Japan, but they flexed their might in Europe by controlling and limiting access to Berlin.

The United States now entered what became known as the Cold War* with the Soviet Union. The Joint Chiefs of Staff, aware that America lacked intelligence about the Soviets and that the State Department had not followed Truman's directions to assume the intelligence lead, made their own proposal to the president. On January 22, 1946, Truman signed a directive forming the National Intelligence Authority (NIA) composed of the president's

---

*Shortly after the end of World War II, President Truman appointed Bernard Baruch to head a committee to investigate the possibility of internationally banning the Bomb and such future developments. The Soviets flatly refused to participate, and a dejected Baruch returned to civilian life in South Carolina, where he said in an interview, "Today, we are in the midst of a cold war." The phrase instantly became the label for the tense U.S.-Soviet relationship that followed.

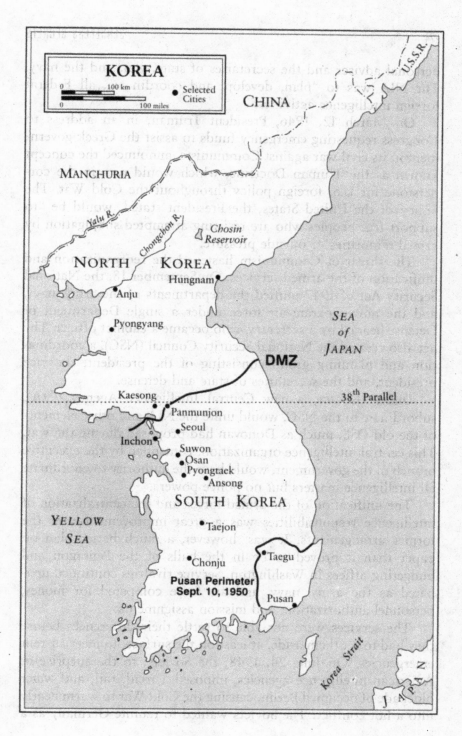

KOREA

0 ——— 100 km

0 ——— 100 miles

Selected Cities

CHINA

MANCHURIA

Yalu R.

Chongchon R.

Chosin Reservoir

NORTH KOREA

Hungnam

Anju

Pyongyang

SEA of JAPAN

DMZ

Kaesong

38th Parallel

Panmunjon

Seoul

Inchon

Suwon

Osan

Pyongtaek

Ansong

SOUTH KOREA

YELLOW SEA

Taejon

Taegu

Chonju

Pusan Perimeter Sept. 10, 1950

Pusan

Korea Strait

JAPAN

U.S.S.R.

personal adviser and the secretaries of state, war, and the navy. The NIA was to "plan, develop, and coordinate...all Federal foreign intelligence activities."

On March 12, 1946, President Truman, in an address to Congress requesting emergency funds to assist the Greek government in its civil war against Communists, announced the concept known as the Truman Doctrine, which would remain the cornerstone for U.S. foreign policy throughout the Cold War. The policy of the United States, the President stated, would be "to support free peoples who are resisting attempted subjugation by armed minorities or outside pressure."

The threat of Communism hastened the reorganization and unification of the armed services. On September 18, the National Security Act of 1947 unified the departments of the army, navy, and the now separate air force under a single Department of Defense headed by a secretary, who became a cabinet officer. The act also created the National Security Council (NSC), a coordination and planning group consisting of the president, the vice president, and the secretaries of state and defense.

Under the act, a new Central Intelligence Agency (CIA), subordinate to the NSC, would unite the NIA and other elements of the old OSS, much as Donovan had proposed during the war. This central intelligence organization, controlled by the executive branch of the government, would have the authority to coordinate all intelligence matters but no police powers.

The unification of the armed forces and the centralization of intelligence responsibilities was a great improvement over the former arrangements. It was, however, a much better plan on paper than it proved to be in the halls of the Pentagon and budgeting offices in Washington. Service rivalries continued unabated as the army, navy, and air force competed for money, personnel authorization, and mission assignments.

The services were not able to settle their differences before they had to set them aside, at least on the surface, to meet current emergencies. On June 24, 1948, the Soviets, to the surprise of American intelligence agencies, imposed a road, rail, and water blockade of occupied Berlin, causing the Cold War to warm nearly into a hot conflict. The Soviets wanted to reunite Germany as a

Communist state, but the remaining Allies resisted. The United States began a massive airlift of fuel, food, and other necessities to Berlin. To ensure the air armada would not be attacked, B-29s, capable of delivering atomic bombs, were transferred from the United States to forward bases within striking range of the Soviet Union. After 321 days and 277,000 American air sorties into Berlin, the Soviets lifted their blockade.

Later in 1949, Germany was formally divided into the Federal Republic (West Germany) and the Democratic Republic (East Germany), with Berlin remaining occupied by the United States, the Soviet Union, Great Britain, and France. The division did more than just create a divided Germany; it signified the division of the rest of the world into two spheres, one influenced by the United States and one influenced by the Soviet Union.

Weeks before the Berlin blockade ended, the United States had entered into its first peacetime military alliance on April 4, 1949. The North Atlantic Treaty Organization (NATO), popular at inception with the American government but not the American people, committed the United States to the defense of Europe and to providing a "nuclear umbrella" for the cosigners. A short time later, the Soviet Union and its allies signed the Warsaw Pact, further polarizing the world into West and East.

The Cold War became even chillier for NATO members in September when they learned that the Soviets had set off their first atomic explosion. The intelligence estimate had said the "backward" Russians would take up to twenty years to develop the Bomb; instead they had done so in less than four. The Soviet acceleration was influenced by U.S. counterintelligence failures within the Manhattan Project, including an incident in which an army enlisted man, David Greenglass, had secured atomic secrets to sell to the Soviets. In exchange for leniency, Greenglass revealed a larger espionage network headed by his sister, Ethel, and her husband, Julius Rosenberg. A longtime member of the Communist Party, Julius Rosenberg had been recruited by the Russians while working in sensitive civilian engineering positions for the U.S. Army Signal Corps.

On June 19, 1953, the Rosenbergs were electrocuted at the prison at Sing Sing, New York. Both had the option of lesser punishment if they revealed information about the Soviet spy operations in the United States, but neither did, maintaining their innocence all the way to the execution chamber. Speculation then and since has centered on the possibility that the Rosenbergs were scapegoats for the U.S. intelligence community, which had failed to maintain the security of the development of the atomic bomb. The Rosenbergs may have been much less involved than suspected, revealing no further information because they had none.

Now that the Soviets had the Bomb, the United States increased its conventional military efforts to stay abreast of the Soviets. Rivalries between the services for funding for the latest weapons and increased personnel reached new heights—or more accurately, new lows. The air force believed air power, particularly with its atomic bomb delivery capability, was the cornerstone of American defense; the navy saw the defense future as depending upon aircraft carriers and nuclear submarines armed with long-range missiles; the army remained confident that no conflict could be resolved without soldiers occupying ground positions.

Maneuvering by the services for resources came to a head on October 5, 1949, when the secretary of defense canceled funding for the construction of the supercarrier *United States*. Navy leaders went public with their displeasure and eventually stated their complaints to a special congressional hearing on national defense policy. This unusual protest by the navy command structure was not popular with the elected officials or with the public, and the press went so far as to label the complaints as "a mutiny" and "the revolt of the admirals."

The immediate result of "the revolt of the admirals" was the replacement of the chief of naval operations, Admiral Louis E. Denfeld. Nonetheless, the foray focused attention on defense and the need to increase spending to meet possible threats from spreading communism. The importance of increased readiness was soon to become dramatically obvious on the peninsula of Korea.

In the final days of World War II, the Soviets had declared war on Japan in accordance with the Allies' agreement to do so within three months of the defeat of Germany. Entering the Pacific war six days before the Japanese surrender and two days after the

United States dropped the first atomic bomb, the Soviets found the agreement fortuitous. With the war nearly over, they shared in the spoils of the defeated Japanese Empire with a minimum of effort. When the Japanese surrendered, Korea, which had been claimed by Japan since 1895, was occupied by the Soviets in the northern part of the country and by the Americans in the south. The 38th parallel, an arbitrary line that followed no topographical feature of the country, became the divider between the two occupying forces.

The United Nations had hoped to sponsor general elections in Korea by 1947 to reunite the country, but the Soviet Union opposed the election and prevented voting in the northern portion of the peninsula. On May 10, 1948, the people of South Korea elected a national assembly and established the Republic of Korea. Communists in the North, with the support of the Soviets, established the Democratic Republic of Korea on September 9. Both of the new governments claimed to represent the whole of the country, and the armed forces of each soon occupied positions along the 38th parallel.

The backbone of the People's Army of North Korea, or the "Inmun Gun," consisted of two divisions of Koreans who had fought with Mao Tse-tung in his successful Communist takeover of China. Seven additional infantry divisions and an armored brigade, organized after the formation of the Inmun Gun, brought North Korea to a strength of more than 135,000 men supported by tanks, artillery, and military advisers from the Soviet Union.

The Republic of Korea (ROK) army, formed almost as an afterthought by the Americans, had forces numbering only 95,000 with no tanks and little artillery. To keep the aggressive South Korean President Syngman Rhee from attacking the North to reunite the country, the U.S. deliberately kept his army small, apparently never considering the possibility that the North Koreans might have Rhee's idea in reverse.

Until 1949, more than 16,000 American troops remained in Korea to organize and train the South Korean army. On June 30 of that year, all but 500 of the U.S. Korea Military Advisory Group (KMAG) withdrew. Although a major general headed the KMAG, the top adviser to the ROK chief of staff and to President Rhee was an army captain. The American advisers were confident that the South Koreans had excellent potential as soldiers and that they could handle the skirmishes that had begun to develop along the 38th parallel.

Border clashes continued into 1950, but, while threats of an invasion from the North existed, no one took them seriously. To most Americans enjoying the prosperity of post–World War II peace, Korea remained a remote area of little interest.

In North Korea, Premier Kim Il-sung, a veteran of the civil war in China, continued preparations for a forceful reunification of the two Koreas into a single Communist country. The only thing restraining him was the threat of U.S. retaliation. Early in 1950, Secretary of State Dean Acheson, speaking at the National Press Club in Washington, unknowingly gave Kim the go-ahead to invade the South when he said that the American Pacific defensive perimeter included Japan. Because Acheson made no mention of Korea, Kim and his advisers interpreted the speech as a clear message that the Americans would not defend South Korea.

North Korea began a buildup just north of the 38th parallel and by June was prepared to attack. In the South, neither U.S. nor ROK intelligence assets had a hint of the impending invasion. Nearly one-third of the ROK army was on home leave to assist in the summer harvest. In mid-June, intelligence officers briefed Secretary of Defense Louis Johnson, who was visiting the U.S. Far East Command in Japan, that there was no evidence of any imminent hostilities on the part of the North Koreans. On June 20, Assistant Secretary of State for Far Eastern Affairs Dean Rusk, testifying before the House Committee on Foreign Affairs, said, "We see no present indications that the [North Koreans] have any intentions of fighting a major war for that purpose [of taking over South Korea]."

Five days later, at 4:00 A.M., 100,000 North Korean troops, supported by 1,400 artillery pieces and 125 Russian T-34 tanks, poured across the 38th parallel. Six hours later, the United Press International office in New York received its first news of the invasion. This was an hour and a half before the U.S. State Department was aware and nearly two hours before President Truman was informed. The CIA was the last to find out about the invasion, and then it was from sources outside rather than inside the agency.

The American diplomats and military remained so confident in their intelligence, which indicated no possibility of a North Korean attack, that they did not believe the initial reports. During the early hours of the invasion, intelligence officers at the U.S. embassy in Seoul assured reporters that the reports were only rumors. KMAG continued for several more hours to reiterate that the attack was merely a "border incident," while General Douglas MacArthur, in charge of the Far East Command in Japan, informed Washington that the attack was no more than a reconnaissance in force.

Forty-eight hours after the invasion began, the North Koreans were on the outskirts of Seoul with most of the South Korean army in retreat. The few who stood and fought discovered that they had no weapon in their U.S.-supplied arsenal capable of stopping the Soviet T-34 tanks. Bazooka rounds, the principal antitank weapon, bounced off the thick steel of the T-34s. Americans in KMAG joined the withdrawal south while they, like their compatriots in Japan and back in the United States, were finally admitting that the invasion was real.

Truman's immediate response to the invasion was to order the U.S. representative to the U.N. Security Council to present a resolution demanding the North Koreans stop their attack and withdraw back behind the 38th parallel. The Russians, who could have vetoed the resolution, continued their boycott of meetings in protest of the membership of Nationalist China on the council. The resolution passed with ease.

North Korea ignored the resolution's demands and entered Seoul on the 27th, causing the U.N. Security Council to pass a second resolution, again with the Soviets absent, asking that "members of the United Nations furnish such assistance to the Republic of Korea as may be necessary to repel the armed attack and to restore international peace and security in the area." Although the United States ultimately provided 90 percent of the manpower, military equipment, and food supplies of the U.N. efforts, sixteen countries did send troops, and another forty-one contributed food and medical supplies for the military and South

Korean civilians. For the first time in its short history, the United Nations was committed to combat.

On the 28th, Truman ordered MacArthur to provide air and sea support to the South Korean army and to assist in the evacuation of American citizens from the area. The president also approved the immediate airlift of an infantry regimental combat team from Japan into Korea and its reinforcement by division-sized units as soon as possible. When asked at a press conference if the United States was at war, Truman responded that the situation could better be called a "police action" under the auspices of the United Nations. Although in the next few years it would look, act, smell, wound, maim, and kill like a real war, it would officially remain a "police action."

Whatever its label, neither the U.S. military nor its intelligence organizations were prepared for it. At the end of World War II the U.S. Army had nearly 100 well-equipped, well-trained divisions. At the outbreak of conflict in Korea, only nine divisions remained. They were equipped mostly with World War II weapons and supplies. The Marine Corps, at a strength of almost half a million in 1945, had only 86,000 men. About one-fourth of these soldiers and marines were stationed in Japan or on nearby Pacific islands, growing soft through occupation duty in which local nationals did all the manual labor, including polishing the soldiers' shoes and keeping their barracks clean. Because few funds were available to finance field exercises, these servicemen trained little and worked less.

The national and military intelligence services were in no better condition for war. Compounding the CIA's failure to predict the North Korean invasion were the efforts it made to place the blame elsewhere. Agency Director Roscoe H. Hillenkoetter informed the *New York Times* that the CIA had been aware of the conditions in Korea and had warned the White House, as well as the Defense and State departments. A few days later, Hillenkoetter made the same claims as he testified before a special Senate committee.

Hillenkoetter desperately justified his agency's failure with reports the CIA had rendered about a buildup of North Korean forces along the 38th parallel—news to no one, since the year-long increase in North Korean forces was general knowledge. While the CIA had reported the capability of the North Koreans, it had not made the vaguest prediction that they would actually initiate hostilities. Truman was extremely angry, and more than a little frustrated, that the agency he had established to prevent just such a surprise had let him and the country down. The CIA's denial of failure to the press and Congress only worsened the situation. Truman did not fire Hillenkoetter; rather, he "allowed" him to resign to return to his position as an admiral in the navy. In an odd tradition, which dated back several wars, of apparently rewarding naval officers for intelligence failures, Hillenkoetter took command of the U.S. Navy 7th Task Force, which had the sensitive mission of protecting Nationalist China.

Military intelligence was as inept as the CIA in predicting the invasion—and improved little during the conflict. Since North Korea had no sea force of any substance, the U.S. Navy intelligence efforts focused on mainland target acquisitions in support of army and marine ground operations. The Office of Naval Intelligence continued its minor role of providing general assistance to the navy's Plans and Operations Division and coordinating with the intelligence units of the other sections of the Defense Department.

After the air force became a separate service in 1947, its A-2 (Intelligence Section) remained subordinate to its A-3 (Operations) instead of having equal status with personnel, operations, and supply.* During the first days of the conflict, the air force supported the withdrawal south from Seoul. Indicative of future intelligence difficulties in differentiating enemy from friendly troops, the U.S. Air Force bombed the South Korean 1st Division attempting to cross the Han River in one of its first air-to-ground attacks.

The Korean War was fought essentially in the boggy or frozen rice paddies and on the rugged mountain ranges that dominated the peninsula. As a result, the bulk of the intelligence responsibilities fell to the U.S. Army. Unfortunately, army intelligence

---

*The A-2 would not gain equal status until 1957.

entered the war woefully unprepared, with critical shortages in trained personnel for the Counter-Intelligence Corps and the Army Security Agency. Particularly in short supply were photo interpreters and Korean and Chinese linguists, a result of post–World War II cutbacks. While training infantrymen required a relatively short time, training qualified photo interpreters and linguists took almost as long as the war lasted.

The Joint Services Far East Command in Japan was also deficient in supporting intelligence efforts. Early in the war it attempted to establish a network of agents in North Korea, but all of the Korean-born agents disappeared without a trace. The command trained more operatives, even though resources and priorities were so minimal that prospective agents practiced airborne infiltrations by stepping off the back of moving jeeps instead of jumping out of airplanes. When these "trained" agents infiltrated into North Korea, few were ever heard from again, and those who did communicate made conflicting reports of little use to analysts and planners.

By the end of the first week of the war, one-half of the South Korean army was dead, wounded, or missing. The first American ground force to join the fight was Task Force Smith—406 men of the 1st Battalion, 21st Infantry Regiment of the 24th Infantry Division, under the command of Lieutenant Colonel Charles B. Smith. The unit immediately moved into blocking positions along the main route south of Seoul at the villages of Pyongtaek and Ansong. Lead elements of the North Korean army encountered Task Force Smith on the morning of July 5. When the Americans fired their 2.36-inch antitank bazookas, round after round bounced off the steel hulls of the Soviet tanks, just as they had for the ROK shooters.

Task Force Smith soldiers attempted to fight a delaying battle, but they were barely able to slow the enemy because they had no weapons to stop the tanks, little ammunition, and no accurate maps of the area. By the end of the day, more than half of Task Force Smith were casualties. The rest of the 24th Infantry Division, under the command of Major General William F. Dean, reinforced the task force a few days later to slow the North Korean invasion.

On July 8, with the approval of the U.N. Security Council, Truman named General Douglas MacArthur the commander-in-chief of the United Nations Command and dispatched other American units stationed in Japan to Korea, where on July 13 Lieutenant General Walton H. Walker assumed command of the U.S. 8th Army. By July 19, the 1st Cavalry and 25th Infantry divisions had joined the 24th as part of the 8th Army. At the end of the month, the 2d Infantry Division and the 1st Marine Provisional Brigade arrived to reinforce Walker's command.

The 8th Army and the ROK troops attempted to stop the invasion about 150 miles south of the 38th parallel at Taejon, but the Communists took the city on July 21. The U.N. forces then fell back to what became known as the Pusan Perimeter, where during the month of August the American and U.N. forces fought to hold a defensive rectangle seventy miles wide and sixty miles long around the port of Pusan on the southeast coast of Korea. At times the ability of the defense to hold was in doubt, creating talk of a Dunkirk-like withdrawal to the sea. Finally, American tanks and 3.5-inch antitank guns arrived in sufficient quantities to stop the North Korean armor. Unopposed U.S. air support also contributed to breaking the Communist attack.

Intelligence had been nearly nonexistent during the Communist offensive. Walker and his division commanders were forced to conduct their own reconnaissances by air and jeep to determine enemy dispositions and intentions. On one of these reconnaissances, General William Dean of the 24th Infantry Division became trapped behind enemy lines. Although he made a valiant effort to escape and make his way to friendly forces, Dean was eventually captured, becoming the highest-ranking American POW of the conflict.

Walker's lack of intelligence for his defense of Pusan was in sharp contrast to the North Koreans' ability to readily gather information about the Americans. Agents had infiltrated south for months before the beginning of the conflict, and the Communists had established an extensive intelligence network. Many of the North Korean soldiers changed their uniforms for civilian clothes when it was advantageous to gather information or to conduct guerrilla operations.

Basic information about the enemy's strength and fighting ability continued to elude American intelligence. Even after two months, intelligence sources could only estimate that the Communists outnumbered the 92,000 U.N. troops four to one, when in fact the North Koreans had only 70,000 soldiers in the south. While intelligence sources overestimated the number of North Koreans, they underestimated the fighting ability of the Communist troops, describing them as inferior and ignorant.

Walker's 8th Army had barely contained the North Korean attack against the Pusan Perimeter when MacArthur announced a bold amphibious counterattack at the northwest port of Inchon, just twenty-four miles from Seoul. MacArthur's intelligence officers, as well as his army and navy commanders, advised against the plan because the landing site was too far north and Inchon itself, surrounded by mud flats and buffeted by tides that varied thirty feet, was a poor site for an amphibious assault. They also noted that with air and sea superiority, the Allies could chose any site they desired for the counterattack. MacArthur, experienced in amphibious warfare during World War II, replied that all the negatives would only make the surprise greater.

MacArthur was not without sound intelligence as he prepared to launch the Inchon attack. He became his own intelligence chief, personally organizing an information-gathering effort. Days before the invasion, MacArthur dispatched a naval officer, Lieutenant Eugene F. Clark, on a ground and sea reconnaissance of the islands and coastline around Inchon. Clark, accompanied by a dozen hand-picked South Korean civilian agents, landed in the area of Inchon two weeks before the scheduled invasion. The team's radio reports provided accurate tide information and pinpointed sea and beach obstacles to the landing. When the attack actually began, Clark lit a guide beacon for the main force and, along with his team, rowed out to meet the invading fleet.

On September 13, the U.N. forces launched a counterattack from the Pusan Perimeter. Two days later the U.S. X Corps, assembled in Japan from the army's 7th Infantry Division and the 1st Marine Division, landed at Inchon virtually unopposed. The X Corps, under command of Major General Edward M. Almond, then moved toward Seoul, meeting progressively stronger resistance. The Americans, supplied from the air and from the port at Inchon, soon outmatched the North Koreans, who relied on constantly bombed supply lines that reached overland all the way to China. When the X Corps cut the supply lines to the North Koreans opposing Walker's 8th Army, the Communists were forced to withdraw northward. Most were killed or captured. Seoul was back in the X Corps's control by September 26, and the 8th Army arrived from the south two days later.

Inchon had been a brilliant move on the part of MacArthur, and Clark's intelligence work had certainly been a factor in its success. Inchon, however, could just as easily have been a disaster for the Americans because of an intelligence failure that occurred several weeks before the invasion. Intelligence operators in Communist China had received reports from their agents in the South about the force buildup and had predicted the invasion would come at one of only five sites that would support such an attack. They had further decided that Inchon was the most likely target since it was the site closest to Seoul.

Two days before the invasion, South Korean officers inadvertently leaked the invasion site and date to American reporters. It is not known if Kim Il-sung learned of the press reports, but he was definitely informed by the Chinese of their intelligence about the attack. Instead of shifting forces to defend Inchon, however, Kim decided an immediate attack against Pusan would defeat the U.N. forces there, stop the invasion plan, and end the war with the Communists as the victors.

Kim's error in pushing the offensive at Pusan rather than defending Inchon left his army in tatters. His few remaining forces withdrew north of the 38th parallel to prepare defensive positions while waiting to see if the U.N. forces would pursue. MacArthur and Rhee wanted to cross the parallel immediately and clear Korea of the Communists all the way to the Yalu River border with China. Both the CIA and MacArthur assured President Truman that an invasion of North Korea would not cause either China or the Soviet Union to enter the war in support of Kim.

Rhee and his South Korean army, not waiting for a decision from Washington or the United Nations, crossed the 38th parallel on October 1. The Soviets, convinced after Inchon that Korea was a lost cause, took no action. Mao, on the other hand, responded that China would not stand aside while a neighbor was in mortal danger.*

China's warning went unheeded. In Washington, the CIA and the military chiefs of staff, who were relying on reports from their own intelligence services, assured Truman that the Chinese were bluffing and had no intention of entering the war. Encouraged by the United States, the U.N. General Assembly voted on October 7 for the restoration of peace and security "throughout" Korea—interpreted as approval for U.S. and U.N. forces to cross into North Korea.

On October 8, the 8th Army crossed the 38th parallel and attacked northward along the western half of the peninsula while the X Corps paralleled them in the eastern half of Korea.† The poorly supplied North Koreans retreated rapidly. Pyongyang, the capital of North Korea, fell to the Americans on October 19.

As U.N. forces swept northward on two axes, aerial reconnaissance continued to be the primary means of intelligence gathering. Air force, navy, and marine aircraft provided aerial photographs while the U.S. Army used small, single-engine aircraft for both visual and photo reconnaissance. Commanders at all levels, including Walker and Almond, continued to conduct personal aerial visual reconnaissance to fill in the gaps in information provided by their intelligence sections. At the division level, intelligence was so limited that commanders had to spend much of their time in the

---

*What Mao did not mention was that 80 percent of China's heavy industry was in Manchuria, which shared a border with North Korea. Defending a neighbor against anti-Communists might also mean defending one's self.

†Normally the X Corps would have been subordinate to the 8th Army, but MacArthur kept the two commands separate with equal priorities. He was criticized for "splitting" his command, and it was common knowledge that he favored Almond, his former chief of staff, over Walker, whom he personally disliked. In fairness to MacArthur, however, it should be noted that the Korean peninsula is divided by large north-south mountain ranges that naturally separate the country into two distinct areas; thus "splitting" the command may have been the best, if not the only, available course of action.

air or on the ground at the immediate front to evaluate the enemy situation.

The assigned intelligence units available to division commanders were reconnaissance companies, seventeen-man Counter-Intelligence Corps detachments, and a few photo interpreters assigned to the G-2 section. Infantry or other combat arms officers, who had little or no experience in the information field, filled the intelligence officer positions at regimental and battalion levels. It was not unusual for the intelligence officer in units lower than division level to have gained his position by being relieved for inefficiency from infantry, artillery, or armor duty.

One of the most qualified, but misused, intelligence resources at the corps and army levels was the rangers. Two months into the Korean police action, the army reauthorized the formation of fourteen ranger companies, six of which deployed to the war zone. These units of elite soldiers should have been ideal resources for the cross-line gathering of intelligence and the capture of prisoners; instead, commanders used the ranger companies mostly as infantry, assigning them missions better suited to full battalions.

While the fighting abilities of the rangers were respected by all, many American commanders believed the special units drained the regular infantry of superior soldiers. Others complained that the austerely organized rangers required too much support in the way of supplies and transportation when attached to the divisions. In the fast-paced events of the Korean War, the rangers never found their proper place or appropriate missions. Before the war concluded, the ranger companies were disbanded.

None of these internal intelligence resources, or the CIA, provided any indication of the massing of Chinese forces along their border, even though China renewed its warnings about entering the war as the U.N. forces neared the Yalu River. In fact, Mao had ordered thirty-nine combat divisions to Korea, and about one-third—260,000 troops—had already crossed the Yalu. On October 25, U.S. and Chinese forces made their first contact. The fight continued until November 6, when the Chinese suddenly broke off combat. MacArthur and his intelligence staff remained convinced that the Chinese intervention was minor and that the war would soon be over. "Home by Christmas" were the watchwords sweeping through the U.N. command.

Reports from Chinese prisoner interrogations nonetheless continued to yield information about the massing of forces along the Yalu. MacArthur ignored this information, unconfirmed by allied air reconnaissance or agent reports, and on November 24 ordered his commanders to close on the Yalu. This was exactly what Mao had anticipated and what he wanted. His strategy was simple. Mao would allow the Americans to penetrate just so far before the vastly superior numbers of Chinese would attack the flanks, closing the trap with lightning speed and explosive combat.

On November 26, nearly 300,000 Chinese—fighting under the guise of "volunteers" to the North Korean army so as to maintain a semblance of Chinese neutrality—struck the U.N. flanks and front. A major portion of the attack was along the mountainous seam between the 8th Army and the X Corps, effectively preventing mutual support between the two commands. For a full day, senior commanders in Korea, Japan, and the United States refused to believe that such an enormous enemy attack was occurring. Commanders continued to accept their prior intelligence that the Chinese would not intervene and that no substantial Chinese units were in the vicinity. Not until the casualty figures started to roll in with reports of entire units killed, captured, or cut off from support did the realities of another intelligence failure begin to sink in. Troops on the front line, however, felt the impact immediately. Typical of the combat was what the 3d Battalion, 9th Infantry Regiment experienced when it attempted to break out of the Chinese encirclement on November 30. Running a gauntlet of more than six miles to escape encirclement, only 37 of more than 600 managed to escape.

By December 4, the American and U.N. forces on the western side of the peninsula were in full retreat, withdrawing from Pyongyang in central North Korea as they continued south. On the eastern front, the X Corps was experiencing even greater difficulty as the Chinese moved to encircle the entire command. Unable to continue the land withdrawal because of Chinese troops to their south, U.N. troops, led by U.S. Marines, fought their way south in freezing weather and mounting snowfall to the port of

Hungnam on the Sea of Japan. By Christmas Eve, more than 100,000 allied troops, 90,000 Korean refugees, and 17,500 vehicles were evacuated by sea and reinserted farther down the peninsula.

On December 23, General Walker was killed in a jeep accident while en route to visit the front lines. He was replaced by Lieutenant General Matthew B. Ridgway, who had to stop the Chinese immediately and defend Seoul. The Chinese Communists attacked the city on New Year's Eve and by January 4, 1951, again occupied the South Korean capital. Ridgway withdrew and by January 10 had established a fairly stable defense twenty-five miles south of the city. As had happened to the North Koreans during their invasion the previous summer, the Chinese began to outdistance their lines of supply and reinforcements.

The new 8th Army commander took firm charge of the U.N. forces. He quickly replaced or fired six of the eight U.S. division commanders and secured MacArthur's approval for the X Corps to become subordinate to his headquarters. Ridgway was even bolder than his predecessor in making low-level and behind-the-lines aerial reconnaissance to assess the battlefield and to gather his own intelligence. While news stories in the United States described the Chinese offensive as the worst defeat of American forces in history, Ridgway rallied his troops and reinforced with men and materials as he planned his counterattack. Less than a week after stalling the Chinese advance, the 8th Army moved northward. On March 14, Ridgway retook Seoul, forcing the Chinese to withdraw to positions north of the 38th parallel. The allies took up positions just south of the invisible line as maneuver warfare gave way to static combat that more closely resembled World War I trench fighting than the mobile operations of the past ten months.

Most of the intelligence activity now focused on the questioning of prisoners about Chinese intentions, supplies, and morale. At the same time, one of the few CIA agents still operational in North Korea provided another intelligence fiasco. In March 1951, the agent reported that Chinese soldiers and Korean civilians at Wonsan were dying of what appeared to be the bubonic plague.

U.N. soldiers had been immunized against smallpox and typhus but not against plague, which created the fear that the disease could spread across the lines and wipe out the allied force.

The United Nations inserted two teams of twenty-two South Koreans in the Chinese-held area to bring back a sick prisoner to be examined by Brigadier General Crawford F. Sams, the only person in MacArthur's headquarters qualified to diagnose the plague. None of the agents was ever heard from again. Six more attempts to air-drop teams into the area met with the same results. On March 13, Sams, accompanied by Lieutenant Eugene Clark, who had performed the reconnaissance at Inchon, rowed ashore from a navy destroyer. With more luck than skill, the two officers linked up with the original reporting agent and made their way into a village where Sams quickly discovered that hemorrhagic small-pox rather than the plague was the problem.

Sams and Clark returned safely to their boat and back to Japan with the good news. The officers' daring visit into North Korea in search of a "deadly epidemic" made its way into international headlines, which allowed the Chinese to distort the news stories to support their claims that the United States was waging germ warfare. American prisoners of war were tortured into signing confessions confirming the Communists' claims.

For the next two years, offensives and counteroffensives by each side did little except increase the ranks of dead and wounded. Along the front, 350,000 U.N. troops faced an enemy force of 350,000 Chinese and 140,000 North Koreans. Battles such as Bloody Ridge, Pork Chop Hill, Finger Ridge, Old Baldy, and Heartbreak Ridge resulted in negligible accomplishments, despite the bravery exhibited by the participants.

During the stalemate, the addition of Soviet-made jet fighters flown by North Korean and Chinese pilots failed to give the Communists an advantage. American pilots shot down the enemy in ratios of more than ten to one until the skies once again were clear of enemy air support. Meanwhile, the air force pounded targets in North Korea and leveled what was left of Pyongyang. Outside the North Korean capital, it bombed dikes and dams to flood farms and villages and limit agricultural production. U.N., and particularly American, air power ruled the skies, with the only controversy being over use of aircraft. Navy and Marine Corps airplanes proved responsive to the marines on the ground, but the U.S. Army claimed the air force was much more interested in producing "aces" from air-to-air combat than in attacking targets in the North or in providing close air support to the infantry. Service rivalries over aircraft and missions remained as hot in war as in peace.

Disputes over how to conduct the war occurred at other levels as well. General MacArthur complained privately and publicly about the constraints placed on him by Washington, making it clear that nothing short of total victory was satisfactory in his mind. Finally, on April 11, 1951, President Truman, no longer willing to tolerate MacArthur's disagreement with national policy or his insubordination, relieved him of duty. Ridgway assumed command of the U.N. forces, while Lieutenant General James A. Van Fleet became the 8th Army commander.

Both Ridgway and his successor, General Mark W. Clark, who replaced him in May 1952, were aware that Truman and the American people were not willing to use atomic weapons or to commit the necessary conventional resources to win the war. The Chinese had likewise discovered that their best efforts were not sufficient to push the U.N. forces off the peninsula. On July 10, 1951, the two sides had their first meeting at Kaesong, just south of the 38th parallel and northwest of Seoul, to begin truce negotiations. For weeks the negotiators argued about chair size, flag placement, and other minor issues not remotely associated with any actual peace settlement. At times, the two sides merely stared in silence at each other for as long as two hours. Negotiations ceased in August and did not resume until November 12 at the village of Panmunjon.

For more than eighteen months, the fruitless talks continued, with the primary issue being the voluntary repatriation of prisoners. The United Nations demanded that those prisoners not wishing to return to Communist Korea or China not be required to do so; while the Communists, not wanting to lose face by having their soldiers stay in the South, insisted they return. Meanwhile, along the front, soldiers of both sides continued to fight and die for territory measured in yards rather than miles.

Finally, on March 28, the Communists agreed to the exchange of sick and wounded prisoners, and in April to the voluntary repatriation of POWs. On July 17, 1953, the two belligerents signed a ceasefire agreement that provided a buffer between them of four kilometers, called the Demilitarized Zone (DMZ), very near the old 38th parallel boundary. During three years of warfare, more than 115,000 allies were killed. The United States suffered 54,246 dead, with another 103,000 wounded and more than 5,000 missing in action. U.N. estimates put the North Korean and Chinese casualties at 1.5 million, with 1 million Korean civilians on each side killed during the war and several million more left homeless. Considering the number of participants, the Korean "police action" was one of the bloodiest wars in history.

Three years of conflict ended where it began. The United States proved it would make a stand against Communist aggression, while at the same time it revealed that its efforts might not result in total victory. In Korea, the United States had attempted a "limited war," a new concept foreign to any rational military mind. The limited war produced neither victory nor resolution; a tie was the most it could claim.

Americans, providing no homecoming parades for their returning warriors, seemed to have forgotten about the Korean war almost before it was over. Along the DMZ today, Americans and South Koreans still face North Korean forces more than forty years after the ceasefire. A truce ended the war, but peace has yet to come to Korea.

★ 12 ★

The Only War We Had: Vietnam

The failure of the CIA to provide warnings about the North Korean attack in 1950 and, later, the Chinese entry into the war brought no punitive consequences to the agency. Ironically, its ineptitude led instead to more manpower, additional funding, and increased authority to conduct covert operations worldwide. The CIA reinstated OSS veterans of World War II and recruited more agents from the same eastern elites and Ivy League school network that had dominated the service since its beginnings. Soon the agency, headed and manned by self-professed "swashbucklers," was conducting operations outside the normal government chain of command.

For more than a decade following the Korean War, the CIA assisted in propping up friendly governments, overthrowing regimes considered hostile to the United States, and establishing new governments friendly to the West. In addition to direct military assistance, the CIA financially subsidized political leaders; recruited labor, business, youth, church, academic, and criminal leaders; and established radio stations and news services. Meanwhile, the arms race between the United States and the Soviet Union, which paralleled the two world powers' efforts to impose their ideas of government around the globe, offered great opportunity to gather and protect intelligence. The same elites who had affectionately labeled intelligence "the grand game" in earlier decades now contended they were in the "golden age of covert action."

The golden age, marked by tremendous successes and even greater failures, lasted only until questions of legality, morality, and efficiency tarnished the CIA's image and increased controls on its operations. Many details of the CIA, particularly the failures, during the golden age remain classified and probably will not be opened for public scrutiny until far into the next century.

Using the Korean War to increase its number of agents and its budget, the CIA enjoyed several intelligence successes while the conflict was still going on. During the early 1950s, Colonel Edward G. Lansdale and the CIA assisted the armed forces of the Philippines in resisting an effort by Communist Huk guerrillas to overthrow the government, and in 1953 the agency helped the Filipino government hold free elections, resulting in the selection of a pro-American candidate. Also in 1953, the CIA orchestrated a coup d'état in Iran that removed the Communist leadership of the country and restored the shah to power. In Guatemala, during the same year, the CIA backed a military junta that took over the government from a leftist reformer.*

Failures, too, plagued the CIA in the early 1950s. During the first two years of the decade, the CIA air-dropped cash, weapons, ammunition, communications gear, and other supplies to what it thought was the anti-Soviet underground in Poland. In December 1952, the Communist Polish government revealed that it had penetrated and controlled the so-called underground throughout the period of CIA support. At the same time, a joint CIA-British venture of sending agents and supplies into Albania proved even more of a disaster when Albanian Communists captured and executed more than 500 Western agents. The infamous British turncoat Kim Philby and his cohorts had kept the Albanians informed about each insertion and the internal organization of the entire operation.

Other CIA operations failed even without the treachery of internal moles. Agents in Hungary were captured or killed in 1956

---

*CIA actions in these countries, at the time labeled successes, ultimately led to complex difficulties, which in hindsight make the actions subject to reevaluation.

when the Soviets crushed the revolt. In Indonesia, a CIA plan to overthrow the Sukarno government failed in 1958. The following year, the Chinese Communists destroyed agency-trained and -armed guerrillas in Tibet.

While it experienced repeated failures in its covert operations, the CIA succeeded in the area of overhead reconnaissance. In 1956, the United States made its first U-2 aerial reconnaissance flights over the Soviet Union. The U-2 possessed a cruising altitude of 85,000 feet, a range of 3,000 miles, and the ability to fly over the entire Soviet Union beyond the range of Soviet antiair weapons. The spy plane carried cameras reputedly so powerful they could record vehicle license plates from more than 60,000 feet. Pilots for the U-2 flights were U.S. Air Force aviators "sheep-dipped" with fake discharges and new records as civilian contract pilots. Once the aviators completed a tour with the U-2s, they returned to the regular air force with gaps in their official records marked as "classified access only."

The U-2 flights produced vast amounts of intelligence about Soviet strategic weapons production and new navy and air force bases as well as providing previously unknown geographic information useful in map production. The Soviets, who knew about the flights but were powerless to stop them, complained bitterly to the United States about the invasion of their air space, but all they received was a denial that flights were taking place.

In the spring of 1960, the Soviets claimed that they had shot down an American spy plane. President Dwight Eisenhower, relying on CIA information that such an incident was impossible, publicly denied the report and the accusation of spying. A few days later, Nikita Khrushchev revealed the wreckage of a U-2 shot down on May 1 and paraded before the cameras the plane's pilot, Francis Gary Powers, who had failed to follow CIA orders to commit suicide rather than be captured. Powers also carried identification and other papers in violation of CIA procedures.

As a result of the Powers incident, the United States no longer sent U-2s over the Soviet Union but relied instead on overhead reconnaissance via satellite technology recently developed jointly by the CIA and the U.S. Air Force. Satellite reconnaissance provided a photographic overview of not only the Soviet Union but also China and other potential "hot spots."

CIA covert action produced another fiasco in 1961, involving Cuba. Fidel Castro, with the assistance of guerrilla leader Che Guevara, had begun an improbable revolution in the mountains in the early 1950s to overthrow the harsh dictatorship of Fulgencio Batista. The United States, officially staying out of the conflict, recognized the Castro government within a week of its January 1, 1959, takeover of the island.

Soon, however, the United States was denouncing Castro for his execution of opposition leaders and other heavy-handed practices. As many as 50,000 Cubans who opposed Castro sailed to Florida and settled in the United States, where some of them began planning to regain control of the island government. The United States denied Castro's demands for the return of several Batista government officials for trial.

U.S.-Cuban relations further deteriorated when Castro nationalized landholdings, hotels, refineries, and other businesses owned by American individuals and corporations. The United States limited exports to Cuba in October 1960 and severed diplomatic relations the following January. Castro, who had denied being a Communist during the revolution, turned to the Soviet Union for support.

By March 1961, the CIA actively supported exiled Cubans in their plan to depose Castro. On April 15, B-26s, owned and flown by the CIA, attacked airfields to destroy the Cuban fighter force. The pilots' cover story was that they were defectors from Castro's air force, but reporters discovered their true identity shortly after the first raid. President John Kennedy ordered the CIA to postpone a planned second air raid to finish off the Cuban fighter fleet until Cuban exiles, trained and armed by the CIA, could secure a beachhead on the Cuban coast at the Bay of Pigs. Despite intelligence leaks that led to the U.S. press's printing details about the invasion force's training and plans, 1,400 Cuban exiles boarded landing craft, so noisily they could be heard for miles, and headed for Cuba.

On April 17 a mix-up by the CIA in coordinating time zones with the U.S. Navy delayed air cover, forcing the exile flotilla to wait for hours offshore. Castro's warned and unopposed air force destroyed part of the invasion force before it landed. Over the next two days, the Cubans killed or captured most of its remaining members.

When the largest single disaster in CIA history was finally over, 114 invaders were dead and 1,189 were prisoners. Charges and countercharges filled Washington as everyone tried to place the blame on someone else. The embarrassment to the United States and the Kennedy administration was compounded when the president had to appeal unofficially to private American sources for the $62 million worth of medicine and food to ransom the prisoners from Cuba. A large shake-up in the CIA's leadership and authority followed, curtailing the agency's opportunities to swash-buckle.

The Soviet influence in Cuba continued to concern the Kennedy administration, which feared the Soviet Union might establish military bases and nuclear missile sites on the island. Kennedy directed the CIA to concentrate on Cuba to determine if the Soviets were delivering long-range weapons there. The CIA responded by compiling information on ship movements, from refugee reports of Cubans who recently had left the island, from agents within Cuba, and from U-2 aerial reconnaissance.

None of these sources revealed any unusual Soviet activity. In September 1962, the CIA's Board of National Estimates reported to the president that the Soviets definitely would not deploy missiles to Cuba. The only dissenter was CIA Director John McCone, who had been appointed to the position in the shake-up following the disastrous Bay of Pigs invasion. McCone, a former defense contractor with no intelligence training or experience, could convince no one in his own agency, much less the president, that the Soviets were deploying missiles to Cuba.

In a matter of weeks, the CIA's failure to provide early detection of the Soviet buildup in Cuba would lead to the brink of nuclear war between the United States and the Soviet Union. It would be the most dangerous direct confrontation between the two superpowers during the Cold War.

On October 14, an American U-2 reconnaissance flight, launched on the recommendation of military intelligence officers rather than the CIA, detected a Soviet missile site under con-struction 100 miles west of Havana near San Cristobal. Two days later, additional flights detected the assembly of Soviet IL-28 bombers at Cuban airfields. Kennedy immediately began mar-athon meetings with his civilian advisers, the Joint Chiefs of Staff, and the CIA. The chiefs, supported by the civilian advisers, wanted to make surgical air strikes to destroy the missile sites but could not guarantee the president they would be totally successful or that Soviet advisers and technicians would not be killed. The CIA advised the president that only a land invasion of Cuba would convince the Soviets to withdraw their missiles and bombers.

Kennedy followed neither the recommendations of the Joint Chiefs nor those of the CIA. On October 22, the president appeared on national television to announce that he was imposing a naval blockade on Cuba effective on the 24th. The quarantine was successful: The U.S. Navy boarded and checked all regular shipping before allowing vessels to proceed into Cuba. Khrushchev, not yet ready either materially or emotionally to initiate a nuclear war, "blinked" and ordered Soviet ships bearing additional arms to Cuba to turn back.

Over the next month, the Soviets recalled missiles and bombers from Cuba, while the United States, in a conciliatory measure, removed its missiles positioned in Turkey. American losses during the crisis amounted to a single U-2 and its pilot, shot down by the Cubans during a reconnaissance mission on October 27. By the end of November, the crisis was over; Kennedy had regained much of the prestige he had lost at the Bay of Pigs, and Khrushchev was soon ousted from office in disgrace.

During the following years, the CIA made several attempts to assassinate Castro through various means, including enlisting the cooperation of the Mafia and other underworld figures. None succeeded.* Despite the American blockade of Cuba during the

*Finally, President Ronald Reagan in 1981 issued Elective Order Number 12333, which states, "No person employed by or acting on behalf of the United States Government shall engage in, or conspire to engage in, assassination."

missile crisis and all the CIA's efforts to overthrow him, Castro remained in power.

While the CIA was getting most of the attention and funding during the "golden age of covert action" of the post-Korea decade, the armed service intelligence organizations were undergoing change. In 1949, the military combined strategic communications intelligence with communications security functions of the services to form the Armed Forces Security Agency (AFSA), which evolved into the National Security Agency (NSA) in 1952. As NSA, the organization became a civilian agency of the Department of Defense.

The armed services lost more of their intelligence missions with the formation of the Defense Intelligence Agency (DIA) in 1961. The DIA, which still exists, assumed the responsibility for intelligence collection requirements, current intelligence production, operation of the military attaché system, and the production of the National Intelligence Estimate.* This concentration of intelligence responsibility at the Department of Defense level left the army, navy, and air force with limited roles in intelligence training, internal security and counterintelligence, combat intelligence, and technical intelligence regarding tactical weapons, mapping, and charting.

With this reorganization, each of the three services adjusted and adapted its intelligence organizations. Within the navy, acoustic intelligence to track foreign submarines became a priority. The air force placed emphasis on overhead reconnaissance, eventually regaining control of reconnaissance aircraft like the U-2s and their replacement, the SR-71s. Satellite reconnaissance, however, was placed under the National Reconnaissance Office, which, although directed by an undersecretary of the air force, is supervised by a board that includes the CIA director.

Within the army, several changes in the names and structure of

---

*The National Intelligence Estimate is a strategic estimate of capabilities, vulnerabilities, and probable courses of action of foreign nations. It is produced at the national level as a composite of the views of the intelligence community.

intelligence organizations occurred in the decade following the Korean War. On July 1, 1962, the Army Intelligence and Security (AIS) branch became an official part of the regular army; on July 1, 1967, it changed its name to the Military Intelligence (MI) branch. This organization created a permanent military occupation specialty (MOS) for enlisted personnel and officers serving in MI units and detachments. These units, assigned down to division level, remained at less than full strength, however, with their personnel frequently assigned nonintelligence duties such as mess officer and fund drive chairman. Even if they were few in number, little respected, and often misused, the army at last had military intelligence personnel supposedly dedicated to the needs of combat commanders. It was not long before actions in Southeast Asia tested the system.

The Southeast Asia region that eventually became Vietnam has rarely seen as much as a decade without bloodshed. In the nineteenth century, Western invaders entered the area, and after more than twenty years of warfare France took complete control of the region in 1881. With its colonialism so entrenched in the country it renamed Indochina, France was able to send 100,000 Vietnamese to Europe to fight in World War I under the tricolor.

During World War II, the Japanese occupied Indochina. The French offered no resistance to the occupation, but Vietnamese Communists, known as the Viet Minh, under the leadership of Ho Chi Minh, mounted an armed revolt in the northern part of the country. Ho, supported by advisers and arms from the American OSS, declared Vietnam an independent republic when Japan surrendered to the Allies. When the French ignored the declaration of independence and moved back to regain their prewar control, the Viet Minh merely changed their enemy from the Japanese to the French and continued the fight.

Ho submitted at least eight formal appeals asking the United States for support against the French. The Americans, fearing Ho's past Communist sympathies, answered by providing economic and military aid to France. Always more a nationalist than a Communist, Ho turned to China, and later to the Soviet Union. Had the United States supported Ho, or at least remained neutral, the next thirty years of warfare might have been avoided.

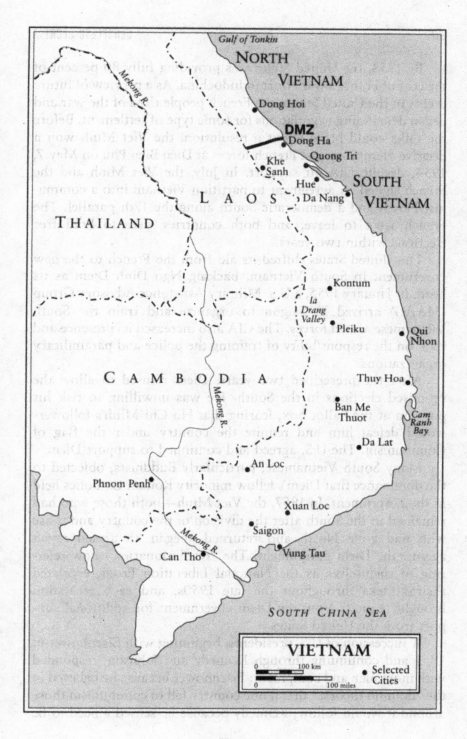

Gulf of Tonkin

NORTH
VIETNAM

• Dong Hoi

DMZ
• Dong Ha

Khe • Quong Tri
Sanh •

Hue • **SOUTH**
Da Nang • **VIETNAM**

LAOS

THAILAND

Kontum •

*Ia
Drang
Valley*
Pleiku •

Qui •
Nhon

CAMBODIA

Thuy Hoa •

Ban Me •
Thuot
*Cam
Ranh
Bay*

Da Lat •

An Loc •

Phnom Penh •

Xuan Loc •

Saigon •

Mekong R.

Can Tho • Vung Tau •

SOUTH CHINA SEA

Mekong R.

VIETNAM

0 _____ 100 km
0 _____ 100 miles
• Selected
Cities

By 1953, the United States was providing fully 80 percent of the cost of France's war effort in Indochina. As a preview of future events in the United States, the French people tired of the war and began demanding negotiations for some type of settlement. Before the talks could bring about a resolution, the Viet Minh won a decisive victory against French forces at Dien Bien Phu on May 7, 1954, despite CIA air support. In July, the Viet Minh and the French signed an agreement to partition Vietnam into a communist North and a democratic South along the 17th parallel. The French were to leave, and both countries were to hold free elections within two years.

The United States shifted its aid from the French to the new government in South Vietnam, backing Ngo Dinh Diem as its head. In January 1955, a U.S. Military Assistance Advisory Group (MAAG) arrived in Saigon to organize and train the South Vietnamese armed forces. The CIA also increased its presence and took on the responsibility of training the police and paramilitary organizations.

After the prescribed two years, Diem refused to allow the promised elections in the South. He was unwilling to risk his position at the ballot box, fearing that Ho Chi Minh's followers would defeat him and reunite the country under the flag of Communism. The U.S. agreed and continued to support Diem.

Many South Vietnamese, particularly Buddhists, objected to the dominance that Diem's fellow minority Roman Catholics held in the government. In 1957, the Viet Minh—both those who had remained in the South after the division of the country and those who had gone North and returned—began an armed revolt against the Diem government. The "revolutionaries," now referring to themselves as the National Liberation Front, escalated their attacks throughout the late 1950s, and each escalation brought requests from the Diem government for additional support from the United States.

A succession of U.S. presidents, beginning with Eisenhower in 1955 and continuing through Kennedy and Johnson, responded with more men and equipment: Eisenhower because he believed in the "domino theory," that if one country fell to communism those around it would follow; Kennedy because he sensed a need to be "tough on communism"; and Johnson because, as he later admitted, he did not want to be the first U.S. president to lose a war.

The year 1959 marked a turning point in Vietnam's history. That was the year that the North Vietnamese began developing a supply route, later known as the Ho Chi Minh Trail, to South Vietnam along a series of roads and trails in Laos and Cambodia. It was also the year that the Americans suffered their first casualties in what would become the longest war in U.S. history.

Another pivotal year was 1963, when the CIA and President Kennedy supported the overthrow of the Diem government on November 1—though both later disavowed approving Diem's assassination. A succession of regimes followed, with officials and the military focused on controlling the government instead of combating the Communist rebels, or Viet Cong, as the Americans and South Vietnamese referred to the guerrillas.

In 1964, with the Viet Cong controlling well over half of the countryside, President Johnson authorized secret operations—advised by the U.S. military and undertaken by the South Vietnamese—against North Vietnam to gather intelligence and conduct guerrilla operations against the Communists. Operation 34-A produced little and resulted in the death or capture of most of its operatives. Recently disclosed evidence indicates that Communist agents infiltrated 34-A, making its activities anything but secret.

U.S. involvement in Southeast Asia continued to intensify when, on August 2, North Vietnamese patrol boats attacked the U.S. Navy destroyer *Maddox*, patrolling in international waters in the Gulf of Tonkin thirty miles off the coast. The North Vietnamese fired at least two torpedoes at the *Maddox* and the navy sank one of the attacking boats during the twenty-one-minute-long engagement. Two days later, on the evening of August 4, the *Maddox* and the *Turner Joy*, on patrol in the Tonkin Gulf, picked up radar contacts they identified as North Vietnamese patrol boats. Following the spotting, the ships, supported by aircraft from the carrier *Ticonderoga*, fired and maneuvered for more than four hours, though they could not confirm an attack by enemy vessels. Later speculation blamed the radar blips on the weather.

Even though the Tonkin Gulf provocation may never have

occurred, President Johnson retaliated on August 5 with air strikes against naval bases, patrol boats, and oil storage depots along 100 miles of the North Vietnamese coast. The strike's sixty-four sorties damaged or destroyed twenty-five patrol boats and more than 90 percent of the petroleum sites in the area. North Vietnamese gunners shot down two navy planes, resulting in the first navy pilot death and the first navy POW of the expanding conflict. On August 7, the U.S. Congress relinquished its war-making powers to the president by authorizing him to "take all necessary measures to repel any armed attack against forces of the United States...and to assist any member or protocol state..." of applicable treaties. The Gulf of Tonkin Resolution provided Johnson the leeway to expand the role of the U.S. military in Vietnam. The resolution received overwhelming support, passing the House of Representatives 416 to 0 and the Senate 88 to 2.

U.S. armed forces in Vietnam quickly rose to 60,000 by mid-1965 and continued to escalate to a peak of more than 543,000 by 1969. Entire military intelligence units joined MI advisers, in Vietnam since 1962, as American combat brigades and divisions arrived in country. The first U.S. military intelligence ground units to report to Vietnam accompanied the 9th Marine Expeditionary Brigade when it landed to secure the Da Nang air base on March 8, 1965. In May, the army's 172d MI Detachment arrived with the 173d Airborne Brigade. Other army divisions and brigades, as well as marine, air force, and naval units, soon followed, adding to the number of dedicated intelligence units in country.

Overseeing the U.S. buildup was the commander of the Military Assistance Command Vietnam (MACV), General William C. Westmoreland, who had assumed the position on June 20, 1964. Heading Westmoreland's joint staff intelligence section was Major General Joseph A. McChristian. Recognizing the large number of different and complex intelligence organizations spread across Vietnam, he created four "combined intelligence" centers within his J-2 organization. These centers included intelligence, interrogation, document exploitation, and material exploitation branches. Computer hardware and supporting software, elementary by today's standards, assisted the centers in analyzing the massive amount of data they received from the plethora of U.S. and Vietnamese intelligence sources.

The CIA's role in Vietnam also continued to increase as the agency added agents and increased its budget. Few official records have been declassified about this period of the agency's history, but those in Vietnam who observed CIA operations saw luxury villas rented for offices and personal quarters, as well as free-flowing money spent on local agents whose loyalties were often in question—but few significant intelligence contributions.

Without a doubt, the combined intelligence-gathering and -analyzing assets in Vietnam exceeded those of any previous American conflict. The intelligence organization was adequate, and its ability to process massive amounts of raw intelligence was superior to what it had been in earlier wars. Intelligence-gathering equipment on the ground, at sea, and in the air had reached the zenith of the current technology. Yet the intelligence community in Vietnam failed to warn the allied forces of a single enemy offensive and never gained the confidence of the forces it was supposed to support, constantly underestimating the numbers of Viet Cong (VC) and the North Vietnamese army (NVA) as well as their will to fight. Ultimately, with their abundance of organizations and information, the various military intelligence factions in Vietnam issued dozens of daily, weekly, and monthly estimates of probable enemy actions, on the theory that surely one of the guesses would be correct. Commanders in the field learned that the only information they could rely on was what they saw or gathered themselves.*

While the mission of the United States in Vietnam was never clear, the objectives of the Viet Cong and North Vietnamese army were. As early as 1952, they documented their purpose, stating, "The ultimate aim of the Vietnamese Communist leadership is to

---

*In all fairness to military intelligence in Vietnam, it should be remembered that neither intelligence officers nor Military Assistance Command Vietnam—or anyone else, for that matter—knew exactly what the mission really was. No overall purpose or objective for U.S. troops in Vietnam was ever defined by the succession of American presidents who shepherded the war.

install Communist regimes in the whole of Vietnam, in Laos, and in Cambodia." Although some observers saw the conflict as a civil war in South Vietnam and compared the National Liberation Front to the revolutionary army of George Washington, nothing could have been further from the truth. The VC were puppets of the Hanoi government, used in whatever manner Hanoi deemed necessary to bring the South under the control of North Vietnam.

The North Vietnamese basically relied on the same strategy against the Americans and the Army of South Vietnam (ARVN) that they had successfully employed against the French. Their effort to conquer the South revolved around a three-phase plan. In Phase One, the insurgents remained on the defensive while conducting guerrilla and terrorist operations to control as much of the population as possible. In Phase Two, regular military forces formed and attacked isolated government outposts. In the climactic Phase Three, large units undertook a full offensive to defeat the government force and to establish full control over the civilian population. The concluding step of the final phase was *khoi nghai,* a general uprising of the people to assist in the overthrow of the government.

Throughout the war, the VC and NVA were consistently able to accomplish the first two phases. Despite overwhelming U.S. superiority in firepower, mobility, and technology, the Communists conducted guerrilla warfare at will and frequently massed for small-scale attacks against ARVN and American units and bases. Whenever they felt threatened, they either withdrew to sanctuaries across the border in Cambodia or changed into civilian clothes and blended in with the local population. Hanoi was patient in its war to conquer the South, willing to lose over more time than the Americans were prepared to spend to win. While the United States won every major battle for many years, the ultimate victory belonged to the Communists.

Despite their patience, the Communists did mount three major offensives in an attempt to gain an early victory. When the first U.S. units arrived in 1965, they were consistently successful in combat with the Viet Cong. The VC had difficulty escaping the helicopter mobility of the Americans, and their best defense against ground attacks supported by artillery and air was to withdraw as quickly as possible.

Intelligence failures in the early months of U.S. ground forces involvement centered on the inability to find the enemy. Most contacts were the result of patrolling by American units, which produced engagements marked by intense firefights that lasted only as long as it took for the VC to break contact and escape. An indication of the lack of intelligence about the location of the VC during this period was that they initiated the contact in more than 65 percent of the engagements, usually by ambush. Intelligence on enemy locations did not improve as the war progressed. Within a year after the arrival of U.S. combat units, the number of engagements initiated by the enemy rose to 88 percent and in some regions as much as 95 percent.

Intelligence about the type and size of enemy forces was as rare as data on their locations. In each of the three major Communist offensives, American military intelligence failed to provide warning or to have any idea about the size of the mounting enemy forces. When the Hanoi government recognized in 1965 that its Viet Cong subordinates were losing ground, it decided to execute a plan of escalation. Beginning in 1964, the Communists had infiltrated regular army forces from North Vietnam into Cambodian marshaling areas. Late in 1965, Hanoi committed these NVA units into South Vietnam in an attempt to escalate the war into Phase Three.

On October 19, the NVA, assisted by local VC, attacked the U.S. Special Forces at Plei Me in the Central Highlands, almost overrunning the camp before ground and air units of the 1st Cavalry Division could fly to the rescue. Following the battle, the 1st Cavalry continued operations in the Ia Drang Valley, where the division's 1st Battalion, 7th Cavalry Regiment of 430 soldiers was ambushed at its helicopter landing zone by 2,700 members of the NVA 66th and 33d divisions on November 14. The Americans, taking heavy casualties, were saved only by intense artillery support and air strikes. Being surprised or ambushed by small groups of VC was nothing new to the Americans; being almost wiped out by a far superior regular North Vietnamese army force was. Like the unannounced Chinese entry into the Korean War, the size of the NVA force was a surprise to American soldiers.

Units that reinforced the 7th Cavalry were also ambushed as they continued operations in the Ia Drang. Despite heavy losses, the American commanders were satisfied with the action because the enemy had suffered substantial casualties by finally standing to fight rather than running away. The NVA, despite its losses, was also content with the outcome. It had proven that it could sustain a protracted battle against the Americans and their supporting firepower. Although the NVA had determined that Phase Three was not yet within its grasp and had been forced to withdraw back into Cambodia, the Communist leadership had learned valuable lessons. Ho Chi Minh ordered his troops to fall back to phases One and Two combat levels, explaining that they could wait for ten or twenty years to wear down the Americans' will to fight. He added that eventually the war would be won as much on the streets and campuses of the United States as it would be on the battlefields of Vietnam.

Between the time of the 1965 battles in the Ia Drang and 1967, American operations in Vietnam were characterized by search and destroy missions and armed reconnaissance efforts to find and eliminate the Communists. Viet Cong guerrillas continued their terrorism, murdering and torturing civilians, and filling the rice paddies and jungles with booby traps to maim pursuers. Pitched battles only occurred when U.S. units encountered NVA units. Mostly, however, the VC and NVA avoided contact unless everything was in their favor for a quick victory. As soon as a fight was over, or more often during the actual battle, the Communist soldiers melted back into the jungle or to their cross-border havens. The Americans took villages and hilltops at great expense in blood and munitions only to leave them behind for the enemy to reoccupy when the battle concluded. The U.S. Army and Marine Corps won every major engagement, but North Vietnam continued to replace men and resupply its forces with equipment and arms from China and the Soviet Union.

Bombing operations during this period continued in both the North and South, but air force and naval air operations in North Vietnam were hindered by various halts and other restrictions unlike any other in the history of warfare. Bombing targets had to be approved by the secretary of defense, the State Department, and the White House. President Johnson was often the final authority for a single airplane strike on a minor target.

Most of Hanoi, including its military targets, was off limits, as were the major port at Haiphong and the railway link with China. American pilots observed missiles and antiaircraft guns being shipped in by train or unloaded from freighters but were allowed to attack only those weapons deployed into defensive or offensive positions. Not until the major bombing offensive of Operation Linebacker II in late 1972 did the bombing of the North have any significant role in the war. All the while, Hanoi manipulated the bombing damage to gain support within the antiwar movement in the United States and around the world. In North Vietnam itself, the bombings united the population in support of the war effort. The bombings also provided a prime source of the Communists' most significant bargaining chips during the peace negotiations: Most of the POWs freed by Hanoi at the end of U.S. participation in the war were air crew members.

While the intelligence involved in target selection in the North was rarely accurately tested because of the many self-imposed political barriers, bombing was freer in the South. Much of the exact nature of acquiring targets in South Vietnam is still classified, but the results paint a picture of failure. More tons of explosives were dropped on, and near, South Vietnam than were expended in all theaters of World War II. Almost three-quarters of a ton of bombs were dropped for every living person—friendly or enemy—in the entire country.

Even so, the war plodded along into 1968, but a resolution to the conflict seemed no nearer than it had been in 1965. Military intelligence continued to create massive numbers of reports and analyses without any real understanding of, or knowledge about, the enemy. In January 1968, military intelligence reported that the enemy might try to take advantage of the upcoming Vietnamese lunar New Year holiday of Tet but that no major offensive was possible or imminent.

American intelligence had failed to detect the Communist buildup of men and equipment across South Vietnam and in

Cambodia as the VC and NVA once again prepared to move into Phase Three of combat. So confident were the American and ARVN commanders that Tet '68 would be nothing more than a traditional celebration that more than half of South Vietnam's 730,000-man army was granted holiday home leave. On January 30, the Communists launched their largest offensive of the war. Surprise was total as they attacked Saigon, Hue, Quang Tri, Da Nang, Kontom, and other major cities in South Vietnam. Of forty-four provincial capitals, thirty-six came under attack, and ten were briefly occupied.

Their surprise had been complete, and they held on to parts of Hue for almost a month, but the VC and NVA were no match for the Americans in direct combat. The Tet Offensive ended as a total defeat for the Communists. There had been no *khnoi nghai,* or rising up of the people, to support the offensive. In fact, in Hue the VC and NVA had murdered 5,000 South Vietnamese they considered "political enemies."

Much of the coverage of the Tet Offensive by the American media centered on a suicide squad of fifteen sappers, who penetrated the grounds of the U.S. embassy in Saigon and killed five before they themselves were killed. Across Vietnam, 32,000 Viet Cong were killed and 5,800 captured, casualties so severe that the VC ceased to be a viable force. Some North Vietnamese replacements were later brought in, but the primary purpose of the Viet Cong after Tet was to lend credibility to the Communist claims that a civil war was raging in the South.

American losses during the offensive were less than 1,000, with ARVN battle deaths numbering 2,800. The Communist defeat on the battlefield had been complete in the short term, but in an amazing turn of events, Hanoi was able to move closer to overall victory in the long run. The offensive was brought into the living rooms of the war-weary American people via their television screens, and its psychological impact transformed the Communist debacle on the battlefield into a political victory on the streets of the United States.*

---

*With the passage of time and increased access to North Vietnamese leaders and records, more and more evidence indicates that the Commu-

In the end, the impact of Tet was decided neither on the battlefield nor in the political centers of Hanoi, Saigon, or Washington. Instead, the decisive voice came from the television studios of CBS News. On February 27, 1968, Walter Cronkite, America's most trusted newsperson, delivered the deepest knife-in-the-back to the American military that has ever come from a "friendly" source when he decided to influence rather than report events.

Instead of accurately reporting the facts about the U.S. rout of the VC during Tet, Cronkite delivered an address that Hanoi could not have written better when he said, "We have been too often disappointed by the optimism of the American leaders.... To say that we are closer to victory today is to believe, in the face of the evidence, the optimists who have been wrong in the past.... To say that we are mired in stalemate seems the only realistic, yet unsatisfactory conclusion.... It is increasingly clear to this reporter that the only rational way out will be to negotiate, not as victors, but as an honorable people who lived up to their pledge to defend democracy, and did the best they could."

Following the Tet Offensive, the NVA and the few surviving VC again withdrew to their sanctuaries deep in the jungles. Tet had taught them two important lessons: They were still unable to achieve Phase Three against the superior Americans, and they could attain much better results, with far fewer casualties, by continuing phases One and Two operations while the U.S. press and campus demonstrations worked in their favor to end the war.

The American military could only continue the war as directed by the political leaders in Washington. While the armed forces were impotent in combating the peace movement at home, they could and did try innovative technological devices to find and destroy the elusive enemy, such as fielding various detection equipment. Military intelligence personnel dropped motion and audio sensors, costing up to $10,000 each, into the jungle from the air or had ground patrols place them along trails and supply

---

nist objective was not an actual Phase Three victory but rather the continued erosion of America's will to persevere in the war. If that is the case, they certainly attained their goal.

routes. They also mounted devices in aircraft that supposedly could detect the enemy by their body heat. Few of the sensors worked for any length of time, if at all, and more often than not they detected only flocks of birds or groups of monkeys. In the end, this high tech, high-cost intelligence effort accomplished little except to expend combat resources.

The CIA and the U.S. Army Special Forces formed various other intelligence-gathering organizations throughout the war with varying degrees of success and failure. Civilian Irregular Defense Groups (CIDG), organized as early as 1962, prepared the local populace to defend their villages against the Viet Cong. When composed of ethnic South Vietnamese, CIDG units were easily and often infiltrated by the VC, making them, at best, worthless. On the other hand, when composed of ethnic minorities, such as the Montagnards, the CIDGs were extremely successful, more because of the Montagnards' traditional hatred of all Vietnamese, North or South, than for any other reason. The Special Forces–sponsored Studies and Observations Group (SOG), which had conducted Operation 34-A, also sponsored various other clandestine activities in North Vietnam and across the border into Laos* and Cambodia.

In 1967, the U.S. military, the State Department, and the CIA initiated the Civil Operations and Revolutionary Development Support (CORDS) program. Part of CORDS focused on civic action and the local militias to improve village security and quality of life. Another part of CORDS, the Phoenix Program, gathered intelligence to target Viet Cong leaders and suspected sympathizers. Phoenix, while achieving moderate success, received wide criticism for its abuse of prisoners and free use of assassination.

None of the technology or programs had any great influence

---

*More than two million tons of bombs were dropped on Laos, mostly on the Ho Chi Minh Trail, from 1965 to 1973. This bombing, and various other operations by the CIA and Special Forces against the Communist Pathet Lao, was kept secret from the American public until late 1969.

on the basic war in the jungles between infantrymen of each side. The intelligence activities that had the greatest impact and paid the greatest dividends were perhaps the simplest and easily the least expensive. As army separate brigades and divisions arrived in Vietnam, their commanders recognized that traditional ground and air cavalry were not sufficient in providing viable reconnaissance and intelligence. Long Range Reconnaissance Patrol (LRRP) units were formed on a provisional basis to field six-man patrols to penetrate deep into enemy-held areas and provide information and targeting data. These LRRPs, pronounced "lurps," were so successful in gathering intelligence and eliminating enemy soldiers that the army formally recognized them in the fall of 1967, providing them official unit designations. In February 1969, the LRRP companies and detachments were redesignated as ranger units of the 75th Infantry.

The Marine Corps arrived in Vietnam more prepared than the army for intelligence-gathering patrols with their Force Reconnaissance (Force Recon) Companies already formed and trained. Navy Sea, Air, and Land (SEAL) teams also conducted successful reconnaissance operations. The greatest obstacle for the LRRPs, Force Recon, and the SEALs consisted of convincing the various levels of intelligence officers to believe the information gathered. Higher headquarters often discounted intelligence gained by direct observation at great risk to small patrols, especially if the information contradicted what they had already assessed as the enemy situation and intentions.

The successes of a few elite units did not, however, influence the direction of the war. After the 1968 Tet Offensive, the American political leadership and public did not seek victory but rather pursued "peace with honor"—with very little consideration for the "honor." President Johnson, himself a political casualty of Tet, announced his decision in March 1968 not to seek reelection. Richard Nixon won the presidency with vague promises to end the war as he and his foreign policy adviser, Henry Kissinger, started peace talks with the North Vietnamese. The president also began a strategy of "détente" to promote harmony with the Soviets in hopes of their encouraging Hanoi to agree to a peaceful settlement. In the fall of 1969, Nixon began to withdraw ground combat troops from Vietnam while attempting to appease the protest groups with a lottery draft system.

Nonetheless, the protest movement stepped up its antiwar and antimilitary efforts. When U.S. newspapers and television learned in late 1969 of the massacre of more than 300 civilians at the village of My Lai, the various protest factions portrayed this isolated occurrence as normal operating procedure for the American armed forces.

Despite the rising number of Americans who professed to be against the war, President Nixon continued efforts to bring the conflict to a resolution that would not abandon the South Vietnamese to the Communists. In April 1970, Nixon authorized large-scale cross-border operations into Cambodia to sever the Ho Chi Minh Trail and to destroy the supply and refitting bases that served the NVA. The operation was a huge success in destroying enemy soldiers and equipment but served only to increase the war protests on American campuses and streets.

A few months later, Nixon approved one of the most dramatic operations of the war. On November 21, 1970, a joint Army–Air Force team conducted a raid to rescue American POWs held at the Son Tay prison in North Vietnam. On November 24, Secretary of Defense Melvin Laird held a press conference to announce the details of an "operation that took place north of the 19th parallel." Laird explained that a raid had been conducted on a prison camp "approximately 20 miles west of Hanoi" with the purpose of "rescuing as many of our prisoners as possible."

Laird introduced the army and air force commanders of the raid to the press. Excitement and anticipation were building in the briefing room before Laird, several minutes deep into his briefing, announced, "Regrettably, the rescue team discovered that the camp had recently been vacated. No prisoners were found."

The defense secretary explained that for "security reasons" he could not discuss details of the raid. During the question period that followed the briefing, a reporter summed up the operation with a question to Laird. "On whom do you blame the intelligence failure?" he asked.

Without a doubt, the raid on Son Tay was a failure in that it did not accomplish its mission. Although Laird and other Pentagon officials later made the excuse that overhead reconnaissance could not "see through the roofs of buildings," there obviously should have been other means of confirming the presence or absence of prisoners. The irony, however, is that of all the intelligence endeavors during the war, the Son Tay raid was probably the best planned and executed and, in that respect, one of the most successful.

Son Tay was selected for two reasons: because it was the only known site where POWs were held outside heavily defended Hanoi, and because overhead photos, agent reports, and other sources that remain classified revealed that seventy or more prisoners were there, sixty-three of whom were identified by name and service. Planners constructed exact replicas of the camp at Eglin Air Force Base, Florida, for rehearsals and assembled a team of the army's best Special Forces and rangers along with top air force pilots and support personnel.

Quite simply, Son Tay should have worked and likely would have had it had been conducted earlier. A series of delays based on weather and political indecision on the part of the White House, however, postponed the raid until after the POWs had been moved. The raid itself, supported by wide-scale bombing across North Vietnam as a diversion, was a complete surprise to the enemy. Even though some of the army raiders were mistakenly landed in darkness 400 meters from the actual camp and became engaged in a heavy firefight, the NVA were so unprepared for such an action that the rescuers were still able to confirm the absence of prisoners and escape unscathed. The failure of the operation did not lie with the raiders but rather with an intelligence system that had been unable to determine that the POWs had been moved months earlier.*

The Son Tay raid was successful in boosting the morale of those Americans still serving in Vietnam, and the worldwide

---

*There is evidence that U.S. intelligence suspected that the POWs might have been moved from Son Tay because of flooding of a nearby river. They were unable to confirm these suspicions, and apparently Nixon felt the chance to free a large number of POWs was worth the risk of another intelligence failure.

attention the operation had placed on the Communists caused the
North Vietnamese to ease somewhat their brutal treatment of the
POWs. However, Son Tay was nowhere near significant enough to
make a long-term impact on the declining spirit of the American
military in South Vietnam, which was being further eroded by the
protest movement back home and the open visits to and support of
Hanoi by American entertainers, journalists, and academic
leaders. U.S. military personnel could not achieve a clear-cut
victory because of the political limits placed on them, yet they
feared the consequences of abandoning their South Vietnamese
allies.

By 1971, many U.S. ground units had withdrawn, leaving the
South Vietnamese, supported by U.S. artillery and air power, to
assume the combat role. Most U.S. intelligence-gathering units
remained in country, but the South Vietnamese could take little
advantage of what information was available because their ranks
had been infiltrated by the enemy. In February 1971, South
Vietnamese units, without U.S. advisers or support, crossed the
border into Laos to cut the Ho Chi Minh Trail and to destroy
NVA sanctuaries. The North Vietnamese army learned of the
offensive through their agents in South Vietnamese intelligence
and was able to prepare a massive trap for the invading force.
South Vietnamese casualties neared 50 percent and would have
gone much higher if U.S. air power had not come to the rescue.

By 1972, fewer than 95,000 Americans remained in Vietnam
compared to 535,000 only three years earlier—and only 6,000 of
those were actual combat troops. Hanoi, for the third time,
decided the circumstances were right to escalate into Phase Three.
On March 30, the NVA launched a coordinated attack of twelve
divisions, supported by artillery and tanks, into the northern
portion of South Vietnam and the Central Highlands. Once again
the Communist attack came as a complete surprise to American
and ARVN military intelligence. The Easter Offensive drove deep
into South Vietnam, but once again the South Vietnamese populace did not rally to the Communists. U.S. air power supported the
South Vietnamese and also increased its bombing of North
Vietnam. The United States also finally mined the Haiphong
harbor. It was midsummer before the South Vietnamese were able

to stop the advancing NVA, and several more months passed before the situation stabilized.

Peace negotiations resumed in earnest following the Easter Offensive. Kissinger and Le Duc Tho, the North Vietnamese representative, came to a tentative agreement in October 1972, but the South Vietnamese did not concur, causing the angered Communists to withdraw from the negotiations. Nixon, following his reelection in November by a large majority, resumed heavy bombing of the North and quickly brought the Communists back to the bargaining table.

The Paris Peace Accords were signed on January 31, 1973, by the United States and North Vietnam. South Vietnam refused to sign but did not oppose the agreement. Over the next few months, Hanoi returned 591 American POWs, and by the end of March the few remaining U.S. troops departed Vietnam, ending more than ten years of military action there. The last Americans returned from Vietnam by air to bases on the West Coast. They arrived mostly in the middle of the night and were met by no bands or parades. The more than 2.7 million Americans who had served in Vietnam, and the war itself, would trouble the conscience of the United States for future decades.

Only a Defense Attaché Office and a few marine guards remained in Saigon. Without the assistance of the U.S. military, South Vietnam was doomed to fall to the Communists eventually. When the U.S. Congress passed a series of bills in 1974 limiting financial and equipment support to the South Vietnamese, their fate was sealed. Despite the empty promises made in the peace agreements, the Communists continued their plans to occupy all of Vietnam. The U.S. abandonment of the South made execution of those plans all that much easier.

In January 1975, North Vietnam again entered into Phase Three, with an overall plan for a two-year offensive to defeat the South, but it took only three months for the Communists to overrun the entire country. On April 30, South Vietnam surrendered, and the last Americans were airlifted from the roof of the Saigon embassy to offshore navy ships. Unlike the earlier major offensives, the final one was no surprise to either South Vietnamese or American intelligence. The end of South Vietnam was inevitable; the only surprise was the short duration of its final defense.

America's longest and most divisive war left more than 58,000 of its finest dead. Another 2,000 are still missing in action. Vietnamese losses are estimated in the range of 2 to 3 million. The Communists sent hundreds of thousands of South Vietnamese to "reeducation centers," more akin to concentration camps than schools. Thousands more South Vietnamese boarded leaky boats and rafts to freedom. Peace was not lasting for the victors either. By 1978, they were in combat against China.

★ 13 ★

Weekend Wars: Grenada, Panama, and More

No more Vietnams" became the watchword for the American public and political establishment in the postwar years. The military, including all aspects of military intelligence, was looked upon with suspicion and blamed for the problems and failures of the war in Southeast Asia. Regardless of the popularity of the antiwar, antimilitary movement, however, the United States as a world power continued to assume responsibilities to preserve democratic freedoms abroad. While avoiding conflicts that might escalate into "another Vietnam," the United States reacted to crises and made stands when necessary—now through short confrontations, or "weekend wars." Unfortunately, failures in military intelligence would continue to plague each and every military operation.

The involvement of the United States in limited offensive and defensive actions actually began before the conclusion of the Vietnam Conflict. During the Six Day War in the Middle East, Israeli aircraft and torpedo boats attacked the U.S.S. *Liberty* in international waters fourteen miles off the Sinai peninsula in the Mediterranean Sea on June 8, 1967. The *Liberty*, a converted freighter used by the U.S. Navy and the National Security Agency as a signal intelligence platform, was hit by rockets, napalm, and machine-gun fire for more than two hours. Lifeboats prepared for launching by the American sailors were machine-gunned on the deck by the Israelis. Although a large American flag flew from the mast and the vessel was clearly marked as a ship of the United States, the Israelis continued their attack. Before they withdrew from pounding the defenseless *Liberty* and her crew of 297, the Israelis had killed thirty-four Americans and wounded 171 others.

During the attack, the crew of the *Liberty* requested air support from a nearby carrier. Planes were dispatched, then mysteriously recalled. This was only the beginning of a series of cover-ups, by either destroying information or classifying it to restrict access, to prevent bad feelings by the American public against the government of Israel.

Israel's excuse for the attack was that the 455-foot, 10,680-ton *Liberty* had been mistaken for the 275-foot, 2,640-ton Egyptian transport *El Quesir*; the Israeli pilots and boat crews claimed not to have seen the U.S. flag on the ship's mast. Eventually, Israel apologized for the incident and provided more than $3 million in compensation to the families of the dead. Many years since the assault on the *Liberty*, some evidence indicates that the Israelis launched the attack to conceal the fact that they, and not the Egyptians, initiated the Six Day War, while still other reports indicate that the *Liberty* was attacked because it was passing intelligence to the Egyptians. There is also evidence that the CIA received warnings from the Israelis to keep the signal intelligence ship out of the area but did not pass along the information to the navy. Whatever the real reasons for the attack, the United States accepted the Israeli excuse of a mix-up in target identification.

Less than a year later, another incident occurred on the other side of the world involving a signal intelligence ship. On January 23, 1968, the U.S.S. *Pueblo* was collecting communications intelligence in international waters off the coast of North Korea when four North Korean torpedo boats and two submarine chasers, supported by fighters, fired warning shots at the ship and demanded permission to board. When Commander Lloyd M. Bucher refused, the North Koreans fired on the vessel, killing one and wounding three others. The *Pueblo* had only two .50 caliber machine guns frozen fast under protective tarpaulins, a maximum speed far slower than the Communist boats, and no hope of support from other U.S. Navy ships or planes that were too far away to come to the rescue. The North Koreans took Bucher and his crew of eighty-two, including two Navy Security Group civilian technicians, as prisoners and held them for nearly a year. They also captured the *Pueblo*, her state-of-the-art communications gear, classified files, codes, and records.

At the time, the *Pueblo* was acting as a part of Operation Chickbeetle, which was in its third year of operation. Chickbeetle gathered signal intelligence from North Korea as well as Soviet naval craft in the northern Pacific Ocean. Several weeks before the seizure of the *Pueblo*, there had been an increase in border incidents along the Korean DMZ, and two days prior to the ship's capture, a group of thirty-one North Korean commandos crossed the border with the intention of assassinating the South Korean president.

The National Security Agency warned the Joint Chiefs of Staff about the potential for these incidents, but the Joint Chiefs took no action. The *Pueblo* was not warned of an increased threat nor had any ships been repositioned to provide security.

A complete accounting of classified materials lost aboard the *Pueblo* has never been released. No explanation has been provided as to why the ship was in such a vulnerable, indefensible position or why the crew had to make a vain attempt to burn classified data on the deck during the boarding process rather than having access to destruction devices or apparatus on board.

The mystery of the unpreparedness of the U.S. Navy is almost as deep as the true motivation of the North Koreans for the incident. Some have theorized that the Communists wanted to increase tension so that South Korea would withdraw its forces supporting the United States in Vietnam. Others have supposed that the seizure of the ship had something to do with the Vietnamese Tet Offensive that began a few days later. A more likely explanation is that the North Koreans saw an opportunity to capture sophisticated signal intelligence equipment with little risk. Whether it was for their own use or for their Soviet or Chinese friends remains unknown.

On April 24, 1969, the North Koreans again took advantage of the failure of the United States to secure its intelligence-gathering resources. North Korean fighters shot down a U.S. Navy EC-121 signal intelligence reconnaissance aircraft over the international waters of the Sea of Japan a full ninety miles off their coastline. The entire flight crew and intelligence staff composed of thirty naval personnel and one marine, were lost. Other than a brief show of force by a navy fleet in the Sea of Japan, the United States took no retaliatory action. It had finally learned its lesson about security, however. Fighter escorts accompanied future EC-121 missions in the area.

The conclusion of the U.S. involvement in the Vietnam War and the fall of Saigon brought no end to continuing American intelligence failures in the region. On May 15, 1975, Cambodian Communist (Khmer Rouge) naval craft in the Gulf of Siam fired upon and seized the U.S.-registered container ship *Mayaguez* and her crew of forty en route from Hong Kong to Thailand. President Gerald Ford, who had replaced Nixon after he resigned over the Watergate controversy, demanded its immediate release, but the Khmer Rouge refused. Ford, aware of the Khmer Rouge murder of more than six million of their fellow Cambodians and not wanting a hostage crisis, ordered a rescue mission.*

With a minimum of preparation, and even less accurate intelligence, the rescue mission began on May 15. Planes from the carrier *Coral Sea* struck air and naval facilities on the Cambodian mainland while marines, deployed from Okinawa, and sailors from the destroyer *Harry E. Holt* boarded the *Mayaguez* only to find the crew had been removed from the ship undetected by American intelligence. A company of marines, in search of the crew, landed on nearby Koh Tang Island, where they met heavy resistance from the Khmer Rouge and lost three helicopters to ground fire.

Unknown to the attackers and military intelligence, the Khmer Rouge had released their captives from another island, and the crew of the *Mayaguez* was already back on their ship when the

---

*More than a few observers have commented that Ford's quick action was also based on his desire to reinstate some of the prestige lost by the United States after its abandonment of South Vietnam to the Communists.

marines assaulted Koh Tang. By the time the *Mayaguez* resumed its voyage, thirty-eight marines were dead and fifty wounded—all needless casualties that could have been prevented by accurate intelligence about the location of the *Mayaguez* crewmen or the intentions of their Cambodian captors.

This series of intelligence failures, internal and external to the Vietnam War, left the American public and political structure extremely doubtful about the effectiveness of its intelligence community. In response to the criticism, the CIA and the military underwent changes in leadership and organization but did not actually alter their way of doing business or improve their effectiveness. The army, in 1975, disbanded the Army Security Agency (ASA) and integrated its units into the regular army command structure, including merging its personnel into tactical military intelligence units. Other parts of the ASA reorganized under a new command, known as the U.S. Army Intelligence and Security Command. The air force underwent a similar reorganization in 1972, reforming its information units into the Air Force Intelligence Service. The navy also restructured its organizations, but the Office of Naval Intelligence title survived, with the assistant chief of naval operations also serving as the director of the Office of Naval Intelligence.

Despite these reorganizations, a great deal of mistrust in overall intelligence operations, particularly as to the legality and morality of CIA activities, continued. Congress conducted several investigations of the CIA in the years after the fall of Saigon, and the findings were leaked to the press. Many of the previously classified misdeeds and errors of America's most secret organization appeared on the front pages and in bookstores, compromising parts of the CIA's worldwide intelligence apparatus and causing many friendly governments, who shared information, to distrust the agency's security. In Washington, the CIA was considered to be such a "loose cannon" that in 1976 both the Senate and the House established permanent select committees on intelligence.

As a result of the embarrassing revelations about its activities and weaknesses, the American intelligence community faced difficulties in recruiting career intelligence personnel and in retaining assistance formerly provided by the academic and business communities. The situation did not improve, and, in 1980, the total bankruptcy of the American intelligence community was exposed to the entire world through the disastrous failure of the American rescue mission of hostages held in Iran.

On November 4, 1979, a mob of 3,000 Muslim "students"— actually fundamentalist followers of the Ayatollah Khomeini— attacked the U.S. embassy in Teheran, seizing the staff of diplomats and marine guards. American intelligence had provided no warning of the assault. After a few days, the students released thirteen women and black hostages, reducing their number of captives to fifty-three. They then announced that they would free the hostages only if the United States extradited the deposed shah back to Iran for a trial by a revolutionary tribunal. At the time, he was in New York for medical treatment. President Jimmy Carter wanted to avoid "another Vietnam" and keep peace with Iran's neighbors. Consequently he pursued a diplomatic rather than a military solution to the hostage situation. The Iranian fundamentalists ignored Carter's impotent actions as American television newscasts began a count of the days of captivity and featured chanting students burning the U.S. flag on practically every telecast.

Carter finally ordered a rescue operation and directed it be "quick, incisive, surgical" with "no loss to American lives" and "minimal suffering to the Iranian people." The president had assigned an impossible mission to an inept force supported by inferior intelligence. What resulted was surely the most complex military rescue operation ever attempted—and it was doomed to failure from its very beginning.

The rescue plan, Operation Eagle Claw, centered around a Delta Force team of ninety-three commandos, who would free the main body of hostages held in the U.S. embassy, and thirteen army rangers, who would free four other Americans held in the Iranian Foreign Ministry. These strike forces were accompanied by a ranger security team, an army antiair missile section, and eleven soldiers fluent in Farsi as interpreters. They would fly by six air force C-130s to a staging area 200 miles from Teheran called Desert One. At the staging area, the rescue teams would link up with eight navy RH-53D helicopters from the carrier *Nimitz* in the Gulf of Oman. The helicopters would refuel from air force tankers at Desert One and then fly the rescue teams to Desert Two, a hiding place just outside of Teheran. The next day the rescue teams would board trucks provided by agents within Teheran and drive to the sites where the hostages were being held. Following rescue, the hostages would then be flown by helicopter to an abandoned airport near the city of Manzariyeh, secured by still another group of rangers, where they would board air force transports and fly to freedom.

Never in the history of the American military has such a complex operation depended so much on intelligence only to have little, or none, available. In fact, later investigations placed much of the operation's failure not only on a lack of information but also on security measures so strict that they prevented the sharing of information and the coordination of resources. Intelligence personnel of each of the participating groups seemingly believed that none of the others had a "need to know" and refused to share the little information that was available. The first time many of the participants talked with each other was when they met at Desert One, where they discovered no one knew such basic information as the exact locations where the hostages were being held within the embassy, the thickness and composition of the embassy's outer walls, or the number of guards or how they were armed. Many of the rescuers later admitted that they had no information about the target area whatsoever before beginning the mission.

On April 24, 1980, Operation Eagle Claw kicked off with eight poorly maintained helicopters flown by marine pilots* who had been "volunteered" for the mission with no screening of their qualifications. Having no information about weather conditions or possible radar and antiair emplacements, the helicopter pilots

---

*More highly qualified air force pilots were available to fly the helicopters, but navy and marine intelligence officers claimed having air force officers on a carrier might compromise the secrecy of the mission. The more likely explanation is that senior marine commanders wanted a "piece of the action," which they thought would bring glory for their rescue service and increased funding for their budget.

flew close to the ground and encountered thick dust storms. By the time the helicopters reached Desert One, two of the choppers had turned back due to maintenance difficulties, and another had warning lights indicating that it should not be flown farther without repair.

Problems with the helicopters were an indication of disaster to come. At Desert One, the Delta Force and rangers had failed to complete unloading their C-130s before a large Mercedes bus, complete with bright headlights, drove down the road that traversed the improvised landing strip, proving incorrect the preoperations intelligence report that the road was "lightly used." Minutes later, a gasoline tanker and a small pickup truck appeared at the west end of the landing strip. After the rangers failed to stop the tanker by shooting at its tires, they fired an antitank rocket, which exploded the vehicle into a huge fireball. The pickup and its occupants escaped. Confusion now reigned as the explosion convinced many that they were under attack. Poor communications contributed to the chaos: Delta Force soldiers could talk around the world on their satellite-linked equipment, but their radios were incompatible with those of the rangers.

Adding to the overall problems at Desert One, there was no unity of command over the entire operation. Each of the services, and teams within each service, had leaders who answered to no one on the ground at Desert One. Finally, Delta Force leader Colonel Charles "Charging Charlie" Beckweth, after learning he had only five operational helicopters when six were required, took charge and canceled the rescue mission. As the various groups prepared to evacuate the Desert One site, one of the helicopters collided with one of the C-130 refueling tankers. Fire engulfed both aircraft, killing five airmen and three marines. Panic swept across Desert One as the other marine pilots abandoned their helicopters to board the remaining C-130s, some leaving in such haste that their helicopters' engines remained running with arms, equipment, and classified documents left behind.

On the morning of April 25, world television carried gruesome pictures of charred American corpses exhibited by Iranian soldiers and Muslim holy men. In the background were the aircraft and equipment abandoned at Desert One. Any confidence in the

American intelligence and special operations communities that might have survived the blunders of Vietnam and the postwar era disappeared within those flickering television images.

Each of the armed services blamed the others for the disaster in the desert, but neither the military nor the government could offer an explanation about why the world's supposedly most powerful country was ineffective in an operation against a tenth-rate nation. No one was willing to admit that the true causes of the failure were the lack of intelligence and a plan so flawed even Hollywood would have rejected it. The United States made no further attempts to rescue the hostages. After 444 days as prisoners, they were released within hours of the inauguration of Ronald Reagan, who succeeded Jimmy Carter as president.

As humiliating as Desert One proved to be, it could have been much worse. Members of the rescue unit and the hostages held in Teheran later conceded that the casualties would have been far greater if the mission had proceeded. Even a well-rehearsed rescue unit with excellent intelligence would have had little chance of success. The actual situation of no intelligence and an unrehearsed rescue team offered opportunities for even greater losses in personnel and prestige.

The Iranian hostage situation and the debacle in the desert did nothing to teach the Americans how to gather intelligence about, or conduct direct combat against, terrorism. Military men and women continued to be sent into harm's way without benefit of a unified command structure, a clearly defined mission, or adequate intelligence.

In August 1982, just months after the release of the hostages from Iran, the United States deployed marine units to Lebanon to provide a buffer between the invading Israelis and the various Christian, Muslim, and hoodlum factions who were warring over control of the country. The marines, with no defined mission, were ordered only to present "an American military presence." Shortly after their arrival, though, the marines themselves described their purpose—referring to themselves as "targets."

In September, the marines occupied the Beirut airport, situated on low ground surrounded by mountains and the sea. It could not be realistically defended. The marine commander's request to move to the high ground, or at least conduct patrols there, was denied. Over the next year, the United States managed to anger all of the many factions, including Israel, fighting over Beirut. When the United States attempted to establish and train a Lebanese army, the Muslims interpreted the move as American assistance to the Christian faction. By the spring of 1983, the Shiite and Sunni Muslims became convinced that the Americans were siding against them and began a campaign of violent terrorism.

On April 18, a truck bomb destroyed the Beirut American embassy and killed fifty-seven, including seventeen U.S. citizens. Marine commanders received no after-action briefings on the bombing or the possible threat against their units. What little intelligence they obtained was outdated, disorganized, inapplicable, or contradictory. In the meantime, marine guards at garrison and camp sites were not allowed to chamber rounds in their rifles unless they faced a specific threat to themselves.

At 6:20 A.M. on October 23, men of the 24th Marine Amphibious Group paid the ultimate price for the confusion of their mission and the absence of warning. A Mercedes truck, loaded with 12,000 to 18,000 pounds of explosives enhanced with pressurized butane canisters, drove though marine checkpoints and guardposts before the sentries could load their weapons. The driver, reportedly with a smile, crashed the truck into the lobby of the multistoried airport headquarters building, which housed 300 marines. When the driver detonated the bomb, the building lifted from its foundation and collapsed. The destruction was complete. Marine dead totaled 241, with seventy more wounded. The single deadliest blow to the U.S. military since Pearl Harbor had been delivered at the cost of one religious extremist truck driver.

During the following months, the marine leadership received great criticism for concentrating units in one location and being lax in security. These were mostly unfair accusations, since the real culprits were an undefined political policy and inadequate intelligence to evaluate the threat and to provide proper warning. Other than returning the body bags to America for burial, the United States took no substantial action as a result of the tragic event. In 1984, the marines withdrew from Lebanon. To date, the

Muslim extremists responsible for the bombing have gone unpunished.

The Beirut bombing did not occupy the front pages and television news leads for long before U.S. troops became involved in another situation. In 1979, the Marxist New Jewel Movement, led by Maurice Bishop, had overthrown the prime minister of the 133-square mile Caribbean island of Grenada. Under Bishop, the former British colony had begun receiving aid and assistance from Cuba and started construction on an airfield capable of handling military aircraft on the western tip of the island at Port Salines. An even more radical faction of the New Jewel Movement had murdered Bishop and encouraged an increase in the Communist buildup on the island. Concerned about the developing Communist stronghold, U.S. officials also worried about the presence of about 1,000 American students attending the island's St. George's University Medical School.

On October 22, 1983, the Organization of Eastern Caribbean States, fearing that Grenada might become a Cuban-Soviet outpost, formally requested that the United States intervene. President Ronald Reagan, sharing the organization's concerns as well as fearing that the American students might be taken hostage, ordered a mission to liberate the students and to establish an interim government.

Navy Vice Admiral Joseph Metcalf III commanded the rescue/liberation mission. Army Major General H. Norman Schwarzkopf later joined him as the operation's deputy commander. Operation Urgent Fury, conceived by military planners as a one-punch knockout or "coup de main," would begin early on the morning of October 25, 1983. Under the plan, the navy would cordon off the island with ships and aircraft while the marines made an amphibious landing on the island's eastern shore to secure Pearls Airfield, Grenada's only operational airport. Army rangers would focus on the military airfield under construction at Port Salines and then rescue the American medical students at the nearby campus called True Blue.

Meanwhile, special operations teams of SEALs and Delta Force would fly by helicopter into the capital city of St. George's to free the British-appointed governor general, who was being held prisoner by the Marxists. They would also secure the radio station, Richmond Hill Prison, and several other key sites. Several battalions of the 82d Airborne Division would join the other forces after the initial assault to assist in taking over the entire island.

The plan for Urgent Fury was satisfactory, but intelligence to support it was not. Intelligence briefing officers told the rangers and marines that the Grenada army of 2,000 active duty troops and about that many more reserves would not oppose the landing. They acknowledged that Port Salines was ringed with antiaircraft guns but said that the poorly trained crews would offer little threat. Finally, the intelligence briefers stated that the 600 to 800 Cubans on the island were lightly armed construction workers who would not fight.

Operation Urgent Fury began with the insertion of SEAL teams at both the eastern and western tips of the island. SEALs successfully accomplished their reconnaissance at the eastern objective of Pearls Airfield and recommended the marines arrive by helicopter rather than landing craft because of the rocky coast. As a result, the marine landing went mostly unopposed and quickly secured Pearls.

The western SEAL team was to determine if the runway at Port Salines was usable or if the rangers would have to deploy by parachute. But unpredicted currents and winds prevented the SEALs from accomplishing their mission—several died when they were swept out to sea. When the SEALs encountered difficulties off Port Salines, the rangers began their flight with no current information about their landing zone.* Air force navigation equipment failures delayed their planes so that the rangers, trained and better suited for night operations, had to make a daylight assault.

---

*The rangers, from battalions at Fort Lewis, Washington, and Fort Stewart, Georgia, assembled at Stewart for the invasion with minimal advance notice and preparation time. Many thought their objective might be somewhere in the Middle East, in retaliation for the Beirut bombing, until the final hours before the invasion.

With no knowledge of the airfield condition, the rangers prepared to parachute into the operation. As their planes neared Port Salines, the "poorly trained" anti-aircraft crews filled the air with explosives and machine gun rounds, forcing the planes to drop to 500 feet to get below the trajectory of the fire. At that altitude the Rangers would not have time to deploy reserve chutes if problems developed with their main canopies, so they left their reserves aboard the aircraft and stepped out into the sky above Grenada.

On the ground, the rangers quickly discovered the Cuban "construction workers," supported by armored vehicles, to be highly trained, well armed, and motivated to fight. Heavy combat broke out all around the airfield, with both sides taking casualties before the rangers secured the area and began removing vehicles and other obstacles from the runway so that the follow-on forces could land.

Two of the helicopter gunships supporting the attacks across the island were shot down. One crew survived, only to be summarily executed by either Grenadians or Cubans on the ground. Battle-damaged army choppers, barely able to stay in the air, and those low on fuel flew to the navy ships off shore, where initially they and army medevac helicopters were waved off because the navy believed the army pilots were not qualified for shipboard landings. Clearer heads finally prevailed, and the choppers landed on the ships, but refueling airworthy birds was delayed while administration and supply personnel all the way back to Washington tried to determine how the other services would be billed for the fuel.

Maneuver on Grenada was restricted by more than the Cuban resistance. Hurriedly prepared maps with inconsistent grid coordinate numbers made normal procedures for the calling of artillery and other support missions impossible. Several of the ranger commanders later admitted that small-scale automobile road maps printed by a well-known oil company proved to be the best maps they had during the entire operation. Incompatibility of radios and radio frequencies caused other difficulties, preventing marines and rangers from communicating with each other or with the support ships off shore.

The operation achieved its primary objective within hours of the invasion—securing the True Blue medical campus—only to expose another intelligence failure. Unknown to American intelligence, the majority of the students did not live at True Blue but rather at a beachfront hotel two miles away at Grand Anse. No one in intelligence had asked the families back in the States about the students' location or looked up the medical school's catalogs readily available in public libraries—omissions intelligence later hurriedly dismissed as a matter of operational security.

By the end of the first day of the Grenada invasion, it was obvious that the one-punch knockout had failed. More than half the medical students remained unprotected, and the enemy had a U.S. special operations unit surrounded and in danger of being overrun in St. George's. The enemy who was not supposed to fight was doing very well for itself.

The first day did end on a positive note with the landing of 250 marines just north of St. George's at Grand Mal Bay. Early the next morning the marines rescued the surrounded special operations teams as well as the governor general and his followers. A helicopter assault by the rangers landed at Grand Anse late in the afternoon and, after a brisk firefight with Grenadian and Cuban infantrymen, removed the remainder of the students, all unharmed, to Port Salines for airlift to the United States. Communications with the students during the rescue was not by secret agent or sophisticated spy technology, but rather by commercial telephones.

By October 27, most of the island was secure. Soldiers of the 82d Airborne, however, took days instead of the mere hours it should have required to clear the remainder of Grenada. They were forced to proceed so slowly and cautiously because of the lack of viable intelligence about the enemy. American forces discovered large amounts of Communist-supplied weapons and ammunition, confirming the U.S. claim of the Cuban-Soviet buildup on the island. Casualty figures totaled 18 Americans dead and 116 wounded. Grenada lost 45 soldiers killed. Cuban losses numbered 24 dead, 59 wounded, and 650 captured.

For the first time in nearly forty years, the Americans had achieved a clear-cut military victory. And the U.S. public had supported the operation and its participants, restoring a bit of the military's prestige. Without a doubt, Grenada was a success. However, it had been gained by brave soldiers, airmen, marines, and sailors, assisted by overwhelmingly superior equipment and technology. The operation itself had been marred by failures—and poor intelligence was at the top of the list. General Schwarzkopf later provided an excellent summation of the short conflict when he wrote, "Above all I was proud that we'd gotten the job done and elated that the American public—at least from my observation—had come out in support of its troops. At the same time, we had lost more lives than we needed to, and the brief war had revealed a lot of shortcomings—an abysmal lack of accurate intelligence, major deficiencies in communications, flare-ups of interservice rivalry, interference by higher headquarters in battlefield decisions, our alienation of the press, and more."

The post-Grenada period brought improvement of special operations capabilities and the intelligence efforts to support such operations. Military intelligence focused on combating worldwide terrorism, especially the anti-U.S. operations conducted by Libyan-sponsored agents. Libya's leader, Colonel Muammar Gaddafi, was the source of funding for many terrorists' activities and also allowed international terrorists to use his country as a training area and a refuge.

An explosion on April 5, 1986, at a West Berlin disco packed with American servicemen, killed a U.S. Army sergeant and a Turkish national and wounded another 230, including 79 Americans. U.S. communications intelligence failed to provide forewarning of the bombing but in the following days intercepted messages between Libya and its embassy in East Berlin confirming Libyan participation. The United States began planning to punish Gaddafi and to put a stop to Libyan-sponsored terrorism.

On April 14, the United States launched a "surgical strike" against three objectives in and around Tripoli. Targets included the military portion of the city's airport, a terrorist commando school at the Sidi Bilal naval base, and Bab al Azizia barracks, where Gaddafi reportedly lived. F-111s from Lakenheath Air Force Base in England conducted the main strike. Support aircraft from the United States and other bases provided in-flight refueling and other aid to get the eighteen fighters to their targets. Thirteen of the F-111s made the actual attack. One, along with its crew of two, was lost, likely shot down by ground fire.

During the attack on Tripoli, twelve A-6 attack bombers from carriers in the Mediterranean attacked the Bengazi area to the east and destroyed a military barracks, four MIG-23s, and several other aircraft on the ground. All of the A-6s returned to their carriers unharmed.

The raid on Tripoli was far from the surgical strike planned and promised. Gaddafi, who the American State Department claimed was not a direct target, escaped injury, but, according to Libyan claims, the raid killed the colonel's fifteen-month-old daughter and wounded two of his sons. Some bombs missed their targets altogether, slamming into residential buildings, including those next to the French embassy. The Libyans later claimed the raid killed thirty-seven of their people and injured another ninety-three.

The raid on Libya did not by any means end terrorism, including violent attacks sponsored by Libya. Gaddafi, however, lowered his profile and became less vocal and obvious in his support of anti-American activities. More important than the bombing results themselves, the United States and President Reagan demonstrated that Americans would no longer sit idly by and allow their military and citizens to be murdered without consequences, as they had when they let the bombing of the Marine barracks in Beirut go unpunished.

When he assumed the presidency in 1989, George Bush continued Ronald Reagan's policy of combating terrorism around the world. In some instances, intelligence supported such activities, while in others, failures remained the norm.

The next commitment of U.S. military forces after Libya was not to combat international terrorism or Communism but rather to remove the dictator of Panama, a former CIA informant. On December 20, 1989, the United States launched its largest combat operation since Vietnam, including the most massive airborne drop since World War II. The goal of the invasion was threefold: to neutralize the Panamanian Defense Force (PDF) and other organized resistance; to capture Panama's dictator, Manuel Antonio Noriega, and return him to the United States to face drug-running charges; and to install the democratic government elected the previous May, which Noriega had ignored.

During the months before the invasion, Noriega had increased his anti-U.S. rhetoric, encouraging the PDF and other forces to harass American military personnel and their families. Both the CIA and President Bush supported a Panamanian overthrow of the dictator, but Noriega's control remained intact. The closest Noriega had come to being deposed had been on October 3, 1989, but a failure of American intelligence allowed him to escape.

Late in September, the U.S. Southern Command (Southcom) intelligence office had been approached by representatives of Major Moises Giroldi Vega requesting assistance in a coup attempt against Noriega. Southcom commander General Max Thurman, an intense staff officer with a background in intelligence, consulted his J-2 (Intelligence Section) and the CIA only to conclude that Giroldi's proposal was merely an attempt to embarrass the United States and that the Panamanian officer was in collusion with Noriega.

Thurman and his intelligence staff were wrong. Giroldi went through with his coup attempt, and it would likely have succeeded had the United States provided minimal support. Instead, the coup failed, and Giroldi, after horrible torture and sexual violation, was murdered. The opportunity to remove Noriega without shedding the blood of U.S. military personnel had passed because of a military intelligence failure.

After the failed coup attempt, Noriega increased his rhetoric and direct action against Americans. On December 16, PDF soldiers at a roadblock shot and killed a marine officer returning to his base from a Panama City restaurant. The next day, a U.S. Navy lieutenant was beaten and his wife threatened with rape after being stopped at another roadblock. President Bush, unwilling to delay any longer, ordered the invasion of Panama.

Over the previous quarter century, the U.S. leadership had learned many lessons that would pay great dividends in Panama. It would not be a "limited" engagement, nor would the 24,000-man American force be micromanaged from the White House. Once Bush gave the order for the invasion, the president, unlike Johnson and Nixon during Vietnam, let his military commanders conduct the operation without intervention.

During the planning phase, Operation Blue Spoon was the top secret code name for the Panama invasion. When the mission received the go-ahead from President Bush, its name was changed to the more glamorous and, in the eyes of Americans, more descriptive Operation Just Cause.

Usual attempts were made to keep the operation secret, but several incidents compromised much of the plan as well as its actual start time. Several U.S. soldiers stationed in Panama mentioned the upcoming operation during telephone conversations with friends and families back home. Noriega's brother-in-law owned and controlled the Panamanian telephone system, so there is no doubt that many if not all of these calls were monitored. Another tip-off to the Panamanians was the tremendous increase in the number of aircraft landing at Howard Air Force Base to bring in additional troops and supplies during the days before the anticipated attack hour. Other lapses in security at the Southcom headquarters, and information released by the international media, compromised any chance for surprise. In fact, several hours before H-hour, widespread messages circulated within the PDF stating, "Party starts tonight at 0100."

The compromise of the attack time did not overly concern the U.S. planners because of the overwhelming force assembled. Military intelligence estimated that even an alerted PDF would not put up much of a fight. As usual, military intelligence proved to be in error.

Operation Just Cause, composed of five separate task forces, focused on neutralizing the PDF or blocking their means of movement and reinforcement. Special operations teams were ordered to seize Noriega and block his various means of exit.

Initially, Just Cause was primarily an army, marine, and air force operation, but the navy demanded a "piece of the action," too. As a result, one of the earliest missions of the invasion called for a SEAL team to infiltrate Paitilla Airport and neutralize Noriega's personal Lear jet, which he might use for escape.

The SEALs were anxious to participate in the operation to redeem their lackluster performance in Grenada, where several had drowned and others had to be rescued by marines after being surrounded. Paitilla Airport looked like an easy mission. Intelligence reported that the airport was lightly guarded.

Approaching the beach near the airport, a Panamanian fishing boat spotted the SEALs and turned a spotlight on the invaders. Things got no better when they reached the airfield. Rather than a few civilian night watchmen, the SEALs encountered PDF soldiers armed with machine guns and assault weapons. Other well-armed men, later identified as security personnel for various drug-running operations, opened fire on the SEALs as they approached across an open runway. During the bitter fight that followed, communications with overhead gunships failed, preventing delivery of supporting fire. By the time the SEALs managed to put an AT-4 antitank rocket into the fuselage of the Lear jet, four members of the team were dead.

During the main attack, several of the units making up the five task forces, particularly those of the 82d Airborne Division, were delayed by a severe winter storm at their East Coast launching bases. These and other units met much stiffer resistance than anticipated when they did arrive, but their overwhelming numbers and firepower subdued the PDF and the organized groups of pro-Noriega thugs known as the Dignity Battalions. The PDF soldiers, contrary to intelligence estimates, did not give up easily. During the early hours of the invasion they managed to conduct a "drive-by" attack, using rocket-propelled grenades and automatic weapons, on the American embassy in Panama City. At the Marriott Caesar Park Hotel, PDF forces took American civilians and news personnel hostage for a brief period.

Although maximum planning and precautions had taken place to prevent "collateral damage" to civilian life and property, destruction and casualties did occur. The specific U.S. unit designated to secure the Panama City shopping districts was delayed by bad weather, allowing an unexpected outbreak of looting by Panamanian civilians. Factions within Panamanian and American peace groups made claims on the major television networks that the civilian death toll was as high as 8,000. Reports of mass graves and a cover-up by the U.S. military lingered long after the invasion was complete. Actual figures of Panamanian deaths during Just Cause, however, are more in line with the Southcom estimate of 314 military and 202 civilian deaths, a total of 516.

Two of the three Just Cause objectives fell to the invaders during the first twenty-four hours of the operation: the U.S. forces routed the PDF and cleared the way for the installation of the government elected in May. One objective, the primary target of the entire operation, remained unfulfilled—Manuel Noriega was still free. For four days after the opening shots of Just Cause, military units, including special Delta Force teams, zipped from site to site, following intelligence tips about the dictator's whereabouts. None were successful. More than 24,000 Americans, with the loss of twenty-three military men killed and 347 wounded, failed to capture a single man because of the lack of accurate intelligence.

U.S. military forces sealed off the Cuban and Nicaraguan embassies to prevent Noriega's seeking asylum there, while intelligence continued unsuccessfully to track the dictator. President Bush offered a $1 million reward for the capture of Noriega, with no results. Despite other successes of Just Cause, if Noriega escaped, the entire operation would be labeled a failure.

On Christmas Eve, Noriega entered a Toyota sedan flying the papal flag in the parking lot of a Dairy Queen near San Miguelito in accordance with the agreement he had made by phone with the head of the Vatican embassy in Punta Paitilla. Within minutes, Noriega was secure behind the walls of the embassy. Listening to civilian news reports, American intelligence finally learned the location of Noriega.

Negotiations between Washington and Rome began immediately. The United States agreed to respect the embassy's diplomatic sanctity but stated emphatically that Noriega would not be allowed to depart to a safe-haven exile.

During the following days, what is surely the most ridiculous psychological operation in U.S. history took place outside the embassy. High-power loudspeakers blasted rock music toward the building. After three days, the ambassador informed the U.S. military that negotiations would stop until the noise ceased.

After extensive discussion, Noriega surrendered on January 3, 1990. His request to surrender in uniform was permitted. Delta Force operators took Noriega into custody and transported him via Howard Air Force Base to Miami, where they turned him over to federal law enforcement officials. Operation Just Cause was finally over.

★ 14 ★

Today and Tomorrow: Can Failures Become Successes?

More than two centuries of U.S. intelligence failures have not gone unnoticed by the country's elected leadership. In addition to the recent intelligence failures during Operation Desert Storm, noted in the August 1993 report by the House of Representatives Armed Services Subcommittee on Oversight and Investigations, the intelligence community has been plagued by moles, spies, and turncoats who have revealed U.S. secrets to potential enemies and friends alike. Although the fall of the Berlin Wall, the liberation of Eastern Europe, and the collapse of the Soviet Union are certainly welcome events, there is no evidence that the American intelligence community foresaw these developments, nor did it provide any warning of them to the U.S. political or military leadership.

Late in 1994, Senator Dennis DeConcini of Arizona, a member of the Senate Intelligence Committee, summed up the current status of the American intelligence community in a damning understatement: "The American public deserves better than it gets for the $28 billion spent on intelligence in this country annually."

The $28 billion intelligence budget for 1995 is only an estimate. Since the end of World War II, accounting of intelligence expenditures has remained classified on the basis of national security. Hidden in false line items and deleted passages in Pentagon accounts, the specific content of this multibillion-dollar "black budget" is known only by a few members of Congress and, of course, the intelligence staffers who expend the funds.

Information about how much it costs to maintain the massive amount of secret information is also classified. A study of the 1991 federal budget by the General Accounting Office revealed that the Department of Defense spent about $6 billion that year on security activities to safeguard information, personnel, and property. Some expenditures were for such simple security items as safes and secure rooms, while more than a quarter of a billion dollars was spent to verify individual security clearances.

Gross expenditures for intelligence security are not limited to internal government activities. In 1989, the last year for which figures are available to the public, civilian defense contractors billed Washington $13.8 billion for their classification and security requirements.

Within the U.S. government today are more than 31,000 full-time employees dedicated to managing and safeguarding classified documents. According to the Senate Intelligence Committee, these workers classify seven million documents each year, about one per second during a forty-hour work week. No one in the government has been able to make an accurate estimate of how many documents are currently classified, but "billions of pages" is the standard guess. According to the current guidelines, documents should remain classified for no more than thirty years. However, in the National Archives alone, more than 300,000 documents dated prior to 1960 remain classified. In these post–Cold War days, with no Soviet "evil empire" posing a threat, it is certainly appropriate to ask just what the country is receiving for its intelligence funding and for the billions of dollars spent to keep this information secret from outside sources, including the American public who pays the bills.

Today's intelligence community has thirteen members: the Central Intelligence Agency; the Defense Intelligence Agency; the National Security Agency; the Central Imagery Office; the National Reconnaissance Office; the Federal Bureau of Investigation; the U.S. Army, Navy, Air Force, and Marine Corps; and the Departments of State, Energy, and Treasury. An exact, or even general, accounting of the budget of each of these thirteen members is classified, as are the numbers of personnel dedicated to intelligence within each agency, department, and service. Further complicating any analysis of today's intelligence community is that the collapse of the Soviet Union has forced intelligence staffs to look beyond military intelligence to pursue other responsibilities to justify their future existence. By 1994, parts of the intelligence community had turned from military matters to focus on economic, scientific, and technical intelligence, with particular interest given to counterterrorism activities and drug trafficking. Current reductions in force of the military and possible cutbacks in the CIA and other intelligence organizations add to the confusion.

Despite these new areas of interest, the primary focus of the intelligence community continues to be military intelligence, and it remains a tremendous consumer of manpower. In 1994, of the more than 73,000 active duty army officers, nearly 5,000, or 7 percent, were members of the Military Intelligence Corps; only the infantry with 6,800, the Field Artillery with 5,300, and the Medical Corps with 5,200 had more officers than Military Intelligence. About the same percentage of the U.S. Army enlisted ranks is dedicated to intelligence specialties. U.S. Air Force and Navy military intelligence personnel figures are similar to the army's.

Despite these huge numbers of dedicated personnel and these billions-of-dollars budgets, the intelligence community continues to fail to provide timely, accurate information to the combat commanders on the ground, at sea, and in the air who are dedicated to defending the United States and the free world. The deplorable two-and-one-quarter-century history of military intelligence failures has been compounded during the past decade by the intelligence community's ineptitude in preventing and detecting internal compromises of classified information.

Traitors within the American military and its intelligence community are nothing new. From Benedict Arnold betraying the army at West Point during the American Revolution to Julius and Ethel Rosenberg selling atomic secrets during the Cold War, classified information critical to American security has regularly been sold or given away. Some of the spies have been caught, while others escaped to take refuge in the countries to which they delivered their secrets. Far more worrisome are personnel within the U.S. intelligence and military communities who continue to compromise secrets without being detected.

During the past decade, the compromise of spies within the intelligence community has increased. The inability of the United States to safeguard its secrets came to the forefront in 1985 with three major spy scandals. John Walker Jr., a U.S. Navy careerist, was arrested for delivering to the Soviets code data that provided locations of the navy's surface and subsurface fleets and access to their secure communications worldwide. Walker's treachery likely dated back to the 1960s and may have compromised the time and location of air strikes as well as ground and sea operations during the Vietnam War. Walker recruited fellow sailors and his own children, one of whom served in the communications center of the U.S.S. *Nimitz,* to increase the amount of purloined information he could sell to his Soviet handlers. When finally apprehended, Walker matter-of-factly stated, "K-Mart has better security than the U.S. Navy."

Another of the American Spy Class of '85 was Ronald Pelton. Pelton, an employee of the National Security Agency, sold top secret signal intelligence to the Soviets for five years before being caught. About the same time Pelton was taken into custody, another turncoat, Edward Lee Howard, escaped to the Soviet Union after his CIA employers discovered his espionage. Howard, whose treachery was revealed by a Soviet defector to the United States, was under investigation and observation by the FBI but still managed to elude capture. Several FBI agents were disciplined for failing to apprehend Howard, but evidence now indicates that the CIA was lax in providing the bureau timely information. Although the CIA was much more at fault in the inept handling of the Howard case, none of its agents or administrators were disciplined.

Army communications proved to be as vulnerable to internal spies as those of the navy, National Security Agency, and CIA when Warrant Officer James Hall III, a communications special-ist, was caught providing information about U.S. electronic-spying capabilities in Europe to representatives of the Soviet bloc in 1988. During the same time period, still another member of the American intelligence community demonstrated that secrets could be sold to friends, as well as enemies, when Jonathan Pollard was exposed for providing classified information to Israel.

In intelligence and government circles, 1985 is known as the "Year of the Spy." With the arrest of CIA agent Aldrich Hazen Ames in 1994, the recent history might better be labeled the "Decade of the Spy."

Ames, described by colleagues as unsophisticated and lazy, had a longtime reputation within the CIA for being much more interested in pursuing women and alcohol than in performing any real intelligence work. Still he managed to progress in the CIA system and in 1984 assumed control of supervising counterintelligence operations against the Soviets in Washington, D.C. Instead of recruiting Russians to spy for the United States, Ames himself became a Russian recruit. By 1985, he was on the Soviet payroll.

Over the next nine years, Ames delivered so much quality information to the Soviets that the Senate Intelligence Committee would later describe him as having "caused more damage to the national security of the United States than any spy in the history of the CIA." Information compromised by Ames resulted in the execution of at least ten Soviet citizens who had been providing information to the CIA. Ames also provided additional documents detailing more than 100 U.S. intelligence operations on subjects as diverse as defense capabilities and international narcotics trafficking.

The total impact of Ames's treachery is unknown and likely to remain that way. Details of exactly what Ames provided remain classified and available only to congressional investigators and the CIA itself. Consequences of the losses, other than the execution of the Soviet informants, are also difficult to evaluate. Because the United States won the Cold War, the Soviet Union never had the opportunity to take advantage of much of the military information Ames leaked.

Despite the Senate Intelligence Committee announcement of the grave damage done by Ames, the greater compromise may very well be to the reputation and future of the CIA. The agency's inability to provide timely, accurate information during the Gulf War and previous conflicts is now multiplied by its failure to maintain its own secrets and to detect traitors within its midst.

That there was a mole within the CIA was no great surprise to those inside or outside the agency. Although the CIA blamed Edward Howard and other spies for much of the information obtained by the Soviets, evidence remained that a mole still existed. In the end, the surprise was that no one had suspected Ames earlier.

Ames, a twenty-five-year veteran of the agency, and the son of a career CIA agent, proved to be either an extremely naive, or an unbelievably careless, spy. In addition to having a drinking problem, he had divorced his first wife and married a Colombian national, whom he had recruited as a spy for the agency while assigned to Mexico. Ames went on the Soviet payroll shortly after his marriage* and in less than a decade received more than $2.5 million from the Russians.

Yet no one in the CIA became suspicious when Ames, whose annual salary was less than $70,000, paid cash for a half-million-dollar house and then made $90,000 in improvements, drove to work in a $65,000 red Jaguar, employed a nanny for his son, ran up credit card bills of $455,000 for furniture, meals, and jewelry, and purchased stocks worth $165,000. Ames and his wife openly discussed their spying on the telephone and kept records of information provided the Soviets on their home computer. There is evidence that the CIA conducted a limited check on Ames as early as 1986, but agents mounted no detailed investigation until about a year before his arrest.

In spite of a security-bankrupt Central Intelligence Agency and

---

*The amount of collusion on the part of Ames's wife, Rosario, is unknown. Officially, the Soviets recruited Ames and he recruited Rosario. Conjecture remains, however, that she may have been the first involved as a Soviet spy. Regardless, Ames pled guilty in a plea bargain to gain his wife a light sentence of a maximum of six years for "aiding, advising and encouraging," so that she would eventually be released to raise their son. Ames is currently serving a life sentence.

a military intelligence community that has consistently failed the U.S. fighting forces, the United States today stands as the world's single superpower. A superior government system and ideology, combined with technology, natural resources, talented leaders, and brave servicemen and women have gained and preserved the freedoms of the nation that today enjoys the world's highest quality of living. With no identifiable national threat, the future challenges of the United States will come from the occasional despot dictator such as Saddam Hussein, organized bandits such as Somalia's Mohammed Aidid, terrorism such as the bombing of New York's World Trade Center, and the international trafficking in illegal drugs.

While none of these threats rival the former dangers of Imperial Japan and Nazi Germany during the Second World War or of the Soviet Union during the Cold War, all must be confronted and removed. Unfortunately, evidence from the past five years indicates that the intelligence community is as ill prepared to meet current and future threats as it has been in combating them in the past. The United States cannot wait for another adversarial world power to appear before it improves its military intelligence capabilities. The country must make changes now to meet current challenges while at the same time preparing to meet those of the future.

The U.S. military intelligence community most recently demonstrated its continued inability to meet the information needs of the armed forces during support of the United Nations peacekeeping mission in Bosnia-Herzegovina, where Muslim, Serbian, and other factions were engaged in a civil war for control of the region that was formerly a part of Yugoslavia. On June 2, 1995, a Bosnia Serb SA-6 surface-to-air missile shot down a U.S. Air Force F-16. Over the next six days, the plane's pilot, Captain Scott O'Grady, managed to elude ground patrols until a U.S. Marine team from the U.S.S. *Kearsarge* in the Adriatic Sea could rescue him.*

*There is no evidence that military intelligence played any role in O'Grady's rescue. Airplanes from his squadron continued to fly near where his F-16 went down and were able to monitor O'Grady's signal from his small hand-held survival radio. O'Grady waited several days to signal his comrades because ground patrols were nearby.

Although it validated Scott's survival training and the operational readiness of the marine rescue force, the incident that placed the men in harm's way and threatened to escalate U.S. involvement in the conflict occurred because of an intelligence failure.

The air force knew nothing about the Serbs' acquisition and deployment of the antiair missiles. As a result, Scott's plane carried no antimissile defenses. Also, with any preflight warning of their location, Scott could easily have avoided flying within the kill zone of the short-range missiles.

The National Security Agency admitted that it had previously detected possible movement of SA-6s into the overflight zone but informed no one in the military. On June 8, 1995, General John Shalikashvili, chairman of the Joint Chiefs of Staff, responded to a congressional committee member's question about the Serbian missile that shot down the F-16. Shalikashvili stated, "We had absolutely no intelligence."

On the same date, one of Shalikashvili's subordinates, Lieutenant General Wesley Clark, director of strategic planning and policy for the Joint Chiefs, outlined the intelligence failure in more detail. According to Clark, the air force had taken no defensive measures to protect the F-16 because no threat had been identified. Clark concluded, "The problem was an intelligence failure that led to a planning failure."

Solutions to the United States' security problems are neither simple nor easily attained. Intelligence operations within a democratic society are much more difficult to maintain and secure than they are in monolithic nations controlled by dictatorships or governed by communists or fascists. Another consideration is that the dynamics of human social and political behavior are not quantifiable. While analysts and consumers of intelligence may rely on facts delineated by numbers and specific descriptions, many aspects of information are not as simple to define. Countries, armies, and individuals are not mechanical, and much of human nature involves emotion rather than logic.

Political and human influences provide an environment where perfect collection, analysis, and dissemination of intelligence is impossible. Intelligence failures—regardless of reforms, changes, and adaptations—will always be a part of military operations.

Yet, despite these inevitabilities, today's intelligence community is so damaged and so desperately in need of immediate change that some of these improvements can be instituted easily. The three primary areas in need of immediate reform are the Central Intelligence Agency, the uniformed military intelligence community, and the overall organization of the U.S. Armed Forces.

Of the three, the CIA may be the most difficult in which to effect change. During his trial, Ames summed up problems within the CIA when he told U.S. District Judge Claude Hilton, "I had come to believe that the espionage business, as carried out by the CIA and a few other American agencies, was and is a self-serving sham. The information our vast intelligence network acquires at considerable human and ethical costs is generally insignificant or irrelevant to our policy-makers' needs."

The CIA's greatest problem, which allowed Ames to practice his treason almost openly, is the club-like atmosphere of the agency's "good old boys," who still see themselves as players in the "grand game" of intelligence. This elitist attitude, nurtured by a tradition of Ivy League and East Coast intellectual influence, has produced an organization that believes neither it nor its members can do wrong and that they are accountable to no one outside their organization. Even the Ames case did not affect their attitude of self-importance and of superior intellect. The only casualty of the decade-long ineptness of the agency was the resignation of director R. James Woolsey. Other than a few minor official reprimands of Ames's supervisors and some general recommendations to increase counterintelligence training and to further limit the access to specific information, business at the CIA has remained unchanged.

While the CIA seemingly does not understand it is time for change, the American people and the Congress certainly do. As Senator DeConcini noted in 1994, speaking about the need to reform the CIA, "Obviously something is broken out there." In the same year, Representative Robert Torricelli, a member of the House Intelligence Committee, even more bluntly declared, "The CIA is incapable of reforming itself."

Reform should not be limited to the CIA alone. The entire intelligence community, including military resources, is in need of a detailed review of performance and organization. This review should produce recommendations for restructuring intelligence resources into an organization that is more efficient, accountable, and aware that the focus of the future must include terrorism and drug trafficking as well as political and economic issues. This reformation of the intelligence community must emphasize dissemination of information, a change in the classification system that would make information more, instead of less, available. Equally important, or perhaps more so, these revisions should include the "old boy elitist" network of intelligence personnel, who must be more carefully scrutinized internally and held responsible for their failures.

The enormity and complexity of the U.S. intelligence community hinders immediate wholesale improvement. However, there are available courses of action that will produce progress. Some of these recommendations are general and apply to the entire community; others are specific to military intelligence alone.

Officials and experts recommend changes within the CIA that range from expanding its responsibilities and awarding its director cabinet rank to dismantling the agency altogether. Somewhere in between lies the best course of action for both military and other intelligence needs. Some of the CIA's functions, including the collection of agricultural, population, and economic data from other countries, could better be performed by the State Department. This would also result in the information's increased availability to U.S. businesses and the public. Likewise, certain technical intelligence collection and analysis currently conducted by the State Department duplicates that of the CIA and should be eliminated.

Reform of CIA functions, operations, and organization will succeed only if senior personnel selection and monitoring are improved. Rather than being political bureaucrats, lawyers, or titans of industry, the director and other senior leaders of the agency should come from the ranks of the military—preferably commanders with experience both in leading ground units, sea fleets, or air armadas and in working with intelligence units. Intelligence is not a grand game but rather a very serious, deadly business. People successful in running for election, trying cases in courtrooms, or manufacturing widgets do not necessarily understand or appreciate how intelligence failures can lead to loss of life.

The CIA leadership must also concentrate on its cooperation with other organizations. Rivalry between the CIA and FBI interferes with the investigation and pursuit of internal moles and external spies. The FBI must have a greater role in maintaining security within the agency and more access to its procedures and personnel during investigations. Turf battles between the CIA and the FBI, which date back to the formation of the CIA, have no place in a successful intelligence community.

The top-level review of the American intelligence community must also reform the extremely costly classification system to limit the number of documents and to prevent the abuse of the system that "hides" failures and inept conduct behind secret covers.* Within today's U.S. government and military, getting permission to require a new report—whether it be an inquiry about the number of paper clips on hand or the number of mechanical mishaps of fighter planes—involves an extensive staffing process.

To classify a document, however, is much simpler. Any junior clerk can do so merely by marking it with the appropriate rubber stamp. On the other hand, declassifying information is a long and painful process. Although the identity of certain information sources and the plans for advanced munitions and weapons certainly may require long-term classification, only a few documents should remain classified for more than ten years. Many, if not most, of the documents that remain classified for over a decade are not protecting national security but rather are covering the mistakes of intelligence operatives, military leaders, and politicians.

---

*In April 1995, President Bill Clinton directed changes in the declassification procedures and limits on how long documents remain classified. Clinton, however, included a statement in the new policy saying it will continue to "maintain the necessary controls over information that legitimately needs to be guarded in the interests of national security." The impact of Clinton's directive, if any, remains to be seen.

Organization within the armed services is also a major factor in the continued failures of military intelligence that is in need of change. Interservice rivalries between the army, navy, and air force greatly hinder their intelligence-gathering and -dissemination capabilities. The services frequently are unable to communicate and transfer information, and even when capabilities do exist for joint intelligence operations, the services often fail to share the findings.

Coordination and cooperation difficulties between the services are not limited to military intelligence. Rivalries for funding and missions, combined with individual jealousies, have hindered combat preparedness since the beginnings of the armed services. The Department of Defense Reorganization Act, also known as the Goldwater-Nichols Act, signed into law on October 1, 1986, was supposed to solve many of the problems when it strengthened the role of the Joint Chiefs of Staff and the unified service commanders by increasing their authority in operational and budget decisions.

The 1986 act provided improvements, but the operational and intelligence difficulties experienced during the Gulf War exposed that "jointness" of the services is still far from reality. Almost hidden by the massive number of failures that resulted in the deaths of eighteen soldiers in Mogadishu, Somalia, on August 21, 1993, was the fact that a navy P-3 crew flying above the city gathered much-needed intelligence for the army helicopters, but had no compatible communications means to relay the information to the soldiers.

Joint policy failures, including intelligence, remain so prevalent that the Chairman of the Joint Chiefs of Staff, General John Shalikashvili, in a September 1, 1994, speech stated that joint service doctrine is in its "infancy" and was "a deep disappointment" to him. The chairman continued by saying that the inability of the services to fight as a joint team was "an extraordinarily dangerous oversight and shortcoming." Shalikashvili added that joint training is so ineffective that "I have gone to more joint exercises and walked away embarrassed...than anything else."

Shalikashvili and other Department of Defense officials in

1994 began an annual Chairman's Program Assessment to increase the joint fighting capability. Intelligence, surveillance, and reconnaissance are critical parts of this assessment procedure.

The Goldwater-Nichols Act and the Chairman's Program Assessment are definitely steps in the right direction for the reorganization of the services to achieve an efficient coordinated fighting capability. However, in the post–Cold War era that has reduced the armed forces by one-third, they may not be enough. In this time of downsizing, with no national threat on which to base future military developments, it may very well be time to look at totally restructuring the armed forces—for economic reasons as well as unified action.

A short-term improvement would be to increase the authority of the Chairman of the Joint Chiefs of Staff in budget and command decision making. A far more drastic step is also available if the services prove unable to solve their coordination problems on their own, or if a continually decreasing defense budget no longer permits "business as usual" within the military community. Past performance, traditions, and service loyalties aside, it may well be time to completely restructure the concept of an independent army, air force, and navy-marine corps. Despite its proud service since the beginnings of the United States, the Marine Corps may have outlived its usefulness. Amphibious warfare, the cornerstone of marine operations, has not been used since the Korean War. In Vietnam, in the "weekend wars," and during Desert Storm, the marines performed the same missions as the army. There is no reason the army cannot assume the marine missions and assimilate marine personnel and equipment. Administration, bureaucracy, and duplication of efforts would be eliminated, producing an annual savings of approximately $20 billion.

The elimination of the Marine Corps is not a new concept but rather one that has been proposed on several earlier occasions. A parallel consideration, and one admittedly even more drastic, is the possibility that the time has come to rejoin the air force with the army. The structure of an air corps subordinate to the army worked well during America's largest conflict, World War II. Many army posts and air bases are jointly located, and the two services, dependent on each other in a myriad of ways, have maintained a close relationship. Again, this consolidation of services would yield a great monetary savings from the elimination of duplicated headquarters and staffs. More important, it would reduce service rivalries and increase combat readiness as well as the effectiveness of the intelligence community.

No study of restructuring the armed services can be complete without a look into the National Guard and reserve force structure, where cutbacks and reductions are past due. The highly politicized reserve components, particularly the Guard, are rarely, if ever, at any degree of training readiness to perform their missions. Only with an increased active duty personnel presence and oversight of the remaining reserve components will they ever be anywhere near combat ready.

To get to the root of the cooperation problem, an immediate improvement in reducing service rivalries could be the restructuring of the service academies. Even if the air force retains its separate status, three academies for the commissioning of second lieutenants and ensigns are no longer necessary in the post–Cold War era. A single school, the United States Armed Service Academy, could replace the Military, Naval, and Air Force Academies, resulting in a savings of both money and manpower. Cadets would not decide which service to join until the end of their second year, remaining in their academy units even after making their selection and attending unsegregated core classes. Specific air, sea, and ground branch training would be handled as elective subjects, with more specific instruction provided during the summers at active duty installations and bases.

More important than the financial savings of a single academy is the far-reaching effect it would have on cooperation. A preponderance of the military's senior leaders have in the past, and will in the future, come from the academies. The camaraderie of cadets and the rivalries among those of different academies is typified by the annual fall Army-Navy football game. Players, cadets, and, more important, the "old grads" take the game with a high degree of seriousness, which ultimately turns cadets and alumni from the other academies into "the enemy"—an attitude that carries over into their military career interactions. This current conflict between cadets, and later officers, of the academies could be turned into cooperation by the consolidation of the three schools.

The realignment of the armed forces into only an army and a navy, the reduction and reorganization of the reserve components, and the formation of a single service academy are ideas worthy of study and possible adaptation to improve cooperative effort — including military intelligence. More pressing, however, is the immediate need for improvement of the military intelligence community within the current force structure. The United States today, as the single world power, exceeds every other country in its ability to access intelligence. The U.S. intelligence community currently gathers vast amounts of raw information, but, unfortunately, the capability to collect has exceeded the ability to analyze all of it, or to reduce it to usable, accurate estimates. The bottom line remains that the total military intelligence community is not delivering to the political leadership or to combat commanders the information they need to make decisions or to avoid surprise.

Immediate improvements must be made in the doctrinal, technical, and sociological aspects of military intelligence. Current doctrinal and technical problems within the intelligence community were detailed in the August 1993 U.S. House of Representatives Committee on Armed Services Subcommittee on Oversight and Investigations report "Intelligence Successes and Failures in Operations Desert Shield/Storm." The subcommittee noted especially serious shortcomings: the absence of any joint doctrine on assessing battlefield damage to the enemy; the incompatibility of equipment between services; the failure of the Secondary Imagery Dissemination System, which is supposed to distribute information; and the inability of the intelligence system to reduce large volumes of data to usable information for combat commanders.

To meet wartime commanders' intelligence needs, the subcommittee report recommended closer coordination of resources and more openness on the part of the intelligence community. Recommendations included more peacetime training exercises by the Joint Training Center including national collection assets and analysts; periodic briefings for senior commanders regarding the capabilities and limitations of the national collection systems; establishing permanent CIA liaison positions on the senior level J-2 (Intelligence) staffs; and the creation of a single, national, deployable Joint Information Center that would augment the intelligence staffs of relevant commands in time of crisis.

Because of the post–Cold War austerity of military funding, the armed services, including military intelligence, are scrambling to reduce their numbers by one-third or more. The information needs of the services nonetheless remain much more fundamental than they are complex. A Marine Corps study of intelligence needs, completed in early 1995, offers concepts that are not difficult to grasp. The study states the intelligence mission of the Corps is to "provide commanders, at every level, with tailored, timely, minimum essential intelligence, and ensure that this intelligence is integrated into the operational planning process."

The marine study adds a list of intelligence principles, including, "Orientation is tactical; focus is downward; intelligence must drive operations; intelligence must be directed and managed by a multi-disciplined trained and experienced intelligence officer; and the intelligence product must be timely and tailored to both the unit and mission."

The implementation of these overall doctrinal and technical recommendations by all sources will increase the effectiveness of military intelligence in meeting the needs of combat commanders. These improvements are not, however, all inclusive. There still remains the need for changes in the sociological aspects of intelligence. The mere title of "intelligence" has often attracted those officers and enlisted members who feel intellectually superior to the combat troops. This arrogance has yielded a corps of intelligence personnel who keep themselves separate, withholding instead of sharing information with the people who need it most.

The gap between military intelligence operatives and the combat commanders they are supposed to serve is widening. Intelligence personnel are reluctant to share their information fully—even with those who have "a need to know"—and commanders are suspicious of what little information they do receive. Steps must be taken to reduce the communication gap. One problem that creates a wedge is that specialization by intelligence officers separates them from the ground, air, and sea commanders they are supposed to support. To remedy this, intelligence officers should serve alternate tours, or at least every third tour, outside the field and in direct contact with combat soldiers, airmen, and sailors to gain better understanding of their missions. To reinforce this integration, commanders of military intelligence units and senior staff positions should also come from the combat branches.

Despite a consistent record of intelligence failures dating back to the Revolutionary War, the United States today, because of a superior democratic means of government supported by a dedicated military and abundant natural resources, is the single world power and the beacon of a better way of life for oppressed peoples around the globe. This time of peace, regardless of the reductions in defense expenditures, is the opportune time for the United States to reevaluate, reorganize, and revitalize its military intelligence community. Lessons learned from the intelligence failures of the past offer tremendous opportunities for successes in the future. The viability and longevity of the United States and the American way of life may very well depend upon it.

★★★★★

Source Notes

Sources on the development and evolution of military intelligence are few and outdated. The two primary sources are *History of the Military Intelligence Division, Department of the Army General Staff: 1775–1941* (Frederick, Maryland: University Publications, 1986) by Bruce W. Bidwell; and *The Office of Naval Intelligence, The Birth of America's First Intelligence Agency: 1865–1918* (Annapolis, Maryland: Naval Institute Press, 1979) by Jeffery M. Dorwart. As the titles indicate, the army's history ends in 1941 and the navy's in 1918. A valuable third source, *The Evolution of American Military Intelligence* by Marc B. Powe and Edward E. Wilson, was published as a "supplementary reading" for students at the U.S. Army Intelligence Center and School in 1973 and has never been commercially printed. These three sources are referred to in the following chapter source notes as "Bidwell," "Dorwart," and "Powe and Wilson."

One of the most valuable resources in writing this book, and in understanding the causes and scope of intelligence failures, was the author's personal visits to many of the battle areas. These visits on foot, by automobile or jeep, and by air are included at the end of each chapter notation.

My personal experiences in the U.S. Army are told in detail in *The Only War We Had: A Platoon Leader's Journal of Vietnam* (New York: Ivy Books, 1987); *Vietnam 1969–1970: A Company Commander's Journal* (New York: Ivy Books, 1988); and *The Battles of Peace* (New York: Ivy Books, 1992).

1. Desert Storm and Somalia

The best analysis of intelligence during the Gulf War is in *Intelligence Successes and Failures in Operation Desert Shield/*

Storm, U.S. House of Representatives Committee on Armed
Services Subcommittee on Oversight and Investigations (Washington, D.C., August 1993). General H. Norman Schwarzkopf's *It
Doesn't Take a Hero* (New York: Bantam Books, 1992), and Rick
Atkinson's *Crusade* (New York: Houghton Mifflin, 1993) provide
excellent overviews of the conflict. A ground-level look at the war
from the infantryman's and tanker's view is offered in Tom
Carhart's *Iron Men* (New York: Bantam Books, 1994). My
opinions of Schwarzkopf are based on daily personal contact with
the general when he commanded I Corps and Fort Lewis, Washington, in 1986 and 1987. No book-length study of the operations
in Somalia has yet been published. The best available accounts of
the disaster in Mogadishu appeared in the October 18 and
November 1, 1993, editions of *Newsweek* and the November 8
issue of *Time*. Editions of *Army Times* for October 18 and 25 and
November 1, 8, and 15 provide additional details. An excellent
summary of the battle, "Betrayal in Somalia," by Malcolm
McConnell, appeared in the April 1994 *Reader's Digest.*

2. Beginnings: The American Revolutionary War

Unlike Desert Storm and Somalia, on which books are just
now appearing, the Revolutionary War and other earlier American conflicts have been documented in hundreds, if not thousands,
of books. Most make little or no direct mention of military
intelligence. Bidwell offers the best description of the preliminary
developments of military intelligence during the revolutionary
era. Powe and Wilson add a bit more to the period and include a
brief pre–Revolutionary War history of intelligence. Overviews of
the Revolutionary War that assisted me included *Encyclopedia of
the American Revolution,* Mark M. Boatner III (New York: David
McKay, 1974); *The Secret War of Independence,* Helen Augur
(Boston: Little, Brown, 1955); *The Road to Yorktown,* John Selby
(New York: St. Martin's Press, 1976); *Less Than Glory,* Norman
Gelb (New York: G. P. Putnam's Sons, 1984); *A Short History of
the American Revolution,* James L. Stokesbury (New York:
William Morrow, 1991); and *The Minutemen,* General John R.
Galvin (Washington, D.C.: Pergamon-Brassey's, 1989). The sol-
dier's view of the war is provided in *Voices of 1776,* Richard

Wheeler (New York: Meridian Books, 1991). My visits to Lexington and Concord, Boston, Philadelphia, New York, West Point, and Yorktown added to my understanding of the period and the intelligence requirements.

3. The Second War for Independence: The War of 1812

Bidwell includes information about the exploration of the West and intelligence developments during the war. Powe and Wilson include only a brief paragraph about the period. A bit more information may be found in *The Spy in America,* George S. Bryan (Philadelphia: Lippincott, 1943); and *A Short History of Espionage,* Allison Ind (New York: David McKay, 1963). Numerous reprints of the journals of Lewis and Clark are available, including *History of the Expedition Under The Command of Lewis and Clark,* 3 volumes, edited by Elliott Coues (New York: Dover, 1965). Several biographies of Lewis have been written; none as yet has been published on Clark. Pike's explorations are detailed in *The Journals of Zebulon Montgomery Pike, With Letters and Related Documents,* 2 volumes, edited by Donald Jackson (Norman: University of Oklahoma Press, 1966). Referenced general studies of the war include *The War of 1812,* Harry L. Coles (Chicago: University of Chicago Press, 1965); and *The War of 1812: A Forgotten Conflict,* Donald R. Hickey (Urbana: University of Illinois Press, 1989). Although I have visited the war's battle sites near Washington, D.C., and Detroit, little remains to provide any real feel of the military operations of the period.

4. Expansionism: The Mexican War

Again, Bidwell offers a brief sketch of further western exploration and intelligence developments of the period. Powe and Wilson include three paragraphs. Exploits of the era's explorers are covered in *Stephen Long: An American Frontier Exploration,* Roger L. Nichols (Newark, Del.: University of Delaware Press, 1980); and *The Explorations of John Charles Fremont,* 3 volumes, edited by Mary Spence (Urbana: University of Illinois Press, 1973–84). Referenced general studies of the war include *The War With Mexico,* 2 volumes, Justin H. Smith (Gloucester, Mass.: Peter

Smith, 1963); *The Mexican War 1846–1848*, K. Jack Bauer (New
York: Macmillan, 1974); and "Ethan Allen Hitchcock: Intelligence Leader—Mystic," Rodney Campbell, *Intelligence Quar-
terly* (October, 1986), pp. 13–14. Parts of the Texas border region
and northern Mexico have changed little in the past 150 years.
However, Mexico, as the loser, has preserved little of the actual
battlefields, and the value of visiting these sites is minimal.

5. Brother Against Brother: The Civil War

No other war in American history has produced more books
and other printed materials than the Civil War. Books by and
about the participants were popular during the war and in the
years immediately afterward. The war's centennial renewed a
barely waning appeal, and the tremendously successful Ken Burns
documentary on public television has increased more recent
interest. Bidwell devotes several detailed chapters to intelligence
developments both before and during the Civil War, while Powe
and Wilson surprisingly skim over the period in only a few pages.
Dorwart begins his study of naval intelligence in 1865 and pays
only minimal attention to the Civil War. Without a doubt, the
most concise and accurate study of Civil War military intelligence
is in "The Mythology of Civil War Intelligence," Edwin C. Fishel,
Civil War History (December 1964), pp. 344–67. A research paper
titled "Tactical Intelligence Methods Used During the Civil War,"
June 14, 1974, by Captain Ronald M. Love, on file in the U.S.
Army Intelligence School and Library (USAICS) also provided
assistance. Of general resource assistance were *Civil War Diction-
ary*, Mark W. Boatner III (New York: David McKay, 1959); *The
Centennial History of the Civil War*, 3 volumes, Bruce Catton
(Garden City, N.Y.: Doubleday, 1961–65); and *The Civil War: A
Narrative*, 3 volumes, Shelby Foote (New York: Random House,
1958–74). My own master's thesis (East Texas State University,
Commerce, Texas, 1977) titled "English War Correspondents in
the Confederate States of America" proved beneficial in research-
ing newspapers of the war. Unlike those of the War of 1812 and the
Mexican War, many Civil War battlefields in both the North and
the South have been maintained or restored to their original
condition. Hours and days spent walking the battlefields at Bull

Run, Antietam, Fredericksburg, Chancellorsville, Gettysburg, Appomattox, and other sites greatly benefited my understanding of the intelligence failures there. Many of these visits were timed to coincide with the same time of the year as the original battle so I could experience the weather along with the terrain.

6. Combat on the Plains: The Indian Wars

Bidwell dedicates a chapter each to the Indian Wars and to the origins of the Military Intelligence Department. Powe and Wilson do not discuss the Indian Wars, but they do include several pages on the early organization of MID. The first third of Dorwart concentrates on the origins and development of the Office of Naval Intelligence. Excellent overviews of the Indian Wars are provided in *War Cries on Horseback*, Stephen Longstreet (Garden City, N.Y.: Doubleday, 1970); *Chronicle of the Indian Wars*, Alan Axelrod (New York: Prentice Hall, 1993); and *The Indian Frontier of the American West, 1846–1890*, Robert M. Utley (Albuquerque: University of New Mexico Press, 1984). A thorough account of Forsyth's Scouts is provided in "Rescue at Death Island," E. Lisle Reedstrom, *Old West* (Summer 1994), pp. 24–29. There are more books and articles on Custer than on all other characters of the period combined, and few are without bias. My best resource on Custer was a research paper titled "Intelligence at the Little Big Horn," dated July 21, 1975, by Captain Edward J. Galbierczyk, which is on file in the USAICS Library. Another research paper in the same files, "The Little Big Horn Intelligence Aspects," December 1978, by Captain Paul B. Jarboe was also of assistance. The Custer Battlefield is well preserved, and a walking/driving tour of the Little Big Horn Valley added greatly to my understanding of the fight. Similar visits to the lava beds of northern California and the mountains and desert of southern Arizona aided in understanding the difficulties in pursuing the Modocs and the Apaches.

7. Remembering the *Maine:* The Spanish-American War

Bidwell offers several chapters on army intelligence operations in Cuba and the Philippines, with Powe and Wilson adding several more pages. Dorwart goes into great detail about the development of the ONI during the period and naval intelligence during the war. The most helpful resource for this chapter for an overview of the war, as well as excellent insight into military intelligence of the period, was *The Spanish War: An American Epic—1898,* G.J.A. O'Toole (New York: W. W. Norton, 1984). Also recommended are *The War With Spain in 1898,* David F. Trask (New York: Macmillan, 1981); and *The Spanish American War,* Donald B. Chidsey (New York: Crown, 1971). Access to the landing site at Siboney and the heights above Santiago including San Juan and Kettle hills are not available to Americans today because of limitations on travel to Castro's Cuba.

8. Over There: The First World War

Both Bidwell and Powe and Wilson provide extensive insights into army intelligence developments before and during World War I. Dorwart also goes into great detail about naval intelligence advancements during the period. Evolution of the Military Intelligence Division during World War I is explained at length in "The Military Intelligence Division General Staff," Brigadier General Marlborough Churchill, *Journal of the United States Artillery* (April 1920), pp. 293–315. Another valuable document concerning army intelligence development during the period is the unpublished manuscript of Ralph Van Deman dated April 1949 on file in the USAICS Library titled *Memoirs of Major General R. H. Van Deman.* Additional information about the punitive expedition was gained from "Intelligence Aspects of the Pershing Punitive Expedition," Captain Robert J. McFarland, USAICS Library, 1972. *Blood on the Border: The United States Army and The Mexican Irregulars,* Clarence C. Clendenen (New York: Macmillan, 1969), offered general reference to the expedition. General World War I references include *The War to End All War: The American Military Experience in World War I,* Edward M. Coffman (Madison: University of Wisconsin, 1968); and *The Doughboys: The Story of the AEF, 1917–1918,* Laurence Stallings (New York: Harper & Row, 1963). A train/automobile journey south from El Paso through the Mexican state of Chihuahua added to my understanding of Pershing's expedition. Similar trips

to World War I battle sites across France assisted in writing about
the Great War.

9. World War II: The Pacific Theater

Powe and Wilson continue their detailed coverage of army
intelligence developments before and during World War II. Bidwell's study ends in 1941. Dorwart's study of naval intelligence
ends in 1918. Research for this book occurred during the fiftieth
anniversary of the war's final years, so much material was
available from daily newspapers and periodicals. Details of the
Black Chamber are from *The American Black Chamber*, Herbert
O. Yardley (New York: Ballantine Books, 1981); and "The American Black Chamber," Captain Thomas R. Kelley, USAICS Library,
1974. The disaster at Pearl Harbor is well covered in *At Dawn We
Slept: The Untold Story of Pearl Harbor*, Gordon W. Prange (New
York: McGraw Hill, 1981); *Captains Without Eyes: Intelligence
Failures of World War II*, Lyman B. Kirkpatrick Jr. (New York:
Macmillan, 1969); and "Pearl Harbor Aftermath," Captain
Wilfred J. Holmes *U.S. Naval Institute Proceedings*, December
1978) pp. 68–75. General references on the Pacific War abound,
but particularly useful were *The Pacific Campaign: The
U.S.–Japanese Naval War 1941–1945*, Dan van der Vat (New
York: Touchstone, 1991); *A Short History of World War II*, James
L. Stokesbury (New York: William Morrow, 1980); *The Pacific
War*, John Costello (London: Collins, 1981); *The Thousand Mile
War: World War II in Alaska and the Aleutians*, Brian Garfield
(New York: Doubleday, 1969); and *All the Drowned Sailors*,
Raymond B. Lech (New York: Stein and Day, 1982). In addition to
visits to Pearl Harbor, mainland Japan, Okinawa, and Guam, I
made an overflight of Kiska and then spent two days (as the result
of an aircraft breakdown) on Attu in the Aleutians walking the
battlefield and exploring the well-preserved U.S. and Japanese
positions.

10. World War II: The European Theater

Powe and Wilson provide great detail about intelligence
developments both in the United States and in North Africa and

Europe. Particularly noteworthy for its coverage of European theater intelligence failures is *Captains Without Eyes: Intelligence Failures of World War II*, Lyman B. Kirkpatrick, Jr. (New York: Macmillan, 1969). General references include *A Short History of World War II*, James L. Stokesbury (New York: William Morrow, 1980); *A Soldier's Story of the Allied Campaigns From Tunis to the Elbe*, General Omar N. Bradley (New York: Henry Holt, 1951); and *Crusade in Europe*, General Dwight D. Eisenhower (New York: Doubleday, 1948). During a three-year tour of duty, equally split between Stuttgart and Schweinfurt, Germany, I visited major World War II battle sites all across Europe and North Africa. Included were Tangier in Morocco, the beaches and mountains of central Italy, the French countryside, the bridges "too far" in Holland, and the Ardennes bulge, including the countryside surrounding Bastogne. As a mechanized infantry commander in Germany, I led combined infantry and armor columns across the German countryside during joint maneuvers along the same routes used by Patton's 3rd Army and also trained for urban warfare in the U.S. sector of Berlin.

11. The Unknown War: Korea

Powe and Wilson provide substantial detail on post–World War II and Korean War army intelligence. Details of intelligence failures in Korea are covered in a chapter of *Military Misfortunes: The Anatomy of Failure in War*, Eliot A. Cohen and John Gooch (New York: Free Press, 1990). Recommended general sources on the Korean War include *South to the Naktong, North to the Yalu*, Roy Appleman (Washington, D.C.: U.S. Army, Center of Military History, 1961); *The Forgotten War: America in Korea*, Clay Blair (New York: Times Books, 1987); *U.S. Marine Operations in Korea, 1950–1953*, 3 volumes, Lynn Montross and Nicholas A. Canzona (Washington, D.C.: U.S. Marine Corps, 1955); *The Korean War*, General Matthew B. Ridgway (Garden City, N.Y.: Doubleday, 1967); and *In Mortal Combat: Korea, 1950–1953*, John Toland (New York: William Morrow, 1991). While participating in military exercises in South Korea, I visited Panmunjon and spent extensive time in the field from Seoul south through the Pyongtaek, Ansong, and Osan corridor.

12. The Only War We Had: Vietnam

Powe and Wilson cover the post-Korea period in detail, and, although their study ends in 1973, some information about intelligence in Vietnam is provided. CIA activities of the period are well covered in *The CIA and the Cult of Intelligence,* Victor Marchetti and John D. Marks (New York: Knopf, 1974). Helpful USAICS research papers included "An Analysis of the Bay of Pigs Defeat," by Captain Ronald D. McAdoo, 1975; and "The Bay of Pigs: An Intelligence Analysis and Overview," by Captain Ronald M. Ferguson, 1987. Vietnam War intelligence resources include *Intelligence,* Colonel Hoang Ngoc Lung (Washington, D.C.: U.S. Army Center of Military History, 1982); *The Role of Military Intelligence 1965–1967,* Major General Joseph A. McChristian (Washington, D.C.: Department of the Army, 1974); and a USAICS research paper "Ignoring Intelligence," Captain Norman K. Welch, 1974. Also of particular note is *Tet 1968: Understanding the Surprise* by Captain Ronnie E. Ford, pending publication by Frank Cass in London (Ford graciously provided me a copy in manuscript form). General recommended references are *Prisoners of Hope: Exploiting the POW/MIA Myth in America,* Susan Katz Keating (New York: Random House, 1994); *Summons of the Trumpet,* Dave Richard Palmer (Navato, Calif.: Presidio Press, 1978); *The Raid,* Benjamin F. Schemmer (New York: Harper & Row, 1976); and *Vietnam Almanac,* Harry G. Summers Jr. (New York: Facts on File Publications, 1985). I also referred to my own books about the war, including: *The Only War We Had: A Platoon Leader's Journal of Vietnam* (New York: Ivy Books, 1987); *Vietnam 1969-1970: A Company Commander's Journal* (New York: Ivy Books, 1988); *Inside the LRRPS: Rangers in Vietnam* (New York: Ivy Books, 1988); *Inside Force Recon: Recon Marines in Vietnam,* with Ray Stubbe (New York: Ivy Books, 1989); and *Inside the VC and the NVA: The Real Story of North Vietnam's Army,* with Dan Cragg (New York: Fawcett Columbine, 1992). My greatest understanding of intelligence failures in the Vietnam War during 1969 and 1970 came from my personal experiences as an infantry platoon leader, reconnaissance platoon leader, rifle company commander, and assistant operations officer in the 199th Light Infantry Brigade.

13. Weekend Wars: Grenada, Panama, and More

Little intelligence information of note has been declassified or released to the public for the past twenty-five years, so information about the "weekend wars" is limited at best. In addition to the news magazines *Time* and *Newsweek*, and daily newspapers of the period, the following are recommended: *The Straw Giant*, Arthur T. Hadley (New York: Random House, 1986); *Assault on the Liberty*, James E. Ennes Jr. (New York: Random House, 1979); *Bucher: My Story*, Lloyd M. Bucher (Garden City, N.Y.: Doubleday, 1970); *It Doesn't Take a Hero*, General H. Norman Schwarzkopf (New York: Bantam Books, 1992); *Operation Just Cause*, Clarence E. Briggs III (Harrisburg, Pa.: Stackpole Books, 1990); and *Just Cause*, Malcolm McConnell (New York: St. Martin's Press, 1991). Insights into many of these operations resulted from official and unofficial debriefings of the participants while I was on active duty as well as informal discussions during off-duty hours.

14. Today and Tomorrow: Can Failures Become Successes?

Recommendations in this chapter are based on twenty years of active service in the U.S. Army and a lifetime study of military history. Of particular assistance were the U.S. House of Representatives Committee on Armed Services Subcommittee on Oversight and Investigations Report "Intelligence Successes and Failures in Operations Desert Shield/Storm," August 1993; U.S. General Accounting Office Report, "Classified Information," October 1993; and unpublished position papers and proposals provided by the public affairs offices of the various armed services. Information about the F-16 shot down over Bosnia is from the June 9, 1995, *Wall Street Journal* (p. A-10) and the June 10, 1995, *New York Times* (p. 1).

Index

Acheson, Dean, 228
Adventures of Captain Bonneville
   (Irving), 62
Aerial reconnaissance, 154–55, 163,
   245
Africa in World War II, 203–5
Aguinaldo (Philippino), 132–33
Aidid, Mohammed F., 19, 20–21
Air Force, U.S., 10, 17, 231
Alaska, purchase of, 102–3
Albania, CIA failures in, 244
Alger, Russell A., 121, 130–31
Alien and Sedition Acts of 1798,
   47–48
Allen, James, 85, 88
Alliance (Continental ship), 44–45
Allied Geographical Agency (AGA),
   182–83
Allied Intelligence Bureau (AIB), 182
Allied Translator and Interpreter
   Section (ATIS), 182
Almond, Gen. Edward M., 234
Ames, Aldrich H., 294–95
Andre, Maj. John, 43
Antietam (Civil War battle), 82
Apache Indians, 112–13
Armed Forces Security Agency
   (AFSA), 249
Army, U.S., 10, 17
   General Staff Corps, 134–36
   Intelligence and Security (AIS), 250
   Security Agency (ASA), 273
Arthur, Chester A., 115
Art of War, The (Sun Tzu), 23
Atomic bombs, 193–94, 225

Babcock, John C., 84
Babcock, John V., 158

Baker, Lafayette C., 83–84, 98
Balloons, 85–88, 128
Battle of the Bulge, 219–20
Bay of Pigs, 246–47
Beauregard, P. G. T., 71
Beckweth, Col. Charles, 276
Belknap, William W., 101–2
Belleau Wood (World War I battle),
   158
Berlin, U.S. servicemen attacked in,
   283
Berlin blockade, 224–25
Bible references to intelligence
   gathering, 22–23
Big Foot (Native American), 113–14
Bishop, Maurice, 279
Boerstler, Lt. Col. Charles, 56–57
Bonhomme Richard (Continental
   ship), 44–45
Bonneville, Benjamin, 61–62
Boomer, Gen. Walter, 17–18
Bosnia, U.S. pilot shot down in,
   296–97
Boston campaign in Revolutionary
   War, 28–30
Bradford, Adm. Royal B., 119
Bragg, Gen. Braxton, 68, 92
Brereton, Gen. Lewis H., 177
Brock, Gen. Issac, 52
Brown, John, 76
Bryan, Capt. E. P., 87
Buena Vista Ranch battle in Mexican
   War, 68
Buford, Gen. John, 90
Burgoyne, Gen. John, 38
Burnside, Gen. Ambrose, 84–85
Bush, George, 6–7, 13, 15, 284, 288
Butler, Gen. Benjamin F., 86–87

California declared a republic, 68–69
Cambodian attack on *Mayaguez*,
    272–73
Campanole, Nicholas W., 141
Canada campaigns in War of 1812,
    51–53, 55–58
Canby, Gen. Edward R., 111
Captain Jack (Native American),
    111–12
Carranza, Venustiano, 139
Carrington, Col. Henry B., 105
Carson, Kit, 62
Carter, Jimmy, 274, 277
Castro, Fidel, 246, 248
Central Command, U.S. (Centcom), 6
Central Intelligence Agency (CIA), 6
    Ames, Aldrich, 294–95
    Desert Shield/Storm, 6
    embarrassing revelations, 273–74
    golden age of covert action,
        243–49
    Korean War, 230–31, 235
    National Security Act, 224
    reforming the, 298–300
Cerro Gordo campaign in Mexican
    War, 70–71
Cervera y Topete, Adm. Pascual, 124,
    125, 129–30
Chancellorsville (Civil War) battle,
    89
Chase, Ann M., 69–70
Cheatham, Gen. Benjamin F., 92
Chesapeake (U.S. ship), 57
Cheyenne Indians, 107–11
Chief Joseph, 112
Chinese intelligence gathering, early,
    23
Chinese intervention in Korean War,
    236–40
Chivington, Col. John M., 105
Civilian Irregular Defense Groups
    (CIDG), 262
Civil Operations and Revolutionary
    Development Support (CORDS),
    262
Civil War, vii
    balloon corps, 85–88
    Bureau of Military Intelligence,
        89–91
    cavalry forces, 93–94
    Confederate Signal Bureau, 91–92

indigenous forces as scouts, 99
naval battles, 97–98
newspapers, 95–96
Pinkerton's National Detective
    Agency, 78–83
postwar demobilization, 100
South Carolina seceding, 76–77
telegraph used, 94–95
Clark, Gen. Mark W., 241
Clark, Gen. Wesley, 287
Clark, Harry L., 166
Clark, Lt. Eugene F., 234, 240
Clark, William, 48–50
Classified documents, 291
Clinton, Bill, 15
Clinton, Gen. Henry, 41
CNN (Cable News Network), 9
Cold War, 222, 224–25
Continental Congress, 39
Coordinator of Information (COI),
    168
Coral Sea battle (World War II), 184
Cornwallis, Gen. Charles, 43, 45
Corps Command Group, x
Cronkite, Walter, 261
Crook, Gen. George, 108–9
Cryptology, 148–49, 164–69, 185,
    186–87, 201
Cuba and Spanish-American War,
    118–29
Cuban-U.S. relations, deteriorating,
    246–49
Curtis, Gen. S. R., 99
Custer, Gen. George A., 105, 109–10

Davis, Jefferson, 75
Dawes, William, 27
DeConcini, Dennis, 290
Defense, U.S. Department of, x
Defense Intelligence Agency (DIA),
    15, 249
Delafield, Maj. Richard, 75
Delta Force, ultrasecret, 11, 19–20
Department of Defense
    Reorganization Act of 1986,
    301–2
Desert Shield/Storm
    casualties predicted, U.S., 8–9
    electronic transfer of intelligence
        data, 12–13
    ground attack, U.S., 13–14

House Armed Services
  Subcommittee on Oversight and
  Investigations, 3–4, 15–16
  intelligence failures, 15–18
  media coverage, 7, 9
  oil dispute between Kuwait and
    Iran, 4, 6
  SCUD missiles, 10–12, 15
Detroit campaign in War of 1812,
    51–52
Dewey, George, 122–23
Discorsi (Machiavelli), 24
Dominguez, Manuel, 72
Donovan, William, 167–68, 221
Doolittle, Jimmy, 183–84
Dowling, Richard, 97–98

Eisenhower, Gen. Dwight D., 203,
    245, 252
Emancipation Proclamation, 83
England. See Revolutionary War; War
    of 1812; World War I
Equipment malfunctions hindering
    intelligence dissemination, 16
Espionage Act of 1917, 145
European military schools, 60,
    62–64, 75–76, 101–2, 114–15
Expenditures on intelligence
    community, 290–92

Farragut, Adm. David G., 98
Fetterman, Capt. William J., 105–6
FitzGibbon, James, 56–57
Ford, Gerald, 272
Forsyth, Maj. G. A., 102, 106–7
France
  alliance with U.S., 40
  England at war with, 42
  Napoleon defeated, 57
  U.S military representatives to,
    63–64
  Vietnam, 250, 252
Franklin, Gen. William B., 97
Fredericksburg campaign in Civil
    War, 85
Frederick the Great, 24
Fremont, John C., 62, 68
Frenchtown battle in War of 1812,
    53–54
Frendendall, Gen. Lloyd, 203, 204–5
Funston, Col. Frederick, 132–33

Gadhafi, Muammar, 283–84
Gage, Gen. Thomas, 25–26, 29
Gates, Gen. Horatio, 40
Germany, 136, 224–25. See also
    World War I; World War II
    (Europe)
Geronimo, 113
Ghost dance movement (Native
    Americans), 113–14
Glaspie, April, 6
Grant, Gen. U. S., 91
Gray, Gen. Charles, 39
Great Lakes and the War of 1812,
    55–56
Greely, Adolphus W., 103
Greene, Gen. Nathanael, 32, 42–43
Greenglass, David, 225
Grenada, U.S. invasion of, 279–83
Grierson, Col. B. H., 93
G-staff structure, 152, 162
Guatemala, 244
Guevara, Che, 246
Gulf War. See Desert Shield/Storm

Hale, Samuel, 34
Hall, James, III, 293–94
Hancock, John, 27
Harmer, Gen. Josiah, 103
Harrison, Gen. William H., 56
Hearst, William Randolph, 118–19
Heath, Gen. William, 33
Hessian (German) mercenaries, 30,
    38
Hillenkoetter, Roscoe H., 230–31
Hitchcock, Col. Ethan A., 72
Hitler, Adolf, 220
Ho Chi Minh, 250, 258
Honeyman, John, 38
Hooker, Gen. Joe, 88–89, 96
Hoover, Herbert, 165
Hoover, J. Edgar, 167, 221
House Armed Services Subcommittee
    on Oversight and Investigations,
    3–4, 15–16, 18, 290, 304
Howard, Edward L., 293
Howe, Adm. Richard, 30
Howe, Gen. William, 30, 32, 35
Huerta, Victoriano, 139
Hull, Gen. William, 34, 51–52
Hungary, 244–45
Hussein, Saddam, 4, 6, 10–11, 15

Indian Wars, 104–17
Indonesia, 245
Instructions for His Generals
    (Frederick the Great), 24
Iran, 4, 244, 274–77
Iraq. *See* Desert Shield/Storm
Irish Catholics in Mexican War,
    65–66
Israeli attack on the *U.S.S.
    Liberty*, 269–70
Iwo Jima battle in World War II, 193

Jackson, Andrew, 58–59
Japan, 136–37. *See also* World War II
    (Pacific)
Java (British ship), 57
Jefferson, Thomas, 48
Jodl, Gen. Alfred, 220
Johnson, Louis, 228
Johnson, Lyndon B., 253, 263
Johnson, Stanley, 187
Joint Army and Navy Board, 137
Joint Intelligence Center (JIC),
    Centcom's, 12
Joint Services Far East Command in
    Japan, 232
Jones, John P., 44–45

Kearny, Col. Stephen W., 69
Kearny, Lt. Philip, 64
Kennedy, John F., 247, 248, 252–53
Khan, Genghis, 24
Khrushchev, Nikita, 245, 248
Kim Il-sung, 228, 235
Kissinger, Henry, 263, 267
Knowlton, Lt. Col. Thomas, 33–34,
    35
Knox, Henry, 47
Korean attacks on U.S. ships/planes,
    North, 270–72
Korean War
    Chinese intervention, 236–40
    CIA preparedness for, 230–31
    end of, 242
    Inchon, 234–35
    intelligence services, 213–32
    North invades South, 228–30
    prelude to, 227–28
    Pusan perimeter, 233
    stalemate in, 240–41
    U.S. ground troops, 232
Kuwait. *See* Desert Shield/Storm

Laffite, Jean, 58
Laird, Melvin, 264
Lake Champlain campaign in War of
    1812, 53
Lake Erie and War of 1812, 55–56
La Mountain, John, 86–87
Lansdale, Col. Edward G., 244
Lawrence, Capt. James, 57
Lebanese attacks on U.S. citizens,
    277–78
Le Duc Tho, 267
Lee, Gen. Charles, 37–38
Lee, Gen. Robert E., 71, 76, 80, 82,
    89
Lewis, Meriwether, 48–49
Libya, U.S. attack on, 283–84
Lincoln, Abraham, 95
Lincoln, Gen. Benjamin, 45
Little Big Horn, 108–10
Little Crow, 104
Long, Maj. Stephen H., 61
Long Range Reconnaissance Patrol
    (LRRP) units, 263
Lowe, Thaddeus S. C., 86, 87, 88
Luciano, Lucky, 197
Lusitania (British ship), 146

MacArthur, Gen. Douglas, 181, 229,
    234, 235, 237–38, 241
Macedonian (British ship), 57
Mache, Maj. Hartman, 85
Machiavelli, Niccolo, 24
Madero, Francisco, 138–39
Madison, James, 51
Malaysians, 20
Manifest Destiny, 64
Marines, U.S., 10, 17–19, 230, 263,
    302
Marshall, George C., 173
Mason, Lt. Theodorus B., 115–16
Maxfield, Col. Joseph E., 128
May, Andrew J., 192
Mayaguez, 272–73
McCaffery, Gen. Barry, 8, 14, 15
McClellan, Gen. George B., 71, 75,
    78–80
McCone, John, 247
McKinley, William, 120
McRee, Maj. William, 63
Meade, Gen. Gordon, 89–90
Metcalf, Adm. Joseph, III, 279
Meteorological observations, 100–101

Mexican government instability,
    138–44
Mexican Spy Company, 71–73
Mexican War, 64–74
Mexico City campaign in Mexican
    War, 67, 73–74
Miles, Col. Nelson A., 112–14, 130
Military Information Division (MID),
    116–17, 121, 131–32, 162–63,
    181, 197
*Military Institutions of the
    Romans, The* (Vegetius), 24
Military Intelligence Corps, 292
Military occupation specialty (MOS),
    250
Mississippi River Valley, postwar
    exploration of, 61
Mitsuo, Fuchida, 174
Modac Indians, 111–12
Monroe, James, 62
Montgomery, Bernard, 205, 215, 217
Montojo y Pasaron, Adm. Patricio,
    123
Mordecai, Maj. A., 75
Moro tribe (Philippines), 133–34
Mussolini, Benito, 208
My Lai massacre, 264

Napoleon, 57
National Guard, 7, 303
National Intelligence Authority
    (NIA), 222, 224
National Security Act of 1947, 224
National Security Agency (NSA), 249
National Security Council (NSC),
    224
Native Americans, 42, 48–49, 56, 99,
    103–17
Navy, U.S., 17, 114, 130
New Orleans campaign in War of
    1812, 58–59
Nez Perce War of 1877, 112
Ngo Dinh Diem, 252, 253
Niagara campaign in War of 1812,
    52–53, 56–57
Nimitz, Adm. Chester W., 181, 185
Nolan, Maj. Dennis, 152, 155
Noriega, Manuel A., 284–86,
    288–89
Norris, Maj. William, 92, 95
North Atlantic Treaty Organization
    (NATO), 225

Office of Naval Communications
    (ONC), 165–66
Office of Naval Intelligence (ONI),
    115–17, 136–37, 149–50, 164,
    167, 181, 197, 231, 273
Office of Strategic Services (OSS),
    182, 197–98, 200, 211, 221–22
O'Grady, Capt. Scott, 296–97
O'Hara, Gen., 45
Okinawa (World War II battle), 193
Organization of Eastern Caribbean
    States, 279

Pakistanis, 20
Panama, U.S. invasion of, 284–89
Paris Peace Accords of 1973, 267
Patton, Gen. George S., 142, 207, 214
Pawnee Indians, 99, 106
Pelton, Ronald, 293
Perry, Oliver H., 55–56
Pershing, Gen. John J., 140–43,
    151–52, 162
Persian Gulf. *See* Desert Shield/Storm
Philippines, 122–23, 131–34,
    176–77, 180, 192–93, 244
Pike, Zebulon, M., 49–50, 55
Poland, CIA failures in, 244
Polk, James, 65
Pope, Gen. John, 82
Powers, Francis G., 245
Prescott, Col. William, 29
Procter, Gen. Henry, 56
Pulitzer, Joseph, 119

Qatar, 10

Radio Intelligence Section (RIS),
    152–53
Raisin River campaign in War of
    1812, 53–54
Randolph (continental frigate), 44
Reagan, Ronald, 277, 279
Reforms needed in U.S. intelligence
    community, 297–306
Remington, Frederic, 119
Reserve force structures, 7, 303
Revere, Paul, 27
Revolutionary War, 24
    Arnold, Benedict, 43–44
    Bunker/Breed's Hill, 29
    Concord, British push to, 27–28
    Continental Secret Service, 36

Revolutionary War (*cont'd.*)
  end of, 46
  Hale, Nathan, 34–35
  intelligence groups, 25–26
  Mechanics, the, 26–27
  mobile strategies, 36–37, 42–43
  Monmouth campaign, 41–42
  New York, 30–33
  Philadelphia campaign, 39–40
  privateers, 45
  Stamp Act, 25
  Trenton campaign, 38
  winter of 1977–78, 40–41
  Yorktown campaign, 45
Reynolds, Col. Joseph J., 108
Rhee, Syngman, 227, 235
Richmond campaign in Civil War, 80
Rickey, Lt. John, 67
Ridgway, Gen. Matthew B., 239, 241
Rivalries within U.S. intelligence
  community, 10, 163, 167–68,
  180–81, 221, 224, 226, 241, 275,
  301, 303–4
Rocky Mountains, postwar
  exploration of, 61–62
Roman empire and intelligence
  gathering, 23–24
Rommel, Gen. Erwin, 203, 204–5
Roosevelt, Franklin D., 167, 169,
  221–22
Rosenberg, Ethel, 225–26
Rosenberg, Julius, 225–26
Rough Riders, 127
Rowan, Andrew S., 121–22
Rusk, Dean, 228

Sampson, Capt. William T., 124–26,
  129
Sams, Gen. Crawford F., 240
Sanger, Capt. J. P., 102
Santa Anna, Antonio Lopez de,
  66–68, 70–71, 73, 74
Saratoga campaign in Revolutionary
  War, 40–41
Satellite reconnaissance, 245–46
Saudi Arabia, 4, 7, 10
Scarface Charley (Native American),
  111
Schley, Winfield S., 124
Schwarzkopf, Gen. Norman, 7–10,
  12, 14, 279, 283

Scott, Gen. Winfield, 58, 67–74
SEAL (Navy Sea, Air, and Land)
  teams, 263
Secondary Imagery Dissemination
  System (SIDS), 16–17
Secord, Laura, 56
Sedition Act of 1918, 145
Seminole people, 103
Serapis (British ship), 44–45
Shafter, Gen. William T., 126
Shalikashvili, Gen. John, 301
Shannon (British ship), 57
Sharpe, Col. George H., 89
Shaw, Henry B., 92
Sheridan, Gen. Philip, vii, 93, 101
Sherman, Gen. William T., 96, 101
Short, Gen. Walter C., 175
Signal Intelligence Service (SIS),
  165–66
Sigsbee, Capt. Charles, 120, 124, 136
Simpson, Henry L., 165
Sims, Adm. William S., 158
Sioux Indians, 103–11
Sitting Bull, 113
Smith, Gen. Jacob, 133–34
Smith, Lt. Col. Charles B., 232
Somalia, 18–21
Soviet Union, 58, 222, 224–27, 247
Spanish-American War
  criticisms after, 130–31
  Cuban-Spanish hostilities, 118
  Maine destroyed, 119–20
  Military Information Division, 122
  naval strategies, 124–25, 129–30
  Philippines, the, 122–23, 131–34
  Santiago attack, 126–29
Special Operations forces, 19–20
Spies, 28
  Arnold, Benedict, 43–44
  Chase, Ann M., 69–70
  Coleman's Scouts, 92–93
  European spies in U.S. government,
    47
  Hale, Nathan, 34–35
  Mexican Spy Company, 71–73
  Philby, Kim, 244
  status of, 33
  Tallmadge, Benjamin, 36
  traitors within U.S. military
    community, 292–95
  women, 98

St. Clair, Gen. Arthur, 103
St. Leger, Col. Barry, 39
Stager, Anson, 94–95
Stoney Creek battle (War of 1812), 56
Stuart, J. E. B., 76, 80, 93
Sullivan, Gen. John, 38
Sun Tzu (Chinese general), 23
Supreme Headquarters Allied
    Expeditionary Forces (SHAEF),
    214, 217

Tallmadge, Benjamin, 36
Tarawa Atoll campaign in World War
    II, 190–91
Taylor, Lt. Daniel, 63–64
Taylor, Zachary, 65–68
Tecumseh (Native American), 56
Texas and Mexican War, 64–65
Thayer, Capt., Sylvanus, 63
Theobald, Adm. Robert A., 185, 186
Thurman, Gen. Max, 285
Tibet, 245
Tonkin Gulf provocation, 253–54
Topographical engineers, 54–55, 60,
    101
Torricelli, Robert, 298
Treaty of Ghent, 58, 60
Treaty of Guadalupe Hidalgo in
    1848, 74
Truman, Harry, 221, 224, 228–30,
    233, 241

U-boats, German, 200–201
U-2 flights, 245, 247–48
United Nations, 229–30, 233, 236
United States (U.S. ship), 57
Upton, Gen. Emory, 101–2

Van Deman, Maj. Ralph, 147–48
Van Rensselaer, Gen. Stephen, 52–53
Vega, Maj. Moises G., 285
Vegetius, Flavius, 24
Veracruz campaign in Mexican War,
    67, 69–70
Vietnam War, viii–ix, 17–18
    bombing operations, 258–59
    Easter Offensive, 266
    end of, 267–68
    intelligence services, 254–55, 262
    political leadership, American,
        263–64

prelude to, 250–54
Son Tay raid, 264–66
TV coverage, 261
Tet Offensive, 260
three-phase plan of the North,
    256–58
Villa, Pancho, 139–44
Von Steuben, Baron Friedrich, 41

Wagner, Col. Arthur L., 121
Walker, Gen. Walton H., 233, 239
Walker, John, Jr., 293
War of 1812, 50–59
Washington, D.C. (burning of), 58
Washington, George, vii, 29, 32–33,
    35–37, 39–40, 45
Wayne, Gen. Anthony, 39
Western frontier, exploring the,
    48–50, 60–62
Westmoreland, Gen. William C., 254
Wheeler, George H., 101
Wilkinson, James, 49
Wilson, Woodrow, 139, 140, 143, 144,
    147
Winchester, Gen. James, 53
Wise, John, 85–86
Witzke, Lothar, 149
Woolsey, James, 298
World War I
    American Expeditionary Force,
        Siberia (AEFS), 160–61
    American Expeditionary Force's
        intelligence organization, 151–55
    American Protective League,
        149–50
    armistice, 159
    Black Chambers (cryptology),
        148–49
    Corps of Intelligence Police (CIP),
        155–56
    demobilization after, 162–64
    fighting ability of U.S. soldiers,
        158–59
    Indianapolis, 194–95
    Military Intelligence Section (MIS),
        147–48
    mine laying, 158–59
    neutrality of U.S., 144–47
World War II (Europe)
    Ardennes offensive, German,
        218–20

World War II (Europe) (*cont'd.*)
    bombing campaign against
        Germany, 205–7
    demobilization after, 221–22
    Dieppe raid, 201–2
    fighting ability of Americans,
        203–4
    intelligence services, 187–200
    Italian campaign, southern, 207–9
    Kasserine Pass, 204–5
    merchant shipping, 200–201
    Operation Market Garden, 215–17
    Operation Overlord, 211–15
    Operation Tiger, 209–11
    Operation Torch, 196
World War II (Pacific)
    air strikes against Japan, 183–84

Aleutian Islands, 189–90
atomic bomb used, 193–94
Guadalcanal, 187–88
intelligence organizations,
    181–83
Midway campaign, 185–86
Pacific battles of 1944, 191–93
Pearl Harbor, 169–76
Philippines attacked, 176–77,
    180
Yamamoto, Adm. Isoroku, 170, 172,
    188–89
Yardley, Herbert O., 148, 164–65
Yarmouth (British ship), 44

Zapata, Emiliano, 139
Zimmermann, Arthur, 146